Lee Marvin

Lee Marvin

His Films and Career

by
Robert J. Lentz

McFarland & Company, Inc., Publishers
Jefferson, North Carolina, and London

Frontispiece: Businessman Jack Osborne (Lee Marvin) prepares for some lethal business in *Gorky Park* (1983).

The present work is a reprint of the library bound edition of Lee Marvin: His Films and Career, *first published in 2000 by McFarland.*

LIBRARY OF CONGRESS CATALOGUING-IN-PUBLICATION DATA

Lentz, Robert J.
    Lee Marvin : his films and career / by Robert J. Lentz
      p.   cm.
    Filmography: p.
    Includes bibliographical references and index.

    ISBN-13: 978-0-7864-2606-5
    (softcover : 50# alkaline paper) ∞

    1. Marvin, Lee.   I. Title.
PN2287.M523L46   2006
791.43'028'092—dc21   99-43492

British Library Cataloguing-in-Publication data are available

©2000 Robert J. Lentz. All rights reserved

No part of this book may be reproduced or transmitted in any form or by any means, electronic or mechanical, including photocopying or recording, or by any information storage and retrieval system, without permission in writing from the publisher.

Cover image ©2005 PhotoSpin

Manufactured in the United States of America

McFarland & Company, Inc., Publishers
  Box 611, Jefferson, North Carolina 28640
    www.mcfarlandpub.com

For my wife Barbara
who has supported me in all ways

Contents

ACKNOWLEDGMENTS ix

INTRODUCTION 1

Feature Films

You're in the Navy Now (aka *U.S.S. Teakettle*) (1951) 3
Teresa (1951) 6
Hong Kong (aka *Bombs Over China*) (1951) 8
Diplomatic Courier (1952) 9
We're Not Married (1952) 11
The Duel at Silver Creek (1952) 14
Hangman's Knot (1952) 16
Eight Iron Men (1952) 19
Seminole (1953) 21
Down Among the Sheltering Palms (1953) 23
The Stranger Wore a Gun (1953) 25
The Glory Brigade (1953) 28
Gun Fury (1953) 30
The Big Heat (1953) 32
The Wild One (1954) 36
Gorilla at Large (1954) 40
The Caine Mutiny (1954) 42
The Raid (1954) 45
Bad Day at Black Rock (1955) 48
Violent Saturday (1955) 52
Not as a Stranger (1955) 55
A Life in the Balance (1955) 58
Pete Kelly's Blues (1955) 60
I Died a Thousand Times (1955) 62
Shack Out on 101 (1955) 64
Seven Men from Now (1956) 66
Attack (1956) 69
Pillars of the Sky (aka *The Tomahawk and the Cross*) (1956) 74
The Rack (1956) 77
Raintree County (1957) 79
The Missouri Traveler (1958) 82
The Comancheros (1961) 84
The Man Who Shot Liberty Valance (1962) 88
Donovan's Reef (1963) 92
The Killers (aka *Ernest Hemingway's The Killers*) (1964) 95
Cat Ballou (1965) 98
Ship of Fools (1965) 103
The Professionals (1966) 106
The Dirty Dozen (1967) 110
Point Blank (1967) 116

Sergeant Ryker (1968) (Filmed in 1963) 119
Hell in the Pacific (1968) 122
Paint Your Wagon (1969) 125
Monte Walsh (1970) 129
Pocket Money (1972) 132
Prime Cut (aka *Kansas City Prime*) (1972) 134
Emperor of the North (aka *Emperor of the North Pole*) (1973) 136
The Iceman Cometh (1973) 139
The Spikes Gang (1974) 143
The Klansman (aka *The Burning Cross*, and *KKK*) (1974) 145
The Meanest Men in the West (1976) 148
The Great Scout and Cathouse Thursday (aka *Wildcat*) (1976) 151
Shout at the Devil (1976) 153
Avalanche Express (1979) 156
The Big Red One (1980) 160
Death Hunt (1981) 164
Gorky Park (1983) 167
Dog Day (aka *Canicule*) (1984) 170
The Dirty Dozen: The Next Mission (1985 TV movie) 172
The Delta Force (1986) 175

Documentaries, Short Films and Stage Plays 180

Television Appearances

M Squad 182
Lawbreaker 193
Other Television Episodes 194
Variety Shows and Interviews 202

BIBLIOGRAPHY 203
INDEX 219

Acknowledgments

I would like to thank everyone who helped make this book a reality. Jim Shepard of Collectors Book Store was especially helpful with still selection. I thank Hugh Muir for his technical computer wizardry. Special thanks go to my father and stepmother, James and Vera Lentz, for their support; to my wife and proofreader, Barbara Lentz; and to my best friend, Michael Ferguson, who led by example.

Introduction

Lee Marvin was twenty-seven years old when his first motion picture appearance was projected onto America's movie screens, and forty when he received his first starring film role. In between, Marvin made more than thirty films, supporting and later co-starring with past, present and future movie stars. Marvin also stepped away from movies for three years to concentrate on a highly successful television series, *M Squad*.

After thirteen years in Hollywood, Marvin's popularity suddenly exploded, and he found himself accepting an Academy Award for Best Actor in *Cat Ballou*. In 1967, with the success of *Cat Ballou*, *The Professionals* and especially *The Dirty Dozen*, forty-three-year-old Lee Marvin became the most popular film actor in America. He then spent five years on the list of annual top ten box office stars next to names such as Sidney Poitier, Barbra Streisand, Steve McQueen, Dustin Hoffman, Clint Eastwood, Jack Lemmon, Julie Andrews and Sean Connery.

At fifty, Marvin's career began its inevitable descent, and within five years, after bombs such as *The Klansman* and *The Great Scout and Cathouse Thursday*, he was widely considered washed up. His notoriety increased in 1979, when he was dragged into court by former companion Michele Triola in the infamous "palimony" suit in which Triola claimed half of Marvin's income as her own.

Marvin worked little in the late 1970s, preferring to spend his time with his second wife and go fishing for marlin in the Pacific. There was one final flash of glory in the early 1980s as Marvin starred in *The Big Red One* and *Gorky Park*, proving that he could still command the screen. But Marvin became a shell of his old self over the next few years, still making the action movies that his fans wanted. He died of a heart attack brought on by respiratory problems in Tucson, Arizona, in 1987.

But Lee Marvin's film career is much more substantial and influential than that brief description implies. No such overview can convey the professionalism of an actor who learned his craft by experience and who always strove to make his co-stars comfortable and relaxed. Nor can it communicate Marvin's creativity and the acting risks that he took to elevate his various performances to something above the ordinary. And it doesn't begin to describe Marvin's work.

That is the purpose of this book.

Lee Marvin was a fascinating, frightening man, a loving husband and father, a brave soldier (with scars, both physical and psychological, to prove it), a reluctant public figure and one of the most natural, effective actors of his time. However, this book is not meant to be Marvin's biography. It is, rather, an examination of his working life, based on the thesis that a film actor's career can (and perhaps should) be evaluated on his legacy of performances and films rather than on the personal details of his life—his personal habits, his family and friends and lovers, the famous people with whom he became acquainted—however entertaining those details may be. In this book, Lee Marvin's film appearances are discussed in detail, with particular attention to his importance to each film and his effectiveness in each of his roles.

Lee Marvin worked as a film actor for thirty-five years and made sixty films. Some of his films are classics, most are of at least good quality, and a scant few are pretty poor. Through them all, Marvin maintained his dignity, striving to contribute *something* to make the experience worthwhile, to justify his paycheck. Marvin was often quoted as saying that acting was a silly way to make a living, that it didn't seem to be a real job. Fans of his films disagree, noting that however Marvin downplayed his chosen profession, he always took his roles seriously and understood better than many of his colleagues what to show to the camera and what to hide.

As an actor, Lee Marvin was widely respected for his abilities by fellow filmmakers and audiences alike. His death scenes in particular (in films such as *The Stranger Wore a Gun*, *The Raid*, *Violent Saturday* and *Seven Men from Now*) were often singled out as memorable. As a movie star, Marvin's persona took shape in the mid–1950s as a sadistic, brutal heavy and gradually changed over the next decade into a lethal anti-hero, similar to that of Steve McQueen, but tougher and more violent. This persona has remained strong years after Marvin's death and has only gained in stature as home video has widened audience exposure to Marvin's acting. What's more, various odd products, organizations, and movie and television references demonstrate that his legacy exists outside of his own film and television work.

For example, in June of 1968 Adventure House Press published a single issue of a comic book called *His Name Is...Savage!*, chronicling the efforts of Savage, "a man without plans, hopes, or dreams," intent on eliminating the enemies of the United States that cannot be destroyed by regular agencies. Though the character of Savage does not look anything like Lee Marvin, the cover of the comic features a hand-colored photograph of Marvin, complete with smoking gun—evidently an image from *The Killers*. Marvin is not mentioned anywhere inside and seems to have no other connection to the "fearless, sinister, threatening" character—yet the producers of this comic evidently felt that Marvin best represented the image they wished to convey. "Savage" only lasted for one issue and is difficult to find, though there does not seem to be much of a demand for the comic.

References to Lee Marvin pop up more and more frequently in films and television as time passes. *Sleepless in Seattle* features a scene in which Tom Hanks, who is tired of hearing about how Rita Wilson is affected by a scene in *An Affair to Remember*, emotionally (and hilariously) recalls the scene in *The Dirty Dozen* in which Jim Brown is killed. Marvin, along with Charles Bronson, is prominently referred to in *Reservoir Dogs*. Jim Jarmusch's western *Dead Man* features two bounty hunters: one named Lee, the other Marvin. In the animated prime time television series *The Simpsons*, one episode shows Homer Simpson bringing home a video copy of *Paint Your Wagon* and being mortified by the fact that both Lee Marvin and Clint Eastwood *sing* rather than shoot people.

There is a semi-secret organization, many of its members from the Hollywood community, titled "The Sons of Lee Marvin." It is a shadowy brotherhood, made up of famous men who appreciate Marvin's no-nonsense style, blunt honesty and prowess with women and firearms. In addition, there is another organization, the BSOL or "The Bastard Sons of Lee," comprised of non-celebrities who simply like Lee Marvin as an actor and who get together to screen Marvin's films, lighting up cigars whenever Marvin does so on-screen. Such is Lee Marvin's lasting fame.

Robert J. Lentz

Feature Films

You're in the Navy Now (1951) (aka *U.S.S. Teakettle*)

CREDITS: 20th Century–Fox. *Directed by* Henry Hathaway. *Produced by* Fred Kohlmar. *Screenplay by* Richard Murphy. *From an article in* The New Yorker *by* John W. Hazard. *Music by*: Cyril Mockridge. *Musical Direction*: Lionel Newman. *Orchestration*: Edward Powell. *Director of Photography*: Joe MacDonald, A.S.C. *Film Editor*: James B. Clark, A.C.E. *Art Direction*: Lyle Wheeler, J. Russell Spencer. *Set Decorations*: Thomas Little, Fred J. Rode. *Sound*: W.D. Flick, Roger Heman. *Wardrobe Direction*: Charles Le Maire. *Makeup Artist*: Ben Nye. *Special Photographic Effects by* Fred Sersen, Ray Kellogg. *Technical Advisor*: Joseph Warren Lomax, Chief Boatswain, U.S.N. Not Rated. Black and White. Flat (1.33:1). 93 minutes. Released in February 1951 as *U.S.S. Teakettle*. Re-released in April 1951 as *You're in the Navy Now*. Not currently available on home video.

CAST: *Lieutenant John W. Harkness*, Gary Cooper; *Ellie Harkness*, Jane Greer; *Chief Boatswain Mate Larrabee*, Millard Mitchell; *Lieutenant Bill Barron*, Eddie Albert; *Commander Reynolds*, John McIntyre; *Admiral L. E. Tennant*, Ray Collins; *Captain Eliot*, Harry Von Zell; *Ensign Anthony Barbo*, Jack Webb; *Ensign Chuck Dorrance*, Richard Erdman; *Norelli*, Harvey Lembeck; *Chief Engineer Ryan*, Henry Slate; *Port Commander*, Ed Begley; *Battleship Admiral*, Fay Roope; *Houlihan*, Charles Tannen; *Wascylewski*, Charles Buchinski (Bronson); *Morse*, Jack Warden; *Crew members*, Ken Harvey, Lee Marvin, Jerry Hausner, Charles Smith; *New Sailor*, James Cornell; *Shore Patrolmen*, Glen Gordon, Laurence Hugo; *Doctor*, Damian O'Flynn; *Sailor Messenger*, Biff McGuire; *Admiral's Aide*, Norman McKay; *Naval Commander*, John McGuire; *Admiral's Wife*, Elsa Peterson; *Naval Captain*, Herman Cantor; *Mess Boy*, Joel Fluellen; *C.P.O.*, William Leicester; *Naval Officer*, Ted Stanhope; *Lieutenant Commander*, Rory Mallinson; *Tugboat Sailor*, Bernard Kates.

Lee Marvin made his motion picture debut as a serviceman, a characterization which would become common for the actor. Over the following thirty-five years, Marvin would appear as a sailor, soldier or military officer some twenty times, covering almost one-third of his screen roles. Only John Wayne, and perhaps Gary Cooper, became more identified with various armed service uniforms during their careers than Lee Marvin.

While most of Marvin's military roles would be in gritty war dramas, this case is the opposite. *You're in the Navy Now*, as this film has best become known, is one of the many military comedies that followed World War II as Hollywood looked for ways to continue making films featuring the military during peacetime. By the mid-1950s, this wave of comedies, which crested with the slapstick adventures of Martin and Lewis in various armed services, turned bitter (*Mister Roberts*) and began to subside. Of all of the wacky military comedies of the early 1950s, *You're in the Navy Now* was considered one of the funniest, at least at the time of its original release.

The PC-1168 is a Navy patrol cruiser fitted with a steam (instead of the standard diesel) engine. The ship, dubbed the U.S.S. *Teakettle* by its crew, is a top secret World War II research experiment designed to determine whether or not a self-sufficient steam turbine engine can result in faster, yet still reliable, Naval service. The officer chosen to helm the ship is Lt. John W. Harkness (Gary Cooper), fresh out of the Navy's three-month training course. He is quite nervous about his first command, as well as having to leave behind Ellie (Jane Greer), his wife of seven years, who has joined the WAVEs.

After meeting his officers (Eddie Albert, Jack Webb, Richard Erdman), all "90-day wonders" like himself, Harkness' first task is to get the ship underway. The officers eventually figure out how to start the steam engine, lose control of the ship and plow into the side of an aircraft carrier. With the help of experienced Chief Boatswain Mate Larrabee (Millard Mitchell), Harkness is able to test the *Teakettle*, which speeds along nicely until the engine overheats and stalls, leaving the ship slowly drifting out to sea without electrical power. Further humiliation follows as a passing oil tanker fires upon them, and they are towed back to base the next day.

Similar misadventures follow as each sea trial fails miserably. To raise morale, one of the crew (Charles Bronson, making *his* film debut, as Wascylewski) enters a boxing match at the base. In order to return in time for the fight, extra distilled water is smuggled aboard to keep the engine running and the *Teakettle* passes its first test without incident. However, Wascylewski falls in the engine room and breaks his ribs, causing Ensign Barbo (Jack Webb) to take his place in the ring to fight for the base championship.

For the *Teakettle*'s final test, Admiral Tennant (Ray Collins) comes onboard to personally inspect the ship. As it speeds along, he sees how Harkness and Larrabee have trained the crew, especially in the engine room, where sweating sailors are busy twirling, pushing and hammering away at the recalcitrant steam engine, keeping it running. On the way back to base, the throttles freeze up, and the *Teakettle* again speeds into the harbor, barely missing drawbridges and other ships until it finally ends up in the side of another aircraft carrier.

Billed twenty-eighth, Lee Marvin first appeared on screen in *You're in the Navy Now*.

Despite the ship's failures, Admiral Tennant calls the experiment a success, noting that steam engines obviously aren't right for patrol cruisers, but that they may prove useful elsewhere. He commends Harkness and his crew for their determination and improvisational skills. As Ellie watches, the U.S.S. *Teakettle*, equipped with a brand new diesel engine, pulls away from the dock and proudly heads for sea duty.

You're in the Navy Now is an uneasy blend of satire and slapstick, entertaining to watch but rarely more than amusing. Though critics and audiences of 1951 seem to have truly enjoyed the antics of the *Teakettle*'s crew, this comedy now seems quaint and labored, much as British comedy often appears to American audiences. Some of the cinematic tricks, such as speeding up the film during the climactic race up the river, do not work at all today (and probably didn't then, either). One problem is that the film's main gimmick, its massive steam engine, is bad-mouthed regularly by the crew but only rarely made part of the on-screen action. "That *thing* in the engine room," as Larrabee refers to it, could have been used to much greater comic effect, but it is all but ignored until the film's climax when Admiral Tennant makes his inspection and sees the noisy behemoth in action.

Some of the human actors are given more to do. This is the kind of film in which the supporting players can outshine the leads, and they certainly do here. Eddie Albert is absolutely energized as the ship's executive officer, Jack Webb is surprisingly animated and cynical, and Harvey Lembeck practices the *schtick* he would later use in *Stalag 17*. This was one of Jack Warden's first films; he plays Morse, the sailor asked to take Wascylewski's place in the boxing tournament. Other familiar faces include Millard Mitchell, Ed Begley and Ray Collins, reliable character actors who could always be counted on to provide strong support. As the *Teakettle*'s new captain, Gary Cooper seems ill at ease, having to play the straight man to the hijinks of the crew. And as his wife Ellie, Jane Greer does her best in a sprightly manner with a thankless role.

Two new faces made their debuts in *You're in the Navy Now*, men whose careers would cross several times over the next thirty years. Charles Bronson made sixteen films under his birth name, Buchinski; this was his first. Bronson was studying acting at the Pasadena Playhouse when that theater school received a casting request for "a cross between Humphrey Bogart and John Garfield." The 29-year-old actor was typecast as a heavy from the beginning, but made a respectable career out of humanizing tough guys.

Lee Marvin was 26 when he made *You're in the Navy Now*. Marvin had been working as a stage actor in New York after a stint as a plumber's assistant and various other short-term jobs. After returning from service in World War II and recovering from injuries sustained when he was wounded in the South Pacific battle at Saipan, Marvin had discovered that acting was fun and was a good way to meet girls. He had acted in various plays in his home town of Woodstock, New York, and had made it to Broadway in *Billy Budd*, when he attended a "cattle call" for film work. Marvin was originally hired for three days as an extra, but director Henry Hathaway was impressed enough to gradually increase Marvin's schedule to three weeks.

Marvin's first scene is in the engine room, smoking and sweating, adjusting some part of the monstrous engine. A little later when the ship is stalled and drifting, Marvin appears as the radioman, informing the Captain that he can't contact anyone. When the crew is allowed liberty, Marvin is one of the two guards instructed to bring in the men quietly as they arrive. His longest scene occurs belowdecks, as Norelli (Harvey Lembeck) is figuring out the bets on the upcoming fight and refers to Marvin's unnamed sailor as "Lee." When Wascylewski falls, Marvin is there to help. At the fight he is not seen but his voice can be heard yelling.

Thanks to the miracle of film editing during the final sea test, Marvin is seen at three stations *at the same time*. He is the radioman on the bridge, relaying orders. He is also at the stern, helping to drop depth charges. He is also in the engine room, helping to keep the steam engine from exploding. In his first film, Lee

Marvin was already doing the impossible. He later commented to *Life* magazine: "In my first picture, I played seven sailors. They even had me talking to myself over the intercom." Marvin's total screen time doesn't quite reach five minutes, and his part isn't as large as Warden's, Bronson's or Lembeck's, but his versatility and willingness to work make his part just as visible.

U.S.S. Teakettle received excellent reviews when it premiered in February of 1951. Bosley Crowther of the *New York Times* led the cheers, calling the film "the best comedy of the year." *Variety* labelled it "a spontaneous and explosive comedy," while *Boxoffice* called it "a bright, fresh and frequently hilarious piece of celluloid." The *Hollywood Reporter* termed the film "a happy, imaginative and offbeat entry," and all of these industry trade reviews predicted handsome box office success. This was not to be.

After disappointing box office returns under the title *U.S.S. Teakettle* in February of 1951, 20th Century–Fox changed the film's name to *You're in the Navy Now* and re-released it two months later. The new title didn't help and the film sank from sight. Today it is hardly remembered, except as a footnote: this is the film which, thanks to director Henry Hathaway, introduced two of the silver screen's greatest tough guys. Both would go on to much bigger and better things.

Teresa (1951)

CREDITS: Metro-Goldwyn-Mayer. *Directed by* Fred Zinnemann. *Produced by* Arthur M. Loew, Jr. *Screenplay by* Stewart Stern. *Based upon a story by* Alfred Hayes and Stewart Stern. *Music by* Louis Applebaum. *Musical Director*: Jack Shaindlin. *Director of Photography*: William J. Miller. *Film Editor*: Frank Sullivan. *Associate Film Editor*: David Kummins. *Art Director*: Leo Kerz. *Recording Supervisor*: James Shields. *Script Supervisor*: Arnold Laven. *Technical Advisors*: Bill Mauldin, Captain James B. Anders, Sergeant Walter R. Malott. Not Rated. Black and White. Flat (1.33:1). 102 minutes. Released in April 1951. Not currently available on home video.

CAST: *Teresa*, Pier Angeli; *Philip Quas*, John Ericson; *Philip's Mother*, Patricia Collinge; *Philip's Father*, Richard Bishop; *Susan*, Peggy Ann Garner; *Sergeant Dobbs*, Ralph Meeker; *Grissom*, Bill Mauldin; *Teresa's Mother*, Ava Ninchi; *Sergeant Brown*, Edward Binns; *Frank*, Rod Steiger; *Professor Crocce*, Aldo Silvani; *Walter*, Tommy Lewis; *Mario*, Franco Interlenghi; *Mrs. Lawrence*, Edith Atwater; *Cheyenne*, Lewis Cianelli; *Boone*, William King; *G.I. Cook*, Richard McNamara; *Soldier on troop ship standing at rail with cigarette*, Lee Marvin.

Lee Marvin's second film appearance, in *Teresa*, is also his briefest. Watch closely during the sequence when Philip Quas (John Ericson) is traveling back to America from Europe by troop ship. There are two shots of Philip standing at the rail of the ship along with four other G.I.s. The soldier at the extreme right with a cigarette in his hand, talking to another soldier, is Lee Marvin. His total screen time lasts about five seconds.

Teresa is a sensitive story regarding a timely issue of the late 1940s: war brides. Director Fred Zinnemann summed it up this way: "The war brides were girls in England, France, Italy and Germany who had married U.S. soldiers serving abroad during the war. All these foreign wives, who had been left behind while their G.I.s were sent home, were 'processed' and followed months later, landing in America in the thousands. Many conflicts arose when they met their new families, who did not always receive them with open arms; often these new relatives could not even converse with each other, and strong clashes of alien cultures were bound to happen. Many girls found it difficult to adjust to their new lives. Some managed; others didn't."

In *Teresa*, the G.I. in question is young Philip Quas (John Ericson), a shy young man with no confidence. After cowardly running away from battle, he meets and falls in love with beautiful Teresa (Pier Angeli) and matures somewhat. He marries her and waits for her arrival in New York. The second half of the film depicts the difficulties Philip and Teresa encounter with Philip's family, especially with his domineering mother (Patricia Collinge), who doesn't want Philip to grow up. Philip and Teresa grow apart and actually separate, but the birth of their son brings them back together and gives Philip the impetus he needs for achieving his independence.

The story, written by Stewart Stern and Alfred Hayes, was nominated for an Academy Award but lost to *Panic in the Streets*. *Teresa* is John Ericson's debut before the cameras, and he registers strongly as weak-willed Philip, but within a few years he would be a supporting player in films like *Bad Day at Black Rock*. Rod Steiger also makes his film debut as a psychiatrist with whom Philip has weekly visits in New York. Steiger was able to build his film career into something more substantial.

Pier Angeli became a star virtually overnight in her first American film and went on to a very respectable career in the 1950s. Unfortunately, her star dimmed in the 1960s and she committed suicide after her appearance in the dreadful *Octaman* in 1972. Other familiar faces in the cast include character actors Ralph Meeker and Edward Binns, former child star Peggy Ann Garner, and actor-journalist-cartoonist Bill Mauldin, who is actually credited as a technical advisor on *Teresa*.

Teresa was not very successful, despite strongly favorable reviews and its timely subject. It was made in the European neo-realistic style which stressed authenticity but perhaps was not entertaining enough for American audiences. Director Fred Zinnemann ultimately termed it "a lost cause despite some good scenes and the best intentions: a film divided against itself."

Teresa is merely a footnote in Lee Marvin's career. He has no lines and is next to invisible as an extra in his one scene. His part is so small that Zinnemann doesn't even mention Marvin's involvement in the book he wrote about his own career, *A Life in the Movies*. Extras are an important aspect to virtually every film, yet few extras, no matter how often they appear, ever gain stardom of any sort. Lee Marvin was one of the few actors who only appeared as an extra once or twice and went on to a tremendous career.

Lee Marvin (far right, with cigarette) in his only appearance in *Teresa*. Philip Quas (John Ericson) is in the middle.

Hong Kong (1951)
(aka *Bombs Over China*)

CREDITS:. Paramount. *Directed by* Lewis R. Foster. *Produced by* William H. Pine, William C. Thomas. *Written for the Screen by* Winston Miller. *Based on a story by* Lewis R. Foster. *Music Score by* Lucien Cailliet. *Director of Photography*: Lionel Lindon, A.S.C. *Film Editor*: Howard Smith. *Art Direction*: Lewis H. Creber. *Set Decoration*: Alfred Kegerris. *Sound Recording*: Harold C. Lewis, Walter Oberst. *Wardrobe*: Charles Keehne. *Costumes for Miss Fleming*: Edith Head. *Hair Stylist*: Kay Shea. *Makeup Artist*: Norman Pringle. Not Rated. Technicolor. *Technicolor Color Consultant*: Robert Brower. Flat (1.33:1). 90 minutes. Released in November 1951 as *Hong Kong*. Re-released in 1962 as *Bombs Over China*. Not currently available on home video.

CAST: *Jeff Williams*, Ronald Reagan; *Victoria Evans*, Rhonda Fleming; *Mr. Lighton*, Nigel Bruce; *Mrs. Lighton*, Lady May Lawford (Mary Somerville); *Too Liang*, Marvin Miller; *Hotel Clerk*, Claud Allister; *Wei Lin*, Danny Chang; *Police Inspector*, Lowell Gilmore; *Bit Part*, Lee Marvin?

If viewers blink during *Teresa*, they might miss Lee Marvin's bit part (it lasts fewer than five seconds). In *Hong Kong*, Marvin's role may be even smaller. In fact, there is some doubt as to whether Lee Marvin appears in *Hong Kong* at all. For years *Hong Kong* has been listed in Lee Marvin's filmography, but a close scrutiny of the film cannot locate him. He may be on the British patrol ship which rescues Ronald Reagan, Rhonda Fleming and Danny Chang at the climax of the film, but the shots of the ship are too far away to properly view any of the ship's crewmen.

The possibilities that Marvin is either onboard that ship (he would be a natural choice for a sailor) or that he may appear as an extra in a crowd scene explain why *Hong Kong* is included in this book. His presence cannot be ruled out, but neither can it be confirmed, despite the film's inclusion in Marvin's filmography.

Hong Kong is a pleasant little potboiler involving ex-G.I. Jeff Williams (Ronald Reagan) in some shady post-war shenanigans in China. Jeff helps Red Cross worker Victoria Evans (Rhonda Fleming) evacuate a group of Chinese peasants to Hong Kong, including a cute Chinese boy named Wei-Lin (Danny Chang). The boy carries with him a golden idol that money-hungry Jeff covets. Jeff makes an attempt to pawn the idol to an art dealer, but his conscience won't let him betray the boy's future. He also takes some time to fall in love with Victoria Evans.

The art dealer (Marvin Miller) kidnaps Wei-Lin and asks for the idol in return. Jeff and Victoria try to make an exchange but fail, resulting in the loss of the idol. They find the art dealer and force him to take them to Wei-Lin, who is being held captive on a sampan in Hong Kong's crowded harbor. A gunfight ensues, which leads to a fire. The art dealer and his henchmen are killed, and Jeff, Victoria and Wei-Lin are rescued by a British patrol ship. The happy ending finds Mr. and Mrs. Jeff Williams visiting Wei-Lin at the orphanage where they have temporarily placed him until they can provide him with a home.

Hong Kong is a routine B-movie, an "adventure quickie" destined to fill half of a double bill (in this instance, with *Flaming Feather*) and disappear into oblivion; or so the filmmakers thought. *Hong Kong* was re-issued by another distributor in 1962 as *Bombs Over China*, both to capitalize on (and ridicule Ronald Reagan's oratories against Communism as he became more immersed in the American political arena. Just four years later, Reagan would become Governor of California. Later, of course, Reagan became the first actor to be elected President of the United States.

The best performance in the film is given by young Danny Chang as Wei-Lin, whom, according to Lawrence J. Quirk in *The Films of Ronald Reagan*, Reagan praised as "the finest and most natural scene stealer he had met during his career." Most critics agreed, complimenting the boy on his natural performance and screen presence. The other actors and behind-the-scenes folk didn't fare nearly as well; the film was noted as "a corn meal special, with chop suey added" by Howard Thompson of the *New York Times* and "a slow-moving adventure tour" by *Newsweek*. Two decades later Leonard Maltin termed it "strictly backlot Hong Kong" in his *TV Movies and Video Guide*. Except for the novelty of seeing Ronald Reagan play a somewhat crooked character, and the question of Lee Marvin's trivial involvement, *Hong Kong* deserves its obscurity.

Diplomatic Courier (1952)

CREDITS: 20th Century–Fox. *Directed by* Henry Hathaway. *Produced by* Casey Robinson. *Screen Play by* Casey Robinson, Liam O'Brien. *Based on the novel* Sinister Errand *by* Peter Cheyney. *Music by* Sol Kaplan. *Musical Direction by* Lionel Newman. *Orchestration*: Edward Powell. *Director of Photography*: Lucien Ballard, A.S.C. *Film Editor*: James B. Clark, A.C.E. *Art Direction*: Lyle Wheeler, John De Cuir. *Set Decorations*: Thomas Little, Stuart Reiss. *Sound*: W.D. Flick, Roger Heman. *Wardrobe Direction*: Charles Le Maire. *Costumes Designed by* Elois Jenssen. *Makeup Artist*: Ben Nye. *Special Photographic Effects*: Ray Kellogg. Not Rated. Black and White. Flat (1.33:1). 97 minutes. Released in June 1952. Currently available on VHS videotape.

CAST: *Mike Kells*, Tyrone Power; *Joan Ross*, Patricia Neal; *Colonel Cagle*, Stephen McNally; *Janine*, Hildegarde Neff; *Ernie*, Karl Malden; *Sam Carew*, James Millican; *Platov*, Stefan Schnabel; *Arnov*, Herbert Berghof; *Max Ralli*, Arthur Blake; *Airline Stewardess*, Helene Stanley; *Ivan*, Michael Ansara; *Chef De Train*, Sig Arno; *Cherenko*, Alfreed Linder; *Military Policeman at Trieste*, Lee Marvin; *Zinski*, Peter Coe; *Watch Officer*, Tyler McVey; *Butrick*, Stuart Randall; *Intelligence Clerk*, Dabbs Greer; *Brennan*, Carleton Young; *French Ticket Agent*, Charles La Torre; *Bill*, Russ Conway; *Cherney*, Tom Powers; *French Stewardess*, Monique Chantal; *Jacks*, Lumsden Hare; *Russian Agents*, Charles Buchinski (Bronson), Mario Siletti; *Second Military Policeman at Trieste*, E. G. Marshall; *Narrated by* Hugh Marlowe.

Lee Marvin is a bit more visible in his next film, *Diplomatic Courier*, a routine espionage thriller, wherein he portrays a military policeman in two scenes who questions diplomatic courier Tyrone Power. While this is not a large part, it does give Marvin the chance to act with a bona fide movie star, however briefly, and he holds his own.

Mike Kells (Tyrone Power) is a diplo-

An early portrait of Lee Marvin, who may or may not appear in *Hong Kong*.

matic courier in Europe who is given a special assignment to contact fellow courier and close friend Sam Carew (James Millican) and receive a top secret document in Salzburg. Carew ignores his friend when the time comes to make the document transfer. Bewildered, Kells follows Carew onto a train, tries to make contact in vain, and eventually finds his friend dead. C.I.D. officer Colonel Cagle (Stephen McNally) persuades Kells to continue the hunt for the document and has Kells flown to Trieste. Kells follows the trail to Janine Betke (Hildegard Neff), who claims to have been working with Sam Carew, and whom Kells had seen with Carew on the train. Kells is attacked outside her apartment by Russian agents but is rescued by Col. Cagle's aide, Ernie (Karl Malden), who has been assigned to protect Kells.

The top secret document is a timetable for an imminent Russian invasion of Yugoslavia, and Kells is ordered to continue to search for it. Kells gets back on the trail but is interrupted, again, by the attentions of a wealthy American jet-setter, Joan Ross (Patricia Neal), who has been amorously following him since they met on the plane to Salzburg.

Janine reveals that she has found and hidden the document, which was passed on to her by Sam Carew on the train before his death. She makes a deal with Kells for safe passage to America, but the deal falls through. Joan Ross reveals that she is actually a Russian agent and corners Kells, but Ernie arrives and easily captures Joan. Kells receives a phone call and falls into a Russian trap, and when the Russians do not find the document on him, they dump him in a river, to be rescued by Ernie—again.

Janine makes a deal with the Russians for her life but secretly leaves the location of the document for the Americans. Col. Cagle tells Kells that it has been retrieved and admits that he was wrong about Janine whom he had always considered an enemy agent. Kells insists on trying to rescue Janine, and is reluctantly aided by Ernie. Kells boards a train headed for Russia, finds Janine and her Russian captor, and bravely spirits her off the train to freedom.

As in most espionage thrillers, there is an abundance of story threads to follow, and much attention is needed to keep track of the characters and their allegiances. Much of the dialogue in this type of film is expository in nature, revealing plot information rather than character development. The result is that the thriller seems slow and ponderous, becoming boring despite its often breakneck pace. This is certainly true of *Diplomatic Courier*. Despite a first-rate cast and some interesting action sequences, the film rarely rewards the viewer attention which it demands.

One of the movie's more interesting aspects is that the men in the film are all pretty straightforward, and it is the women who are the duplicitous double agents. The female characters seem much more cunning and smart than the men who follow them. Hildegarde

Lee Marvin (as a military policeman) in the first of his two scenes with Tyrone Power in *Diplomatic Courier*.

Neff and Patricia Neal give stronger performances than their male counterparts, probably because their roles are juicier; they don't have to play by the numbers like Tyrone Power and Stephen McNally. Neff gives Janine enough shading to make it plausible that she truly is a Russian agent, while Neal is aggressively sexy and surprises as the true Russian agent. However, the best performance is given by Karl Malden, who blusters and cajoles his way through the bureaucratic red tape of his job, trying to keep Mike Kells alive.

Director Henry Hathaway had hired Lee Marvin for *You're in the Navy Now*; here he used him again, giving Marvin a larger, more dynamic role. As the unnamed Military Policeman in Trieste, Marvin provides Mike Kells with information about Janine Betke, enabling him to track her down, and he later checks with Kells to see if he has seen her.

It is a solid little performance, giving Marvin a chance to exhibit some of his natural authority.

Along with Marvin, Hathaway also hired Charles Buchinsky (Bronson) again for this film. Bronson, who, like Marvin, had made his film debut in *You're in the Navy Now*, portrays one of the Russian agents trailing Sam Carew on the train. It is a small role with virtually no dialogue, but Bronson certainly looks the part and plays it well. Two other actors appear in small roles who would go on to impressive careers: Michael Ansara and E. G. Marshall.

Critics were divided on the film's merits. *Newsweek* called it "a satisfactory entertainment," and Howard McClay of the *Los Angeles Daily News* deemed it "an intriguing film," while the *New York Times*' Bosley Crowther wrote: "And yet it (20th Century–Fox) has a picture of no more than middling appeal." *Diplomatic Courier* did moderate business and was soon forgotten.

We're Not Married (1952)

CREDITS: 20th Century–Fox. *Directed by* Edmund Goulding. *Produced by* Nunnally Johnson. *Screenplay by* Nunnally Johnson. *Adapted by* Dwight Taylor *from a story by* Gina Kaus, Jay Dratler. *Music by* Cyril Mockridge. *Musical Direction*: Lionel Newman. *Orchestration*: Bernard Mayers. *Director of Photography*: Leo Tover, A.S.C. *Film Editor*: Louis Loeffler. *Art Direction*: Lyle Wheeler, Leland Fuller. *Set Decorations*: Thomas Little, Claude Carpenter. *Sound*: W. D. Flick, Roger Heman. *Special Photographic Effects*: Ray Kellogg. *Costumes Designed by* Elois Jenssen. *Wardrobe Direction*: Charles LeMaire. *Makeup Artist*: Ben Nye. Not Rated. Black and White. Flat (1.33:1). 85 minutes. Released in July 1952. Currently available on VHS videotape.

CAST: *Ramona Gladwyn*, Ginger Rogers; *Steve Gladwyn*, Fred Allen; *Melvin Bush (Justice of the Peace)*, Victor Moore; *Annabel Norris*, Marilyn Monroe; *Jeff Norris*, David Wayne; *Katie Woodruff*, Eve Arden; *Hector Woodruff*, Paul Douglas; *Willie Fisher*, Eddie Bracken; *Patsy Fisher*, Mitzi Gaynor; *Freddie Melrose*, Louis Calhern; *Eve Melrose*, Zsa Zsa Gabor; *Duffy*, James Gleason; *Attorney Stone*, Paul Stewart; *Mrs. Bush*, Jane Darwell; *Attorney General Bush*, Tom Powers; *Governor Bush*, Victor Sutherland; *Detective Magnus*, Alan Bridge; *Radio Announcer*, Harry Golder; *Wife*, Kay English; *Pinky*, Lee Marvin; *Potman*, O. Z. Whitehead; *Ruthie*, Marjorie Weaver; *Mississippi Governor*, Forbes Murray; *Organist*, Maurice Cass; *Daughter on Radio*, Margie Liszt; *Autograph Hound*, Maude Wallace; *Mr. Graves*, Richard Buckley; *Men in Radio Station*, Alvin Greenman, Eddie Firestone; *Wife*, Phyllis Brunner; *M.P.s at Railroad Station*, Steve Pritko, Robert Dane; *Master Sergeant Nuckols*, James Burke; *M.P.s*, Robert Forrest, Bill Hale; *Counterman*, Ed Max; *Brigadier General*, Richard Reeves; *Twitchell*, Ralph Dumke; *Justice of the Peace*, Harry Antrim; *License Bureau Clerk*, Byron Foulger; *Postman*, Harry Harvey; *Doctor Ned*, Selmer Jackson; *Chaplain Hall*, Harry Carter; *Man at Miss Mississippi Contest*, Dabbs Greer; *Beauty Contest Announcer*, Emile Meyer; *State Troopers*, Henry Faber, Larry Stamps.

We're Not Married is a star-studded comedy of five couples who discover that they are not legally married some two-and-a-half years after their weddings. The marital mistake is due to Melvin Bush (Victor Moore), a bumbling Justice of the Peace who marries six couples days before his appointment actually commences. The problem is discovered when a couple in another state ask for a divorce and find that they were never legally married. That leaves five couples, each of whom are notified by official letter.

The Glad Gladwyns (Ginger Rogers, Fred Allen) are a popular radio morning show couple who bicker constantly off the air. Their regular battle is interrupted one morning when they receive the fateful letter. Both agree that marrying again is out of the question; their unexpected freedom is too valuable. However, they must be married to collect their paychecks. Their bickering is cut short as their radio show begins and they earn their money by cooing at each other and engaging in non-stop product selling.

Annabel Norris (Marilyn Monroe) wins the Mrs. Mississippi contest in a swimsuit as husband Jeff (David Wayne) and baby son watch proudly. Personal appearances follow and Jeff's temper rises as he is left home to do the housework and take care of the baby, until the letter arrives. He informs the national committee of his wife's ineligibility, but rather than cry, Annabel is delighted. She walks down a runway in a swimsuit, again, this time as Miss Mississippi. Jeff, with son, cheers as his beautiful fiancé takes the crown.

Katie (Eve Arden) and Hector Woodruff (Paul Douglas) are the third couple, who barely talk to each other anymore. After dinner Hector opens the mail and to his immediate delight finds himself a bachelor again. He then imagines women for each day (excepting Sunday, his day of rest), kissing them and dancing the night away. His fantasies come to an abrupt end when he imagines the bill for an evening of celebration. He frowns and burns the letter.

Millionaire oil man Freddie Melrose (Louis Calhern) is framed for adultery by wife Eve (Zsa Zsa Gabor), who immediately files divorce papers. At his office, while Eve and her attorney begin to divy up his loot, Freddie escapes to his outer office, where he distractedly glances at the mail. A few minutes later, he rejoins them in a different frame of mind. He presents her with "the most important asset I have" and calmly lights a cigar while she reads the letter and faints.

Willie Fisher (Eddie Bracken) receives his letter just as he is shipping out to serve in Korea. As his train leaves, wife Patsy (Mitzi Gaynor) arrives, yelling to him that she's pregnant. Faced with having an illegitmate child, Willie goes AWOL and telegraphs Patsy to meet him so they can remarry. She arrives in time to get the license, but trying to arrange a quick blood test and M.P.s on the lookout for Willie sink their plans. From the brig on a ship headed for Korea, Willie is called up to the radio room, where an Army chaplain marries the couple over the air.

The montage ending of the film sees Annabel remarry Jeff (presumably after her tour as Miss Mississippi), Katie remarry Hector (despite her ignorance of the letter, which he burned), and Ramona remarry Steve Gladwyn.

We're Not Married follows the episodic structure of such popular hits as *Tales of Manhattan* (1942), *A Letter to Three Wives* (1949), *Phone Call from a Stranger* and *O. Henry's Full House* (both 1952), but this is the only one that is wholly comedic, poking fun at relationships, gender roles, money, radio, greed, beauty contests, advertising, nepotism and marriage in its many forms.

The first sequence is the funniest, as Rogers and Allen first ignore each other, then spew epithets at each other like cobras, then turn sickly-sweet for their radio gab-fest, which lampoons such radio shows and their advertisements with gusto. Their byplay is both real and funny. The second segment is the most memorable, due to the photogenic presence of Marilyn Monroe, shown to advantage in swimsuits during most of her fourteenth film appearance. Though the quiet marriage between Arden and Douglas is the most realistically filmed, it is also the most boring of the quintet.

Much more contemporary is the segment wherein Gabor tries to fleece Calhern of his millions. The situation captures the ring of authenticity yet is highly comical as well. Calhern is especially fun to watch. The final episode is tragic in implication yet almost slapstick in execution. It's an uneasy blend, but leads to a touching finale involving radio, which was lambasted in the first segment.

Lee Marvin appears in this last segment

Willie Fisher (Eddie Bracken) tells his buddy Pinky (Lee Marvin) that he'll be back in *We're Not Married*.

as Willie's army buddy Pinky, who tries to explain Willie's predicament to their sergeant, then watches Willie go AWOL. It's a nice, sensitive little two-minute performance that helps establish just how desperate Bracken is to get remarried and furnish his unborn child with a last name. Marvin is billed twentieth in his fifth film, and it was the second comedy for the lanky actor, but that trend died quickly as producers discovered his darker side. He would not make another true comedy until *Cat Ballou*, some thirteen years and thirty-two films later. This is also Marvin's first appearance on film as a soldier going to Korea, a role which he would repeat three more times during his career.

We're Not Married garnered favorable reviews from all over the country. The *New York Times* called it "…a tailored entertainment that is one of the snappiest of the year," while the *New Yorker* named it "…excellent entertainment…." *Newsweek* decreed it "…superior stuff…," while *Time*, in a mixed review, noted that the opening wedding of the Glad Gladwyns was "…one of the funniest marriage ceremonies ever seen on the screen."

Life wrote, "The brightest spot in a sad cinematic summer, *We're Not Married* takes a few snappily satiric cracks at certain features of contemporary American life—beauty contests, suburban comfort, a dyspeptic radio couple who gurgle to each other over breakfast beverages which they refer to in private as 'laundry juice.' It mixes its satire with proper doses of sentiment so that the final verdict of the picture is that marriage is a worthwhile thing after all."

The *Motion Picture Guide* describes *We're Not Married* as "the perfect TV movie, made in the days before they produced TV movies." It's an apt description due to the film's episodic nature, its mix of familiar veteran performers and young future television and movie stars, and even the subject matter. Indeed, it is surprising that *We're Not Married* has not been remade as a TV movie, as so many other film projects have been in recent years.

The Duel at Silver Creek (1952)

CREDITS: Universal. *Directed by* Don Siegel. *Produced by* Leonard Goldstein. *Screenplay by* Gerald Drayson Adams and Joseph Hoffman. *Story by* Gerald Drayson Adams. *Musical Direction by* Joseph Gershenson. *Director of Photography*: Irving Glassberg, A.S.C. *Film Editor*: Russell Schoengarth, A.C.E. *Art Direction by* Bernard Herzbrun, Alexander Golitzen. *Set Decorators*: Russell A. Gausman, Joe Kish. *Sound by* Leslie I. Carey, Corson Jowett. *Costumes by* Bill Thomas. *Makeup by* Bud Westmore. *Hair Stylist*: Joan St. Oegger. Not Rated. Technicolor. *Technicolor Color Consultant*: William Fritzche. Flat (1.33:1). 76 minutes. Released in August 1952. Currently available on VHS videotape.

CAST: *Luke Cromwell ("The Silver Kid")*, Audie Murphy; *Opal Lacey*, Faith Domergue; *Marshal "Lightning" Tyrone*, Stephen McNally; *Dusty Fargo*, Susan Cabot; *Rod Lacey*, Gerald Mohr; *Johnny Sombrero*, Eugene Iglesias; *Pete Fargo*, Walter Sande; *"Rat Face" Blake*, Kyle James; *Tinhorn Burgess*, Lee Marvin; *Jim Ryan*, George Eldredge; *Claim Jumpers*, Forest Burns, Carl Andre, John Carpenter; *Dan Musick*, Griff Barnett; *Dr. Clayton*, Frank Wilcox; *Sheriff Barton*, Steven Darrell; *Abe Cooney*, Jeff York; *Dr. Hargroves*, Wheaton Chambers; *Sam*, Stanley Blystone; *Stagecoach Driver*, Jennings Miles; *Dad Cromwell*, Harry Harvey; *Bit Parts*, David Newell, Sailor Vincent, Frank Hagney, Cap Sommers, Taylor McPeters, Alma Maison, Emile Avery, William Bailey, Monte Montague, Lee Morgan, George Brand, James Anderson.

All but forgotten now, *The Duel at Silver Creek* is definitely a minor western, but is notable as a stepping stone on the career paths of director Don Siegel and star Audie Murphy—and to a much lesser degree, Lee Marvin.

A band of ruthless claim jumpers is terrorizing the area around Silver City, forcing gold miners to sign over their claims and then killing them. Luke Cromwell (Audie Murphy) is able to shoot three of them down, but not before they kill his father at their mine. The action jumps to Silver City where Marshal "Lightning" Tyrone (Stephen McNally) organizes a posse to pursue the claim jumpers after another raid. The posse finds them, but they escape, wounding Lightning in the process. Recuperating at a nearby army hospital, Lightning meets Opal Lacey (Faith Domergue), a "fancy filly" traveling to Silver City to join her brother Rod. She flirts with Lightning and strangles a wounded man who has seen the claim jumpers firsthand.

When Lightning returns to Silver City, he finds that his best friend has been killed. He instantly blames local gunfighter Johnny Sombrero (Eugene Iglesias) and confronts him, but Johnny has an alibi. He's working for Opal and her brother Rod (Gerald Mohr). Opal implicates a drifter named the "Silver Kid," who arrived just before the murder. Lightning finds the Silver Kid at the saloon playing poker—it's Luke Cromwell. Luke settles a disagreement over poker with local tough Tinhorn Burgess (Lee Marvin) by shooting him in the hand, and Lightning is impressed enough to offer him a job as deputy. Together they go after the claim jumpers.

Luke catches "Rat Face" Blake (James Anderson) trying to kill Lightning. He is jailed, but Johnny Sombrero and an unwitting Tinhorn Burgess lead a lynch mob to the jail to string him up. As Lightning calms down the mob, a jailbreak does take place and Blake is supposedly freed (though Blake really isn't rescued because he isn't there; he's been safely hidden away). Later that night, Opal tells lightning that Rod has been kidnapped by the claim jumpers, who want to trade him for Blake.

Lightning and Luke argue about Opal;

all Lightning can see is her beauty, while Luke doesn't trust her. Lightning loses his temper and fires the deputy. Opal overhears the argument and learns that Lightning's hand is crippled from the earlier shooting. She gets word to Johnny Sombrero, who calls him out for a showdown. Dusty (Susan Cabot), a local tomboy who likes Lightning, begs Luke to help him; Luke wings Lightning in the arm and takes his place against Johnny Sombrero, whom he shoots down easily. Before he dies, Sombrero tells all about Opal. Lightning and Luke make a deal with Opal, round up a posse and attack the claim jumpers' hideout. The villains are either captured or killed, including Opal, who is shot by Rod for leading the posse to their hideout.

Despite its obvious origins as a "B" western, *The Duel at Silver Creek* does have some positive aspects. It's a slam-bang actioner directed with a fast pace by Don Siegel, who would become one of the masters of the crime thriller later in his career. The film zips along from gunfight to chase and back to gunfight, only interrupted by a lynch mob, a jailbreak or a kiss. Siegel originally brought the film in at just fifty-four minutes, causing some consternation at Universal. Siegel added the prologue in which Luke's claim is jumped, and the epilogue in which Dusty and Luke finally kiss to fatten the film to its final length of a still-lean seventy-seven minutes.

Unlike most other dry, dusty oaters of the time, *The Duel at Silver Creek* doesn't take itself so seriously. The film is enjoyably tongue-in-cheek, poking a little fun at some of the familiar conventions of the genre. The character names reflect the attitude of the film: Lightning, Brown Eyes, Silver Kid, Johnny Sombrero, Rat Face, Tinhorn, Dusty. The dialogue, for the most part, is sharp as well. There are genuine laughs and some

Tinhorn Burgess (Lee Marvin) has just been called "Sheep Dip" by the Silver Kid (Audie Murphy) in *The Duel at Silver Creek.*

cutting insults thrown around with aplomb. In the poker game scene, Audie Murphy refers to Lee Marvin as "Sheep Dip."

The characters are well drawn and competently acted. Gerald Mohr's Rod Lacey dispatches people with no remorse, yet seems convincingly honest. He is outdone in villainy by his sister Opal (Faith Domergue), who will do *anything* for money, including murder. This is probably Domergue's best performance over her very spotty film career. Lightning is not very smart, but Stephen McNally plays him with integrity and doesn't mind that he occasionally appears foolish. Audie Murphy's Luke seems too fast and smart for his youth, which is the foundation for most of the film's humor. By this, his ninth movie, Murphy had attained an easy grace in front of the camera, which would see him through some forty films. And Eugene Iglesias just about steals the show as Johnny Sombrero, the flamboyant Spanish gunfighter who aligns himself with the Laceys.

Lee Marvin is fine as a local tough in his first of some fifteen westerns. Tinhorn Burgess is one of those guys who is always hanging around the saloon looking for action. He isn't a villain, but doesn't mind joining in for a bar fight or a hanging. Burgess plays poker against the Silver Kid (and loses), helps lead the mob to the jail to lynch Rat Face Blake, and delivers the message to Lightning that Johnny Sombrero wants a showdown. He also has a few of the film's funniest lines, insulting anyone smaller than himself.

The Duel at Silver Creek received generally favorable reviews. Arthur Knight in the *Saturday Review* wrote, "*Duel at Silver Creek* is a neat stand-out among recent Westerns—not the big *High Noon* type of Western with big stars and careful production, but that more standard brand of action film that every studio has learned to turn out quickly, efficiently and profitably." *Newsweek* praised the film as "...a cracking good Western for any number of sound reasons. It has pace, characterization, a suspenseful plot, and reels of arresting camera angles in vivid Technicolor." Philip K. Scheuer of the *Los Angeles Times* stated that, "*The Duel at Silver Creek* gets going with a bang and never lets up. It's not a Civil War yarn, as its title might suggest, but a 'little' western that might well be the envy of bigger ones."

For Lee Marvin, *The Duel at Silver Creek* was a fast-paced introduction to the Old West, a setting to which Marvin would return again and again over the course of his thirty-five year acting career. Marvin and Siegel would join forces again twelve years later for *The Killers*.

Hangman's Knot (1952)

CREDITS: Columbia. *Written and Directed by* Roy Huggins. *Produced by* Harry Joe Brown. *Executive Producer*: Randolph Scott. *Music by* Mischa Bakaleinikoff. *Director of Photography*: Charles Lawton, Jr., A.S.C. *Film Editor*: Gene Havlick, A.C.E. *Art Director*: George Brooks. *Set Decorator*: Frank Tuttle. *Sound Engineer*: Frank Goodwin. *Assistant Director*: Jack Corrick. *Second Unit Director*: Yakima Canutt. *Assistant to the Producer*: Herbert Stewart. Not Rated. Technicolor. *Technicolor Color Consultant*: Francis Cugat. Flat (1.33:1). 80 minutes. Released in October 1952. Currently available on VHS videotape.

CAST: *Major Matt Stewart*, Randolph Scott; *Molly Hull*, Donna Reed; *Jamie Groves*, Claude Jarman, Jr.; *Cass Browne*, Frank Faylen; *Captain Peterson*, Glenn Langan; *Lee Kemper*, Richard Denning; *Rolph Bainter*, Lee Marvin; *Mrs. Harris*, Jeanette Nolan; *Plunkett*, Clem Bevans; *Quincey*, Ray Teal; *Smitty*, Guinn "Big Boy" Williams; *Maxwell*, Monte Blue; *Egan Walsh*, John Call; *Hank Fletcher*, Reed Howes; *Cavalry Officer*, Edward Earle; *Stagecoach Driver*, Post Park; *Bit Parts*, Frank Hagney, Frank Yaconelli.

Hangman's Knot was Lee Marvin's second western, his first with Randolph Scott, (with whom he would appear in two more), and represented, more than any other early film appearance, Marvin's big break. After bit parts as military policemen or servicemen, this was the first time that Marvin embodied a fully-written character, an equal in importance to any other character in the film, including star Randolph Scott's. This was also the first villainous role which Marvin played, and his success here was to spur him on to much more movie villainy over the next thirty-four years.

Major Matt Stewart (Randolph Scott), leads a group of Confederate soldiers who ambush a Union gold shipment in Nevada, killing all of the Union troops before hearing from one of the dying Union soldiers that the Civil War has ended. After the ambush, the most hot-headed member of the group, Rolph (Lee Marvin), kills their contact—the man who deliberately sent them on the ambush knowing that the war was over—before Matt can stop him, causing the Rebels to start for home carrying a load of stolen gold bars. The Confederates encounter a posse, which chases them to the nearest stagecoach station, capturing rebel Cass Browne (Frank Faylen) during the chase.

The southerners hole up at the station, using the two stagecoach passengers, nurse Molly Hull (Donna Reed) and trader Lee Kemper (Richard Denning), as hostages, as well as the elderly man and his daughter-in-law who run the stagecoach stop (Clem Bevans, Jeanette Nolan). A night escape is attempted, but Kemper calls out, warning the posse and halting the escape in mid-flight. One man is wounded and tended to by Molly, while Rolph beats and gags Kemper for his outburst. Later that night, the posse threatens to hang Cass, but Matt uses the last of their dynamite to disrupt the hanging and rescue his friend. Cass tells the Confederates that the posse is made up of drifters looking not for justice but for the gold. Two of the drifters burrow under the station for an assault but are stopped by Cass, who drives them away.

Rolph takes a liking to Molly, but she recoils and Matt steps in to teach him a lesson. Matt and Rolph have a huge, very entertaining fight which Matt finally wins, but Rolph attacks again when he sees Matt and Molly embrace. Rolph is killed by Jamie (Claude Jarman, Jr.), the youngest member of the Confederates, the one who didn't kill any Union soldiers in the ambush, not wanting to spill blood. Kemper makes a deal with Matt, informing him of an escape route in exchange for his own life and two gold bars, but his luck runs out when the posse begins to burn down the station. Kemper runs outside, calling out his identity, and is shot down anyway. As the station roof burns and caves in, rain miraculously begins (which Kemper predicted) and the sky becomes so dark that the Confederates are able to escape into the night and engage the posse in battle.

As the rain starts, some of the drifters take off to find the gold but are shot down by the others before they can leave. The remainder of the drifters are killed by the Confederates, but Cass is also slain. In the end, only Matt, Jamie, Molly and the two station keepers remain. The old man and his daughter-in-law offer their home to Jamie, essentially adopting him, and Jamie accepts. Matt and Molly embrace again, and Matt and Jamie ride off into the sunset to deliver the gold to the South, promising to return.

Hangman's Knot is an action-packed western which caused some controversy upon its release because of its extreme violence. It was deemed violent enough by the film boards of Sweden, Norway and Denmark to be banned in those countries until alterations were made. The reviewer for *Cue* magazine claimed that he counted 54 corpses in the film—three times the number of the listed cast members. Indeed, the opening sequence, when the Confederates use dynamite and rifles to wipe out a Union convoy without any warning, leaves a bad taste in the mouth, exciting as it is. The excuse that it is an act of war, and therefore not robbery, seems extremely hollow.

It is the gold which raises the moral issues of the film. The Confederates, once they find out that the war is over, rather naturally want to keep it for themselves. Matt argues that the South can use the bullion for reconstruction and that they cannot keep it, because then their ambush *would* become a cold-blooded robbery. This moral dilemma is never really solved, while the drifters who make up the posse don't have any compunction about killing the Rebels—or the hostages—and taking the gold for themselves.

Hangman's Knot is tightly written and directed by Roy Huggins, and the stock characters are fleshed out more fully by a stronger

Matt (Randolph Scott) warns Rolph (Lee Marvin) to keep his hands off of nurse Molly Hull (Donna Reed) in *Hangman's Knot*.

cast than that found in most other B-westerns. The relatively small groups of characters—the Confederates, their prisoners, the posse—make it easy to set up memorable personalities, conflicts and dynamics within each group, as well as between the three groups. It is the characters and their circumstances, rather than trite plot devices, which propel the film forward. And for all of the action and gunplay, at its core the film is about the importance of personal honor.

Indeed, the only survivors of the siege are the people who hold onto their honor, valuing it above instant wealth. Everyone else dies, killed by other characters willing to do anything to get their hands on the stolen gold. Only the death of Cass Browne strikes a tragic chord rather than one of moral justice.

Randolph Scott made exactly one hundred movies; this was his eighty-first. It was also his biggest hit, helping him reach the number eight slot in the annual top ten movie stars poll for 1952. He also served as executive producer for the film, which garnered generally good reviews, though many critics noted its violence quotient. Scott, who had been a star for more than a decade, believed in giving newer faces exposure—particularly as flamboyant villains—and went out of his way to cast lesser-known actors (such as Lee Marvin) in important roles.

Thus, the cast is peppered with familiar faces: Donna Reed (who would win an Oscar the following year for *From Here to Eternity*), Claude Jarman, Jr. (who had won a special Oscar for *The Yearling* six years earlier), reliable character actors Ray Teal, Frank Faylen, Jeanette Nolan, Clem Bevans and Monte Blue, all of whom were familiar to film fans—and Lee Marvin.

Marvin plays the role of Rolph Bainter like a seasoned professional. Rolph is a quick-tempered, greedy man with an itchy trigger finger. Marvin plays him laconically, but with a steely reserve. Selfishness is Rolph's most obvious characteristic; he wants to keep the gold, he wants to have Molly Hull and he wants Matt Stewart to get off his back. It is only when Rolph's interest in Molly becomes physical that Matt steps in, and then the two men have a dandy fight, destroying the interior of the stagecoach stop. Marvin stands up to Scott in the acting department as well, holding his own against the veteran.

For Lee Marvin, *Hangman's Knot* resulted in recognition. For the first time, his name began to appear in newspaper reviews, with appreciative comments surrounding it. *Variety* noted that "Lee Marvin stands out as the killer in Scott's group...," while the *Hollywood Reporter*'s critic wrote: "Lee Marvin does an excellent job as a trigger-happy Southerner and stages a whale of a fight with Scott." Marvin was also mentioned by name in the *New York Times* and *Newsweek* reviews, though without any superlatives. Marvin had become, in his seventh film, a face to watch, a rising star.

Eight Iron Men (1952)

CREDITS: Columbia. *Directed by* Edward Dmytryk. *Produced by* Stanley Kramer. *Associate Producers*: Edna and Edward Anhalt. *Screen Play by* Harry Brown. *Adapted from his play* A Sound of Hunting. *Musical Score by* Leith Stevens. *Musical Director*: Morris Stoloff. *Director of Photography*: Roy Hunt. *Film Editor*: Aaron Stell, A.C.E. *Art Director*: Robert Peterson. *Set Decorator*: James Crowe. *Production Design by* Rudolph Sternad. *Production Manager*: Clem Beauchamp. *Sound Engineer*: Lambert Day. *Editorial Supervision*: Harry Gerstad. *Assistant Director*: James Nicholson. Not Rated. Black and White. Flat (1.33:1). Released in December 1952. Not currently available on home video.

CAST: *Colucci*, Bonar Colleano; *Carter*, Arthur Franz; *Sergeant Mooney*, Lee Marvin; *Coke*, Richard Kiley; *Sapiros*, Nick Dennis; *Ferguson*, James Griffith; *Muller*, Dick Moore; *Small*, George Cooper; *Captain Trelawny*, Barney Phillips; *Walsh*, Robert Nichols; *Lieutenant Crane*, Richard Grayson; *Hunter*, Douglas Henderson; *Girl*, Mary Castle; *Cafferty*, David McMahon; *Bit Parts*, Dorothy Turley, Mona Knox, Sue Casey, Angela Stevens, Carolyn Collins, Joan McKellem, Kathleen O'Malley, Evelyn Lovequist, Jill Jarmon; *Minister*, Pat O'Malley.

The war drama *Eight Iron Men* gave Lee Marvin his biggest part yet and was his first film for producer Stanley Kramer, with whom he would make four others. Marvin again plays a serviceman, this time the line sergeant of an eight-man army squad. It was his first real role of authority, yet Marvin fills the role more than capably, drawing on his personal wartime experience to infuse the character with authenticity.

The exact location and time of *Eight Iron Men* are not defined; it takes place somewhere in Europe sometime during World War II. An American squad, never named or numbered, is occupying the ruins of some devastated unnamed European town. It rains most of the time and there's very little to break up the monotony between patrols.

On one such patrol, a newly installed German machine gun nest pins down Private Small (George Cooper). Two other soldiers escape and return to the bombed-out house where the squad is quartered with the news of Small's predicament. Hot-headed Coke (Richard Kiley) prods Sergeant Mooney (Lee Marvin) for a rescue attempt and Mooney is game, but Captain Trelawney (Barney Phillips) rejects the idea, fearing the loss of still more men.

After hours of waiting and discussing the situation, Mooney and Coke finally defy orders and make an attempt with a mortar, but to no avail. Then the squad's daydreaming lothario, Colucci (Bonar Colleano), goes out on his own, eliminates a neighborhood sniper, and single-handedly knocks out the machine gun nest with a lucky grenade toss. He rescues Small, only to find that the wayward soldier had sprained his ankle, given himself a shot to ease the pain, and slept away the afternoon. The squad, whole once more, pulls back from the ruined town.

There isn't much plot to digest, nor much action to excite, in *Eight Iron Men*. This is a character-driven piece, based on the author's Broadway play *A Sound of Hunting*, meant to express the actual *experience* of the war in all its banality and boredom. The movie takes place in the cave-like house which the soldiers have called their own for the past seventeen days, and the dialogue is the small talk of soldiers—stories about women, grumbling about the army, and complaints about the food—the talk of lonely, tired men just trying to relieve the relentless boredom.

Critic Robert Kass in *Catholic World* summed up the situation perfectly: "Authentic almost to the point of dullness and conveying exceptionally well the boredom of war itself, *Eight Iron Men* is a tricky film to review. Personally, I found it one of the best war pictures I have ever seen and yet I hesitate to recommend it indiscriminately since its appeal will depend entirely upon your susceptibility to an hour-and-a-half of rugged, realistic male war talk."

Eight Iron Men is a fine little film that succeeds in its ambition to capture some of the day-to-day drabness of warfare. It does so because of the finely detailed, often humorous script, which is acted out by a cast of relatively fresh faces, many of whom went on to become familiar faces in movies and television. It doesn't have the pretentions of some war films which are fashioned into allegories about good and evil; it's merely a glimpse into the lives of eight men who are trying to survive another day.

The main point of the story is articulated by Carter (Arthur Franz) late in the film when he justifies Sergeant Mooney's insubordinate rescue attempt to Captain Trelawney. "Captain, if they don't bring him (Small) in, or find out what happened to him, they'll never be the same. If they leave him out there, it'll be as though they left a part of themselves, and they'll feel guilty—it'll keep them awake maybe the rest of their lives. But if they bring him in, it'll be all right. Even if they find him dead, it'll be all right. It will hurt, and they won't forget it. But they'll know they did all they could. Their luck ran out, that's all."

In three dream sequences the war is forgotten. Mary Castle appears as the pin-up queen (and Rita Hayworth double) whom Colucci dreams of wooing and Ferguson (James Griffith) dreams of marrying. Some critics found the dreamy departures a welcome

Captain Trelawney (Barney Phillips) refuses to grant Sergeant Mooney's (Lee Marvin) request to make a rescue attempt in *Eight Iron Men*.

relief from the tedium of the war, but they seem forced and inappropriate for the tone of the film, as if a producer had demanded that there be included some kind of "love interest."

The cast is uniformly fine, but Richard Kiley and Lee Marvin stand out with their realistic portrayals. Marvin plays Sergeant Mooney as a soldier with a conscience, fed up with a chain of command which has failed him. "We came up here with eight men and we're going back with eight men," declares Marvin doggedly. His stubborn streak works both ways however; when the mortar attack doesn't work, Mooney considers Small dead and insists that the rest of the squad do the same. Mooney must walk the tightrope between his duty and his conscience, and the mental battle between those two often disparate perspectives can be seen in Lee Marvin's eyes.

Eight Iron Men inspired wildly different reviews. Critics who liked it noted its stark realism, excellent ensemble acting and eloquent mixture of comedy and drama. Critics who didn't like it noted its pointlessness and harped on the boredom factor. Even producer Stanley Kramer was disappointed in the film—he had hoped to cast the stars of the play, Burt Lancaster and Frank Lovejoy, but scheduling difficulties and a low budget prevented him from attracting them. The lack of big-name stars certainly didn't help the film's box-office performance, which was poor.

Titles are changed on Hollywood projects all the time. *A Sound of Hunting* was the original play's title, and it eventually became *Eight Iron Men*. In between, however, it was known for a time as *The Dirty Dozen*, changed because the squad only contained eight men.

Seminole (1953)

CREDITS: Universal. *Directed by* Budd Boetticher. *Produced by* Howard Christie. *Story and Screenplay by* Charles K. Peck, Jr. *Musical Direction*: Joseph Gershenson. *Director of Photography*: Russell Metty, A.S.C. *Film Editor*: Virgil Vogel, A.C.E. *Art Direction*: Alexander Golitzen, Emrich Nicholson. *Set Decorations*, Russell A. Gausman, Joseph Kish. *Sound*: Leslie I. Carey, Glenn E. Anderson. *Costumes*: Rosemary Odell. *Hair Stylist*: Joan St. Oegger. *Makeup*: Bud Westmore. *Assistant Director*: Tom Shaw. *Military Technical Adviser*: Colonel Paul R. Davison, USA Retired. Not Rated. Technicolor. *Technicolor Color Consultant*: William Fritzsche. Flat (1.33:1). 87 minutes. Released in February 1953. Not currently available on home video.

CAST: *Lieutenant Lance Caldwell*, Rock Hudson; *Revere Muldoon*, Barbara Hale; *Osceola / John Powell*, Anthony Quinn; *Major Harlan Degan*, Richard Carlson; *Kajeck*, Hugh O'Brian; *Lieutenant Hamilton*, Russell Johnson; *Sergeant Magruder*, Lee Marvin; *Kulak*, Ralph Moody; *Zachary Taylor*, Fay Roope; *Corporal Gerard*, James Best; *Scott*, John Day; *Captain Streller*, Don Gibson; *Corporal Smiley*, Howard Erskine; *Trooper*, Frank Chase; *Hendricks*, Duane Thorsen; *Farmer*, Walter Reed; *Corporal*, Robert Karnes; *Trader Taft*, Robert Dane; *Major Lawrence*, John Phillips; *Mattie Sue Thomas*, Soledad Jimenez; *Officer*, Don Garrett; *Captain Sibley*, Robert Bray; *Troopers*, Earl Spainard, Scott Lee; *Sentry*, Peter Cranwell; *Officer*, Alex Sharp; *Guards*, Jack Finlay, Jody Hutchinson; *Bit Parts*, William Janssen, Dan Poore.

Lee Marvin's first film of 1953 was the Florida western *Seminole*, in which he once again plays a soldier, this time a Dragoon. It was Marvin's most physical role since his debut film, *You're in the Navy Now*, as he sweated in full military uniform in the sultry Florida Everglades, helping to drag a wagon of supplies through the swamps along with the rest of the cast.

In 1835 a garrison of soldiers at Fort King, located just outside of the Florida Everglades, is preparing to force the Seminole Indians living in the swamps to move out west to a reservation. Second Lieutenant Lance Caldwell (Rock Hudson), straight out of West Point, is assigned for scouting duty at the fort because of his knowledge of the area and its people. Caldwell finds to his dismay that Major Degan (Richard Carlson), the fort commander, doesn't care how the Seminoles are moved; he's perfectly willing to kill them if they don't leave peacefully.

Caldwell also finds that the woman he loves, Revere Muldoon (Barbara Hale), still cares for him but has fallen in love with his former best friend John, who, unbeknownst to

Sergeant Magruder (Lee Marvin) stands at attention as Lieutenant Caldwell (Rock Hudson) confers with Major Degan (Richard Carlson) in *Seminole*.

Caldwell, is Osceola (Anthony Quinn), the leader of the Seminoles. Major Degan decides to sneak into the Everglades and attack the Indians on their home ground, forcing Lt. Caldwell to speak up against the action and incurring Degan's wrath. Degan doesn't trust Caldwell and orders Sergeant Magruder (Lee Marvin) to carefully watch him.

A group of about 20 men march into the Everglades in full uniform along with a wagon full of supplies and arms that have to be manhandled through the swamps. On the first day, a soldier (James Best) is injured, run over by the wagon. On the second day, the wagon is lost in quicksand and Caldwell rescues the injured soldier rather than the arms, further infuriating Degan. Finally, the exhausted men reach the Indian camp. They wait until the Indians are asleep, then attack with guns blazing. All the Seminoles are in the trees, however, and they counterattack the soldiers, killing all but a few—Magruder, Degan, who is wounded, and Scott (John Day). Magruder watches as the Seminoles, led by Osceola, rescue the wounded Caldwell.

After the disastrous battle, Caldwell recuperates while Osceola reveals his identity to his old friend. Revere talks to Degan and arranges for Osceola to visit the fort under a flag of truce. Osceola and Caldwell travel to the fort, where Degan has Osceola beaten and locked up. Caldwell confronts Degan, angrily demanding Osceola's freedom, and is confined to quarters. Magruder arranges for Caldwell to rescue Osceola, but the Indian leader is killed by Kajeck (Hugh O'Brian), the warrior who has opposed Osceola's peace efforts all along. Caldwell is blamed for Osceola's death, accused of treason, and sentenced to a firing squad by Zachary Taylor (Fay Roope). Caldwell is saved at the last possible moment by Kajeck, who interrupts Caldwell's execution, demands the body of Osceola, and admits to the killing of his former chief. As the Seminoles leave with the body of Osceola, Zachary Taylor clears Caldwell's name and hopes that the two peoples can learn to live together.

Seminole is a strange little film—it's part western, part war film and part character study. Unfortunately, this combination, which could have produced a unique, intriguing motion picture, only works to split the movie's cohesiveness and break it down into disparate elements. It is weakest as a western, since it is not set in the west and has few of the familiar accoutrements of the genre. As a military film, it is more successful at depicting the strategies of battle and the personal elements that cannot help but influence military decision-making. The scenes of the soldiers mucking their way through the swampy Everglades in full uniform, as quietly as possible, are striking.

The film is most interesting—and disturbing—as a character study. Major Degan is a Napoleonic martinet, much shorter than his fellow Dragoons, playing at war and doing whatever it takes to further his own career. He follows military procedure precisely, not even allowing the men to open their collars on the march through the steamy swamps. Degan's obstinacy and lack of regard for the Indians are infuriating to watch, but drive the film's drama. On repeat viewings, Richard Carlson's performance as Degan gains empathy for its desperate, tragic edge.

As the hero, Rock Hudson is stalwart and strong, making the proper stands at the proper times. Anthony Quinn is miscast but earnest as Osceola, while Barbara Hale gives Revere Muldoon a toughness that belies her beauty. Hugh O'Brian is almost unrecognizable as Kajeck, the Seminole warrior, but is quite impressive in the small role. And Lee Marvin is competent in the ambiguous role of Sgt. Magruder, the soldier asked to spy on Lt. Caldwell and who ultimately turns against his own commander to help Caldwell sneak Osceola out of camp. As Magruder gets to know Caldwell, he does learn to respect the other soldier's moral stands and eventually is persuaded to favor them. Marvin doesn't have much to do other than sweat and salute, but he does both well.

Seminole gathered mostly unfavorable reviews (*Time* called it "swampy melodrama") and faded quickly into oblivion. The film was based on at least one historical character but, like so many other films, bears little resemblance to actual history. The real Osceola was arrested in 1837 (also under a flag of truce!) and died the following year in a South Carolina fort.

Down Among the Sheltering Palms (1953)

CREDITS: 20th Century–Fox. *Directed by* Edmund Goulding. *Produced by* Fred Kohlmar. *Screenplay by* Claude Binyon, Albert Lewin, Burt Styler. *Based on a story by* Edward Hope. *Music*: Harold Arlen. *Lyrics*: Harold Arlen, Ralph Blane. *Musical Direction*: Lionel Newman. *Incidental Music*: Leigh Harline. *Orchestration*: Herbert Spencer, Earle Hagen. *Vocal Direction*: Ken Darby. *Songs*: "All of Me" (*written by* Seymour Simons, Gerald Marks), "Down Among the Sheltering Palms (*written by* Abe Olman, James Brockman), "I'm the Ruler of a South Sea Island," "What Makes de Difference?," "When You're in Love," "Who Will It Be When the Time Comes?" *Dances Staged by* Seymour Felix. *Director of Photography*: Leon Shamroy, A.S.C. *Film Editor*: Louis Loeffler. *Art Direction*: Lyle Wheeler, Leland Fuller. *Set Decorations*: Thomas Little, Stuart Reiss. *Sound*: Alfred Bruzlin, Roger Heman. *Wardrobe Direction*: Charles Le Maire. *Costumes Designed by* Travilla. *Makeup Artist*: Ben Nye. *Special Photographic Effects*: Fred Sersen. Not Rated. Technicolor. *Technicolor Color Consultant*: Leonard Doss. Flat (1.33:1). 86 minutes. Released in June 1953. Not currently available on home video.

CAST: *Captain Bill Willoby*, William Lundigan; *Diana Forrester*, Jane Greer; *Rozouila*, Mitzi Gaynor; *Lieutenant Carl Schmidt (Smitty)*, David Wayne; *Angela Toland*, Gloria De Haven; *Reverend Edgett*, Gene Lockhart; *Lieutenant Mike Sloan*, Jack Paar; *Corporal Kolta*, Alvin Greenman; *King Jilouili*, Billy Gilbert; *First Sergeant*, Henry Kulky; *Major Curwin*, Lyle Talbot; *Lieutenant Everly*, Ray Montgomery; *Lieutenant Homer Briggs*, George Nader; *Colonel Parker*, Fay Roope; *Witch Doctor*, David Ahdar; *Toami*, Sialofi Jerry Talo; *Colonel's Aide*, Clinton Bagwell; *Radio Operator*, Charles Tannen; *Woolawei*, Claude Allister; *Mrs. Edgett*, Edith Evanson; *Officers*, Steve Wayne, Richard Grayson, John Baer; *Native Girl*, Jean Charney; *Murphy*,

Lee Marvin, as he looked around the time of *Down Among the Sheltering Palms*.

Barney Phillips; *Snively*, Lee Marvin; *Thompson*, Henry Slate; *Harris*, Joe Turkel; *G.I.s*, David Wolfson, James Ogg, Ray Hyke, Roger McGee, Richard Monohan.

In 1950 a new Rodgers and Hammerstein musical called *South Pacific* blew onto Broadway and became a smash hit. With its romantic songs and exotic locale, it was only a matter of time (eventually eight years) before it became a big budget motion picture. Hoping to cash in on its success, producer Fred Kohlmar commissioned a film which would beat *South Pacific* to release yet still contain many of the same elements. The result is *Down Among the Sheltering Palms*.

Captain Bill Willoby (William Lundigan) is assigned to take an Army force to occupy Midi island in the south Pacific. Once there, he receives a non-fraternization order from headquarters just as dozens of native lovelies have introduced themselves to his men. Orders are orders, so Willoby focuses his men on ping-pong, volleyball and softball.

When Willoby is named Governor of the island, King Jouilili (Billy Gilbert) presents him with a wife, Rozouila (Mitzi Gaynor). Willoby tries to return her to no avail, so he hides her in a nearby bungalow, resisting her advances by avoiding her.

He and his fellow officers are much more interested in Diana Forrester (Jane Greer), niece to missionary Reverend Edgett (Gene Lockhart). Willoby reminds his officers that the non-fraternization order applies to them equally, but that doesn't keep them from buzzing around Diana like bees when she assumes secretarial duties at the post for Lieutenant Schmidt (Smitty), Willoby's right-hand man. Smitty (David Wayne) hires her because she can type.

So can Angela Toland (Gloria DeHaven), a newspaper columnist-author who tours the island looking for a story. She falls for Willoby (who only wants Diana) and stumbles across a story when she finds Rozouila, who states, "I belong to Captain Willoby; I am his woman." She writes her story, which leads to an investigator coming to Midi island and sorting out the mess. Smitty calls Angela a brat, but settles for her anyway. The King allows Willoby to give Rozouila away and Willoby makes up with Diana, who was jealous of the native girl. Midi is declared a "friendly island" and the troops sail away.

Down Among the Sheltering Palms is, at best, a pleasant diversion. It's as light as a warm sea breeze, enjoyable but as utterly forgettable as a change in wind direction. There's absolutely nothing of any lasting value about this movie: the songs are bland, the locale is strictly Hollywood backlot, the comedy is tepid. The romantic goings-on are uninspired, despite an attractive, if not very talented, cast and some nice color cinematography. This truly is escapist fare, pleasant but mindless and non-involving.

Of the songs, "I'm the Ruler of a South Sea Island" is interesting, primarily because it was filmed entirely in one take. The title song, which became popular after being recorded by Bing Crosby, is not even given a full treatment in the film; it is sung as background by a male chorus and partially warbled by Angela Toland while she is romancing Captain Willoby during their picnic scene.

Lee Marvin appears about halfway through the film, in the scene when all of the lonely soldiers are crowding into Captain Willoby's office to get a good look at Diana. He bursts into the room just as Willoby is yelling and receives his share of Willoby's anger. Marvin adapts a nasal whine for his two lines, as if deriding his own part. Who could blame him? It is his only scene. Future *Tonight Show* host Jack Paar can be seen as one of the officers; it was the last of his few film appearances.

Down Among the Sheltering Palms did beat *South Pacific* to the big screen, but few people bothered to see it. Rodgers and Hammerstein had nothing to worry about.

The Stranger Wore a Gun (1953)

CREDITS: Columbia. *Directed by* Andre de Toth. *Produced by* Harry Joe Brown. *Associate Producer*: Randolph Scott. *Screenplay by* Kenneth Gamet. *Based upon* Yankee Gold *by* John M. Cunningham. *Musical Director*: Mischa Bakaleinikoff. *Director of Photography*: Lester H. White, A.S.C. *Film Editors*: Gene Havlick, A.C.E., James Sweeney, A.C.E. *Art Director*: George Brooks. *Set Decorator*: Frank Tuttle. *Sound Engineer*: Lambert Day. *Assistant Director*: William Reineck. *Assistant to Producer*: Herbert Stewart. Not Rated. Color by Technicolor. *Technicolor Color Consultant*: Francis Cugat. Flat (1.33:1). Originally 3-D. 83 minutes. Released in July 1953. Currently available on VHS videotape.

CAST: *Jeff Travis*, Randolph Scott; *Josie Sullivan*, Claire Trevor; *Shelby Conroy*, Joan Weldon; *Jules Mourret*, George Macready; *Degas*, Alfonso Bedoya; *Dan Kurth*, Lee Marvin; *Bull Slager*, Ernest Borgnine; *Jason Conroy*, Pierre Watkin; *Dutch Mueller*, Joseph Vitale; *Jim Martin*, Clem Bevans; *Poley*, Paul Maxey; *Red Glick*, Frank Scannell; *Harve Comis*, Reed Howes; *Milt Hooper*, Roscoe Ates; *Jeb*, Edward Earle; *Ike*, Guy Wilkerson; *Bit Parts*, Mary Newton, Mary Lou Holloway, Franklyn Farnum, Barry Brooks, Tap Canutt, Al Haskell, Frank Hagney, Frank Ellis, Francis McDonald, Phil Tully, Al Hill, Harry Mendoza, Terry Frost, Diana Dawson, Richard Benjamin, Herbert Rawlinson, Britt Wood, Harry Seymour, James Millican, Jack Woody, Rayford Barnes, Rudy Germaine, Edith Evanson, Guy Teague.

Outlaws Dan Kurth (Lee Marvin) and Bull Slager (Ernest Borgnine) await a passing stagecoach to rob in *The Stranger Wore a Gun*.

The second of Lee Marvin's three films with Randolph Scott is the weakest of the trio and the only one filmed in 3-D. *The Stranger Wore a Gun* rode into theatres in 1953 as one of about ten 3-D westerns (including *Gun Fury*, also with Marvin, and the two best— *Hondo* and *The Charge at Feather River*) of that era. In two scenes in particular, knives, chairs, crockery and even fire are thrown toward the camera in an effort to provide the "YOU-ARE-THERE!" excitement of three-dimensional viewing. Thanks to Ernest Borgnine's aim, a few of the 3-D effects remain startling, even on a flat print.

Jeff Travis (Randolph Scott) is the title character in *The Stranger Wore a Gun*, which is somewhat puzzling because for much of the film he does *not* wear a gun. Travis is a Confederate soldier working as a spy in Lawrence, Kansas, waiting for his commanding officer, William Quantrill, to arrive. Quantrill does and sacks the town, looting, burning and killing indiscriminately. Sickened by what his actions have wrought, Travis leaves Quantrill's Raiders and heads out on his own.

Some time later, Travis is recognized as a Raider while playing poker on a Mississippi riverboat with Josie Sullivan (Claire Trevor). He is attacked but escapes with the aid of Josie and a mystery man. Travis flees Prescott, to Arizona and meets the mysterious friend, tycoon Jules Mourret (George Macready), who had saved Travis' life in order to hire him again as a spy. Travis is to sign on with Prescott's local stagecoach company to discover where gold shipments are being hidden, so that they can be stolen with little trouble.

The stagecoach company is run by Shelby Conroy (Joan Weldon) and her father Jason (Pierre Watkin). Travis, posing as stage line investigator Mark Stone, likes Shelby instantly and begins to have second thoughts about his assignment. Complicating matters is Degas (Alfonso Bedoya), a Mexican bandit whom Mourret has evicted from Prescott (Mourret has also run out the government; the opening scene in Prescott has the state capitol moving to Phoenix and the not-so-law abiding citizenry cheering). Degas still wants his share of the gold shipments, and says so to Mourret.

Travis supplies the shipment information to Mourret, but, unknown to Travis, no gold is shipped. As a result, the stagecoach driver is beaten and killed by Mourret's men, Dan Kurth (Lee Marvin) and Bull Slager (Ernest Borgnine). Seeing the result of his duplicity (again), Travis searches for a way out. He talks Shelby into another stagecoach run and tells both Mourret and Degas that it will carry $100,000 in gold, knowing that both men will attempt to rob it at Raccoon Pass. Travis drives the stage himself, but is surprised when Kurth buys a ticket and accompanies him.

At Raccoon Pass Travis knocks Kurth off the stage and heads back to Prescott, leaving Degas and his men to shoot it out with Mourret and his men. Before killing Degas, Mourret learns that Travis has betrayed him and sends Kurth and Slager to get him. Travis is captured but gets away from Slager by appealing to his greed, then beating him up in the film's best 3-D sequence. Travis shoots it out with Kurth and kills him. The next day he faces Mourret and Slager in the hotel's saloon and kills both men while a roaring fire burns the place down around them. His reputation finally cleared, Travis gets on the stage once again, this time accompanied by Josie, and heads for a new life in California, leaving Shelby behind.

The Stranger Wore a Gun is a film which does not stand up to close scrutiny. It noticeably glosses over relevant details, such as having Mourret openly talk in the street—where anybody could hear—to Kurth and Slager about robbing the stagecoach, and having Kurth and Slager brazenly walk around town even though a witness had seen them beat the stage driver to death. These kind of inconsistencies make the film difficult to accept. Further undermining the effort is poor staging of the gunfights, particularly on the riverboat and at Raccoon Pass. Quick cuts and reaction shots do not comprise exciting gunplay.

The film's biggest weakness is the character of Jeff Travis. Based on what he did in the opening scene in Lawrence, Kansas, Travis does not deserve to live and escape on the riverboat, nor get a chance to redeem himself later in the film. Travis wants to live, and does eventually tell the truth about himself to the Conroys, but his actions to rid Prescott of Jules Mourret and his henchmen does not seem near enough penance to make up for the immeasurable destruction and loss of life caused by his actions in Lawrence. Another actor might have been able to express some regret and misery in the part, giving Travis some real emotional depth, but Randolph Scott is his usual granite-faced self and does not permit any real emotional connection with his flawed character.

Also ordinary in the film are Lee Marvin and Ernest Borgnine as Mourret's main henchmen, and Joan Weldon as Shelby Conroy, the beautiful and brave stagecoach line owner. There is nothing of note about any of these characters or performances. George Macready is fine as Jules Mourret, using his modulated voice to give his character an extra ounce of intelligence. Alfonso Bedoya is amusing as Degas, though his character borders on the unbelievable. Most unbelievable is Claire Trevor as Josie Sullivan, the gambler who has always carried a torch for Jeff Travis. Trevor works too hard at making Josie tough; she seems ill at ease in the part and more suited to Mourret than to Travis. When Travis ends up with Josie at film's end, it is something of a surprise, because he seems more suited to Shelby than to Josie.

Ultimately, despite a few startling 3-D effects, *The Stranger Wore a Gun* is a run-of-the-mill western saga, with nothing fresh or new to contribute to the oldest and largest genre of American film. Like its nondescript misnomer of a title, the film is completely ordinary in most ways and doesn't really deliver what it promises. In the text of Lee Marvin's career, it is a run-of-the-mill villainous role, just a footnote of little interest.

The Glory Brigade (1953)

CREDITS: 20th Century–Fox. *Directed by* Robert D. Webb. *Produced by* William Bloom. *Written by* Franklin Coen. *Musical Direction*: Lionel Newman. *Director of Photography*: Lucien Ballard, A.S.C. *Film Editor*: Mario Mora. *Art Direction*: Lyle Wheeler, Lewis Creber. *Set Decorations*: Fred J. Rode. *Sound*: W. D. Flick, Harry M. Leonard. *Choreography by* Matt Mattox. *Special Photographic Effects*: Ray Kellogg. *Makeup Artist*: Ben Nye. *Assistant Director*: Eli Dunn. *Technical Adviser*: Captain William J. Knickerbocker, C.E., U.S.A. Not Rated. Black and White. Flat (1.33:1). 82 minutes. Released in August 1953. Not currently available on home video.

CAST: *Lieutenant Sam Prior*, Victor Mature; *Lieutenant Niklas*, Alexander Scourby; *Corporal Bowman*, Lee Marvin; *Sergeant Johnson*, Richard Egan; *Corporal Marakis*, Nick Dennis; *Sergeant Chuck Anderson*, Roy Roberts; *Private Stone*, Alvy Moore; *Private Taylor*, Russell Evans; *Sergeant Smitowsky*, Henry Kulky; *Private Ryan*, Gregg Martell; *Captain Adams*, Lamont Johnson; *Captain Davis*, Carleton Young; *Major Sauer*, Frank Gerstle; *Lieutenant Jorgenson*, Stuart Nedd; *Private Nemos*, George Michaelides; *Captain Charos*, John Verros; *Sergeant Lykos*, Alberto Morin; *Sergeant Kress*, Archer McDonald; *Colonel Kallicles*, Peter Mamakos; *Chaplain*, Father Patrinakos; *Greek Soldiers*, John Haretakis, Costas Morfis, David Gabbai, Nico Minardos; *Medic*, George Saris; *Colonel Peterson*, Jonathan Hale.

The Glory Brigade gave Lee Marvin his first cinematic taste of the Korean War. Though he was enroute to the conflict in *We're Not Married*, that doesn't really count as a war film. Marvin would experience court-martials in *The Rack* and *Sergeant Ryker* later in his career, but his only Korean conflict combat comes in this movie.

The film opens with American forces retreating across a river on a pontoon bridge, which they promptly blow up before North Korean forces can use it against them. Soon enough, a mission calls for a platoon of American soldiers to ferry a platoon of Greek soldiers across that river for reconaissance. Lieutenant Sam Prior (Victor Mature) volunteers his squad because he is half Greek himself and is anxious to introduce his men to some genuine Greeks. The river crossing goes well, but just after the Greeks set off, a skirmish with Communist forces leads Sam to believe that the Greeks have surrendered. He sends most of his platoon back to the river to cross and bring back heavy weapons, but the entire platoon is killed on the beach.

When part of the Greek force arrives, Sam doesn't believe their battle story because their bayonets are clean. He takes command, striking inland to finish the necessary reconaissance, against the wishes of the Greek leader, Lieutenant Niklas (Alexander Scourby). They destroy an enemy tank and raid an enemy ammo dump, replenishing their dwindling supplies. Sam is surprised to find that the Greeks clean their weapons *immediately* after battle, explaining why there had been no blood stains on them earlier.

At the ammo dump, a wounded New Zealander informs the men that the North Koreans are establishing an armored force to attack soon. Lt. Niklas retakes command and starts the group heading back to the river, using a bulldozer and trailer to transport the wounded. Another Communist tank arrives and is destroyed by American demolitions expert Corporal Bowman (Lee Marvin). It becomes clear that the force will not reach the beach by daylight, so the Greeks resign themselves to fighting, sending the four Americans ahead to pass on the vital information.

Sam and his men reach the river and find that the North Koreans are building an underwater bridge to cross the river. At the beach rendezvous point, the Americans are joined by the rest of the Greek regiment and, more importantly, their radio. Sam radios the news to headquarters, then leads all of the men back to the remaining Greek force. They head for the highest hill and are rescued by helicopter as the Communist forces futilely attack from below while being fire-bombed by American jets.

The Glory Brigade is a routine war film with an agreeable premise: that all of the national fighting forces in Korea need to work together, without rancor, to complete their military objectives. It is an obvious point, one worth repeating, though perhaps not to the

Corporal Bowman (Lee Marvin, at left, with glasses), Lieutenant Prior (Victor Mature) and the other men in thier platoon watch the unusual battle preparations made by a Greek platoon in *The Glory Brigade*.

extent of this film. The American squad is comprised of many nationalities already, further making the point that skin color and ethnic origin should not matter when it comes to working together to win a war. Once the mutual trust between the groups is established, they help each other and support each other when the going gets rough. The film works a little too hard to make this point, occasionally becoming melodramatic and using some cornball dialogue, but it certainly means well.

As a war film, *The Glory Brigade* is strictly routine. There is no real sense of time or place; the men could be in any war at any time fighting any battle. The message, not the details, is the important thing. While the script is not firmly rooted in Korean War details, it certainly does convey the difficulties of fighting a war in a foreign land, and does express the horror of war to strong effect, particularly when Sam and his men find the remains of their platoon on the beach. Unfortunately, the production values do not support the script as well as they should. The river doesn't seem nearly as difficult to cross as it is said to be, and the terrain looks like any number of southern state parks.

Victor Mature has the lion's share of the dialogue and gives a steady, understated performance. Lee Marvin, as the demolitionist, Bowman, has little to do other than grumble once in a while about the Army and explode something. This is the only film in which he wears glasses throughout. It's a different look for him, making him seem more intelligent, at least enough to handle high explosives. Bowman is a soldier's soldier, doing his job as methodically and efficiently as possible, and Marvin lets that simple philosophy rule his acting as well. He doesn't stand out in the cast, but he's not supposed to. Like the United Nations forces, the film's cast is an ensemble meant to work smoothly, with each man doing his part. Though the movie certainly practices what it preaches, it could have used a bigger budget, a better script and some exciting action sequences.

Like most other Korean War films, this one passed through theaters without much fanfare or business. Critics found the film routine and repetitious, and audiences stayed away—despite its timeliness and worthwhile message.

Gun Fury (1953)

CREDITS: Columbia. *Directed by* Raoul Walsh. *Produced by* Lewis J. Rachmil. *Screenplay by* Irving Wallace and Roy Huggins. *Based upon the novel* Ten Against Caesar *by* The Grangers. *Music Director*: Mischa Bakaleinikoff. *Director of Photography*: Lester H. White, A.S.C. *Film Editors*: Jerome Trome, A.C.E., James Sweeney, A.C.E. *Art Director*: Ross Bellah. *Set Decorator*: James Crowe. *Sound Engineer*: Josh Westmoreland. *Assistant Director*: Jack Corrick. Not Rated. Technicolor. *Technicolor Color Consultant*: Francis Cugat. Flat (1.33:1). Originally 3-D. 83 minutes. Released in October 1953. Currently available on VHS videotape. Previously available on laserdisc.

CAST: *Ben Warren*, Rock Hudson; *Jennifer Ballard*, Donna Reed; *Frank Slayton*, Phil Carey; *Estella Morales*, Roberta Haynes; *Jess Burgess*, Leo Gordon; *Blinky*, Lee Marvin; *Brazos*, Neville Brand; *Doc*, Ray Thomas; *Curly Jordan*, Robert Herron; *Jim Morse*, Phil Rawlins; *Weatherby*, Forrest Lewis; *Westy*, John Cason; *Vincente*, Don Carlos; *Johash*, Pat Hogan; *Pete Barratto*, Mel Welles; *Billy*, Post Park; *Lieutenant Wherry*, Bob Morgan; *Sheepmen*, John Dierkes, Dan White; *Sheriff*, Robert E. Griffin; *Barber*, Carl Harbaugh; *Second Poker Player*, Henry Rowland; *First Poker Player*, Frank Fenton; *Old Man*, Jim Reeves; *Florid Man*, Drake Smith; *Fat Mexican Waitress*, Rosa Turich; *Mrs. Rogers*, Maudie Prickett; *Francesca*, Charlita; *Elena*, Christey Marlo; *Second Mexican Girl*, Alma Beltran.

Gun Fury was, along with *The Stranger Wore a Gun*, one of about ten 3-D westerns of that era. At various times during the film, rocks, knives, logs and even kitchen utensils are thrown toward the camera in an effort to frighten and excite audiences. Most of the effects are woven into the script pretty well; only the stock shot of the rattlesnake that menaces Donna Reed and jumps toward the camera seems inappropriate.

As *Gun Fury* opens, Jennifer Ballard (Donna Reed) is traveling in a stagecoach to meet her fiance when fellow passenger Mr. Hampton (Phil Carey) takes a liking to her. That evening Jenny is surprised by her fiance, Ben Warren (Rock Hudson), who has traveled to meet her earlier than expected. At dinner, though Hampton is obviously disappointed by Ben's arrival, he and Warren talk of the recently ended Civil War and its drastic effect upon the South and the men who served. Ben wants only peace, to work his California ranch. Hampton is far more bitter about the destruction of the South.

The following day all passengers are aboard the stage when it is held up, and Mr. Hampton turns out to be Frank Slayton, a renegade outlaw who has engineered the heist. Ben is shot and left for dead during the robbery, and Slayton and his gang take Jenny with them. The gang's second-in-command, Jess Burgess (Leo Gordon), tries to persuade Slayton to leave Jenny, to no avail. When Slayton menaces her, Jess interrupts and for his chivalry is tied to a fence post in the blistering Arizona sun and left to die.

Ben wakes up, groggy but unhurt(!), follows the trail, and finds Jess. When Jess swears revenge, they team up to rescue fair Jenny. They try to recruit help at the nearest town, but the sheriff won't even bother forming a posse. An Indian trails them out of town and attacks Jess that night, recognizing him as one of his wife's killers. Ben saves Jess' life and, after conferring, they let the Indian join their efforts to stop Slayton.

Slayton's Mexican girlfriend Stella (Roberta Haynes) welcomes Slayton back to the gang's stopover hideout, but he is only passing through and pays her no mind. When Stella sees Jenny she knows why she has been ignored and flies into a rage. One of the gang, Blinky (Lee Marvin), is told to guard her but she knocks him senseless and attacks Jenny. Stella is locked inside the hideout but she escapes and follows the gang into the desert.

Blinky frightens her horse away, leaving her to die. She is picked up soon afterwards by Ben, Jess and the Indian.

Slayton's gang holes up in a Mexican bordello. Stella sneaks in and tries to kill Slayton but is caught. She tells him that Jess will finish him; Slayton is surprised that Jess is still alive. He decides to make a deal and sends back an offer: Jenny for Jess. Though wary, Ben and Jess agree to Slayton's terms. The trade is made, but Slayton finishes off Jess once and for all. Ben loses his temper and goes after the murdering scoundrel, chasing and fighting him up and down rocky hills before Slayton is finally killed by the Indian as he is about to finish off Ben. Ben and Jenny finally ride off toward California.

Gun Fury is a fast-paced oater from Raoul Walsh, an action director better known for gangster films (*The Roaring Twenties*, *High Sierra*, *White Heat*) and Errol Flynn adventures (*Gentleman Jim*, *They Died with Their Boots On*, *Objective Burma*) than his westerns. It is a minor Walsh film, yet styled with his best qualities: vigorous action sequences, snappy dialogue, quick plot development. It is filmed in gorgeous Technicolor with spectacular scenery and lots of action and gunplay. The 3-D effects don't interfere with the story, which is fairly complex and very entertaining. The film's flaws are due to some unbelievable plotting, such as Ben Warren being shot only to wake up later unhurt.

At the center of the story is Jenny, a beautiful, well-mannered and educated lady of the East who travels into the untamed western frontier and is shocked by the boorishness and vulgarity she encounters. Ben promises her a fine California ranch where, as Slayton points out, her beauty will be buried beneath the dust of toil. Slayton tries to keep her for himself, though he would be defiling

Outlaws Frank Slayton (Phil Carey) and Blinky (Lee Marvin) discuss the fate of tempestuous Stella (Roberta Haynes) in *Gun Fury*.

the very beauty and civility by which he is entranced. It is this constant tension between East and West, refinement and coarseness, passivity and aggression that sets the characters against each other. Ultimately the film hopes that Jenny and Ben can find courtesy further west, in California.

Acting honors in *Gun Fury* belong to the bad guys: Phil Carey and Leo Gordon. Carey is confident, callous and even debonair. He seems a natural leader and a man to be reckoned with, unhibited on-screen—brutal, playful, romantic, menacing. It's really quite a performance. Gordon, compared to Carey, is stone-faced. Yet it is this lack of expression that makes Jess' stubbornness and vengeance more purposeful. Jess' sincerity is never questioned because he could not possibly be duplicitious. Their opposites, whether with or against one another, make for good drama.

Rock Hudson's performance as a pacifist is convincing if rather superficial. After Jess is killed, Ben's moral outrage and sudden vengefulness is abrupt but believable, despite some critical response to the contrary. Donna Reed looks beautiful and acts commendably. She won the Best Supporting Actress Academy Award for a very different performance in 1953 for *From Here to Eternity*. As Blinky, Lee Marvin is rather bland. As the third most prominent member of Slayton's gang, he sports a moustache and has one amusing scene where Roberta Haynes throws things at him (in 3-D!) and knocks him senseless. But Marvin has little else to do afterward except grumble and die without note in the final reel.

Gun Fury received mixed reviews. The *Hollywood Citizen-News* called it "…a topnotch Western on all counts," and *Variety* said, "Even without 3-D Columbia's *Gun Fury* would be a superior western." The *Hollywood Reporter* labeled it "…a hard-driving affair smacking of authenticity and well thought out construction," and *Commonweal* described it as "…a lot of exciting cinema." On the other hand, both *Time* and *Newsweek* found the film completely ordinary. The *New York Times* didn't even bother to review it.

The film, like most of the other 3-D films of the period, soon passed from memory. It did little for Lee Marvin other than further typecast him as a western villain and provide him with a paycheck.

The Big Heat (1953)

CREDITS: Columbia. *Directed by* Fritz Lang. *Produced by* Robert Arthur. *Screenplay by* Sydney Boehm. *Based upon the* Saturday Evening Post *serial by* William P. McGivern. *Musical Director*: Mischa Bakaleinikoff. *Director of Photography*: Charles Lang, A.S.C. *Film Editor*: Charles Nelson, A.C.E. *Art Director*: Robert Peterson. *Set Decorator*: William Kiernan. *Sound Engineer*: George Cooper. *Gowns by* Jean Louis. *Hair Styles by* Helen Hunt. *Makeup by* Clay Campbell. *Assistant Director*: Milton Feldman. Not Rated. Black and White. Flat (1.33:1). 89 minutes. Released in November 1953. Currently available on VHS videotape. Previously available on laserdisc.

CAST: *Dave Bannion*, Glenn Ford; *Debby Marsh*, Gloria Grahame; *Katie Bannion*, Jocelyn Brando; *Mike Lagana*, Alexander Scourby; *Vince Stone*, Lee Marvin; *Bertha Duncan*, Jeanette Nolan; *Tierney*, Peter Whitney; *Lieutenant Wilks*, Willis Bouchey; *Gus Burke*, Robert Burton; *Larry Gordon*, Adam Williams; *Commissioner Higgins*, Howard Wendell; *George Rose*, Cris Alcaide; *Hugo*, Michael Granger; *Lucy Chapman*, Dorothy Green; *Doris*, Carolyn Jones; *Baldy*, Ric Roman; *Atkins*, Dan Seymour; *Selma Parker*, Edith Evanson; *Dr. Kane*, Joe Mell; *Bartender*, Sid Clute; *Jill*, Norma Randall; *Joyce*, Linda Bennett; *Martin*, Herbert Litton; *Mrs. Tucker*, Ezelle Poule; *Dr. Jones*, Byron Kane; *Butler*, Ted Stanhope; *Segal*, Mike Ross; *Reds*, Bill Murphy; *Mike*, Phil Arnold; *Dixon*, Mike Mahoney; *Intern*, Pat Miller; *Fuller*, Paul Maxey; *Hopkins*, Charles Cane; *Marge*, Kathryn Eames; *Harry Shoenstein*, Al Eben; *Hank O'Connell*, Harry Lauter; *Hettrick*, Phil Chambers; *Bill Rutherford*, Robert Forrest; *Al*, John Crawford; *Mark Reiner*, John Doucette.

The Big Heat was Lee Marvin's fourteenth film, and it is the first true movie classic with which he was involved. It was Marvin's fourth villainous role and the one that really registered with audiences and typecast him as a heavy for the following decade. Director Fritz Lang saw in Marvin the potential for sudden, brutal, explosive violence and made use of that potential where previous directors had not. For Marvin, Vince Stone was more than just another role; it became his calling card.

Less than ten seconds into the film, Tom Duncan shoots himself at a desk. His wife (Jeanette Nolan) finds the body and a suicide note...and makes a telephone call. The cover-up begins. Detective David Bannion (Glenn Ford) believes the widow Duncan's story until it is refuted by bar hostess Lucy Chapman (Dorothy Green), who had been seeing Duncan for over a year. Mrs. Duncan admits the affair, but still insists that her husband's suicide was due to worries over poor health. Bannion begins to wonder about the real cause of Duncan's suicide.

Bannion learns that Lucy Chapman has been murdered after being tortured (she was covered with cigarette burns), and he questions Mrs. Duncan. His boss, Lieutenant Wilks (Willis Bouchey), urges Bannion to lay off, but he doesn't listen. Bannion visits crime boss Mike Lagana (Alexander Scourby) at his home, beats up one of Lagana's men and vows to get to the bottom of the Duncan-Chapman mystery. Lt. Wilkes reprimands him again, but Bannion's cheery wife Katie (Jocelyn Brando) tells him not to compromise. Shortly thereafter, she is killed by a car bomb meant for her husband.

Assured by corrupt Police Commissioner Higgins (Howard Wendell) that his wife's killers will eventually be brought to justice, Bannion resigns from the police force and warns Lt. Wilks and former partner Gus Burke (Robert Burton) to stay out of his way while he tracks down the killers himself. Meanwhile, Mike Lagana's right-hand man, Vince Stone (Lee Marvin), has his hands full with sarcastic girlfriend Debby Marsh (Gloria Grahame), who constantly teases him about jumping through Lagana's hoops like a trained animal, and about the bungling of Larry Gordon (Adam Williams), whom Vince had trusted to dispose of Lucy Chapman and Bannion.

While tracing Larry, Bannion runs into Vince and Debby at a bar, where he sees Vince burn a woman's hand with a cigarette. Bannion steps in and forces Vince to leave, then refuses Debby's offer of a drink. Debby follows Bannion outside and persuades him to take her to his hotel. He pumps her for information about Larry but gets nowhere and sends her back home. Debby lies to Vince about where she has been, and Vince angrily twists her arm behind her back, then throws a pot of scalding coffee into her face. Vince forces his poker buddy, Police Commissioner Higgins, to take her to a doctor.

Debby escapes and returns to Bannion, begging him to help her and making sure he understands that her face was scalded because she was seen with him. She tells him about Larry, whom Bannion tracks down and beats up for information. Larry blames the murders on Vince, and Bannion leaves him alive to run, knowing that he won't get far. Larry is killed (offscreen) by Vince, who tells Mike Lagana straight out that he won't be the fall guy if Bannion exposes them. They agree to put pressure on Bannion's most vulnerable point—his young daughter.

Bannion tells Debby that Larry confirmed that Mrs. Duncan has her husband's records on Lagana, and that they would be brought to the public's attention if anything were to happen to her. That is why Lagana wants her kept alive. Upon hearing of his daughter's danger, Bannion rushes to her side to find that she is well protected. Even Lt. Wilks and Gus Burke arrive to help. Meanwhile, Debby takes matters into her own hands, visiting and killing Mrs. Duncan.

Bannion goes to Vince Stone's apartment, but Debby has beaten him there. She surprises Vince with a pot of scalding coffee of her own and tells him that she has killed Mrs. Duncan. He shoots her, then shoots at Bannion as he arrives. They have a brief gunfight, which ends as Vince runs out of bullets and tries to run away. Bannion beats him up but can't bring himself to kill him. Lt. Wilks and Gus Burke arrive and take Vince into custody as Debby dies on the floor, tenderly consoled by Bannion. In the last scene, Detective Bannion sits at his desk in the police station, gets a call and joins Gus Burke to investigate another crime.

The Big Heat is an old-fashioned police

34 The Big Heat

Vince Stone (Lee Marvin) is captured by detectives Dave Bannion (Glenn Ford), Gus Burke (Robert Burton) and Lieutenant Wilks (Willis Bouchey) in *The Big Heat*.

procedural, dressed up with all the style and finesse of a top director with a contemporary sensibility. While some older film noirs have lost their effect because of their overly familiar style and plot elements, *The Big Heat* contains more than enough vitality to keep the familiar from becoming old while providing striking contrast and depth through the use of light, camerawork and characterization. The film continues to pack an emotional wallop, not only because of its superior writing, but due to the way director Fritz Lang tells the story.

Lang begins with characters that are neither wholly good nor wholly evil, places them in a setting where they must make tough, difficult choices, and gives them various motivations and rationale for their actions. He then paints his picture with broad, sure strokes, contrasting the dimly lit, unsafe, outside world with the brightly lit, happy Bannion home; comparing the luxurious, seemingly ceilingless Lagana house to the messy, cramped police station where Bannion works and the plain hotel room where he later stays; dressing the criminals and their molls much more glamourously than the working-class cops and their wives. The effect is obvious, but it works: the criminals make and have money and its benefits, but the working-class detective is the one who has the inner satisfaction and, ultimately, the happy home.

Bannion's home life is explored in some detail so that when it is ripped apart by the sudden, unexpected murder of his wife, his grief means more to the audience. It isn't a coincidence that before the car bombing, Bannion tries to help his daughter build a castle out of blocks but clumsily knocks it down, just as he is about to destroy his own family life due to his investigation. The tragedy extends to the death of Debby as well, who is scarred because she was seen with Bannion and who ultimately sacrifices herself trying to finish what Bannion started. The only times Bannion ever shows real human empathy are when he's at home with his wife and daughter, and when he's comforting dying Debby by telling her about his wife.

Another familiar element is the line between good and evil, or in this case the line between Dave Bannion and Vince Stone.

When Bannion talks to Debby about his desire to kill Mrs. Duncan, she reminds him that he couldn't have done it, or else he would have become the same type of man as Vince. Bannion has the same capacity for violence as does Vince but, unlike the psychopathic killer, he doesn't *like* it. Vince thinks nothing of putting out a cigarette on somebody's hand or literally twisting an arm or two to get what he wants. That's why Vince Stone is such a frightening character.

As played by Lee Marvin, Vince is almost suave, nicely dressed in suit and tie, intelligent, sharp—and deadly. For Vince, violence is a necessary part of business, and is sometimes necessary in his personal life as well. The really frightening thing about Vince is his temper; when he loses it, he grabs the nearest weapon and attacks without thinking. It is this brutality, this out-of-control ferocity, which makes such an impact on audiences because it comes so suddenly and violently. Marvin succeeds at making the rampaging Vince both a frightening monster and a desperate man unable to control his raw emotions.

Marvin's true acting ability shines later, however, after his character's rampages subside and he struggles to control himself and continue to lead a civilized existence. The inner struggle within Vince is apparent: he wipes back his hair as if trying to soothe his brain, darts his eyes around to see if his momentary loss of control will lead to any further consequences, and gradually lowers his voice from a shout to a loud roar of dialogue. There would be times later in his career when Marvin would go from quiet to shout to quiet again without transition, but here he is masterfully in control of the tone and inflection of his voice and body language.

Though Marvin is superb in the film, he is matched by the acting of Glenn Ford and

Vince Stone (Lee Marvin) is scalded with hot water by his girlfriend Debby Marsh (Gloria Grahame) soon after disfiguring her in the same way in *The Big Heat*.

Gloria Grahame. Ford is excellent as Dave Bannion, convincingly conveying the detective's unshakable sense of right and wrong. Even better is Gloria Grahame as Debby, the bubbly B-girl who endures Vince's occasional tantrums for the sake of her preferred lifestyle. Grahame had won 1952's Best Supporting Actress Academy Award for her role in *The Bad and the Beautiful*, and she's better here. She infuses Debby with sarcasm, wit and genuine warmth early on and, after the scalding, brings to the surface a newfound maturity and sense of justice.

Debby proves that she also is capable of the same destructiveness as Vince, but because (unlike Vince) she acts to set things right, she remains redeemable and is seen as such at film's end. In fact, Debby's killing of Mrs. Duncan and attack on Vince save Bannion from the moral repurcussions of killing them himself and thus becoming the same kind of criminal as Vince Stone. His conscience is free to continue the good fight, while Debby has become, through a temper tantrum of Vince's, an instrument of justice.

Ultimately, justice is what *The Big Heat* is all about. At the end of the film Bannion is back where he belongs, Mike Lagana and Police Commissioner Higgins are indicted, the secret which killed Tom Duncan is out in the open, and the key members of Lagana's gang are dead. The price for the clean-up is high—especially for Dave Bannion—but necessary. Justice has also arrived over time—for this unheralded gem, as *The Big Heat* has slowly been recognized as a classic of the cynical, hard-boiled school of mystery-thrillers, a worthy successor to Howard Hawks' *The Big Sleep*.

Critical response to the film was generally good, though like *High Noon*, *The Man Who Shot Liberty Valance* and many others, it's reputation has soared over the years since its original release. All of these films were somewhat ahead of their times and remain contemporary today.

In terms of Lee Marvin's career, *The Big Heat* is one of his best performances and one of the best films in which he ever appeared. It also ensured that he received steady work over the next decade as a heavy, for the impact that Marvin made on audiences in this role cannot be overstated.

The Wild One (1954)

CREDITS: Columbia. *Directed by* Laslo Benedek. *Produced by* Stanley Kramer. *Screenplay by* John Paxton. *Based on a story* (The Cyclists' Raid) *by* Frank Rooney. *Musical Score by* Leith Stevens. *Musical Director*: Morris Stoloff. *Director of Photography*: Hal Mohr, A.S.C. *Film Editor*: Al Clark, A.C.E. *Production Design*: Rudolph Sternad. *Art Direction*: Walter Holscher. *Set Decoration*: Louis Diage. *Sound Engineer*: George Cooper. *Assistant Director*: Paul Donnelly. Not Rated. Black and White. Flat (1.33:1). Filmed with Garutso Balanced Lens. 79 minutes. Released in February 1954. Currently available on VHS videotape, laserdisc and DVD.

CAST: *Johnny*, Marlon Brando; *Kathie*, Mary Murphy; *Harry Bleeker*, Robert Keith; *Chino*, Lee Marvin; *Sheriff Singer*, Jay C. Flippen; *Mildred*, Peggy Maley; *Charlie Thomas*, Hugh Sanders; *Frank Bleeker*, Ray Teal; *Bill Hannegan*, John Brown; *Art Kleiner*, Will Wright; *Ben*, Robert Osterloh; *Wilson*, Robert Bice; *Jimmy*, William Vedder; *Britches*, Yvonne Doughty; *Gringo*, Keith Clarke; *Mouse*, Gil Stratton, Jr.; *Dinky*, Darren Dublin; *Red*, Johnny Tarangelo; *Dextro*, Jerry Paris; *Crazy*, Gene Peterson; *Pigeon*, Alvy Moore; *Go-Go*, Harry Landers; *Boxer*, Jim Connell; *Stinger*, Don Anderson; *Betty*, Angela Stevens; *Simmonds*, Bruno VeSoto; *Sawyer*, Pat O'Malley; *Chino Boy*, Timothy Carey; *Cyclist*, Wally Albright; *Dorothy*, Eve March; *Mrs. Thomas*, Mary Newton; *Racer*, Ted Cooper.

"This is a shocking story. It could never take place in most American towns—but it did in this one. It is a public challenge not to let it happen again."

So begins *The Wild One*, the first major American film to feature alienated youth in leather jackets riding motorcycles and looking for some sort of existential fulfillment. The film was based on Frank Rooney's story *The Cyclists' Raid*, a fictional chronicle of an actual incident which occurred over the Fourth of July weekend in 1947, when an estimated 4000 motorcyclists rolled into Hollister, California and trashed the town. Producer Stanley Kramer read Rooney's story in *Harper's* and bought the rights to it.

After their fight, Johnny (Marlon Brando) and Chino (Lee Marvin) try to show the local police that they were just fooling around in *The Wild One*.

"[The story] touched my sense of social responsibility," stated Kramer, "and I thought that it would make a good movie." Kramer's sense of the story's possibilities was keen, but he never dreamed that his movie would become a *cause celebre* for the disaffected youth of America.

A group of leather-jacketed motorcyclists roars down the road and into a small town where they interrupt a motorcycle race. They are driven off by the local sheriff, but not before one of the gang steals a trophy, which he presents to Johnny (Marlon Brando), the leader of the Black Rebels Motorcycle Club, who proudly mounts it on the front of his Triumph motorcycle. Their next stop is a small town where one of the Rebels is injured while "dragging for beers." The other twenty or so members of the gang fill up the town's only watering hole or hang out on the street, needling the town's conservative residents. Johnny takes a liking to Kathie (Mary Murphy), who works in her uncle's bar, and tries to talk to her, even offering to give her the trophy, but she won't accept it.

The Rebels are about to leave when Chino (Lee Marvin) and his motorcycle gang, the Beetles, arrive. Chino, a former Rebel, picks a fight with Johnny and they go at it in the middle of the main street. Johnny wins the fight, but it is Chino who goes to jail for disturbing the peace. Tension rises as the sun goes down; the bar is becoming rowdier and the residents are afraid to walk the streets. The Rebels break Chino out of jail, but he's too drunk to move. Some of the townspeople arm themselves and search for Johnny, who is searching for Kathie. He finds her being tormented by some of his own gang, rescues her, and takes her on a sensuous moonlit ride through the night.

Johnny brutishly kisses Kathie, but she does not respond. She tries to appeal to his sensitivity, but he cannot respond. She runs away, inadvertantly leading him into the hands of a small mob who try to beat some sense into him. Kathie's father, the town cop (Robert Keith), stops the angry men from beating Johnny, who breaks free and flees. He rides away from a larger mob of angry townspeople when someone throws a tire iron, knocking him off of his Triumph; it rolls on and runs down an old man who also worked at the bar, killing him.

The county sheriff (Jay C. Flippen) shows up just in time to arrest Johnny for manslaughter. Kathie tries to get Johnny off the hook, but it isn't until two witnesses to the accident tell the sheriff that it wasn't Johnny's fault that the sheriff lets him go. The sheriff issues a stern warning to the cyclists never to enter their county again, and the Black Rebels ride off. A little while later, Johnny rides back into town, stops at the bar, enters, looks longingly at Kathie, puts the trophy on the bar, smiles warmly at her (for the first time), and leaves silently, riding out of town alone.

Though the film has not aged well, *The Wild One* remains a powerful and sometimes disturbing glimpse into a misunderstood segment of our society. When Johnny is asked, "What are you rebelling against?" he replies, "Whattya got?" This offhand remark is at the heart of the film, causing either consternation or appreciation in viewers. *The Wild One* is deliberately ambiguous, asking viewers to judge the characters for themselves. The clearest explanation the film provides for the Rebels' destructive behavior is Johnny's taunt while being beaten up: "My old man hit harder than that."

It is interesting that the Rebels are portrayed not so much as a gang of thugs but more like adolescent boys looking for new toys. During one sequence in town they take turns on a pogo stick; later they dance outside the beauty shop with each other, clowning

This advertisement for *The Wild One* appeared in 1968, when the film was finally released in Britain. Its stars, Marlon Brando and Lee Marvin, are featured at bottom right.

around with a wig and a hair dryer. Only after dark do they become sinister. On the other hand, the town's citizens are purported to be greedy moneygrubbers, willing to tolerate the mayhem as long as the money flows in and the damage isn't too great. Many critics felt that by undermining the respectable townspeople and sugar-coating the motorcycle gang, the film was delivering an un-American message to its youthful audience.

The Wild One, even more than *A Streetcar Named Desire*, made Marlon Brando a cultural superstar. The teenagers who hadn't seen *Streetcar* took Brando's offhanded attitude, macho postures and ultra-cool costuming to heart. His performance gave the entire subculture of rebellious teens and disenchanted drop-outs a look and a voice that it hadn't yet found. With this one movie role, Brando became an icon to a generation. But Marlon Brando didn't want to become an icon and fought the image for several years. Originally thrilled by the project, Brando became disillusioned as the social commentary that had attracted him in the first place was gradually removed. *The Wild One* found controversy everywhere it played (and didn't play; it was banned in Britain until 1968 for its violence).

Lee Marvin's character and performance are the antithesis of Brando's. Johnny is a soft-spoken, reserved, even isolated leader, one who lets events take their course and only gets involved to settle disputes. Chino is a loud, coarse, brutish bully, constantly talking or yelling, threatening people and pushing them around. While Johnny's intelligence and sensitivity is gradually revealed by his dialogue, Chino sounds more infantile the more he rambles on.

Physically, Johnny glides along with little extraneous movement, acting quickly only when attacked. Chino moves with sweeping arms, dangling legs, darting eyes and booming voice. Even their costumes are contradictory—Johnny is ultra-cool in his shiny black leather jacket while Chino looks like a jailbird in his horizontally striped shirt and scraggly beard. Yet Chino holds his own against Johnny, and their turbulent relationship provides the film with a dangerous edge—as well as an undeniable subcurrent of sexuality. Chino calls Johnny "sweetheart" and "baby" several times and exclaims that he loves him at least twice.

Keenan Wynn was the first choice to play Chino, but he wanted more money than Kramer was willing to spend. Wynn recommended one of his riding buddies, Lee Marvin, for the part in his stead. Marvin was at home on motorcycles and seems a whole lot more authentic as a motorcycle gang leader than the moody but charismatic Brando. Marvin and Wynn often rode together on weekends and even entered cross-country races together on their Triumphs for years afterward.

The Wild One is also notable for its Leith Stevens score; it was the first Hollywood film to use a score completely comprised of jazz music. Stevens was also innovative in using on-screen sources for the music, such as juke boxes and radios. Another musical trivia note: After watching the film, a young British band took the name of Chino's gang for their own, though they changed the spelling somewhat.

Critics were divided in their responses to *The Wild One*. Bosley Crowther of *The New York Times* applauded its intention more than its execution: "...it is a tough and engrossing motion picture, weird and cruel, while it stays on the beam. ...So long as the makers of this picture permit it to stay in the realm of graphic examination of the behavior and depredations of this mob, it is a powerful and terrifying survey. ...they briefly project their film onto the elevated level of social drama with significance and scope.

"...Withal, *The Wild One* is a picture of extraordinary candor and courage—a picture that tries to grasp an idea, even though its reach falls short. It is too bad that some mutterings in the industry have seemed to deprecate it..."

Crowther also gives this description of Lee Marvin's Chino: "And in a second wolf-pack leader, whom Lee Marvin gruesomely portrays as a glandular 'psycho' or dope-fiend or something fantastically mad, there is briefly injected into this picture a glimpse of utter monstrosity, loose and enjoying the privilege of hectoring others in a fair society."

Hollis Alpert of the *Saturday Review* also appreciated the film: "It's first-rate moviemaking, and I'd say also something in the way of a public service. It's pleasant to report such conscientiousness in a Hollywood seemingly so consecrated at present to tricks and novelties." Earlier in his review, Alpert had noted that, "The nice thing about Mr. Kramer's movie is that it doesn't preach or ever state directly what the sources of the trouble are. It's done largely through implication and is helped no end by an astonishing performance on the part of Marlon Brando."

Other critics, however, took the opposite view. *Newsweek* claimed that the film "…lacks both the social signficance and the dramatic resolution to justify the heavy going." *Time* stated that, "*The Wild One* has the disturbing shock of reality but its main purpose seems to be to shock. No one can doubt that the movies are highly skillful at picturing brutality and violence but *The Wild One* suggests that Hollywood may be making too much of a bad thing."

Catholic World called both producer Stanley Kramer and his film irritating: "What is so irritating about *The Wild One* is the feeling of frustration which it churns up inside you. Mr. Kramer has neatly set up his problems and then blandly rides off saying that there it is and there isn't anything you can do about it. Marlon Brando is at his most repulsive as the arrogant leader of the cyclists."

Repulsive or sensual, Marlon Brando had struck a nerve. The success of *The Wild One* (it didn't make much money, but everybody talked about it whether they had seen it or not) inspired a spate of juvenile delinquency and biker films in the following years, finally culminating in the *other* landmark biker film, *Easy Rider*, in 1969.

Gorilla at Large (1954)

CREDITS: Panoramic Productions and 20th Century–Fox. *Directed by* Harmon Jones. *Produced by* Robert L. Jacks. *Executive Producer*: Leonard Goldstein. *Written by* Leonard Praskins, Barney Slater. *Musical Direction by* Lionel Newman. *Director of Photography*: Lloyd Ahern, A.S.C. *Film Editor*: George A. Gittens. *Art Direction by* Lyle Wheeler, Addison Hehr. *Set Decorations by* Al Orension. *Sound Engineered by* Clayton Ward, Harry M. Leonard. *Costumes Designed by* Renie. *Wardrobe Direction by* Charles LeMaire. *Makeup Artist*: Frank Westmore. Not Rated. Technicolor. Widescreen (1.66:1). Originally 3-D. 84 minutes. Released in April 1954. Not currently available on home video.

CAST: *Joey Matthews*, Cameron Mitchell; *Laverne Miller*, Anne Bancroft; *Sgt. Garrison*, Lee J. Cobb; *Cyrus Miller*, Raymond Burr; *Audrey Baxter*, Charlotte Austin; *Kovacs*, Peter Whitney; *Shaughnessy*, Lee Marvin; *Mack*, Warren Stevens; *Morse*, John G. Kellogg; *Owens*, Charles Tannen.

In between parts in two major, popular films, *The Wild One* and *The Caine Mutiny*, Lee Marvin appeared in what must surely rank as his silliest movie, *Gorilla at Large*, a low-budget melodrama shot in 3-D to take advantage of that short-lived movie craze. It is a departure from Marvin's usual roles in that he plays a cop rather than a criminal, and that he provides the comic relief in the movie.

The most popular act in an amusement park (never named) is the gorilla act, in which trapeze artist Laverne Miller (Anne Bancroft) swings tantalizingly out of reach of Goliath the gorilla, "who cost the lives of a thousand men before his capture!"

Laverne only teases the gorilla, saving her charms for husband Cy Miller (Raymond Burr), the owner of the park. Miller makes his rounds and after hours fires a lazy employee, who later is found with a broken neck. The prime suspects of the murder are Goliath and Joey Matthews (Cameron Mitchell), a young carnival barker who will be assisting Laverne with her new gorilla act by donning an ape suit, replacing Goliath in the cage, and capturing her as she swings past.

The detective on the case, Sergeant Garrison (Lee J. Cobb), assigns a cop named Shaughnessy (Lee Marvin) to guard Goliath, but the ape imposter knocks Shaughnessy out and frees Goliath. Joey's fiancee, Audrey Baxter (Charlotte Austin), is attacked by Goliath in the new mirror maze, and Miller's press agent is killed. More blame falls on Joey when

At right, Patrolman Shaughnessy (Lee Marvin) tries to explain that an escaped gorilla named Goliath turned on the amusement park's loudspeaker system in *Gorilla at Large*.

his gorilla suit is found. The gorilla's handler, Kovacs (Peter Whitney), finds and hides Goliath, but the gorilla is inadvertently let loose by Shaughnessy. Goliath rambles through the park, activating several rides as it goes, distracting the police. When it threatens Laverne, Goliath is caught by Kovacs and the police and is locked up again. Sgt. Garrison is questioning Laverne when, to everyone's surprise, Miller confesses to the murders and is taken away.

As Laverne and Joey prepare for their new act, Kovacs threatens Laverne but is stopped by Joey. At the police station, Joey proves to Sgt. Garrison that Miller couldn't have committed the murders due to a broken arm that had never healed correctly, so they rush back to the park to protect Laverne from Kovacs. Joey discovers the truth when he finds Laverne's trapeze gloves stuffed inside the hands of his gorilla suit. Kovacs refuses to let him replace Goliath in the act. "She's got it coming to her," says Laverne's former husband. Goliath captures Laverne, rushes though the audience and climbs to the top of the roller coaster with her. Joey climbs to just underneath them and distracts Goliath with his cigarette lighter. Fireworks shoot past the gorilla and further distract him while Joey rescues Laverne. Goliath is shot three times and plummets to his death, and Laverne is led off to jail for murder.

Gorilla at Large is an old-fashioned melodrama with plenty of stock characters with unsavory pasts, driven by sex, money and deceit, hiding secret relationships and showing little love for each other. Three aspects of the film give it some small stature: the 3-D effects (which are minimal and ineffective), the setting at an amusement park and central gorilla figure (which are unusual and fairly interesting), and the surprisingly big-name cast.

This is Anne Bancroft's eighth film and is one of her sexiest performances. She's almost always in skimpy costumes and heating up the screen with whomever will kiss her. Lee J. Cobb is properly dour as the detective who refuses to pin the murders on a gorilla, while Cameron Mitchell (who had a circus background) seems at home in the amusement park surroundings. This was one of Raymond Burr's three 1954 releases, along with *Rear Window* and *Godzilla*, before later becoming television's most famous lawyer.

Then there's Lee Marvin. He clearly has fun with this role, especially in the scene where he and Goliath face off and take each other's measure. Later he brags about how he would be able to solve the case while he inadvertantly lets Goliath out of his submerged hiding place. This is one of the few times when Marvin supplied most of a film's comic relief. *Variety* praised Marvin as "...doing a good study of a talkative policeman..."

Gorilla at Large received mixed reviews, being perceived as one of several routine melodramas trying to capitalize on the current 3-D craze. The *Hollywood Reporter* called it "a diverting, highly exploitable 3-D mystery melodrama that offers a gorilla on the loose, several murders and a baffling maze of mirrors, all set against a carnival background. Persuasively acted out by a fine cast rather unusually strong all the way down the line, this Panoramic production, attractively produced by Robert L. Jacks, should bring in satisfying returns." Despite the stellar cast, the film did little business and vanished quickly.

The film did receive an upsurge of attention in the early 1980s when 3-D movies enjoyed a resurgence, particularly on television. *Gorilla at Large* has aired in 3-D (with special glasses necessary) in Boston, Los Angeles, Hawaii and Japan, among other places. The film still receives (and deserves) little respect, but because of its cast and its 3-D features, it has attained the status of a minor camp classic.

The Caine Mutiny (1954)

CREDITS: Columbia. *Directed by* Edward Dmytryk. *Produced by* Stanley Kramer. *Screenplay by* Stanley Roberts. *Additional Dialogue by* Michael Blankfort. *Based upon the Pulitzer Prize–winning novel by* Herman Wouk. *Musical Score by* Max Steiner. *Song* "I Can't Believe That You're in Love with Me" *by* Jimmy McHugh, Clarence Gaskill. *Song* "Yellowstain Blues" *by* Fred Karger, Herman Wouk. *Director of Photography*: Frank Planer, A.S.C. *Second Unit Photography*: Ray Cory, A.S.C. *Film Editors*: William A. Lyon, A.C.E., Henry Batista, A.C.E. *Production Design by* Rudolph Sternad. *Art Director*: Cary Odell. *Set Decorator*: Frank Tuttle. *Sound Engineer*: Lambert Day. *Special Effects*: Lawrence W. Butler. *Makeup by* Clay Campbell. *Hairstyles by* Helen Hunt. *Gowns by* Jean Louis. *Assistant Director*: Carter DeHaven, Jr. *Technical Adviser*: Commander James C. Shaw, U.S.N. Not Rated. Technicolor. *Technicolor Color Consultant*: Francis Cugat. Flat (1.33:1). 125 minutes. Released in June 1954. Currently available on VHS videotape, laserdisc, and DVD.

CAST: *Captain Philip Francis Queeg*, Humphrey Bogart; *Lt. Barney Greenwald*, Jose Ferrer; *Lt. Steve Maryk*, Van Johnson; *Lt. Tom Keefer*, Fred MacMurray; *Ensign Willie Keith*, Robert Francis; *May Wynn*, May Wynn (originally Donna Lee Hickey—she changed her name when she won the role); *Captain DeVriess*, Tom Tully; *Lt. Commander Challee*, E. G. Marshall; *Lt. Paynter*, Arthur Franz; *Meatball*, Lee Marvin; *Captain Blakely*, Warner Anderson; *Horrible*, Claude Akins; *Mrs. Keith*, Katharine Warren; *Ensign Harding*, Jerry Paris; *Chief Budge*, Steve Brodie; *Stilwell*, Todd Karns; *Lt. Commander Dickson*, Whit Bissell; *Lt. Jorgensen*, James Best; *Ensign Carmody*, Joe Haworth; *Ensign Rabbit*, Guy Anderson; *Whittaker*, James Edwards; *Urban*, Don Dubbins; *Engstrand*, David Alpert.

The Caine Mutiny was one of the biggest productions of the decade. Herman Wouk's mammoth tale of a fictional Naval mutiny during World War II had been published in 1951, spent more than two years on the *New York Times* bestseller list, won the Pulitzer Prize for fiction in 1952 and had been adapted into a hit Broadway play by the author. The film version was eagerly anticipated, and when it came time to make it, Lee Marvin definitely wanted to be included. It was to be his first truly *major* motion picture.

Ensign Willie Keith (Robert Francis), fresh out of midshipmen's school, is assigned to the *Caine*, a tired old minesweeper. He is disheartened by the rundown condition of the *Caine* and its crew and does not respect slovenly Captain DeVriess (Tom Tully), though he does befriend Lt. Maryk (Van Johnson) and Lt. Keefer (Fred MacMurray). When Captain DeVriess is transferred, Keith is relieved that his replacement, Captain Philip Francis Queeg (Humphrey Bogart), seems to be stronger in character.

Queeg's character becomes evident as the ship heads out to sea. During a target towing assignment, the *Caine* steams in a circle and cuts its own towline while Queeg bawls out a sailor. The ship is then sent into battle to lead a flotilla of landing craft to a beachhead. Still 1500 yards from their turning point, Queeg orders the *Caine* turned and a yellow dye marker thrown overboard to guide the Marines to shore. Unable to explain Queeg's behavior except as cowardice, the officers begin to question Queeg's authority.

Queeg finds that a quart of strawberries is missing and convinces himself that a key to the icebox was made. He determines to find the key and has the officers search the ship for it. Keefer persuades Maryk that Queeg is paranoid and delusional but refuses to take the matter to the admiralty. A storm warning is issued and the storm blows into a typhoon. Queeg refuses to change direction into the wind to steady the ship; he will not act without orders. As the *Caine* heels over Queeg freezes, unable to speak or act. Maryk issues orders to change direction and relieves Queeg of command, supported by Willie Keith. Queeg objects and threatens them with a court-martial, but the men stand firm. The ship plows on through the storm in a safer new direction.

In San Francisco Lt. Maryk is to be tried for mutiny. Lt. Barney Greenwald (Jose Ferrer), a hotshot lawyer who would rather prosecute, agrees to defend Maryk. The court-martial begins. Keith testifies, followed by the helmsman, a sailor named Meatball (Lee Marvin), and then Keefer, who lies on the witness stand. One of the Navy's psychiatrists is questioned next, and Greenwald forces him to admit that Queeg has at least the symptoms of a paranoid personality. Maryk testifies, followed by Captain Queeg. Poised and confident, Queeg blames the mutiny squarely on Maryk and "disloyal officers." As Greenwald asks specific questions, Queeg's memory becomes cloudier and his countenance less confident. When Greenwald catches Queeg in an outright lie, Queeg begins to ramble, contradicting himself and blaming everyone else for his own faults. The court-martial judges watch in silence as Captain Queeg crumbles before their very eyes.

After the court-martial the jubilant *Caine* officers throw a party. Keefer shows up, surprising Maryk, the only *Caine* officer to witness his perjury. As they talk, Barney Greenwald arrives, drunk. He tells the officers how much he hated having to destroy Queeg's career, how much they owe men like Queeg and why Tom Keefer deserved to be the man on trial. He describes Keefer's testimony, then throws a glassful of champagne in Keefer's face and challenges him to a fight. One by one, the officers exit, leaving Keefer standing alone, dripping with shame.

First and foremost, *The Caine Mutiny* is a character study. Willie Keith matures from a callow youth into a confident officer as he learns the necessity of taking personal responsibility. Maryk questions authority for the first time and forces himself to take action he believes necessary in spite of his training against it. Keefer discovers that his own thin skin is more important to him than personal honor or the respect of his fellow officers. Greenwald tests himself by taking on a case nobody else wants and by restraining his personal feelings about it until afterward. Queeg deteriorates from a stout, solid Naval officer into a petty tyrant, insecure and intimidated by his own crew, finally unable to muster up enough initiative to control his ship during the typhoon.

The film also presents two opposite viewpoints concurrently. First, that the Navy (specifically, the *Caine*) is run-down and fouled-up, unable to do anything right or on time, wastes its efforts on worthless training exercises and endless routine, monotonous tasks, and basically has no idea how to fight a war; and second, that despite all of its problems, the Navy (the *Caine*'s officers and crew) still manages to work together as a team, keeps outdated machinery operating safely, withstands any barrage that nature or the Japanese throws at them and does so with a captain that seems to be going nuts. This dichotomy of disparagement and approbation was at the heart of Herman Wouk's novel, providing a realistic attitude for the *Caine*'s crew, but it deeply disturbed the Navy.

Four film companies had expressed interest in the novel soon after its publication,

44 The Caine Mutiny

but when word leaked out that the Navy would not cooperate (essential for such a film) unless major changes were made to the story, the offers were rescinded. Producer Stanley Kramer took the risk and optioned the book for just $60,000. As the book won the Pulitzer Prize in 1952 and sales passed the two million level, the Navy brass realized that the story was too well-known to dilute without controversy and eased its restrictions.

Though Wouk had envisioned Fredric March as Queeg, Humphrey Bogart had lobbied for the part and accepted a smaller salary than usual to secure it. It is Bogart's performance—confident yet overwhelmed, poised yet pathetic—that is justly remembered. Van Johnson gives his most thoughtful performance as Maryk, while Fred MacMurray is brilliant as manipulative Tom Keefer and has much of the film's best dialogue. Matching MacMurray's brilliance is Jose Ferrer, the top actor of the early 1950s, who is razor sharp as lawyer Barney Greenwald.

The film's two new stars did not fare quite as well. Though Robert Francis and May Wynn show talent, their characters' relationship is the weakest point of the story, identified in virtually every review. Their love story had somewhat more meaning in Wouk's novel, but it didn't translate to the screen with any power. Robert Francis made two more films before dying in an airplane crash in 1955; May Wynn (Donna Lee Hickey adopted her character's name as her own stage name) made three more films before retiring.

Meatball (Lee Marvin) takes a break from sanding and notices that the *Caine* is about to steam over its own towline in *The Caine Mutiny*.

Lee Marvin and Claude Akins appear as the two most important sailors on the ship, Meatball and Horrible. Marvin has just over two minutes of screen time but is very visible. It is Meatball and Horrible who give Willie Keith a poor impression of the ship when he first comes aboard; Meatball drops the paravane into the water that Maryk retrieves by jumping into the ocean after it; Meatball witnesses the *Caine* cut its own towline; Keith yells at Horrible and Meatball before being called to the Captain's cabin to be chewed out himself, prompting Meatball to grouse about "all these 90-day wonders. Every one of them thinks he's a five-star admiral."

When DeVriess leaves the *Caine*, it is Meatball who presents him with a gold watch from the enlisted men. Later, Meatball and Horrible are stripped (offscreen) and searched for the imaginary key after the strawberries disappear. Marvin's final appearance in the film takes place at the court-martial, a situation which would later prove familiar to the actor (*The Rack, Sergeant Ryker*). Meatball is questioned by the prosecuting attorney about Queeg, then asked by Barney Greenwald what the campaign stars on his uniform are for. He describes the origins of his decorations before being excused. Though Meatball is certainly a slob, his bravery cannot be questioned.

Though his part was small, Lee Marvin was thrilled to be on an A-list film and working with Humphrey Bogart, whose professionalism impressed him. He also worked as an unofficial technical advisor from his own experience, giving director Dmytryk his opinions on various issues involving the Navy. Marvin was learning from the best, contributing and being listened to by Hollywood big boys. And he was getting paid for it.

The Caine Mutiny became one of the big hits of 1954 for Columbia, which had released another wartime drama, *From Here to Eternity*, the previous year. In fact, the release of *The Caine Mutiny* was postponed for six months to separate the two films and keep them from competing against each other for the same audience and awards.

Bosley Crowther of the *New York Times* called it "a vibrant film" and noted that, "...the body of the picture—the good, solid, masculine core—that has to do with the chafing of naval officers under a neurotic captain's command is salty, exciting and revealing. And it is smartly and stingingly played by a cast of able performers..."

Newsweek praised, "One of the year's best films, with a half dozen of the year's best performances." Arthur Knight, in the *Saturday Review*, called the film "...one of the most stimulating and satisfying dramas of the season." Most of the other reviews were favorable; however, reviewers did compare the film to the novel and the current Broadway play *The Caine Mutiny Court Martial* (with Lloyd Nolan as Queeg), mostly unfavorably. They complained that the romance added nothing and should have been scrapped, while the court-martial scenes should have been more detailed and forceful. Even director Edward Dmytryk wasn't satisfied with the finished product. "It's a disappointment in my career, to tell the truth. The film should have been much longer. Stanley Roberts' original script was about 190 pages, even without the romantic subplot involving the ensign and the nightclub singer. It should have remained that—a three and one-half or four hour picture—and it would have been more logically developed, the characters would have been further fleshed out. It would have been perfect."

Despite the film's flaws, it was tremendously popular with the public, grossing $8.7 million, second only to *White Christmas'* $12 million that year. When the Academy Award nominations were announced, *The Caine Mutiny* collected seven, including Best Picture, Actor (Humphrey Bogart), Supporting Actor (Tom Tully, who played DeVriess), Screenplay, Scoring of a Dramatic or Comedy Picture, Editing, and Sound Recording. It was completely shut out on Oscar night, however, losing in three categories to Marlon Brando's triumph *On the Waterfront*.

The Raid (1954)

CREDITS: Panoramic Productions and 20th Century–Fox. *Directed by* Hugo Fregonese. *Produced by* Robert L. Jacks, Leonard Goldstein.

46 The Raid

Screenplay by Sydney Boehm. *Screen Story by* Francis Cockrell. *Based on the story* Affair at St. Albans *by* Herbert R. Sass. *Music by* Roy Webb. *Musical Direction*: Lionel Newman. *Director of Photography*: Lucien Ballard. *Film Editor*: Robert Golden. *Art Direction*: George Patrick. *Set Decoration*: Glen Daniels. *Sound*: Arthur Kirbach, Harry M. Leonard. *Costumes Designed by* Travilla. *Makeup Artist*: Louis Hippe. *Assistant Director*: Ad Schaumer. Not Rated. Technicolor. *Technicolor Color Consultant*: Leonard Doss. Flat (1.33:1). 82 minutes. Released in August 1954. Not currently available on home video.

CAST: *Major Neal Benton / Neal Swayze*, Van Heflin; *Katy Bishop*, Anne Bancroft; *Captain Lionel Foster*, Richard Boone; *Lieutenant Keating*, Lee Marvin; *Larry Bishop*, Tommy Rettig; *Captain Dwyer*, Peter Graves; *Reverend Lucas*, Douglas Spencer; *Colonel Tucker*, Paul Cavanagh; *Banker Anderson*, Will Wright; *Lieutenant Robinson*, James Best; *Corporal Deane*, John Dierkes; *Delphine Coates*, Helen Ford; *Mr. Danzig*, Harry Hines; *Captain Henderson*, Simon Scott; *Lieutenant Ramsey*, Claude Akins; *Confederate Soldier*, William Schallert.

In every film actor's career there are movies that, for better or worse, are remembered, and others that, also for better or worse, remain largely forgotten. *The Raid* is a forgotten little gem of a movie based on a true incident that occurred near the end of the Civil War. It is a suspenseful drama, thought-provoking and entertaining, and well worth anybody's time and attention.

Before *The Raid* can take place, seven Confederate prisoners, led by Major Neal Benton (Van Heflin), must escape from the Union stockade in Plattsburgh, New York, near the Canadian border. One of the escapees is shot in the firefight begun by Lieutenant Keating (Lee Marvin) with the Union guards and is left to die. The others successfully escape into Canada. Two-and-a-half weeks later, Benton arrives in St. Albans, Vermont by train in the guise of a Canadian businessman named Neal Swayze. A local banker advises him of available properties and sends him to Katy Bishop's boarding house to stay.

Major Benton (Van Heflin) and Captain Dwyer (Peter Graves) discuss Lieutenant Keating's (Lee Marvin) request to accompany his fellow Confederates on a daring raid in northern Vermont in *The Raid*.

Benton takes an instant liking to the young widow (Anne Bancroft) and her son Larry (Tommy Rettig) but focuses his energies on mapping the town for an upcoming Confederate raid.

Other Confederates, all in civilian disguise, arrive in St. Albans in twos and threes, converging their main force at an abandoned farm outside of town and across the river. The Confederates prepare for their private act of war, the first of a planned series of raids designed to force the Union to pull troops back from the front to protect the most northern towns from rear attack, and to help finance the Southern war effort with stolen funds from the North. Meanwhile, Katy's attentions are divided between Benton and one of her oldest friends, one-armed Union officer Captain Foster (Richard Boone), who also stays at her boarding house and who is jealous of her attentions to Benton.

On the day of the planned raid, two platoons of Union soldiers arrive in town, forcing its postponement. Lt. Keating takes the news hard, endangering their mission by acting on his own and beating one Union officer to death. Benton orders Keating caught and held, but Keating gets away and disrupts the town's church service, where Benton shoots him down and becomes a town hero. Later that evening Benton is told by the St. Albans town council that he has been given prime acreage and guaranteed future business, which, along with his liking for Katy and the townspeople, nags at his conscience.

Nevertheless, the following day when the Union soldiers leave, the raid proceeds. Larry finds Benton in his Confederate uniform, refuses to listen to his explanations, and escapes to find and bring back the Union cavalry. The Confederate troops take control of the stunned town. They herd all of the townspeople into one group, steal the money from the town's three banks, take all of the town's horses and burn all the buildings around the town square. Captain Foster puts up a fight, killing two of the rebels, but is forced to surrender. Foster's heroics redeem him in the eyes of Katy Bishop.

As the cavalry closes in, Benton uses the townspeople as a human blockade to keep at bay the returning Union soldiers until the last possible moment. Benton and the rebel soldiers escape across the river, burn the bridge behind them, and flee into Canada. As the town burns around them, Larry tearfully hopes that Benton gets away, and Katy reads a note from Benton that asks her to try to understand his actions.

The Raid is one of the most unusual Civil War movies ever made. Not only does it reverse the common scenario of Northern soldiers burning their way through the South, but it asks and expects the audience to withhold any moral or political judgment until the end of the story. Both sides of the issue of war are seen and discussed in detail, and both sides are given justification for their actions. Some people on both sides are inflamed with hatred and the will to destroy, while others are more rational and try to overcome their personal feelings to understand the larger picture of the war. The situations of Benton and Katy Bishop, both of whom have lost loved ones in the conflict, articulate the heartfelt emotion involved on both sides, and their growing feelings for each other argue for reconciliation, though that does not happen.

As Neal Benton / Swayze is embraced by the people of St. Albans and his feelings for Katy deepen, he undergoes such pressure from his conscience that it seems he may forego the raid and rediscover the happiness which he lost when the war destroyed his property and family. Ultimately, though, Benton chooses duty to the South above his own personal happiness and leaves Katy with only a note of regret and contradictory memories of a man she might have loved.

The film is based on a true episode of the Civil War, and it recounts the actual raid pretty closely, though the real Confederates were much younger than their movie counterparts. The real raiders were arrested in Canada, but the Canadian courts eventually ruled that the Confederates were soldiers acting under military orders and released them. No further raids were made, and the war ended soon afterward.

Lee Marvin once again fills the role of the hot-headed, trigger-happy soldier who puts the mission in jeopardy with his aggressiveness. Early in the film, he almost baits one of his fellow Confederate prisoners (who stays behind out of conscience) into a fight; he awakens a Union officer just to club him viciously with the butt of his rifle; and he rashly shoots at the prison guards during the escape, leading to the shooting and unnecessary death of one of his fellow prisoners. That's in the first five minutes of the movie.

Despite his promise to Major Benton to hold his temper and stay out of trouble, when the raid is postponed, Lieutenant Keating (allegedly drinking) goes off on his own and starts his own offensive against the North. His comeuppance occurs in the town church when Reverend Lucas (Douglas Spencer) uses Biblical references to call for the extermination of the South, which is more than Keating can take. He shoots a Union soldier trying to leave the church and is about to kill the Reverend when Major Benton calmly steps into the aisle and guns him down in front of an astonished parish. This is one of the first of Marvin's many memorable death scenes, for which the actor would become well known.

While Marvin instigates and provides much of the violence in the movie, it is Van Heflin who carries the film. He represents the heart and soul of every soldier. Sampling life on both sides of the Mason-Dixon line, he is torn by duty and conscience, tries to do the right thing according to his own beliefs, and follows a moral code, even in war. Heflin does such an able job humanizing his character that it is almost a surprise when he goes through with the raid. During the mid-fifties, from *Shane* through *3:10 to Yuma*, Van Heflin was one of Hollywood's finest actors, and he's at the peak of his powers here.

Along with Lee Marvin, actors Peter Graves and John Dierkes give strong performances in supporting roles as Confederate officers under Heflin, and familiar faces Claude Akins, James Best and William Schallert also appear in gray. Richard Boone is properly strident as the one-armed Union officer who dislikes Major Benton and who finally gets a chance to redeem his wartime cowardice. Anne Bancroft is fetching and has some nice scenes along the way, and Tommy Rettig is fine as her boy Larry; he found lasting fame as the human star of *Jeff's Collie* on television.

The Raid did not perform particularly well at the box office, despite generally favorable reviews and the fresh approach to its Civil War subject. Philip T. Hartung of *Commonweal* give the film its best review:

"The most interesting piece of Americana that has turned up in a movie in a long time is found in *The Raid*, an exciting little item about a group of Confederate Officers who escape from a Vermont [actually New York] prison during the Civil War and carefully plan a raid on a New England town. Directed with suspense by Hugo Fregonese, this picture deliberately builds up its characters, both the Southerners and the Northerners, so that when the big excitement comes, your loyalties are with both groups. Because of the exceptionally fine portrayal by Van Heflin, as the Confederate leader, you are likely to ally yourself with him—and his problem is by no means easy when he realizes the damn Yankees are people too and not just foes. *The Raid* successfully avoids the sentiment that could have been its pitfall. Without getting tricky, it gives you just the facts—and the emotions."

Hartung's concise review says it all. *The Raid* is an exciting, thought-provoking, entertaining history lesson which, thankfully, doesn't provide any easy answers to the questions that it asks. And because it presents both sides as carefully as it can, the film doesn't come across as propaganda. The situations and characters are complex and heartfelt, which makes the action that much more compelling. *The Raid* is certainly one of the finest Civil War films ever produced and is one of the better films in which Lee Marvin ever appeared.

Bad Day at Black Rock (1955)

CREDITS: Metro-Goldwyn-Mayer. *Directed by* John Sturges. *Produced by* Dore Schary. *Associate Producer*: Herman Hoffman. *Screenplay by* Millard Kaufman. *Based on a story* (Bad Time at Honda) *by* Howard Breslin. *Adaption by* Don

McGuire. *Music by* Andre Previn. *Director of Photography*: William C. Mellor, A.S.C. *Film Editor*: Newell P. Kimlin, A.C.E. *Art Directors*: Cedric Gibbons, Malcolm Brown. *Set Decorations*: Edwin B. Willis, Fred MacLean. *Recording Supervisor*: Wesley C. Miller. *Assistant Director*: Joel Freeman. Not Rated. Eastman Color. *Color Consultant*: Alvord Eiseman. CinemaScope (2.35:1). 81 minutes. Released January 7, 1955. Currently available on VHS videotape and laserdisc.

CAST: *John J. Macreedy*, Spencer Tracy; *Reno Smith*, Robert Ryan; *Liz Wirth*, Anne Francis; *Sheriff Tim Horn*, Dean Jagger; *Doc Velie*, Walter Brennan; *Pete Wirth*, John Ericson; *Coley Trimble*, Ernest Borgnine; *Hector David*, Lee Marvin; *Hastings*, Russell Collins; *Sam*, Walter Sande.

1955 was a very good year for Lee Marvin, who starred or co-starred in seven films released during those twelve months. The first of those was *Bad Day at Black Rock*, which was immediately acclaimed as a classic and stands today as one of the best films of the 1950s. It is certainly one of the best films in which Marvin ever appeared.

Bad Day at Black Rock begins as a passenger train urgently races across the California desert. The Streamliner slows and stops, for the first time in four years, at a dusty collection of buildings known as Black Rock. Off the train steps a one-armed man in black, John J. Macreedy (Spencer Tracy), who encounters mistrust and open hostility when he asks about a local Japanese farmer named Komoko. Macreedy is watched and bullied by Coley Trimble (Ernest Borgnine) and Hector David (Lee Marvin), the town's toughs, to find out why he's there. The town sheriff (Dean Jagger) refuses to answer any questions regarding Komoko.

Macreedy is quizzed by Reno Smith (Robert Ryan), the town's unquestioned leader, who reluctantly gives him clues to Komoko's fate. Macreedy hires a jeep from Liz

Hector David (Lee Marvin) prods stranger John J. Macreedy (Spencer Tracy) to talk in *Bad Day at Black Rock*.

Wirth (Anne Francis) and drives out to Adobe Flat to see for himself. He finds the charred remains of buildings, a working well and what seems to be a grave. On the way back to town, Macreedy is run off the single lane dirt road by Coley Trimble and his pickup truck. Returning to town, Macreedy decides that he's had enough and announces that he will be leaving. Unfortunately, the next train isn't due until morning. He tries to take the jeep but is stopped by Liz, who refuses to aid him. He enlists the help of apathetic Doc Velie (Walter Brennan), but Doc's car is openly vandalized by Hector.

Macreedy goes to the diner and is followed by Trimble, who picks a fight. This time Macreedy responds, dropping the big man with a judo chop to the neck. Trimble attacks again and is thrown through the screen door. He attacks one more time and is dropped with quick punches and judo chops from the one-armed man, who knows now that he is under a death sentence. He openly accuses Smith of killing Komoko and warns him that he'll also have to kill all of the witnesses, because eventually someone will talk.

Macreedy is left to wait until dark with Doc Velie. He tells Doc and Pete Wirth (John Ericson) why he came to Black Rock. Komoko's son had died saving Macreedy's life during World War II in Italy and had been awarded a medal. Macreedy simply wanted Komoko to have his son's posthumous medal. Doc convinces Pete to tell Macreedy how Komoko was killed: Reno Smith led a group of six locals to harass the Japanese farmer soon after Pearl Harbor was bombed and ended up shooting him.

After his confession, Pete agrees to help Doc get Macreedy out of town. After dark, Pete and Doc ambush Hector, knocking him out. Macreedy joins Liz in her jeep and they drive into the hills. Liz stops suddenly, and the jeep is bathed in light. Macreedy jumps out as a bullet whizzes past. Liz walks toward the light only to have Reno Smith describe her imminent death and shoot her in the back as she runs away, simply because she knows too much. Meanwhile, Macreedy crawls under the jeep and uses a bottle to make a molotov cocktail to defend himself. He sees Smith circle around for the kill and throws the firebomb, which bursts on a rock in front of Smith and sets him on fire. As Smith rolls on the ground to put the fire out, Macreedy picks up Smith's rifle, safe at last. Back at Black Rock, Macreedy is met by the Sheriff, who has taken one last stab at his job and dignity by locking up Trimble, Hector and the other killers of Komoko. Smith joins them in jail, and Macreedy tells Pete of his sister's death.

While waiting for the train the next day, Macreedy and Doc watch as the state police take away Komoko's murderers. Doc asks Macreedy for the medal, which he hopes will help the town heal its four-year-old wound. Macreedy gives it to him, shakes his hand, and steps back onto the train.

Bad Day at Black Rock is an exploration of guilt, chronicling the moral degeneration and mental anguish of an entire town (albeit a very small town). For four years, a crime in which two-thirds of the population participated has been festering at their souls, as well as those of the people who stood by and did nothing about that crime. The arrival of the mysterious stranger provides a long overdue catharsis for everyone in the town. Macreedy, dressed in black, becomes a confessor for some (Doc, Pete), a punisher for others (Smith, Trimble, Hector, etc.) and an avenging angel for Komoko and Liz Wirth.

The film also questions America's feelings about World War II a decade later, even though it is set soon after the war, in 1945. Contemporary war films such as *From Here to Eternity* (1953), *The Caine Mutiny* (1954) and *Mister Roberts* (1955) explored the psyches and attitudes of our fighting men, but few bothered to investigate larger issues such as racism, ultrapatriotism and post-war depression. *Bad Day at Black Rock* touches upon these subjects subtly, never allowing these thematic elements to get in the way of its suspenseful story. Yet the entire story hinges upon Reno Smith's hatred of the Japanese and the actions to which that hatred has led him, and the heavy atmosphere surrounding the town is due as much to the characters' apathy and lethargy (and collective guilt) as it is to the desert's inescapable heat.

Director John Sturges employs the age-old structure of one man fighting for what is right (and for survival) against many, and it works because of the shading of the characters, the unraveling of the central mystery, and the slow, certain buildup of suspense. None of the characters, not even Reno Smith, are wholly evil, and their reactions to Macreedy and his plight vary enough to give him hope. Because the audience does not know why Macreedy is visiting Black Rock, there is a trace of mistrust about him. And as Macreedy discovers the fate of Komoko, he realizes that the same fate awaits him and that he must use

Bad Day at Black Rock's heavies: Coley Trimble (Ernest Borgnine) and Hector David (Lee Marvin).

every means available to avoid being murdered. His physical handicap only makes the battle for survival that much more exciting.

To tell this story, Sturges assembled an exceptionally strong cast, including past or future Oscar winners Tracy, Borgnine, Marvin, Jagger and Brennan (a three-time winner!), as well as excellent character actors Ryan, Ericson, Russell Collins and Walter Sande. The lone female is Anne Francis, who's as tough as any of the men in the movie.

As Macreedy, Spencer Tracy is intelligent and calm enough to avoid trouble, yet is too curious and stubborn for his own good. It's an excellent performance that was nominated for a Best Actor Oscar in 1955. Ironically, Tracy lost to one of his co-stars, Ernest Borgnine, who triumphed later in the year with *Marty*. The manipulative bully role was becoming standard for Robert Ryan, who had played a similarly sinister part in *Crossfire* and many other films. As in *Crossfire*, prejudice is the key to Ryan's character.

In this all-star cast, Lee Marvin is billed eighth. The role of Hector David allowed him to prod and bully Spencer Tracy, whom he refers to as "boy" in the movie. Marvin moves with grace and confidence, ready for whatever comes. Hector is Reno Smith's right hand man, delegated with enough authority to move on his own, whereas Coley Trimble (Borgnine) is Smith's muscle, always to be ordered. Marvin stands tall and lean in cowboy boots, long blue jeans and a white cowboy hat. This is one of the few films where Marvin is one of the most attractive people in the cast.

Marvin was singled out by John O'Hara in *Colliers*, who wrote, "An actor named Lee Marvin will give you that hint [of immobilizing hostility] playing the kind of small-town lout that you know you're going to have to fight because he isn't going to let you get away without fighting. By the time he gets his head bashed in, you hate him so that you wish you could supply a supererogatory kick in the face." The critic for *Time* noted that "...Lee Marvin is alarmingly mean as a steely, easygoing plotter..." Critics were finally beginning to take notice of the lanky actor. For Marvin it was a wonderful opportunity to work with actors he admired and respected, especially Spencer Tracy. Afterward, he always referred to making the film as one of his favorite experiences.

Bad Day at Black Rock collected excellent reviews. John O'Hara led the parade of praise with this review in *Colliers*: "You are not going to see many pictures as good as *Bad Day at Black Rock*. There just haven't been many pictures as good as *Bad Day at Black Rock*, and mindful of the law of averages, I can predict there won't be many. This is one of the finest motion pictures ever made."

A year later, the Academy of Motion Picture Arts and Sciences agreed, rewarding the film with three Academy Award nominations, further enlarging the statures of Spencer Tracy (for Best Actor), John Sturges (Director) and Millard Kaufman (for Screenplay). Despite brilliant cinematography and film editing, *Bad Day at Black Rock* was not nominated in either of these categories. Nor was it remembered for the top prize, though today it seems like a natural choice for Best Picture. The film lost all three of its Oscar nominations to the feature film version of Paddy Chayefsky's *Marty*.

Violent Saturday (1955)

CREDITS: 20th Century–Fox. *Directed by* Richard Fleischer. *Produced by* Buddy Adler. *Screenplay by* Sydney Boehm. *Based on the Novel by* William L. Heath. *Music*: Hugo Friedhofer. *Conducted by* Lionel Newman. *Orchestration*: Edward B. Powell. *Director of Photography*: Charles G. Clarke, A.S.C. *Film Editor*: Louis Loeffler. *Art Direction*: Lyle Wheeler, George W. Davis. *Set Decorations*: Walter M. Scott, Chester Bayhi. *Sound*: E. Clayton Ward, Harry M. Leonard. *Wardrobe Direction*: Charles LeMaire. *Costumes Designed by* Kay Nelson. *Makeup Artist*: Ben Nye. *Hair Styling by* Helen Turpin. *Special Photographic Effects*: Ray Kellogg. *Assistant Director*: Joseph E. Richards. Not Rated. Color by Deluxe. *Color Consultant*: Leonard Doss. CinemaScope (2.35:1). 91 minutes. Released in May 1955. Not currently available on home video.

CAST: *Shelley Martin*, Victor Mature; *Boyd Fairchild*, Richard Egan; *Harper*, Stephen

McNally; *Linda Sherman*, Virginia Leith; *Harry Reeves*, Tommy Noonan; *Dill*, Lee Marvin; *Emily Fairchild*, Margaret Hayes; *Chapman*, J. Carroll Naish; *Elsie*, Sylvia Sidney; *Mr. Stadt*, Ernest Borgnine; *Helen*, Dorothy Patrick; *Stevie Martin*, Billy Chapin; *Gil Clayton*, Brad Dexter; *Bobby*, Donald Gamble; *Mr. Fairchild*, Raymond Greenleaf; *Georgie*, Richey Murray; *Stan*, Robert Adler; *Mrs. Stadt*, Ann Morrison; *Anna Stadt*, Donna Corcoran; *David Stadt*, Kevin Corcoran; *Mary Stadt*, Noreen Corcoran; *Slick*, Boyd "Red" Morgan; *Conductor*, Harry Seymour; *Amish Children*, Jeri Weil, Pat Weil, Sammy Ogg; *Amish Farmer*, John Alderson; *Amish Woman on Train*, Esther Somers; *Bart*, Harry Carter; *Miss Shirley*, Florence Ravenel; *Bank Customer*, Dorothy Phillips; *Marion, the Secretary*, Virginia Carroll; *Sidney*, Ralph Dumke; *Roy, the Bartender*, Robert Osterloh; *Mrs. Pilkas*, Helen Mayon; *Signalman*, Fred Shellac; *Bank Teller*, Ellen Bowers; *Dorothy*, Joyce Newhard; *Drug Clerk*, Mack Williams; *Bit Part*, Richard Garrick.

In the 1950s, many American filmmakers began to look inward at their own country for their dramas, sensing that there was more than met the eye behind the shiny veneer of middle-class life. One of those explorations is *Violent Saturday*, which is less about its climactic bank robbery than about the neuroses and secrets hidden just beneath the surface of its seemingly placid Arizona town setting.

Into Bradenville wanders Harper (Stephen McNally), a congenial man peddling costume jewelry. Joining him shortly are Dill (Lee Marvin) and Chapman (J. Carroll Naish), who help Harper case the town's bank and plan to rob it just before it closes at noon on the following Saturday. The bank manager, Reeves (Tommy Noonan), doesn't notice the men; he's too busy watching and following nurse Linda Sherman (Virginia Leith).

Copper mining is the town's main industry, but Boyd Fairchild (Richard Egan), the son of the mine owner, is an alcoholic who can't keep his own wife Emily (Margaret Hayes) from sleeping around. His foreman, Shelley Martin (Victor Mature), has a problem of his own—his son thinks of him as a coward and is ashamed because his father didn't fight in the war. Harper studies the town's layout at the library, where he sees librarian Elsie (Sylvia Sidney) steal a woman's purse. Later, Reeves witnesses Elsie trying to dump the evidence and threatens to go to the police. Elsie deduces that Reeves is spying on Linda, and dares him to report her deed. Boyd expresses some interest in Linda, who tells his wife to hang on to her man if she really wants him. The Fairchilds finally have a soul-searching talk and agree to work on their marriage, beginning with a long vacation away from Bradenville.

All of these threads come together on the Saturday of the title, when the bank robbers go into action. They carjack Shelley (by chance) and force him to drive them to an Amish farm, where they stow the getaway vehicle, tying up Shelley and the Amish family (Ernest Borgnine, Anne Morrison and Kevin, Donna and Noreen Corcoran). At the bank, as the robbers open the safe, Reeves goes for a gun and is shot by Dill, who also shoots Emily Fairchild (there buying traveller's cheques) when she moves to help Reeves.

The robbers escape with all of the money in the safe (as well as Elsie's stolen money not yet deposited) and go to the Amish farm where they find that Shelley has escaped, killed their lookout, and is hiding with the Amish family in the barn. They try to deal with Shelley but the Amish farmer refuses, preferring to let God handle the evildoers. The three robbers approach the barn and Chapman is killed by Shelley. Harper and Dill send a car through the barn door and set fire to it, trying to force Shelley out into the open. Shelley and the farmer push the burning car out of the barn, and one of the farmer's children is hit by a stray bullet. Shelley rushes out and kills Harper, but is shot in the leg by Dill. As Dill is about to finish off Shelley, he is stabbed in the back with a pitchfork by the farmer, who has finally taken some action on his own.

The denouement finds Boyd mourning his wife's totally senseless death, Reeves confessing to Linda Sherman his interest in her, and Shelley in the hospital, finally a hero to his son.

Though the bank robbery is the catharsis for all of the intertwining human stories,

During the bank robbery in *Violent Saturday*, Dill (Lee Marvin) takes Elsie's (Sylvia Sidney) stolen money before she can safely deposit it.

the real crux of the film is those stories. The bank robbers are really unknowing intruders into the town's distasteful secret life, unaware and uncaring of the consequences of their actions. As more and more films of the time took a good hard look at the middle-class American way of life, many of them were critical in their views. Bradenville is seen not as a bustling town of industry with interesting citizens, but rather as a snake's nest of adultery, chicanery, lust and social posturing.

It is no coincidence that some of the town's leading citizens—the librarian, the bank manager, the copper mine owner's son and his wife—are the ones with the worst problems and behavior. *Violent Saturday* is an indictment of the social and sexual pettiness that exists in a so-called "civilized society." The robbers actually precipitate a primitive cleansing for the sin-drenched Sodom, a call for basic codes of social behavior to eliminate evil. And as the robbers themselves eliminate some of the evil of the town, they are eliminated themselves by the most righteous citizenry—Shelley and the Amish farmer.

The last third of *Violent Saturday* is dramatic and effective, as the three robbers systematically and professionally rob the bank, shoot Reeves and Emily Fairchild, and make their escape. The sequence at the Amish farm is excellently staged and exciting, smartly made and emotionally satisfying. While one may not agree with or enjoy the view of Bradenville which predominates the first hour of the film, the power of the last third cannot be denied.

Violent Saturday was one of many caper films of the mid–1950s, but is one of the few to depict at least some of the consequences of the caper on the subject town. It also doesn't follow the standard noir look of such caper films. *Violent Saturday* was filmed in CinemaScope, most of it in bright sunshine or brightly-lit interiors, eschewing the more familiar dark, dimly lit world of crime for the glaring blaze of the hot Arizona sun. The result is a more truthful, factual, documentary feel than the moody representations of traditional film noir.

The cast performs well, preferring the low-key approach to the melodramatic. Best are Richard Egan, especially in his scenes with Linda at the bar, Virginia Leith's cool beauty as nurse Linda, Victor Mature in a role tailor-fit for him, and Lee Marvin. *Violent Saturday* marked the third consecutive villainous role for Lee Marvin; in his review of the film, *New York Times* critic Bosley Crowther called Marvin "the Number 1 sadist of the screen."

Well-meaning and complimentary though that remark is, it isn't quite right for this picture. Marvin plays Dill, the benzedrine-sniffing hood who takes a lot of ammo to the bank robbery because he was once caught in a revolving door without enough to make a satisfactory exit. He's just a regular guy who happens to be a bank robber. He stays up late one night reminiscing with Harper about his bad luck with women, preferring to schmooze than to get the requisite rest needed before the big robbery. It's a nice, regular-joe portrayal of a criminal. Of course, it is Lee who gets trigger happy and guns down Reeves and Emily at the bank; such action wouldn't have seemed right if taken by either of the two other bank robbers.

Reaction to the film was mixed. Some critics found it incisive, while others found it incendiary. Most seemed to find it a middle-of-the-road caper melodrama, heavy on the suds but competent in the action department. The mayor of Lancaster, Pennsylvania was more definite, banning the film from his town and making headlines across the country for his action. *Violent Saturday* is dated in the time and place of its story, but it has held up and perhaps improved over time. Its realistic, non-sensationalistic tone serves its subject well, and its cast delivers the drama with power. As time goes on, the film's reputation should gradually grow.

Not as a Stranger (1955)

CREDITS: Stanley Kramer Pictures Corporation. *Distributed by* United Artists. *Produced and Directed by* Stanley Kramer. *Written for the Screen by* Edna and Edward Anhalt. *Based on the Novel by* Morton Thompson. *Music by* George Antheil. *Song* "Not as a Stranger" *by* James Van Heusen and Buddy Kaye. *Music Conductor*: Paul Sawtelle. *Director of Photography*: Franz Planer, A.S.C. *Film Editor*: Fred Knutson, A.C.E. *Art Director*: Howard Richmond. *Set Decorator*: Victor Gangelin. *Production Design by* Rudolph Sternad. *Sound Engineer*: Earl Snyder. *Costumes Supervision*: Joe King. *Gowns*: Don Loper. *Makeup*: Bill Wood. *Hair Styles*: Esperanza Corona. *Camera Operator*: Bud Mautino. *Dialogue Director*: Anne Kramer. *Script Supervisor*: John Franco. *Production Assistant*: Sally Hamilton. *Company Grip*: Morris Rosen. *Production Manager*: John E. Burch. *Assistant Director*: Carter DeHaven, Jr. *Technical Adviser*: Morton Maxwell, M.D. *Assistant Technical Advisers*: Josh Fields, M.D., Marjorie Lefevre, R.N. Not Rated. Black and White. Flat (1.33:1). 135 minutes. Released in June 1955. Currently available on VHS videotape.

CAST: *Kristina Hedvingson*, Olivia de Havilland; *Lucas Marsh*, Robert Mitchum; *Alfred Boone*, Frank Sinatra; *Harriet Lang*, Gloria Grahame; *Dr. Aarons*, Broderick Crawford; *Dr. Dave Runkleman*, Charles Bickford; *Dr. Snider*, Myron McCormick; *Job Marsh*, Lon Chaney; *Ben Cosgrove*, Jesse White; *Oley*, Henry (Harry) Morgan; *Brundage*, Lee Marvin; *Bruni*, Virginia Christine; *Dr. Dietrich*, Whit Bissell; *Dr. Lettering*, Jack Raine; *Miss O'Dell*, Mae Clarke.

While Lee Marvin had been appearing in films of good quality the last few years, only *The Caine Mutiny*, based on a best-selling novel, had been a huge hit at the box office. *Not as a Stranger*, also based on a best-selling novel, repeated that box office success, ending up as the fourth largest grossing movie of 1955 and exposing Marvin's acting to a wider audience than ever before.

The central character of *Not as a Stranger* is Lucas Marsh (Robert Mitchum), a medical intern intent on becoming a great doctor. Though morally supported by his fellow internists Al (Frank Sinatra) and Brundage (Lee Marvin), Marsh is in trouble financially. His poor financial condition leads him to court nurse Kristina (Olivia de Havilland), the "Swedish Nightingale" of the hospital, who puts half of her paycheck into the bank each week. Marsh convinces Kristina that he loves her and they marry, to the chagrin of Al, who knows the truth. Throughout their internship, Marsh and Al keep up their friendship, despite Al's misgivings about the marriage and Marsh's growing arrogance. At one point, Marsh is threatened with expulsion for arguing with a surgeon about one of his procedures. Marsh eventually backs down, even though he was right, and takes his frustrations out on Kristina.

Once he graduates medical school, Dr. Marsh sets up practice in a small town called Greenville with aged Dr. Runkleman (Charles Bickford), and Kristina settles herself into housework. Runkleman introduces him to many patients and their ailments, including Harriet Lang (Gloria Grahame), a lonely widow who likes the look of the new doc. Over time, Marsh finds himself drawn to her and they begin an affair, even as Kristina discovers that she is pregnant. Kristina believes that Marsh doesn't want the baby, so she doesn't tell him about it. Marsh discovers a patient with typhoid at the hospital, isolates him and calls in Kristina as a nurse; together, working all night, they save the man. Not knowing about the baby, Marsh asks Kristina to come back to nursing, thus confirming her fear and breaking her heart. Marsh feels guilty about the affair and breaks it off, just before Al tells him that Kristina is pregnant. Not only is she pregnant, but she's furious about the adultery and his treatment of her, and she throws him out of the house.

Marsh tries to find solace in work, but that backfires when Dr. Runkleman has a heart attack and dies on the operating table as Marsh tries to save him. As Marsh leaves the operating room in a daze, another doctor watches and says, "God help him; he made a mistake." Marsh wanders around town, finally finding himself at home. Kristina opens the door to find her husband in tears. "Help me, Kris, for God's sake, help me," he begs. She holds him, silently forgiving him and accepting him because he finally needs *her*.

Not as a Stranger is a traditional Hollywood melodrama, with its star power and literate script lifting it to a level above the standard soap opera. Though Mitchum, Sinatra and Marvin were all a bit long in the tooth to play medical interns (they were each in their thirties), the other interns are all about the same age, so it doesn't seem so out of place. The medical scenes during their internships are realistic and compelling. Indeed, there are two medical montages which are among the most interesting, truthful and amusing sequences in the film.

The human stories aren't as well executed. Marsh marries Kristina for her money and eventually learns to appreciate her devotion. But his appeal to her remains unexplained. What does she see in cold-blooded Lucas Marsh which causes her to marry him and leave the job she loves? Another problem is the relationship between Marsh and Harriet Lang. Their eventual entanglement is foreseen early on, and the night scene where, with the wind whistling, horses bucking and

As Dr. Aarons (Broderick Crawford) lectures, Brundage (Lee Marvin), Al (Frank Sinatra) and Lucas Marsh (Robert Mitchum), all seated together in the second row, listen intently in *Not as a Stranger*.

neighing, and the music crescendoing, Marsh finally plants a passionate kiss on Harriet's stiff lips is absurdly overstaged.

Nevertheless, Lucas Marsh is a compelling character, and the humanization he finally experiences makes for good, satisfying drama. As Marsh, Robert Mitchum received more criticism than praise for his acting, which many found stultifying. The general consensus was that Mitchum couldn't handle the dramatics and was sorely miscast. Mitchum is, in fact, very good in a role which asks for him to repress his feelings until the final, climactic catharsis. He studied and practiced the medical procedures for realism and delivers a reserved but tenacious portrait of a man subduing his emotions for the sake of his very honorable ambitions. There's even some humor in his portrayal, which most critics either slept through or ignored.

The surprise of the film is Frank Sinatra, who creates a memorably warm portrait of Al, Marsh's best friend. It is a beautifully written characterization of a man who cares deeply about his friends—he is an unassuming, compassionate doctor genuinely interested in his patients as people. As Brundage, Marsh's other friend in medical school, Lee Marvin is fine but has little to do. When the interns discuss the financial rewards of medicine, Brundage suggests that the location where a doctor sets up practice is more important than what kind of medicine he practices, which infuriates Marsh. Brundage is not seen again—other than at the graduation speech scene—after that remark.

Olivia de Havilland has a dramatic but essentially thankless role as Kristina, who subordinates her own desires for those of her new husband. Gloria Grahame is sultry as Harriet Lang, but the wedge of tissue beneath her upper lip (she was told it would make her sexier) keeps her mostly expressionless. As the experienced doctors, Broderick Crawford and Charles Bickford are excellent, dispensing familiar care-phrases with expertise and expounding on the importance of medical care in our society.

Medical dramas have been a staple of television for decades, but there have been relatively few major movies dealing with medicine. Most movies about medicine are sharply-barbed black comedies about the hypocrisy of medical care—how money determines who will get treatment and the greed of doctors. *Not as a Stranger* is one of the few serious dramas which dares to honestly explore, warts and all, what it is like to devote one's life to the calling of medicine, and the rewards—and demands—of that experience. To be sure, it is melodramatic, but its search for Lucas Marsh's heart is certainly in the right place.

Based on the blockbuster novel by Morton Thompson, *Not as a Stranger* substituted cinematic realism and thematic exploration for some (but not all) of the more sundry elements of the novel. The movie, like the book, was a huge hit, becoming one of the highest grossing films of the year and the biggest hit in which Lee Marvin had yet appeared during his brief career.

A Life in the Balance (1955)

CREDITS: Panoramic Productions and 20th Century–Fox. *Directed by* Harry Horner. *Produced by* Leonard Goldstein. *Screenplay by* Robert Presnell, Jr., Leo Townsend. *Based upon a Story by* Georges Simenon. *Music by* Raul Lavista. *Director of Photography*: J. Gomez Urquiza. *Edited by* George Gittens, George Crone. *Art Director*: Bunther Gerzo. Not Rated. Black and White. Flat (1.33:1). 74 minutes. Released in July 1955. Not currently available on home video.

CAST: *Antonio Gomez*, Ricardo Montalban; *Maria Ibinia*, Anne Bancroft; *The Stranger*, Lee Marvin; *Paco Gomez*, Jose Perez; *Lieutenant Fernando*, Rodolfo Acosta; *Captain Saldana*, Carlos Muzquiz; *Sergeant*, Jorge Trevino; *Andres Martinez*, Jose Torvay; *Carla Arlotta*, Eva Calvo; *Carmen Martinez*, Fanny Schiller; *Dona Lucrecia*, Tamara Garina; *Porter*, Pascuel G. Pena; *Pedro*, Antonio Carbajal.

After a brief fling at medical school in *Not as a Stranger*, Lee Marvin returned to his more familiar criminal, psychopathic ways in *A Life in the Balance*, based on Georges Simenon's short story *A Matter of Life and Death*. Though Simenon's original story takes place in Paris, producer Leonard Goldstein changed the locale to Mexico City and used a largely Mexican cast and crew to film his version there. It was Marvin's third, and final, film for Panaromic Productions and is almost impossible to find today.

Widower Antonio Gomez (Ricardo Montalban) is accused of the murder of a woman in his apartment building and is questioned by the police. His son Paco (Jose Perez) knows his father is innocent because Paco has seen the murderer. Paco follows a stranger (Lee Marvin) across Mexico City while his father dallies with Maria Ibinia (Anne Bancroft). Paco smashes police call boxes as he follows the stranger, until the psychotic killer, who murders people whom he believes to be sinners, figures out that he's being followed and grabs the boy. The police arrive and capture the killer before Paco is hurt, resulting in the exoneration of Paco's father.

A Life in the Balance is a thriller that derives much of its atmosphere from the ambiance of Mexico City's urban cityscape, particularly the street festival that always seems within sight or earshot of the action and the huge murals that adorn the University. It changes focus from Paco's determined pursuit of the killer to his father's more relaxed pursuit of the nice neighborhood girl (for whom he has fallen) and back again—until the climax, when the killer captures Paco and desperately searches for a safe place to kill the boy and make his getaway as the police close in.

Paco (Jose Perez) tries to escape the clutches of The Stranger (Lee Marvin) in *A Life in the Balance*.

Simenon's original story takes place in a Parisian police station, in which the authorities learn of a situation in the city when someone begins setting off police alarms, and lights on the huge wall map in the station begin to light up, indicating a trail for the police to follow or intercept. The same device is used in the film version when Paco follows the killer and transmits his location to the police by smashing call boxes along his path—until, of course, the killer realizes that he's being followed.

By taking on villainous roles (this was his eighth), Lee Marvin was carving out a niche for himself as, according to Bosley Crowther in his *New York Times* review of *Violent Saturday*, "the Number 1 sadist of the screen." *A Life in the Balance* presents Marvin with another variation on the theme of evil: an unnamed stranger in a strange land, wandering the world, unconnected to his present situation other than a need (or desire) to punish people whom he considers sinners. This gives Marvin the opportunity to portray a religious fanatic, a man who believes himself to be the instrument of divine retribution. As always, Marvin is up to the task and gives the part his all.

Marvin received good notices for his unnamed role as "The Stranger," as did Ricardo Montalban and Anne Bancroft, but the best reviews went to young Jose Perez who, according to Howard Thompson of the *New York Times*, "acquits himself commendably." The film received little attention, garnered mixed reviews and has since virtually disappeared.

Pete Kelly's Blues (1955)

CREDITS: Warner Bros. *Produced and Directed by* Jack Webb. *Screenplay by* Richard L. Breen. *Song* "Pete Kelly's Blues" *by* Ray Heindorf (music) and Sammy Cahn (lyrics). *Songs* "He Needs Me," "Sing a Rainbow" *by* Arthur Hamilton. *Arrangements for* Pete Kelly's Big Seven *by* Matty Matlock. *Director of Photography*: Hal Rosson, A.S.C. *Film Editor*: Robert M. Leeds, A.C.E. *Art Director*: Feild Gray. *Set Decorator*: John Sturtevant. *Production Design*: Harper Goff. *Sound*: Leslie C. Hewitt, Dolph Thomas. *Wardrobe*: Gene Martin. *Costume Design*: Howard Shoup. *Makeup Supervisor*: Gordon Bau, S.M.A. *Makeup Artist*: Stanley Campbell, S.M.A. *Assistant Director*: Harry D'Arcy. *Chief Set Electrician*: James Potevin. Bayou Exteriors *filmed on* The Fleming Plantation, Lafitte, LA, *with* Teddy Buckner, Cornet, and the Choir of the Isrealite Spiritual Church, New Orleans. Not Rated. WarnerColor. CinemaScope (2.35:1). 95 minutes. Released in August 1955. Currently available on VHS videotape and laserdisc.

CAST: *Pete Kelly*, Jack Webb; *Ivy Conrad*, Janet Leigh; *Fran McCarg*, Edmond O'Brien; *Rose Hopkins*, Peggy Lee; *George Tenell*, Andy Devine; *Al Gannaway*, Lee Marvin; *Maggie Jackson*, Ella Fitzgerald; *Joey Firestone*, Martin Milner; *Rudy*, Than Wyenn; *Bedido*, Herb Ellis; *Guy Bettenhouser*, John Dennis; *Cigarette Girl*, Jayne Mansfield; *Cootie Jacobs*, Mort Marshall; *Pete Kelly's Big Seven*, Dick Cathcart (cornet), Matty Matlock (clarinet), Moe Schneider (trombone), Eddie Miller (saxophone), George Van Eps (guitar), Nick Fatool (drums), Ray Sherman (piano), Jud de Naut (bass); *Squat Henchman*, Nesdon Booth; *Dako*, William Lazerus; *Waiter in Rudy's*, Snub Pollard; *Tuxedo Band members*, Joe Venuti, Harper Goff, Perry Bodkin; The Isrealite Spiritual Church Choir of New Orleans. *Narrated by* Jack Webb.

Jack Webb had co-starred in Lee Marvin's first film, *You're in the Navy Now*, and when Webb began to produce and direct his own films, he remembered Marvin and hired him for a small part in his second directorial effort. Webb eventually produced and directed six movies, including two (one feature film in 1954, one TV movie in 1969) based on

On cornet, Pete Kelly (Jack Webb) leads his band, the Big 7, featuring drummer Joey Firestone (Martin Milner) and clarinetist Al Gannaway (Lee Marvin) in *Pete Kelly's Blues*.

his two trademark television series, *Dragnet*. *Pete Kelly's Blues* was the only one of Webb's films in which Lee Marvin appeared.

Pete Kelly's Blues is a jazzy period piece taking place in Kansas City in 1927. Cornetist Pete Kelly (Jack Webb) fronts a seven-piece band which barely makes enough money to keep its members fed. Local mob boss Fran McCarg (Edmond O'Brien) decides to make Kelly's Big Seven part of his empire, taking a 25% cut of the profits along the way. Clarinetist Al Gannaway (Lee Marvin) chooses to leave the band rather than work for McCarg. He also predicts that McCarg will kill one of the band members if they protest. Drummer Joey Firestone (Martin Milner) does protest—and is indeed murdered.

Kelly has more than the band on his mind—a flapper named Ivy Conrad (Janet Leigh) has danced her way into his life and wants him to marry her. McCarg forces Kelly to take on a singer named Rose Hopkins (Peggy Lee), thus changing the musical focus of Kelly's Big Seven. Rose resents McCarg's control of her career and begins to drink heavily. She makes a fool of herself (and thus, McCarg) during one set when she cannot remember song lyrics, and is beaten (offscreen) by McCarg. Kelly is powerless to prevent the beating, which ultimately sends Rose to an insane asylum with irreparable brain damage.

Al Gannaway returns to the band and offers to help Kelly stand up to McCarg. Kelly discovers McCarg's weakness—some papers that incriminate him in Firestone's murder—and goes alone (knocking out Al, who tries to come along) to get them. Kelly is followed by Ivy and they are confronted by McCarg and two hoods, who initiate a gunfight. Kelly shoots one man and causes the other to accidentally shoot McCarg. The third man gives up and runs away, leaving Kelly and Ivy together and McCarg dying on the floor. The film ends with Ivy watching Pete Kelly and his Big Seven (including Al Gannaway) play to a full house.

Pete Kelly's Blues boasts a colorful musical score and several familiar songs performed by Peggy Lee and Ella Fitzgerald. Fitzgerald, in a small role, croons the title song to Jack Webb and performs "Hard-Hearted Hannah" as well. Lee sings "Sing a Rainbow," "He Needs Me," "Somebody Loves Me" and "Sugar." Other songs include "I Never Knew," "Bye, Bye Blackbird," "What Can I Say After I Say I'm Sorry," "Oh, Didn't He Ramble," "Smiles" and "I'm Gonna Meet My Sweetie Now."

The instrumental jazz played by Pete Kelly's Big Seven is supplied by jazzmen Dick Cathcart (who dubbed Webb's cornet playing), Matty Matlock (who also arranged the music), Moe Schneider, Eddie Miller, George Van Eps, Nick Fatool, Ray Sherman and Jud de Naut. Most critics agreed that the music was the best thing about this movie, noting the fine vocal and instrumental performances.

Some of the movie's acting was also impressive. In the relatively small role of Rose Hopkins, Peggy Lee garnered a Best Supporting Actress Academy Award nomination. She lost to Jo Van Fleet in *East of Eden*. Lee Marvin, also garnered good notices, including Howard Thompson's note in the *New York Times* that, "The best performance comes from Lee Marvin, as Mr. Webb's faithful pal," and Philip Hamburger's comment in *The New Yorker* that, "Lee Marvin deserves honors for his quiet portrayal of a lonesome, wandering musician who just wants to play the music he likes best." Marvin is good in the film but has little motivation for his departure from and later return to the band, and really has very little to do in the movie.

The critics also agreed, however, that Jack Webb's acting was at best wooden and at worst stultifying. Gone is the energetic, expressive Webb of *You're in the Navy Now*; in his place is the dour face and rapid-fire monotone of *Dragnet*'s Sergeant Joe Friday, complete with melodramatic *Dragnet*-like narration. While Webb's direction is interesting and occasionally imaginative (and surprisingly effective), his acting is stiff and one-dimensional, often playing against the tone of a scene he himself has directed. Even his cornet playing (dubbed by Dick Cathcart) looks phony.

Also weak is Janet Leigh as Ivy, the girl who wins his heart. She has no reason to fall in love with Kelly and no reason to stay with him once she does. It is a thankless role, poorly conceived. The script is full of such melodrama, plot threads that lead nowhere, and silliness such as the final poorly-staged shootout in the dance hall. What power the film has is thrown away due to the weaknesses of the script.

According to Moira Walsh in *America*, "the film is a trial balloon to test audience interest in a proposed television series about a cornet-playing band leader of the roaring 'twenties." If so, this never occurred, though the film was surprisingly successful, grossing some $5,000,000, placing it within the fifteen highest-grossing films of 1955. Along with *Not as a Stranger*, which topped $7,000,000 and placed fifth on that list, the success of *Pete Kelly's Blues* ensured that Lee Marvin was a highly visible presence on America's movie screens in 1955.

I Died a Thousand Times (1955)

CREDITS: Warner Bros. *Directed by* Stuart Heisler. *Produced by* Willis Goldbeck. *Written by* W. R. Burnett. *Music by* David Buttolph. *Orchestrations*: Maurice dePackh, Gus Levene. *Director of Photography*: Ted McCord, A.S.C. *Second Unit Photographer*: Edwin DuPar, A.S.C. *Film Editor*: Clarence Kolster, A.C.E. *Art Director*: Edward Carrere. *Set Decorator*: William J. Kuehl. *Sound by* Charles B. Lang. *Wardrobe by* Moss Mabry. *Makeup Supervisor*: Gordon Bau, S.M.A. *Assistant Director*: Chuck Hansen. *Second Unit Director*: Russ Saunders. *Second Unit Assistant*: Al Alleborn. *Dialogue Supervisor*: Eugne Busch. Not Rated. WarnerColor. CinemaScope (2.35:1). 108 minutes. Released in November 1955. Currently available on VHS videotape and laserdisc.

CAST: *Roy Earle (Roy Collins)*, Jack Palance; *Marie Garson*, Shelley Winters; *Velma Goodhugh*, Lori Nelson; *Babe Kosic*, Lee Marvin; *Chico*, Pedro Gonzalez Gonzalez; *Big Mac*, Lon Chaney (Jr.); *Red Hattery*, Earl Holliman; *Louis Mendoza*, Perry Lopez; *Lon Preisser*, Richard Davalos; *Doc Banton*, Howard St. John; *Ma Goodhugh*, Olive Carey; *Pa Goodhugh*, Ralph Moody; *Jack Kranmer*, James Millican; *Sheriff*, Bill Kennedy; *Kranmer's Girl*, Peggy Maley; *Ed*, Dub Taylor; *Deputy*, Dick Reeves; *Mabel Baughman*, Mae Clarke; *Mr. Baughman*, Hugh Sanders; *Bell Boys*, Nick Adams, Darren Dublin; *Joe*, Dennis Hopper; *Margie*, Myra Fahey; *Art*, Herb Vigran; *Officers*, Dennis Moore, Mickey Simpson; *Sheriff's Deputy*, John Pickard; *Man in Tropico Lobby*, James Seay; *Bit Parts*, Ed Fury, Larve Farlow, Hubie Kerns.

With the advent of CinemaScope, executives at Warner Brothers decided to review their library of classic films and remake some of them using color and the new widescreen process to make the new versions bigger, bolder and brighter than their black-and-white predecessors. One of the classics they chose to remake was *High Sierra*, the 1941 crime drama with Humphrey Bogart which had been remade once already as *Colorado Territory* with Joel McCrea in 1949. This second remake was ridiculously titled *I Died a Thousand Times*, with up-and-coming film star Jack Palance tackling the central role.

I Died a Thousand Times follows the exploits of "Mad Dog" Roy Earle (Jack Palance), a criminal who has recently been released from prison. He heads into the mountains of Southern California to rendezvous with the crime kingpin who arranged his parole and who wants Earle to pull a heist for him in return. Earle is met by Jack Kranmer (James Millican), an ex-cop now working for criminal kingpin Big Mac. Earle instantly dislikes Kranmer but follows his instructions to continue into the mountains to join up with the rest of the gang.

On his way, Earle meets the Goodhugh family, who are heading for Los Angeles in a rickety truck with all their belongings. Earle takes a liking to all of them, especially Velma (Lori Nelson), the Goodhugh's adult daughter, but leaves them behind to fulfill his obligation. At the mountain hideaway, Earle meets his partners in crime: two hot-headed hoods named Red (Earl Holliman) and Babe (Lee Marvin), and Marie Garson (Shelley Winters), a dime-a-dance girl Babe picked up in Los Angeles. Earle also meets Pard, a mongrel dog which quickly attaches itself to Earle and soon listens to no one else.

After settling in, Earle visits Big Mac (Lon Chaney, Jr.), who is bedridden with heart trouble and attended to by Doc Banton

(Howard St. John), who tells Earle that Mac isn't doing well. The job turns out to be a half-million dollar jewel heist at the Tropico Hotel in Palm Springs. Earle agrees to knock off the Tropico but complains about the incompetence of his young gang members, who continually fight over Marie. "Punks," he calls them. The inside man at the Tropico, Louis Mendoza (Perry Lopez), finally arrives and describes the setup. Earle cases the Tropico a few days later, making Mendoza nervous, and finds the Goodhughs in trouble out in the parking lot. Earle is startled to find that Velma has a clubfoot. After dinner with them, he arranges to take Velma to a doctor to see what might be done about it. Doc Banton examines Velma and suggests surgery, which is soon performed. Earle comes by, expresses his feelings for her, and asks Velma to marry him. She refuses but thanks him for all he has done for her.

The heist goes ahead as planned, late at night. Earle guards the lobby while Red and Babe rob the security boxes that Mendoza has indicated. Marie and Pard wait outside. When a guard interrupts, Earle shoots him. Earle (with the jewels) joins Marie while Red, Babe and panicky Mendoza jump into the second getaway car. Babe speeds away but refuses to turn on his lights, leading to a fiery crash. Earle takes the jewels to Big Mac but finds that Mac has died in bed. Kranmer tries to make a deal with Earle to split the take between them, but Earle refuses, so the two men shoot it out. Earle is wounded while killing Kranmer but takes the jewels, hides out and is patched up by Doc Banton, who reminds him to visit Velma.

While waiting for his share of the fenced jewel money, Earle and Marie visit Velma, who is dancing away on her repaired foot. Earle makes a scene, realizes his foolishness,

Babe (Lee Marvin) is bullied by Red (Earl Holliman) after he threatens to slap around Marie (Shelley Winters), in *I Died a Thousand Times*.

then confesses his love for Marie instead. Meanwhile, it turns out that Mendoza has lived through the fiery crash and talked, identifying Roy Earle as the gang leader. Earle goes alone to get his share of the take. He is spotted by the police and chased up into the Sierra mountains, where he holds off the cops with a rifle. Marie, with the dog, hears of his situation on the radio and hurries to the scene. When she arrives, Pard escapes and hurries up the mountainside. Earle comes out of hiding to get him and is shot down from above by a policeman at the top of the ridge. The movie ends with Marie crying for Earle's soul, repeating again and again, "He's free! He's free!"

Hollywood has never learned the lesson that it is very difficult to remake a classic film and improve on the original. This is certainly the case with *I Died a Thousand Times*. Despite the rugged beauty—in CinemaScope and WarnerColor—of the Sierra Nevada mountains (not to mention Shelley Winters and Lori Nelson) and the involvement of W. R. Burnett, who penned the original novel and screenplay (John Huston helped out on *High Sierra*), the remake simply doesn't compare well to its first antecedent.

Melodrama is the overriding style here as Winters bounces between most of the leading men and Palance glowers at everybody except Pard the dog. The only humor comes from Pedro Gonzalez Gonzalez, who maintains the mountain hideaway and explains in broken English how Pard brings nothing but bad luck and death to all of his owners. Palance, of course, doesn't listen and even takes the dog to the robbery. The robbery of the Tropico should have been elaborate and exciting, but it isn't. The hotel set is plain and unconvincing, with too little human traffic for such a hot spot. Planning for the robbery is incomplete and the robbery itself is poorly staged. And the film's attempt to give "Mad Dog" a human side by having him help out Velma with her clubfoot only works to show that he should mind his own business.

Jack Palance is a decent choice to play Roy Earle. His menacing voice and looks give him the sinister edge necessary for the role, and his warm, tender scenes are surprisingly strong. Although Palance is alternately tough and tender in the lead role, his taut performance is, and forever will be, overshadowed by Humphrey Bogart's more vulnerable portrayal of the same character some fourteen years earlier.

Poor Lee Marvin. In the gang that takes the Tropico for half a million in jewels, his character is not the leader nor even the second banana. Babe is third in the pecking order and even less important to the robbery than Mendoza, the fourth man. Babe is pushed around by Red and Earle, hits Marie (offscreen), and ultimately kills himself and Red by driving with his lights off. Watching Marvin being bossed around by Jack Palance is one thing, but seeing Earl Holliman (who the very next year played the tipsy cook on *Forbidden Planet*) push him around is stunning in its unbelievability. Whoever cast the film should have switched their roles. At least Marvin got the better billing (fourth to Holliman's seventh). This was not a step forward in Lee Marvin's career.

Shack Out on 101 (1955)

CREDITS: Allied Artists. *Directed by* Edward Dein. *Produced by* Mort Millman. A William F. Broidy Production. *Story and Screenplay by* Edward and Mildred Dein. *Music Composed and Conducted by* Paul Dunlap. *Song* "A Sunday Kind of Love" *by* Barbara Belle, Louis Prima, Anita Leonard, Stan Rhodes. *Director of Photography*: Floyd Crosby, A.S.C. *Film Editor*, George White, A.C.E. *Art Director*: Lou Croxton. *Recorded by* Roger White. *Wardrobe Supervision by* Jerry Bos. *Terry Moore's Wardrobe by* Jax of Beverly Hills. *Makeup by* Don Cash. *Production Supervisor*: A. R. Milton. *Assistant Director*: Bert Glazer. *Dialogue Supervisor*: Murray Alper. *Script Supervisor*: Doris August. *Property Master*: Leo Cornet. *Chief Electrician*: Robert E. Jones. Not Rated. Black and White. Flat (1.33:1). 80 minutes. Released in December 1955. Currently available on VHS videotape.

CAST: *Kotty*, Terry Moore; *Sam (The Professor)*, Frank Lovejoy; *George*, Keenan Wynn; *Slob*, Lee Marvin; *Eddie*, Whit Bissell; *Artie*, Jess Barker; *Pepe*, Donald Murphy; *Dillon*, Frank De Kova; *Perch*, Len Lesser; *Lookout*, Fred Gabourie.

This is probably the strangest film in which Lee Marvin ever appeared, topping even *Gorilla at Large* for eccentricity. Though billed fourth, Marvin is undoubtedly the star of the show, with more screen time than anyone else in the cast. He's the central character of this odd little Cold War melodrama and also provides most of the movie's comic relief.

George (Keenan Wynn) runs a dilapidated little diner on Route 101 along the California coast. His two employees are waitress Kotty (Terry Moore) and cook Slob (Lee Marvin). Kotty is dating a local nuclear physicist, Sam (Frank Lovejoy), also known as the Professor. All of the visitors to the diner, as well as George and Slob, are jealous of Kotty's affections for Sam.

Kotty's affections turn sour as Sam spends more and more time at work (and collecting seashells with Slob) than with her. She doesn't know that Sam is collaborating with Slob to smuggle nuclear technology out of the country. Meanwhile, George pumps iron with Slob and makes plans to go skin diving with his war buddy Eddie (Whit Bissell). One night, one of Sam's scientific friends shows up at the beanery, begging Sam to go with him to the authorities, and Slob kills him.

Kotty grows suspicious, questions Sam, and is warned to keep her mouth shut. On a stormy night she finally accuses Slob of treachery, and he beats her up. Sam arrives and tries to play along, but Slob realizes Sam's duplicity and beats him up. Sam and Kotty make up while Slob makes escape plans. When George arrives, Slob takes him hostage as well and admits that he is actually Mr. Gregory, the mastermind behind the disappearances of three nuclear physicists. Eddie sneaks into the back of the beanery, puts together the spear gun that he and George were planning to use while skin diving, and shoots Slob in the back (offscreen) as he tries to leave the diner (and the country).

Except for a few brief scenes shot outside to take advantage of Terry Moore in swimsuits, most of the film takes place in various rooms of George's beanery, primarily the counter area and the kitchen. The three people who work there also live there; George's room upstairs is the only one never seen. This setting does betray the low budget of the production but also enhances the feel of the piece, as the Shack becomes very familiar and oddly comforting.

Shack Out on 101 is a melodrama with a message: Communist agents can be, and are, anywhere. When Slob takes Kotty, Sam and George hostage, they argue about loyalty and treason, and Sam makes the movie's point— that we have to watch for men like Slob everywhere because they are such chameleons. The following year, *Invasion of the Body Snatchers* made the same point with much more subtlety and finesse.

The spread of Communism was a hot topic at the time and would be for years to come. It certainly provided this film with its dramatic plotline. The movie, however, makes no pretensions about being important. This is a potboiler, more interested in exploring Kotty's love life than the disappearances of three nuclear physicists. Indeed, every male in the film is not only attracted to but makes a pass at the comely waitress (with wardrobe supplied by Jax of Beverly Hills). Terry Moore is the film's only female, and while her acting is not sensational, she certainly makes the part her own.

The rest of the cast is decent, but Lee Marvin completely steals the show as Slob, whose real name is Leo, and who is later revealed to be the mysterious Mr. Gregory. In his *Movie and Video Guide*, Leonard Maltin writes the definitive tagline: "Lee Marvin *is* Slob in this trash classic..." The *New York Times* panned the film, but gushed, "Credit Lee Marvin with a polished portrayal as the tough, sinister and seemingly thick-witted cook." *Time* went even further, to the point of overstatement: "And yet, Actor Marvin, who is easily the most repulsive object that Hollywood has dug up in recent years, is such a skillful performer that when he starts hacking away at a bacon-lettuce-and-tomato on toast, the spectator has all the visceral sensations of watching an MVD interrogator go to work on an enemy of the people."

The *Motion Picture Herald* noted "Lee Marvin's delightful portrayal of a simple-minded

George (Keenan Wynn) and Slob (Lee Marvin) lift weights and compare anatomies.

short order cook, who turns out to be the menace of the film" and predicted, "Marvin will certainly gain in importance as a marquee name with this picture." While the film was nothing to get excited about, Marvin's performance was. Physically, he's as gangly as can be, all elbows and knees, with long, thin arms and a head that seems two sizes too big for his body. Usually dressed in a greasy t-shirt, Marvin often does look repulsive, and he certainly acts like a fool.

When Mr. Gregory's plans are threatened, however, Marvin hardens his voice, steels his gaze and tightens himself into a lethal agent, well versed in the ways of death. Marvin's best scenes are his comedic ones, when Slob is usually the butt of the insults but goes along with them good-naturedly. The weight-lifting scene, wherein Keenan Wynn and Marvin pump iron and then compare anatomies, is so strangely funny it borders on genius.

Shack Out on 101 has developed a small cult following over the years, but most people don't know what to make of the film. It truly is an oddity, with its uneven mixture of exploitation, political message and comedy. And while Lee Marvin made many other, better, films in his long career, this bizarre little movie contains one of his most unique and memorable performances.

Seven Men from Now (1956)

CREDITS: Batjac and Warner Bros. *Directed by* Budd Boetticher. *Produced by* Andrew V. McLaglen, Robert E. Morrison. *Original Story and Screenplay by* Burt Kennedy. *Music Composed and*

Conducted by Henry Vars. *Songs* "Seven Men from Now," "Good Love," *by* Dunham, Henry Vars. *Director of Photography*: William H. Clothier. *Edited by* Everett Sutherland. *Art Director*: Leslie Thomas. *Set Decorator*: Edward G. Boyle. *Sound by* Earl Crain, Jr. *Property Master*: Joseph LaBella. *Script Supervisor*: Catalina Lawrence. *Production Manager*: Nate H. Edwards. *Unit Production Manager*: Gordon B. Forbes. *Assistant Director*: Emmett Morrison. *Makeup Supervisors*: Web Overlander, S.M.A., Norman Pringle, S.M.A. *Hair Stylist*: Lillian Ugrin, C.H.S. *Costumers*: Carl Walker, Rudy Harrington. *Miss Russell's Wardrobe Designed by* Edward Sebesta. Not Rated. WarnerColor. Flat (1.33:1). Released in August 1956. Not currently available on home video.

CAST: *Ben Stride*, Randolph Scott; *Annie Greer*, Gail Russell; *Big Masters*, Lee Marvin; *John Greer*, Walter Reed; *Pate Bodeen*, John Larch; *Clete*, Donald Barry; *Henchman*, Fred Graham; *Clint*, John Beradino; *Jed*, John Phillips; *Mason*, Chuck Roberson; *Lieutenant Collins*, Stuart Whitman; *Senorita*, Pamela Duncan; *Fowler*, Steve Mitchell; *Bit Parts*, Cliff Lyons, Fred Sherman.

Over the previous four years Lee Marvin had assayed many villainous roles and had played them with a great deal of variety. He had been brutish in *The Wild One*, psychotic in *A Life in the Balance*, rather dim-witted in *I Died a Thousand Times* and even diabolical in *Shack Out on 101*. Occasionally, Marvin would get the chance to play stronger characters—intelligent, confident, quick-thinking villains, and in films like *The Big Heat* and *Bad Day at Black Rock* he made the most of those opportunities. His role in *Seven Men from Now* gave Marvin another such opportunity and, once again, the actor took advantage of the challenge, giving his finest performance up to that time.

Seven Men from Now is, like many other westerns, a tale of revenge. Ben Stride (Randolph Scott) is heading south through Arizona, looking for a group of men. He finds John and Annie Greer (Walter Reed, Gail Russell) and their Conestoga wagon helplessly mired in mud, and helps them out of it. Worried that John will not be able to take care of Annie on their journey south, Stride agrees to accompany them. At an abandoned relay station they are joined by two other men, Masters (Lee Marvin) and Clete (Donald Barry), who inform the Greers that Stride is a former sheriff hunting the seven men who robbed a Wells Fargo office and killed his wife in the process. Stride had already caught up to the first two in the opening scene; five are still alive. Masters and Clete are after the stolen gold.

The next morning the group is visited by a small band of hungry, silent Chiricahua Indians; Stride thinks quickly, gives up his spare horse, and the Indians ride off after it. Stride, Masters, Clete and the Greers again head south. A bit later they run into the same Chiricahua chasing a man. Stride and Masters drive the Indians away, but as Stride goes to get the man's horse, he is drawn on by the man. Masters shoots him in the back, saving Stride from the same fate. Now only four men are left for Stride to hunt down. At camp that evening, in the pouring rain, Masters flatters Annie Greer to embarrassment and refers to her husband as "gentle and soft." Stride tells him to mind his own business and then slugs Masters when he doesn't back down, telling Masters and Clete to leave.

In Flora Vista, Masters and Clete meet the robbers' leader, Pate Bodeen (John Larch), and tell him that three of his men won't be joining them because of Ben Stride. Bodeen appeals to Masters' sense of revenge and offers him a cut for knowledge of Stride's whereabouts. Stride leaves the Greers behind and is ambushed and wounded by two of the robbers, whom he kills. The Greers find Stride, who learns that John Greer has been transporting the stolen gold in his wagon, though he wasn't involved in the robbery. The former sheriff confiscates the stolen gold and sends the Greers safely on their way. However, John has an attack of conscience, goes into Flora Vista, informs Pate Bodeen that Stride is waiting for him, and is killed by Bodeen as he heads for the sheriff's office.

Bodeen and his remaining henchman ride into the desert to find Stride, followed by Masters and Clete. Three of the four men kill each other in the rocks, leaving only Stride, Masters and the stolen gold. Masters openly faces Stride, tells him about the death of John Greer, and tries unsuccessfully to talk Stride into letting him take the gold. The two men then shoot it out, leaving Masters dead. Stride rides into Flora Vista and delivers the strongbox to Wells Fargo, tells Annie Greer that he'll be heading back to Silver Springs, and rides out of town. Annie delays her trip to California, intimating that she'll follow him.

Seven Men from Now is a conventional western with a familiar plot; its quality originates in the writing, directing and acting of its story. Burt Kennedy, who over the next twenty years became a respected writer and director of western movies, wrote this simple story of revenge, choosing to focus his talent on character development rather than plot elements. As a result, *Seven Men from Now*, with its memorable characters and tangled interrelationships, is much more effective as human drama than most other oaters of the period. Though the revenge motif is overly familiar to the genre, Kennedy gave his characters more than enough personal motivation to keep their characters fresh and the action lively.

The film was directed by Budd Boetticher, who became, along with John Ford and Anthony Mann, one of the most influential and important western movie directors of the 1950s. This was Boetticher's first feature with Randolph Scott; over the next five years they would team up to make a total of seven films together. Boetticher directs the movie with an eye for the locale—note the variations of the Arizona landscape, from the desolate rocky terrain to the peaceful, quiet, river country to the parched, arid desert—and with a respect for the western genre. He doesn't flaunt western traditions, but flushes them out with

The eyes of Annie Greer (Gail Russell), John Greer (Walter Reed) and Clete (Donald Barry) are focused on Big Masters (Lee Marvin) and his gun in *Seven Men from Now*.

natural and authentic flourishes, such as having Stride sleep underneath the Greer's wagon during the rainstorm (and thus increasing their intimacy).

The third film to pair Lee Marvin with Randolph Scott is easily the best of the trio, providing both men well-written characters to portray. Unlike those in *Hangman's Knot* or *The Stranger Wore a Gun*, Randolph Scott's character is not burdened by the guilt of causing an opening scene massacre, though the death of his wife serves the same psychological purpose. Here, his Ben Stride is an honorable man, trying to do the honorable thing and avenge his wife's death, thus assuaging his own conscience at having put her in harm's way. This to the character results in more identification and empathy, and a greater emotional impact. This also makes it easier for Scott to lower his guard and give one of his better performances.

Lee Marvin is wonderful as Big Masters. He is Scott's equal on-screen and takes a different acting tack than the laconic veteran. Masters is flamboyant and expressive, not asking but *telling* Scott that he and Clete will be accompanying them south to Flora Vista. Marvin's Masters is a tough, independent, virile man with a greedy streak. He stands up to Stride when he first sees him at the deserted relay station, telling Stride that he wasn't involved in the holdup. "Good," Stride states matter-of-factly. "I'd hate to have to kill you." Masters glances over at him and says, nonchalantly, "I'd hate to have you try."

It is from Masters that the Greers learn of Stride's quest for revenge, and it is Masters who breaks up their little group by insulting "short on spine" John Greer and flattering his comely wife. Ultimately, however, it is Masters who gives Greer his final measure of respect. When Greer is shot in the back by Pate Bodeen, Masters stands over the body and says, "I was wrong, Clete. He wasn't half a man," and because *Masters* is saying it, the audience must agree. One of Marvin's finest moments comes when Bodeen tells him that John Greer is transporting the gold to Flora Vista. The look on Marvin's face, as he realizes that it was within his grasp for the past few days, is priceless.

Big Masters is one of Lee Marvin's finest roles and one of his best performances, certainly of Academy Award quality. Marvin reveals all of the various layers of his character to the audience, one by one, until all that's left is the underlying greed that drives him. At that point, Masters faces off against Stride, still looking for a peaceful solution to the situation. Masters does most of the talking then, setting up the inevitable shootout, and finally dies a brave death at the hands of Scott's stoic integrity. Reportedly, at a sneak preview for the film at the Pantages theater in Hollywood, audience members were so enamored of Marvin's death scene that they demanded the final reel (featuring his death scene) be played again after the film had finished.

Seven Men from Now is one of Randolph Scott's better films and is superior to many of the westerns of that period. Perhaps due to its ambiguous title, the film did not do much business and was not heavily reviewed, though the critics that did see it generally recommended it. Though it is very difficult to find today, the film has reached minor classic status, mainly due to Lee Marvin's memorable performance and the wonderfully-written relationship and climactic duel between Marvin and Randolph Scott. For Scott, the film led to an ongoing and very prosperous relationship with director Boetticher and Columbia Pictures. For Marvin, the film was a special western, displaying perhaps the epitome of his screen acting.

Attack (1956)

CREDITS: The Associates and the Aldrich Company. *Distributed by* United Artists. *Produced and Directed by* Robert Aldrich. *Screenplay by* James Poe. *Based on the play* Fragile Fox *by* Norman Brooks. *Produced on the stage by* Paul Vroom. *Music Composed and Conducted by* Frank DeVol. *Photographed by* Joseph Biroc, A.S.C. *Film Editor*: Michael Luciano, A.C.E. *Art Director*: William Glasgow. *Set Decorator*: Glen L. Daniels. *Sound*: Jack Solomon. *Sound Effects*: Robert A. Reich. *Makeup*: Robert J. Schiffer. *Assistant Director*: Robert Justman. *Assistant to the*

Attack

Producer: Adele T. Strassfield. *Dialogue Supervisor*: Robert Sherman. *Casting Supervisor*: Jack Murton. *Special Effects*: David B. Koehler. *Technical Supervisor*: Bud Cokes. *Associate Producer*: Walter Blake. *Production Supervisor*: Jack R. Berne. Not Rated. Black and White. Flat (1.33:1). 107 minutes. Released on September 19, 1956. Currently available on VHS videotape and laserdisc.

CAST: *Lieutenant Joe Costa*, Jack Palance; *Captain Erskine Cooney*, Eddie Albert; *Colonel Clyde Bartlett*, Lee Marvin; *Private Bernstein*, Robert Strauss; *Private Snowden*, Richard Jaeckel; *Sergeant Tolliver*, Buddy Ebsen; *Lieutenant Woodruff*, William Smithers; *Corporal Jackson*, Jan Shepodd; *Private Ricks*, Jimmy Goodwin; *Short German*, Steven Geray; *Tall German*, Peter Van Eyck; *Old Frenchman*, Louis Mercier; *Sergeant Ingersol*, Strother Martin.

Like many actors before and since, Lee Marvin found that there were certain directors with whom he shared a particular affinity or perspective which allowed them to work well together, to their mutual enjoyment and benefit. For Lee Marvin, the director of choice seemed to be Robert Aldrich, and *Attack* was their first film together.

Aldrich was an independent producer-director known as a maverick in Hollywood, renowned for tackling controversial subjects with directness, presenting violence as (a sometimes necessary) part of the modern way of life, casting actors other directors might normally bypass as leads, bringing his films in on time and within their budgets, and creating unique films worth watching and remembering in the process. *Attack* qualifies on all those counts.

Attack is set in Europe during part of the Battle of the Bulge in 1944 and concerns a platoon led by Lieutenant Costa (Jack Palance), who, in the opening sequence, watches one of his squadrons massacred before

Colonel Bartlett (Lee Marvin) accepts Captain Cooney's (Eddie Albert) Southern hospitality in *Attack*.

his very eyes because his superior officer, Captain Cooney (Eddie Albert), cannot muster enough courage to enter battle.

The main action in *Attack* occurs some time later as Costa's Fox platoon prepares to advance into a town thought to be occupied by Germans. Colonel Bartlett (Lee Marvin) explains the situation to Captain Cooney, whom he knows to be cowardly, but whom he leaves in charge in order to curry favor with Cooney's powerful father back in the States. Cooney decides to send in an expeditionary force led by Costa, supported by the platoon and artillery. Costa reluctantly agrees, but before leaving he confronts Cooney directly, telling him that, "if one of my men dies—just one—through your negligence, so help me I'll come back here, stuff a grenade down your throat and pull the pin!"

From a safe point outside the town, the platoon gathers and Costa gives his orders. The men slowly advance down the hill, but when German gunfire erupts, only five men make it to the farmhouse on the edge of town alive and unhurt: Lt. Costa, Sergeant Tolliver (Buddy Ebsen) and privates Snowden (Richard Jaeckel), Bernstein (Robert Strauss) and Ricks (Jimmy Goodwin). When Costa calls for support, Cooney ignores him and argues with the platoon's executive officer, Lieutenant Woodruff (William Smithers), about the wisdom of sacrificing more men for the sake of the six stranded soldiers.

While in the farmhouse, Tolliver picks off a German sniper, and the soldiers find two Germans hiding in the cellar, one of whom is an officer. When the officer refuses to tell him about the German forces in the town, Costa shoves him outside to die in a fusillade of German bullets, convincing the other one to talk. Realizing that help is not forthcoming, Costa radios Cooney that he is coming back for him and sends the soldiers back up the hill one by one, through German gunfire, which kills Private Ricks.

The rest of the platoon returns safely but without Costa. They report as Bartlett announces that the Germans are moving in and that the town must be held at all costs. Cooney asks to be relieved of command, but Bartlett browbeats him into continuing and leaves. As Woodruff watches, Cooney cracks up, reliving a past memory of a beating from his father. Costa suddenly arrives, beaten and bloody, looking to murder Cooney. Woodruff won't let him, and word comes that the remainder of Costa's platoon is in trouble, fighting Germans up the street. Costa leaves again, with a warning that he'll be back to finish the job.

Costa disables a German tank with a bazooka and a grenade but is pinned down and partially run over by a second tank. Meanwhile, Cooney runs through the streets, shooting Germans and shouting like a madman, and somehow finds the platoon, which holes up in a cellar as German soldiers walk through the streets. Cooney decides that the best course of action is to surrender and holds the platoon at gunpoint to do so. He is stopped, however, by the sight of Costa, bloody left arm dangling at his side, slowly coming down the steps to the cellar, asking God for the courage to kill his commanding officer. At the bottom of the stairs, Costa collapses, then dies with a primal scream on his face.

Cooney again tries to make the platoon surrender, but this time is stopped by Lt. Woodruff, who shoots and kills him. When Woodruff states that he wants to be turned in for murder if they survive, the other men in the platoon each pump a bullet into Cooney's corpse and claim that they killed the coward. Col. Bartlett arrives, announcing that the Germans have been driven back, and takes in the scene calmly, realizing that he might gain more personally out of Cooney's death than if Cooney had lived. He pushes Woodruff too far when he decides that Cooney should get a posthumous medal, thus giving Cooney's father the heroic son he never had, and Woodruff refuses to go along with the charade any longer. As the film ends, Woodruff calls headquarters, asking to tell his story to a general.

The Department of Defense found the screenplay, based on Norman Brooks' play *Fragile Fox* (the name of the platoon), so incendiary that they wouldn't support it in any way. This refusal became controversial enough to cause a member of the House Armed Services Committee, Representative Melvin Price, to accuse the DOD of censorship, specifically in regards to this film, on the floor of the U.S. Congress.

To make his movie without official cooperation, independent producer-director Robert Aldrich had to make do with what he could find. For the German tanks, he bought one Japanese tank for $1,040, had it restored for another $1,000, and rented a British model and refit that as well. "The joke of it is that anybody could have stopped the picture cold for about $25,000," recalled Aldrich later, "just by buying up all the uniforms."

Aldrich, who had attempted and failed to get the rights to two other hot war properties, Norman Mailer's *The Naked and the Dead* and Irwin Shaw's *The Young Lions*, was determined to make a war movie that didn't glorify the excessive violence of war, that did not pander to the jingoistic politicism rampant at the time, and that told a dramatic story worthy of his directorial time and effort. "My main anti-war argument was not the usual 'war is hell,' but the terribly corrupting influence that war can have on the most normal, average human beings, and what terrible things it makes them capable of that they wouldn't be capable of otherwise," he stated. In *Fragile Fox*, Aldrich found the ideal vehicle for his sentiment.

Aldrich hired Jack Palance, who had previously starred in his art-house hit, *The Big Knife*, as Lt. Costa, and Palance gives the role his all. As the action increases, Palance responds with an intensity so fierce he almost ignites on-screen. Some critics found his overplaying disturbing, but within the context of the story, it is not only appropriate but necessary. The movie's conscience is represented by Lt. Woodruff, portrayed by William Smithers, in his first film role. Woodruff is the man who walks the middle of the road between the extremes of Cooney and Costa, and who must ultimately decide the fate of the entire platoon by his action, or inaction. To his credit, Smithers never sounds preachy but delivers his dialogue with genuine feeling and emotion.

It is Eddie Albert, however, who steals the show. *Attack* was Albert's thirty-fifth film, and nothing he had done before had prepared audiences for the brittle, indecisive, spiteful character that Albert presented them. Albert not only makes Captain Cooney human, he makes the character real. Douglas Brode, in his book *The Lost Films of the Fifties*, wrote: "Eddie Albert should have won a Best Supporting Actor Oscar (he wasn't even nominated) for his incisive portrayal of a psychologically scarred character, so characteristic of that decade when Hollywood focused on neurotics."

Smaller roles are played with aplomb by film veterans Buddy Ebsen, Robert Strauss and Richard Jaeckel. Buddy Ebsen's role of Sergeant Tolliver was first offered to Lee Marvin, who instead sought the more complex role of Colonel Clyde Bartlett. Marvin recalled that, "Having been a P.F.C. in the Marine Corps, I was aware of officers that didn't come up to the standards and respect of the common man—the dogface. I did know this colonel who had that attitude, browbeating the guys at poker games to win, just covering his own tracks, and I just looked forward to playing that kind of little bastard."

It is Col. Bartlett who causes all of the story's drama, simply because he chooses to leave Captain Cooney in command to further his own political ambitions, gambling men's lives that Cooney won't embarrass him. Bartlett isn't secretive about his intentions; he tells Lt. Woodruff early on what his plans are and why he is leaving an obvious coward in charge. At film's end, Woodruff takes on the Colonel and all that's wrong with political favoritism by making his call to General Parsons. Unfortunately for Costa, the rest of the Fragile Fox platoon, and ultimately Bartlett himself, the Colonel's gamble doesn't pay off.

Marvin, as Bartlett, comes off as a shrewd manipulator, playing poker with the toys of war and the lives of men. With a gentle Southern drawl, Marvin plays Bartlett as an opportunist, looking for the best personal gain in every situation. Despite Bartlett's ambitions, however, he is a fighter, and Marvin portrays that side of the Colonel expertly.

Colonel Bartlett (Lee Marvin) tries to explain his side of things to Lieutenant Woodruff (William Smithers) in *Attack.*

Attack was filmed in 32 days on the backlot of RKO studios, much of it where *The Story of G.I. Joe* had been filmed some dozen years earlier. Robert Aldrich had been an assistant director on *G.I. Joe* and remembered the desolate set when scouting locations for *Attack*. In fact, the sequence involving the German sniper being shot by Sgt. Tolliver and falling out of the church tower is taken directly from the earlier film.

At the time of its release, *Attack* was lauded for its grim, relentless view of war as hell, but faulted for its histrionics and overt Costa-as-Christ references as the story reaches its climax. Most reviewers felt that the story worked up to a point, but lost its footing as Captain Cooney crumbled and Lt. Costa returned from the (presumed) dead to face him. The *Newsweek* review, for instance, began, "Perhaps no picture can be all blood and iron, but this one comes about as close to such a product as has come out of Hollywood. It has its theatricalism, in generous amount, but the iron in it beats the theatricalism into a pulp." The reviewer summed it up this way: "Hard to take, but hard to forget, too." Other reviews are similar enough to make one wonder whether the Department of Defense's refusal to cooperate, which was noted in many of the reviews, had some effect on the reviewers.

Today, *Attack* is viewed as at least a minor classic, a precursor of films such as *The Dirty Dozen*, *M*A*S*H*, *Apocalypse Now* and *Platoon*, which portray military life in unsparing terms and seriously question issues of authority. Historically, *Attack* deserves mention for its status as the first film denied cooperation by the Department of Defense. More importantly, however, *Attack* deserves respect for its realistic attitude toward the military, well spoken by Lt. Woodruff as he faces off against Captain Cooney, and for the authenticity the cast and director bring to the story.

Attack isn't a film which targets the U.S. military; it is a film which tells a taut, dramatic story that explores human nature under stress and shows us the best and worst examples of human behavior under conditions of war. It is among the best films in which Lee Marvin (not to mention Jack Palance and Eddie Albert) ever appeared.

Pillars of the Sky (1956) (aka *The Tomahawk and the Cross*)

CREDITS: Universal. *Directed by* George Marshall. *Produced by* Robert Arthur. *Screenplay by* Sam Rolfe. *From the novel* Frontier Fury *by* Will Henry. *Music Supervision by* Joseph Gershenson. *Director of Photography*: Harold Lipstein, A.S.C. *Film Editor*: Milton Carruth, B.S.C. *Art Direction*: Alexander Golitzen, Bill Newberry. *Set Decoration*: Russell A. Gausman, Oliver Emert. *Sound*: Leslie J. Carey, Frank H. Wilkinson. *Costumes*: Rosemary Odell. *Make-up*: Bud Westmore. *Hair Stylist*: Joan St. Oegger. *Assistant Director*: Marshall Green. Not Rated. Technicolor. *Technicolor Color Consultant*: William Fritzsche. CinemaScope (2.35:1). 95 minutes. Released in October 1956. Not currently available on home video.

CAST: *Sergeant Emmett Bell*, Jeff Chandler; *Calla Gaxton*, Dorothy Malone; *Doctor Joseph Holden*, Ward Bond; *Captain Tom Gaxton*, Keith Andes; *Sergeant Lloyd Carracart*, Lee Marvin; *Timothy*, Sydney Chaplin; *Colonel Edson Stedlow*, Willis Bouchey; *Kamiakin*, Michael Ansara; *Mrs. Anne Avery*, Olive Carey; *Sergeant Dutch Williams*, Charles Horvath; *Malachi*, Orlando Rodriguez; *Lieutenant Winston*, Glen Kramer; *Lieutenant Hammond*, Floyd Simmons; *Jacob*, Pat Hogan; *Lucas*, Felix Noriego; *Morgan*, Paul Smith; *Waco*, Martin Milner; *Albie*, Robert Ellis; *Music*, Ralph J. Votrian; *Major Donohue*, Walter Coy; *Sergeant Major Frenchy Desmonde*, Alberto Morin; *Isaiah*, Richard Hale; *Zachariah*, Frank de Kova; *Captain Fanning*, Terry Wilson; *Major Randall*, Philip Keiffer; *Elijah*, Gilbert Conner.

Of the many westerns in which Lee Marvin performed, this one may be the most unusual, for two reasons. First, Marvin sports an Irish brogue in his part as a cavalry officer. Marvin didn't use accents very often, so this instance stands out. Second, although many westerns have some sort of religious motif supporting the basic good vs. evil plot, *Pillars of the Sky* uses as a foundation the efforts of white men to convert Indians to Christianity and extrapolates much of its plot from the ramifications of those efforts. In fact, the British title for the film is *The Tomahawk and the Cross*.

The *Pillars of the Sky* are what the various Indian tribes in Oregon call the mountains which surround their valley reservation. Though the Indians do not like being limited to the reservation lands, they hold with the treaty, largely due to the efforts of Sergeant Emmett Bell (Jeff Chandler), a cavalry scout who sympathizes with them (much like Kevin Costner learned to do thirty-five years later in *Dances with Wolves*), and Dr. Joseph Holden

(Ward Bond), a medical missionary who teaches and treats the Indians, converts them to Christianity, and gives them Biblical names.

Trouble arrives with a cavalry regiment led by Colonel Stedlow (Willis Bouchey), who has orders to build a road and a fort on the reservation. Indian opposition is led by Kamiakin (Michael Ansara), one of the chief's sons, who has thrown off his Christian name and vows to kill any soldier who crosses the Snake River. Despite the warnings from Bell, Stedlow obstinately follows his orders. Complicating matters is news that Kamiakin is holding two white women hostage, one of whom is the wife of one of the cavalry officers (Keith Andes) and a former love interest of Bell's.

While the Indians prepare for war, Bell leads a rescue party to the women, only to discover that Calla (Dorothy Malone) came out to Oregon to find and stay with him rather than her own husband. They rejoin the regiment, which has crossed the river into Indian country. The regiment is followed, attacked, and forced to fight its way onto a low plateau where it can regroup. Among the many wounded is Sergeant Carracart (Lee Marvin), a close friend of Bell's. During the night, the soldiers and women sneak down the hill, away from the Indians, while Bell and Dr. Holden keep Carracart company for a time before leaving him to die alone at the hands of the Indians. In the escape, Calla's husband is injured as well.

The regiment arrives at Dr. Holden's mission, closely followed by the Indians, who set the mission on fire using flaming arrows. Dr. Holden (unarmed) meets the Indians, confronts Kamiakin, and is shot dead by the warrior. Sgt. Bell follows and humiliates Kamiakin, who tries to kill him as well, but

Sergeant Emmet Bell (Jeff Chandler) and Doctor Holden (Ward Bond) say farewell to their injured friend, Sergeant Carracart (Lee Marvin), in *Pillars of the Sky.*

Kamiakin is shot in the back by his father as he attacks. Bell carries the body of Dr. Holden back to the mission, followed by the Indians, and effectively takes the parson's place by leading the penitent people in prayer.

Pillars of the Sky is a literate, honest attempt at weaving such serious issues as religion and race relations into a fairly standard western context. As such, it deserves some respect. Sam Rolfe's screenplay stresses characterization over action and focuses on the relationships between the characters and how those relationships are affected by the circumstances of the plot. The film tries hard to find a balance between the traditional "white is right" mentality of most westerns and overemphasis of the persecution of the Indian tribes, and succeeds pretty well.

Nevertheless, the religious themes are jarring to watch as they unfold, perhaps because they are so unusual in this setting. While the integration of Indian and white cultures is discussed at the chief's meeting, no character ever questions the wisdom or ramifications of converting the Indians to Christianity. It seems a foregone conclusion to everyone involved, white and Indian, that the Indians should all become God-fearing Christians. Only Kamiakin refutes the white man's ways, throwing off his Christian name of Aaron and choosing to wage war (for rather good reasons).

Pillars of the Sky is based on Will Henry's novel *Frontier Fury* (also known as *To Follow a Flag* and, later, the movie's title), which is based on a true incident that occurred along the Idaho-Washington border in May of 1858. Henry evidently thought it best to change some of the names, however, so real-life Colonel Edward Steptoe became Colonel Edson Stedlow, and so forth. It seems that the religious aspects of the movie were not nearly as prominent in the actual incident, and there were no women present.

The film's biggest problem is the romantic triangle involving Sgt. Bell, Captain Tom Gaxton and his wife Calla. While the script is intelligent and incisive in many ways, when it comes to these characters it becomes melodramatic and unduly obvious. Because Calla is so insensitive to her husband, she solicits no sympathy, and the men seem foolish to be fighting over her.

Despite the literate scope of the script and its beautiful CinemaScope photography, *Pillars of the Sky* remains a minor western, virtually unknown to most audiences today. Part of this is due to the casting, which offers no big names (such as John Wayne, Gary Cooper or even an Audie Murphy), though it does sport some wonderful supporting actors. A lack of action may be another reason for audience apathy; what action there is in the film is small in scale and lackluster in execution. Since this is also a more serious western than most, its thematic subject matter may also be a contributing factor to its continuing obscurity.

Jeff Chandler is fine as Indian sympathizer Sgt. Bell. Chandler plays Sgt. Bell ruggedly, detailing the character's flaws and rebellious spirit nicely. Dorothy Malone's part (and billing) is overblown. Keith Andes is one-dimensional as her rejected husband. It is the supporting cast of Ward Bond, Lee Marvin, Michael Ansara and Sydney Chaplin which brings much of the warmth of the story to the forefront.

Ward Bond, who appeared in most of John Ford's westerns, brings a real compassion to his role and easily makes the strongest impression in the film. Michael Ansara, who played Indians in many Hollywood productions, also leaves a lasting impression as Kamiakin, the one man strong enough to try to lead his people to freedom. Sydney Chaplin has a key role as Timothy, the Indian scout who accompanies Bell and who best articulates the future co-existence of the white and Indian races.

Lee Marvin has a small role as a sergeant accompanying the green troops, trying to whip them into shape by the time they confront any trouble. In a light Irish brogue, Sgt. Carracart (also called Carey) yells a bit and drinks a bit and then gets dramatically speared in the back. Marvin actually has little to do until his death scene but comes across as one of the wiser soldiers in the regiment. His final scene, with Sgt. Bell and Dr. Holden staying with him as long as they can, is nicely done and well-illustrates the feeling that the men in the cavalry had for each other.

If *Pillars of the Sky* had forgotten its love triangle and staged its battle scenes more imaginatively, it might have been a minor classic. Unfortunately, that didn't happen, so the film remains decent but flawed. It received favorable reviews and did solid business upon its release, especially in Great Britain, then lapsed from memory like so many others before and since.

The Rack (1956)

CREDITS: Metro-Goldwyn-Mayer. *Directed by* Arnold Laven. *Produced by* Arthur M. Loew, Jr. *Screenplay by* Stewart Stern. *Based on the teleplay by* Rod Serling. *Music by* Adolph Deutsch. *Director of Photography*: Paul C. Vogel, A.S.C. *Film Editors*: Harold F. Kress, A.C.E., Marshall Neilan, Jr. *Art Directors*: Cedric Gibbons, Merrill Pye. *Set Decorations*: Edwin B. Willis, Fred MacLean. *Recording Supervisor*: Dr. Wesley C. Miller. *Makeup by* William Tuttle. *Assistant Director*: Robert Saunders. *Technical Advisor*: Colonel Charles M. Trammel, Jr., U.S.A.R. Not Rated. Black and White. Flat (1.33:1). 100 minutes. Released in November 1956. Not currently available on home video.

CAST: *Captain Edward W. Hall, Jr.*, Paul Newman; *Major Sam Moulton*, Wendell Corey; *Colonel Edward W. Hall, Sr.*, Walter Pidgeon; *Lieutenant Colonel Frank Wasnick*, Edmond O'Brien; *Aggie Hall*, Anne Francis; *Captain John R. Miller*, Lee Marvin; *Caroline*, Cloris Leachman; *Colonel Ira Hansen*, Robert Burton; *Law Officer*, Robert Simon; *Court President*, Trevor Bardette; *Sergeant Otto Pahnke*, Adam Williams; *Millard Chilson Cassidy*, James Best; *Colonel Dudley Smith*, Fay Roope; *Major Byron Phillips*, Barry Atwater.

The Rack is the second film about the Korean War in which Lee Marvin co-starred, but unlike the straightforward action of *The Glory Brigade*, this film delves into the psychological rather than the physical demands of warfare. Marvin would visit the same territory yet again twelve years later in *Sergeant Ryker*. Though his role in *The Rack* is small in terms of screen time, it is crucial for the development of Captain Hall's character, for the viewer's understanding of conditions in Korea, and for the ultimate conclusion of Hall's court-martial.

Captain Edward W. Hall, Jr. (Paul Newman) returns home from duty in the Korean War with an injured leg and a great deal of guilt. He has a secret, one which will forever alter his relationship with his proud military father (Walter Pidgeon) and his late brother's widow, Aggie (Anne Francis). When he is well enough to leave the hospital, Hall is charged with collaborating with the enemy while being held as a North Korean prisoner of war. Major Sam Moulton (Wendell Corey) finds the case distasteful but takes on the task of prosecuting Hall in the ensuing court-martial, while sympathetic Lt. Colonel Frank Wasnick (Edmond O'Brien) handles Hall's defense. Hall's father learns of the charges through a military friend, loses his temper and harshly condemns his son for his admitted treason, even suggesting that death would have been more honorable. Aggie tries her best to reconcile the two men.

During the court-martial the prosecution uses the testimony of Captain John R. Miller (Lee Marvin) to show that even when physically tortured, most American soldiers did not reach the point where they would give "aid and comfort" to the enemy. Hall was never tortured — at least not physically. He was held for six months in solitary confinement in a small, wet cellar until, when informed that his younger brother had died in combat, he broke down and agreed to sign whatever his captors wanted him to.

Hall's defense is that he was an intensely lonely man — his caring mother died when he was 12 and his father has never embraced him or shown him love — and that the North Koreans used this knowledge against him until he couldn't help himself. Under oath, and honest introspection, however, Hall admits (to the court and to himself) that he never did reach his breaking point, close though he may have come. After this testimony, Hall and his father do their best to start their relationship all over again.

Hall is found guilty, then takes the stand one last time and tells how he had talked to

Sergeant John R. Miller (Lee Marvin) gives testimony in *The Rack*.

Captain Miller that morning. Miller told him that everybody faces a moment of ultimate choice in their lives. If the right choice is made, it becomes a "moment of magnificence"; if not, a moment of regret. Hall wishes that he had not "sold himself short" and prays that other people will choose more wisely than himself. He then stands, ready for sentencing.

One of the most unexpected and least understood aspects of the Korean War was the number of American soldiers who collaborated with the enemy, something that was almost unheard of in World War II. When prisoners of war were being repatriated, 21 American soldiers chose to stay with their North Korean captors rather than return home. Quite naturally, this shocked and angered the American public, who wanted to know how such a change of heart could occur in its proud fighting men.

The term "brainwashing" came into vogue then, as psychiatrists and military experts explained how the North Koreans and Chinese would use psychological tactics to gain prisoners' trust and continually ridicule and condemn their home country. Extra food and privileges were often given to soldiers who cooperated with the Communists, while those who fought the indoctrination were often beaten, or worse. As a result, some soldiers gave in rather than fight. *The Rack* describes this physical and psychological torture in detail and depicts how soldiers attempted to combat these techniques. The film asks how much psychological pressure a soldier must be able to handle and concludes that soldiers must be better prepared for such duress than Captain Hall.

The Rack had its origins as a live television drama by Rod Serling, who tackled the controversial subject soon after his hit teleplay *Patterns* had aired. The original teleplay was produced for the *United States Steel Hour* on April 12, 1955, with Marshall Thompson as Captain Hall. Wendell Corey co-starred as the prosecuting attorney; he was the only major television cast member to repeat his performance in the film. MGM then bought the property and had a film ready for theaters just one year later.

This was Paul Newman's third movie performance, after his inauspicious debut in *The Silver Chalice* (1954) and his excellent portrayal of boxer Rocky Graziano in *Somebody Up There Likes Me* (1956). Newman takes full advantage of the role, showing his range as the character moves from a scared and confused veteran with a hellish secret to a professional soldier on the witness stand describing the harrowing death march to the North Korean prison camp. His sensitivity is highlighted in the film's most moving scene when, in a car with Walter Pidgeon (recalling the famous scene between brothers Marlon Brando and Rod Steiger in *On the Waterfront*), father and son try to find common ground.

The Rack provides Lee Marvin with another opportunity to show his stuff in a classy project. Marvin has a total of four scenes in the film and only speaks in one. But when he does, he holds the audience spellbound. As Captain Miller, he describes what the North Koreans did to him, and others, when they were caught after escaping from the prison camp. His tale of abuse is disturbing to hear, and when he removes his shirt to display the scars of his torture, the camera thankfully turns away. The court audience's reaction is more than adequate to depict the horror of interrogation and physical torture.

Further, it is his character whom, at the end of the film, offers Hall understanding, if perhaps not forgiveness. Miller's change of heart about Hall during the film serves as the audience's as well. From calling him a "lousy yellow crud" when first taking the witness stand, Miller comes to realize that Hall faced as much or more pressure than himself to collaborate. Since it was Miller who was tortured and told that Hall had informed on his escape plans, it is only right that Miller exonerate him from direct blame when shown that Hall could not have known of those plans while in solitary confinement.

Hall quotes Miller during his speech about the "moment of magnificence," a speech which serves to make Miller a more noble figure. It's no wonder Marvin took this role; it's a far cry from the villainous roles for which he was known and continually being offered. Because of parts like this one, Hollywood began to realize that Marvin was capable of more than the roles he was generally offered.

The Rack received mostly favorable reviews, such as this excerpt from Arthur Knight in the *Saturday Review*: "Paul Newman is superb in the complex role of the accused, Wendell Corey and Edmond O'Brien create warm and human figures as the prosecuting and defending officers in the court martial that dominates the film, and Walter Pidgeon gives one of his finest performances as Newman's father, a hard-shelled colonel whose lack of understanding precipitated his son's breakdown under the Red terror. Like *Marty* and *Patterns*, *The Rack* indicates what vital new subject matter the TV screen is opening up for the movies."

Lawrence J. Quirk of the *Motion Picture Herald* praised the film as "...a powerful, moving and adult drama..." and stated that, "*The Rack* is a provocative and creative piece of work." Paul Newman was singled out by nearly every critic for his sensitive portrayal of the unfortunate prisoner of war. Thanks to this film and *Somebody Up There Likes Me*, Newman was on his way to becoming a major star. Lee Marvin was on his way as well, but took a few more years to follow.

Raintree County (1957)

CREDITS: Metro-Goldwyn-Mayer. *Directed by* Edward Dmytryk. *Produced by* David Lewis. *Associate Producer*: Millard Kaufman. *Screenplay by* Millard Kaufman. *Based on the Novel by* Ross Lockridge, Jr. *Music by* Johnny Green. *Song* "The Song of Raintree County" *by* Paul Francis Webster, Johnny Green, *sung by* Nat King Cole. *Director of Photography*: Robert Surtees, A.S.C. *Film Editor*: John Dunning, A.C.E. *Art Directors*: William A. Horning, Urie McCleary. *Set Decorations*: Edwin B. Willis, Hugh Hunt. *Recording Supervisor*: Dr. Wesley C. Miller. *Costumes by* Walter Plunkett. *Make-up Created by* William Tuttle. *Hair Styles by* Sydney Guilaroff. *Special Effects*: Warren Newcombe. *Assistant Director*: Ridgeway Callow. Not Rated. Technicolor. *Color Consultant*: Charles K. Hagedon. MGM Camera 65 (2.75:1). Original Roadshow running time: 187 minutes. Video / Laserdisc running time: 168 minutes. Released in December, 1957. Currently available on VHS videotape and laserdisc.

CAST: *John Shawnessy*, Montgomery Clift; *Susanna Drake*, Elizabeth Taylor; *Nell Gaither*, Eva Marie Saint; *Professor Jerusalem Webster Stiles*, Nigel Patrick; *Orville "Flash" Perkins*, Lee Marvin; *Garwood B. Jones*, Rod Taylor; *Ellen Shawnessy*, Agnes Moorehead; *T. D. Shawnessy*, Walter Abel; *Barbara Drake*, Jarma Lewis; *Bobby Drake*, Tom Drake; *Ezra Gray*, Rhys Williams; *Niles Foster*, Russell Collins; *Southern Officer*, DeForest Kelley; *Lydia Gray*, Myrna Hansen; *Jake the Bartender*, Oliver Blake; *Cousin Sam*, John Eldredge; *Soona*, Isabelle Cooley; *Parthenia*, Ruth Attaway; *Miss Roman*, Eileene Stevens; *Bessie*, Rosalind Hayes; *Tom Conway*, Don Burnett; *Nat Franklin*, Michael Dugan; *Jesse Gardner*, Ralph Vitti (Michael Dante); *Starter*, Phil Chambers; *Man with Gun*, James Griffith; *Granpa Peters*, Burt Mustin; *Madame Gaubert*, Dorothy Granger; *Blind Man*, Owen McGiveney; *Party Guest*, Charles Watts; *Union Lieutenant*, Stacy Harris; *Jim Shawnessy at 2 1/2*, Donald Losby; *Jim Shawnessy at 4*, Mickey Maga; *Pantomimist in blackface*, Robert Foulk; *Photographer*, Jack Daly; *Old Negro Man*, Bill Walker; *Bearded Soldier*, Gardney McKay; *Bit Parts*, William Challee, Frank Kreig, Janet Lake, Luana Lee, Judi Jordan, Phyllis Douglas, Sue George, Nesdon Booth, Robert Forrest, Josephine Cummins, Mil Patrick.

Raintree County was an attempt by MGM to repeat the gargantuan success of *Gone with the Wind*. In this case, the movie itself is gargantuan but its success was only modest. It is easy to compare to *Gone with the Wind* because it covers much of the same Civil War-era romantic ground, takes its characters through years of living and loving, boasts two of the biggest stars of its time along with a strong supporting cast, and ends with the same "new beginning" motif of the earlier blockbuster. However, *Raintree County* is easily the inferior film and is much less effective, for various reasons.

Raintree County is a fictional county in Indiana, an idyllic paradise with a local legend that Johnny Appleseed planted a special "raintree," a tree that represents truth and fulfillment to the person who finds it. When John Shawnessy (Montgomery Clift) hears the story in 1859, he goes into a nearby swamp to find it and nearly drowns. Nell Gunther (Eva Marie Saint), the girl he loves, doesn't believe in the story, but a beautiful woman whom John meets does. Susanna Drake (Elizabeth Taylor) and John immediately fall in love, and Susanna ensures that John will remain with her by telling him, falsely, that she is pregnant. Nell tells John that she loves him, but he is bound by honor to marry Susanna.

After marrying, John and Susanna move to Susanna's native New Orleans, but John doesn't like life in the South, particularly in regards to slavery. Susanna shows some signs of mental illness, so John moves them back to Freehaven, in his beloved Raintree County. Susanna does become pregnant and has a boy, whom they name Jim. They remain fairly happy during the first few years of the Civil War, isolated from the conflict, but Susanna finally goes crazy and takes Jim with her, through the fighting, to Georgia. John enlists in the Union army, joins up with his former athletic rival, Orville "Flash" Perkins (Lee Marvin), and tutor, Professor Stiles (Nigel Patrick), and begins to fight his way toward Georgia to rejoin his wife and son.

John locates and rescues Jim, aided by Flash Perkins, who dies at the hands of a Confederate soldier (DeForest Kelley) while helping them to escape. After the war ends, John finds Susanna in an insane asylum and takes her home to Raintree County. John is encouraged to make a political run against his former rival for Nell's affections, Garwood Jones (Rod Taylor), but John doesn't seem interested. Feeling that she is holding her husband back from his true ambitions, Susanna relapses and rushes into the swamp to find the mythical raintree, and is followed by Jim. The townspeople of Freehaven search and find Susanna, dead from exposure. Young Jim wakes up underneath the golden raintree, hears people calling his name, and rejoins his joyous father while Nell happily watches.

Raintree County was a mammoth production plagued with problems, beginning with the suicide of the novel's author, Ross Lockridge, Jr., in 1948, soon after the film rights to the best-selling novel were purchased by MGM for $150,000. Seven years later, cameras began rolling on a production that cost some $6 million to make and which barely broke even upon its initial release. Halfway through filming, Montgomery Clift was severely injured in a car accident, and the production closed down for two months while Clift recuperated from the accident and the resultant plastic surgery. The most ghoulish aspect of the film is the noticeable difference between Clift's pre- and post-accident scenes.

The film's biggest problem, however, lies in its source material. Though *Raintree County* does cover much of the same ground as the film it most emulates, *Gone with the Wind*, it has little of the technique, artistry or emotional impact of the earlier masterpiece. Where *Gone with the Wind* determined how the tragic destruction of the South during the Civil War eventually forced Scarlett O'Hara to maturity, the war is just another plot device in *Raintree County*. Scarlett is a full-bodied character, one of the great female roles in cinema history; Susanna Drake is a beautiful nutcase, driven to insanity by the thought that she might be carrying Negro blood in her veins. Rhett Butler is a rogue who finds within himself a surprising supply of strength and honor; John Shawnessy is a man destined for great things who settles for a rather ordinary life.

Both films feature sumptuous production values—great music, opulent sets, gorgeous

John Shawnessy (Mongtomery Clift) races Orville "Flash" Perkins (Lee Marvin) on the Fourth of July in *Raintree County*.

costumes, beautiful Technicolor art direction—but these are used to support the story in *Gone with the Wind*, whereas they comprise the bulk of *Raintree County*'s assets. *Raintree County* does have one superior feature: its 2.75:1 MGM Camera 65 widescreen cinematography, making it one of the most panoramic movies ever filmed (CinemaScope and Panavision, the industry's standard widescreen formats, are 2.35:1).

Though the film did not overly impress the critics, *Raintree County* was nominated for four Academy Awards: Best Art Direction—Set Decoration, Best Costume Design, Best Score and a surprising nod for Elizabeth Taylor as Best Actress (her first nomination). The film lost in all four categories to four separate films. If *Raintree County* had been better—quite a bit better—it might have garnered a supporting actor nomination for Lee Marvin.

In his final film before he began his successful television series, *M Squad*, Lee Marvin all but steals the show from star Montgomery Clift. Early on, Marvin puts his physical talents on display as he cavorts in a bar after a few drinks, swinging from a chandelier, doing handstands and impressing the crowd. Marvin then displays his real acting ability by running a foot race with Clift and making his *loss* convincing. Later, in the war scenes, Marvin's Flash Perkins gains in stature as he learns about war the hard way, aiding John in his desperate search. *Raintree County* gives Lee Marvin yet another memorable death scene, as Flash Perkins is belly-shot but holds off tracking Confederate soldiers by talking to them long enough for John and young Jim to safely get away.

Raintree County is an overlong, overblown Civil War tearjerker with not enough realistic human drama to cause tears. It was, unfortunately, beset by many problems, and is known today more for its turbulent history than its quality. It provided Lee Marvin with another strong, yet under-utilized, role and another classic death scene. It would also be Lee Marvin's last major film for four years, as he turned to television and concentrated on his first series, *M Squad*.

The Missouri Traveler (1958)

CREDITS: Buena Vista. *Directed by* Jerry Hopper. *Produced by* Patrick Ford. *Executive Producer*: C. V. Whitney. *Associate Producer*: Lowell J. Farrell. *Screenplay by* Norman Shannon Hall. *Based upon the novel by* John Burress. *Music by* Jack Marshall. *Director of Photography*: Winton C. Hoch, A.S.C. *Film Editor*: Tom McAdoo. *Art Director*: Jack Okey. *Set Decorator*: Victor Gangelin. *Properties*: Irving Sindler. *Special Effects*: Jack Caffee. *Sound*: Stanley Jones. *Men's Costumer*: Frank Beetson. *Women's Costumer*: Ann Peck. *Makeup Artist*: Ray Romero. *Hair Stylist*: Margaret Donavan. *Assistant Director*: Lew Borzage. Not Rated. Technicolor. *Technicolor Color Consultant*: Morgan Padelford. Flat (1.33:1). 103 minutes. Released in February 1958. Currently available on VHS videotape.

CAST: *Biarn Turner*, Brandon de Wilde; *Tobias Brown*, Lee Marvin; *Doyle Magee*, Gary Merrill; *Finas Daugherty*, Paul Ford; *Anna Love Price*, Mary Hosford; *Fred Mueller*, Ken Curtis; *Clyde Hamilton*, Cal Tinney; *Willie Poole*, Frank Cady; *Nelda Hamilton*, Mary Field; *Serena Poole*, Kathleen Freeman; *Sheriff Peavy*, Will Wright; *Reverend Thorndyke*, Tom Tiner; *Henry Craig*, Billy Bryant; *Jimmie Price*, Barry Curtis; *Red Poole*, Eddie Little; *Herb Davis*, Rodney Bell; *Hattie Neely*, Helen Brown; *Pos Neely*, Billy Newell; *Simpson*, Roy Jensen; *Old Sharecropper*, Earle Hodgins.

The Missouri Traveler was the second film in a series conceived by producer C. V. Whitney as a tribute to America. In 1954 Whitney, who had previously financed such blockbusters as *A Star Is Born* (1937), *Gone with the Wind*, and *Rebecca*, was interviewed in *Newsweek* and announced that he intended to film "…what I would describe as an American Series, to show our own people their country and also to make certain that the rest of the world learns more about us. No Whitney picture will ever misrepresent the United States or its people. There will be no hokum in my pictures. There's nothing more interesting than the truth as long as it is faithful and realistic."

The first installment of Whitney's Americana series was *The Searchers*, which has been acclaimed as an American classic since its original release in 1956. His second effort, *The Missouri Traveler*, based on the novel by John Burress, was not as well received. After the lackluster performance of this film, Whitney quietly abandoned his Americana series without further fanfare.

The Missouri Traveler is actually an adolescent runaway orphan named Biarn Turner (Brandon de Wilde) who, while on the road to Florida, is given a ride by farmer Tobias Brown (Lee Marvin) into the sleepy little town of Delphi, Missouri. As Brown himself says to the youngster, "The railroad passed us, we've never been hit by no flood or cyclone, we've never had a murder, bank robbery or a tar-and-feathering. Folks around here just don't amount to much." While Tobias Brown rankles the townsfolk, and specifically Miss Anna Love Price (Mary Hosford), with his arrogance and crudity, Biarn is befriended by newspaper editor Doyle Magee (Gary Merrill), who finds the boy a deserted farm to use as his own and arranges for him to take care of his spirited horse, Twister. Biarn finds friends easy to make in Delphi, except for Brown, who repeatedly teaches the boy hard lessons about life by taking light advantage of him.

Biarn asks the farmer to teach him how to plow, and Brown has Biarn plow one of his fields, then refuses to let the boy use his equipment to plow Biarn's field at the deserted farm. In response, Magee and a couple of the town selectmen, Finas Daugherty (Paul Ford) and Willie Poole (Frank Cady), coerce Brown into repaying the favor and plowing Biarn's field for him, setting up an animosity that lasts until the climax of the film. Brown buys the deserted farm and gives Biarn 30 days to leave, demanding that the horse Twister, whom he had sold to Magee because of its wildness, be taken away immediately. When Biarn tries to defend the horse from Brown, he is accidentally hurt, causing the townsfolk to rise up in anger against the farmer. Biarn recovers and admits that his injury was more his own fault than Brown's. Nevertheless, the town feeling against Brown runs high.

Miss Anna Love Price suggests that Twister be trained to race by Finas Daugherty, a former race horse owner. Meanwhile,

Young Biarn Turner (Brandon de Wilde) asks prosperous farmer Tobias Brown (Lee Marvin) for help in *The Missouri Traveler*.

Magee, a former boxer, starts working out on a punching bag. Together, the two men, with Biarn as jockey, train the horse as a trotter. Brown is challenged to a race on the Fourth of July by Magee, and he accepts. Most of the townsfolk bet against the prosperous farmer. After the annual Fourth of July parade, the race begins. Biarn ignores Daugherty's advice and starts out in front of Brown, who eventually catches and passes the boy, winning the race rather easily. After he is paid off, Brown starts a fight and is taken on by Magee. Their fistfight carries them around the town square and is the liveliest action the town has seen in years. Brown finally gives up and gracefully admits defeat. Then he stuns the crowd by kissing Miss Anna Love Price. Feeling generous, Brown offers to make Biarn a fair deal on the farm, which Biarn accepts, and Brown kisses Miss Anna Love Price again as the townsfolk celebrate.

It's easy to see what charmed C. V. Whitney about this story. Delphi is a Norman Rockwell painting come alive, with immaculately manicured landscaping, engrossing detail of rural life, and homespun characters possessing a simple, upstanding morality. This is the snapshot of rural America that Whitney wanted to present to the world—serene, simple, enjoyable, uplifting. And, up to a point, it works.

As several critics at the time pointed out, the problem with filming a sleepy town where nothing much ever happens is that, on-screen, nothing much ever happens. The film is dull to the point of tedium, up until the climactic fight when slapstick livens things up for awhile. Adding to the general apathy is a musical score played by a single harmonica. C. V. Whitney would not have wanted to present America as being this dull.

The strength of the film lies in its eye for

detail. Small town life is examined, and occasionally lampooned, with warmth and humor. At Finas Daugherty's diner, for instance, there is a sign in the window that falls down — and is picked up and replaced — every time the front door is opened. Finally, Doyle Magee picks it up and rips it in half. The sign was for a tax auction which took place some ten months previously. Characters speak in the small-town idiom which has become so familiar to movie audiences over the years, such as when Tobias Brown tells Biarn that, "A good farmer works from cain't to cain't — when he cain't see in the morning to when he cain't see at night."

Despite engaging performances by Gary Merrill, Paul Ford and young Brandon de Wilde, the film lacks a strong sense of movement and often seems dull. Lee Marvin has a pivotal role as the arrogant farmer whom nobody likes and who takes advantage of Biarn's naivete. Yet Tobias Brown is not as mean as people think; he's lonely and is perhaps even looking for some sign of acceptance from the people who he snubs. His comeuppance (and liberation) comes at the climax of the film when Doyle Magee beats the tar out of him. He is finally able to express himself, kissing Miss Anna Love Price and admitting his human feelings. Marvin is fine in the role, which is nothing special.

The Missouri Traveler is strong on charm and sentimentality, but meanders along at its own pace like a country river on a warm summer day. It paints a picture of life in rural America as idyllic as can be, but audiences didn't seem to care, passing by this quaint, picturesque still-life in favor of other, more active movies. Today it is just a footnote in the histories of its stars and studio, and the end of C.V. Whitney's "Americana" dream.

The Comancheros (1961)

CREDITS: 20th Century–Fox. *Directed by* Michael Curtiz. *Action Sequences Directed by* Cliff Lyons. *Produced by* George Sherman. *Screenplay by* James Edward Grant, Clair Huffaker. *Based on the Novel by* Paul I. Wellman. *Music*: Elmer Bernstein. *Orchestration*: Leo Shukin, Jack Hayes. *Dances Staged by* Hal Belfer. *Director of Photography*: William H. Clothier. *Film Editor*: Louis Loeffler. *Art Direction*: Jack Martin Smith, Alfred Ybarra. *Set Decorations*: Walter M. Scott, Robert Priestly. *Sound*: Alfred Bruzlin, Warren B. Delaplain. *Costumes Designed by* Marjorie Best. *Makeup by* Ben Nye. *Hairstyles by* Helen Turpin. *Assistant Director*: Jack R. Berne. Not Rated. Color by DeLuxe. CinemaScope (2.35:1). 107 minutes. Released in October 1961. Currently available on VHS videotape and laserdisc.

CAST: *Jake Cutter*, John Wayne; *Paul Regret*, Stuart Whitman; *Pilar Graile*, Ina Balin; *Graile*, Nehemiah Persoff; *Tully Crow*, Lee Marvin; *Amelung*, Michael Ansara; *Tobe*, Pat Wayne; *Major Henry*, Bruce Cabot; *Melinda Marshall*, Joan O'Brien; *Horseface*, Jack Elam; *Judge Thaddeus Jackson Breen*, Edgar Buchanan; *Ed McBain*, Guinn "Big Boy" Williams; *Gireaux*, Henry Daniell; *Estevan*, Richard Devon; *Comanchero*, Steve Baylor; *Bill*, John Dierkes; *Bub Schofield*, Roger Mobley; *Pa Schofield*, Bob Steele; *Spanish dancer*, Luisa Triana; *Josefina*, Iphigenie Castiglioni; *Bessie Marshall*, Aissa Wayne; *Iron Shirt*, George Lewis; *Duel Opponent*, Gregg Palmer; *Card Dealer*, Don Brodie.

After three years of starring on television in *M Squad*, Lee Marvin returned to the big screen in a supporting role in a John Wayne western. Despite his television success, Marvin still wasn't seen as a big box-office draw and still wasn't being offered leads, but the magnitude of his co-stars was certainly going up. Instead of shooting it out with Jeff Chandler or Ronald Reagan, he had held the screen against Spencer Tracy, Paul Newman and Montgomery Clift, and now he was duking it out with the Duke himself in the first of three films they made together from 1961 through 1963.

The Comancheros begins with suave New Orleans gambler Paul Regret (Stuart Whitman) forced to defend himself in a duel and becoming a wanted man in the process. On a steamboat some months later, a mysterious woman (Ina Balin) seduces Regret. When the steamboat docks, Texas Ranger Jake Cutter (John Wayne) wakes up Regret, handcuffs him, and leads the gambler off toward New Orleans for a proper trial and hanging. Along the way, Regret clobbers Cutter in the head with a shovel and escapes.

Tully Crow (Lee Marvin) displays his gun-handling ability (and fashion sense) to the man he believes is Ed McBain (John Wayne) in *The Comancheros*.

Cutter returns to the Rangers and is instructed to take the identity of Ed McBain (Henry Daniell), a trader caught taking a wagonload of rifles to the Comancheros, the white men aiding and supplying the Comanche raiding party. Cutter dons McBain's dusty stovepipe hat and travels to the arranged meeting place. There he meets a half-scalped wild man named Tully Crow (Lee Marvin), the Comancheros' contact man. Crow and Cutter size each other up while tearing up the town, drinking, singing and fighting.

The two men decide to join a card game, and the Ranger is surprised to find Paul Regret at the table. Cutter introduces himself as Ed McBain and play begins. McBain wins big and Tully Crow is not amused. He demands that play continue until he wins. McBain tries to exit without violence, but Crow draws on him and the Ranger kills him in self-defense. Then he re-arrests Regret. Cutter and Regret meet up with the Rangers at a grain ranch just as the Rangers are heading out on patrol.

After they leave, Comanches attack, accompanied by a group of white men. While Cutter and the ranchers hold off the attackers, Regret escapes again, but he brings back the Rangers and proves himself a fine shot. The Texas Rangers reward Regret for his actions by inducting him into their ranks, thereby voiding the price on his head. Together the two men venture into Comanche territory with a wagonload of guns to find the Comancheros.

Cutter and Regret contact the Comanches and are led to a valley where the Comancheros live. They are hung up in the sun to fry by Amelung (Michael Ansara), one of the Comanchero leaders. When the mysterious woman from the steamboat rides into the valley and sees the men, she orders them to be cut down and cared for immediately. She is Pilar Graile, daughter of the Comanchero founder. Graile (Nehemiah Persoff), now confined to a wheelchair, explains how his secret society operates by aiding the efforts of the Comanches, and offers Cutter and Regret a chance to join. A group of Comanches arrive and a celebration ensues while Cutter and Regret try to formulate a plan of escape. At dinner that night, Pilar announces to her father that she is leaving with Paul Regret and that he should leave as well. Cutter is revealed as a Texas Ranger, and he holds Graile hostage until dawn, when the group tries to escape. As they are sneaking out of the valley, Graile is killed, and the Comancheros give chase. Just as they close in, the Texas Rangers ride to the rescue and rout the criminals. After the skirmish, Regret says goodbye to the Rangers—with Cutter's blessing—and rides off with Pilar toward Mexico.

The Comancheros is a strange, uneven movie derived from an unusual novel by Paul I. Wellman. The novel follows Paul Regret's adventures as he travels from stylish gambler to abject poverty to forced membership in the Texas Rangers, learning along the way what should be important in his life. The movie shares the same basic plot, yet focuses more on Cutter and the Rangers (in the book, Cutter is named Tom Gatling), while changing some of the action. Most unusual is the fact that Lee Marvin's character, Tully Crow, is not in the original novel at all.

As an action-adventure, *The Comancheros* is fairly successful. The fish-out-of-water plot, with Cutter teaching Regret the ways of the West, works well, and the pairing of Wayne and Whitman as reluctant allies is memorable, particularly when Whitman belts Wayne in the head with a spade, then apologizes to his unconscious victim. The byplay between the two men is quite enjoyable. However, the movie's tone is wildly uneven, veering from broad comedy to life-and-death melodrama, with some romance and philosophy thrown into the mix.

One plot element that doesn't work well is the Comanchero society. The movie (and the book) present the Comancheros as the worst of criminals: white men profiting by providing warring Comanche warriors with guns, and even accompanying them on their murderous raids. But in the secret (!) valley, the Comancheros, who have evidently been operating for years, punish any theft or other crime between members by death. Honor among thieves, indeed. They are led by an old man in a wooden wheelchair who rules the society like a fatherly dictator. It is preposterous, but still entertaining.

Then there's the romance between Regret and the mysterious woman on the steamship who turns out to be the daughter of the founder of the Comancheros. Pilar's mystery originates from her character making absolutely no sense. She seduces Regret on the ship, just because. With the Comancheros, she seems at home, then does an abrupt turnaround when Regret arrives and betrays her father for the sake of rescuing Cutter and Regret. Even as her father is killed during their getaway, she shows no regret.

The Comancheros was the final film to be directed by Michael Curtiz, a veteran Hollywood director, born in Budapest, who had made some of the best films of the thirties and forties for Warner Brothers: *Captain Blood*, *The Adventures of Robin Hood*, *The Sea Hawk*, *Yankee Doodle Dandy*, *Casablanca*, etc. Because Curtiz's health was failing, the more rigorous action sequences were handled by Cliff Lyons, with John Wayne rumored to have also taken the directing reins from time to time.

For John Wayne, *The Comancheros* was part of a career turn which had begun with *Rio Bravo*, in which he leaned toward roles that allowed him to poke fun at his character's advancing age and some of the more familiar Wayne mannerisms. Over the next decade, films like *North to Alaska*, *Hatari!*, *Donovan's Reef*, *McLintock!*, *El Dorado* and *True Grit* were Wayne lite—easygoing made just for the fun of it. These, ultimately, were the more popular Wayne films, outnumbering and outgrossing such serious projects as *The Man Who Shot Liberty Valance* and *In Harm's Way*.

Though Wayne receives top billing, the main character is Paul Regret, and Stuart Whitman plays him with rugged charm. Whitman is convincing as the debonair gambler and generates much of the film's humor as he tries to adapt to Texas ways. 1961 was a

Tully Crow's (Lee Marvin) unusual appearance is due to a near-scalping.

banner year for Whitman; he not only starred in this film, but also in a small British production, titled *The Mark*, about a criminal recently released from prison trying to fit back into society, a performance for which Whitman received his only Oscar nomination.

Lee Marvin, as gun-runner Tully Crow, has a role that allows him to drink, sing, fight and raise hell, play poker, and die violently, all within a ten-minute period. His half-scalped appearance only makes his wild character more grotesque. It's an over-the-top performance, almost burlesque, designed to pop the movie into high gear and keep it moving. The role crosses into self-parody when, after drinking and fighting with Wayne, Marvin casually reminds him that, "I'm only as drunk as I wanna be, same as you."

Bosley Crowther summed up the movie's intent in the *New York Times*: "This new Western film, *The Comancheros*...is so studiously wild and woolly that it turns out to be good fun." On Wayne and Marvin, he wrote: "They play cut-throat poker in Sweet-water, where Mr. Wayne puts a couple of deadly slugs into a scalping-scarred, booze-sogged Lee Marvin, who gets so noisy he just has to be shot."

This is one of those roles—and movies—that just cannot be taken too seriously. Lee Marvin overacts because he can without hurting the film's half-serious tone; he's certainly not the only actor who does. When he's on-screen, Marvin is at least the Duke's equal, and often dominates him. Wayne lets him bully him for a while, then kills him. It was nothing new for a Lee Marvin character.

The Man Who Shot Liberty Valance (1962)

CREDITS: Paramount. *Directed by* John Ford. *Produced by* Willis Goldbeck. *Script by* James Warner Bellah, Willis Goldbeck. *Based on the Story by* Dorothy M. Johnson. *Music Scored by* Cyril J. Mockridge. *Conducted by* Irvin Talbot. *Director of Photography*: William H. Clothier. *Process Photography*: Farciot Edouart. *Edited by* Otho Lovering. *Art Direction by* Hal Pereira, Eddie Imazu. *Set Decorators*: Sam Comer, Darrell Silvera. *Sound Recording*: Philip Mitchell, Charles Grenzbach. *Costumes by* Edith Head. *Makeup Supervision*: Wally Westmore, S.M.A. *Hair Style Supervision*: Nellie Manley, C.H.S. *Assistant Director*: Wingate Smith. Not Rated. Black and White. Flat (1.33:1). 119 minutes. Released in April 1962. Currently available on VHS videotape and laserdisc.

CAST: *Ransom Stoddard*, James Stewart; *Tom Doniphon*, John Wayne; *Hallie*, Vera Miles; *Liberty Valance*, Lee Marvin; *Dutton Peabody*, Edmond O'Brien; *Link Appleyard*, Andy Devine; *Doc Willoughby*, Ken Murray; *Starbuckle*, John Carradine; *Nora Ericson*, Jeanette Nolan; *Peter Ericson*, John Qualen; *Jason Tully*, Willis Bouchey; *Maxwell Scott*, Carleton Young; *Pompey*, Woody Strode; *Amos Carruthers*, Denver Pyle; *Floyd*, Strother Martin; *Reese*, Lee Van Cleef; *Handy Strong*, Robert F. Simon; *Ben Carruthers*, O. Z. Whitehead; *Mayor Winder*, Paul Birch; *Hasbrouck*, Joseph Hoover.

The second of Lee Marvin's three consecutive films with John Wayne is the complete antithesis of the other two. While *The Comancheros* and *Donovan's Reef* are outdoor adventure sagas, colorful and brightly lit, swaggering and played with a wink and a smile, *The Man Who Shot Liberty Valance* is old-fashioned drama, photographed in black and white, mostly on Hollywood soundstages, with much of the action taking place at night. The film was not at all the usual John Ford product that had come to be anticipated. Yet, while the two other films have enjoyed modest reputations over the years, *The Man Who Shot Liberty Valance* has become, though somewhat slowly, acclaimed as an American classic.

Most of the film is flashback, set up by an opening sequence in which Senator Ransom Stoddard (James Stewart) and his wife Hallie (Vera Miles) return to Shinbone for the funeral of a man the local newspapermen have never heard of—Tom Doniphon. At their urging, Stoddard tells of the time, years before, when he first traveled to Shinbone by stagecoach.

Outside of town, the stage is held up by outlaws led by a vicious man with a silver-knobbed whip. When Stoddard objects, Liberty Valance (Lee Marvin) beats him with that whip and leaves him to die. Tom Doniphon (John Wayne) and his manservant Pompey (Woody Strode) find Stoddard and bring him into town where he is cared for by Tom's girl Hallie and a Swedish couple, the Ericsons (Jeanette Nolan, John Qualen), who run the town cafe. Stoddard explains that he is a lawyer and describes Valance to the town marshal, Link Appleyard (Andy Devine), a comic figure who is (rightly) afraid of Valance.

Stoddard stays with the Ericsons while he recuperates, earning his keep by washing dishes and waiting tables. One boisterous Saturday night, Liberty Valance stops in for dinner with his two saddle pals (Strother Martin, Lee Van Cleef). Valance laughs at the sight of Stoddard in an apron and trips him, sending Stoddard and the steak he's carrying sprawling. Doniphon steps forward and tells Valance to pick it up; it was *his* steak. Before the two men shoot it out, Stoddard picks up the steak and restores the peace.

Later, Stoddard teaches some of the townspeople how to read, using a newspaper article by editor Dutton Peabody (Edmond O'Brien) about the fight for statehood as a civics lesson (and outlining the benefits and protection of statehood). Class is interrupted by Doniphon, who announces that Valance is hiring guns for the cattlemen, who oppose statehood and want to keep the ranges open, and that Valance will be arriving in town soon. Hallie discovers that Stoddard has been practicing shooting and asks Doniphon to help him. Doniphon uses his shooting skill to humiliate Stoddard, but gains some respect for the tenderfoot when Stoddard slugs him in return.

Shinbone holds a town meeting to choose local delegates to go to the territorial convention where the statehood issue will be debated; Doniphon is nominated by Stoddard but refuses the nomination on personal grounds. Stoddard and Peabody are nominated as delegates, as is Liberty Valance, who has taught his pals the nominating procedures. By an overwhelming vote, Stoddard and Peabody are chosen. Valance publicly challenges Stoddard to a shootout that night and leaves. Doniphon offers Stoddard a way out, a quiet wagon ride out of town.

That night Valance visits Peabody in the newspaper office, beating the editor viciously and destroying the office in the process. Stoddard, still weighing Doniphon's offer, finds Peabody half dead. Calmly he retrieves the handgun which Peabody had loaned him and goes out into the street to face Valance.

Valance taunts Stoddard, frightening him with one shot, wounding him with another. Both men take aim at each other. Shots ring out and Valance falls, dead. In shock, Stoddard walks back to the Ericsons', where Hallie tends to him and professes her love for him. She turns around to find Doniphon watching bitterly. "I'll be around," he growls. Doniphon goes into a saloon and beats up Valance's two henchmen, who are trying to rouse the town into hanging Stoddard, then drinks heavily. When Pompey gets him home, he sets fire to the addition he had been building onto the house.

Some time later, Stoddard and Peabody arrive at Capitol City for the territorial convention. Peabody nominates Stoddard as a delegate to Washington, but the cattle-men's agent (John Carradine) refers to Stoddard as a murderer and a lawyer who takes the law into his own hands, causing Stoddard to walk out in self-loathing. Doniphon stops him and sets him straight: It was *he* who killed Valance that night, shooting him from the shadows across the street. Doniphon admits to the murder and states that he can live with it, before telling Stoddard to go back in and accept his nomination with a clear conscience. Stoddard does exactly that, and the film then returns to the present.

As Stoddard finishes his story, the newspaper editor tears up his notes and burns them. "You're not going to use the story?" asks Stoddard. "No," replies the editor. "When the legend becomes fact, print the legend." On the train back to Washington, the conductor confirms the Senator's travel arrangements and brags about the train's top speed of 25 m.p.h. "Nothing's too good for the man who shot Liberty Valance!" he exclaims.

The majority of westerns are content to entertain and teach a quick moral in sixty to ninety minutes of trail dust and six-gun action. John Ford, despite his well-known disregard for the label of "artist," was never content with just entertaining. He wanted his films to explore what it was like to live in other times in particular circumstances, and he wanted his characters to reveal essential truths about human nature. To his great credit, much of the time, Ford succeeded. He left behind a long list of excellent films, of which *The Man Who Shot Liberty Valance* is near the top, in terms of both quality and entertainment value. It is most certainly his last great film.

The Man Who Shot Liberty Valance is an atypical John Ford film in some ways, but its themes of the "civilization" of the West, the legacy of history, the use of a violent, unlawful act for the good of society, and the importance (and consequences) of freedom are purely Fordian. And while this is a darker vision of the West than Ford's followers were used to seeing, it still contains the Ford hallmarks of flamboyant, tempestuous characters, the importance of personal honor, and lots of robust humor.

Based on a story by noted western author Dorothy M. Johnson, the film spends most of its time and effort examining the "civilization" of Shinbone. The wild and woolly past is represented by Tom Doniphon and Liberty Valance; the promising, decent future is represented by Ranse Stoddard, and Hallie. Though Hallie loves Tom Doniphon for his strength and freedom, it becomes clear that she cherishes the more idealistic way of life that Ranse Stoddard offers, and that Doniphon eventually loses her not just to Stoddard, but to a more modern sensibility, one against which Doniphon is powerless.

Tom Doniphon and Liberty Valance are indeed two sides of the same coin. Ranse Stoddard notes the similarity early on, when Doniphon tells him that in the West, a man settles his own problems. "You're saying just exactly what Liberty Valance said!" Stoddard exclaims. The difference is that Doniphon exhibits some common decency and a conscience, while Valance is, at heart, a coward and has no scruples. Doniphon is respected in Shinbone, while Valance is feared. Doniphon himself states that, "Liberty Valance is the toughest man south of the Picket Wire [river]. Next to me." Later, to Stoddard he says, "I hate tricks, but that's what you're up against with Valance. He's almost as fast as I am."

The tragic irony, of course, is that in order to save Stoddard's life and eliminate Valance once and for all, Doniphon does stoop to a trick, hiding in the shadows and firing at the same time as Stoddard. Saving Stoddard's life causes him to lose Hallie for good, dashing all his hopes for happiness. Doniphon's act, done for all the right reasons, leads directly to his own disillusionment and heartbreak, gradually reducing his own importance until his eventual, obscure death. Yet, John Ford's perspective is that such sacrifice was, and is, necessary for the taming and civilization of a frontier; that the progress and betterment of a society requires such personal stands and confrontations. This realization is at the heart of all of Ford's greatest films and provides for them the heroic resonance with which they glow.

Along with his role as Ethan Edwards in Ford's *The Searchers*, this role is John Wayne's most complex and demanding—and least likable. In both films Wayne portrays selfish, strong-willed men forced into action by events outside their control but who are determined to control the outcome of their situations. As Edwards in *The Searchers*, Wayne must finally face his prejudice and hatred of the Comanche; as Doniphon, Wayne must make a conscious choice regarding Hallie and their future together and then face the consequences of that decision. These two roles prove conclusively that Wayne was not just a movie star but an *actor*, and a good one.

This film did provide John Wayne imitators with a favorite catch-phrase: "Pilgrim." Doniphon refers to Stoddard as "Pilgrim" throughout the movie, which is perfectly appropriate because Stoddard is indeed journeying into a strange land, one where he may not belong. One repeated complaint about the film is that both Wayne and James Stewart were too old for their parts. There is some truth to this, particularly regarding Stewart early on, but the film also benefits from the superstar stature of its stars, which boosts their characters' heroic and tragic qualities.

James Stewart is fine as idealistic Ranse Stoddard, transplanting his *Mr. Smith Goes to Washington* character to the Old West. Stoddard is just as naive and slow to catch on as Jefferson Smith had been, but *The Man Who Shot Liberty Valance* takes the character type much farther, continuing his story through maturity to show how he would live with the loss of his innocence. The humorous characters are Andy Devine's always-hungry sheriff, Link Appleyard, and Edmond O'Brien's loquacious newspaperman, Dutton Peabody, but they have effective scenes of drama as well, as does Woody Strode as Doniphon's faithful manservant, Pompey.

Almost always overlooked in these male-dominated tales is the wonderful work of Vera Miles. This hard-working actress appeared in several classic films, including *Psycho*, *The Wrong Man*, *The Searchers* and *The Man Who Shot Liberty Valance*, providing, in turn, both dramatic support and comic relief. Here she inspires Tom Doniphon to build an addition onto his house, and Ranse Stoddard to add teaching duties to his work as an attorney. Miles represents the future of the West, courted and finally won by the idealism and promise of democracy and progress. And she's as pretty as a cactus rose.

As Liberty Valance, Lee Marvin plays one of the most despicable roles of his career. His character may seem misnamed, but he really represents the abuse of liberty. Though Doniphon refers to Valance as tough, what he means is that Valance is fast with a gun. Because next to Tom Doniphon—or Ranse Stoddard for that matter—Liberty Valance is a

Liberty Valance (Lee Marvin), about to finish off Ranse Stoddard on the dusty streets of Shinbone, in *The Man Who Shot Liberty Valance*.

coward. He beats and tortures people, assisted by his two cohorts in crime, Floyd (Strother Martin) and Reese (Lee Van Cleef), because he is a sadist. But Valance won't face anyone (except tenderfoot Stoddard) without his men to back him up.

Liberty Valance is the culmination of all of Marvin's villainous roles, a man so cruel and violent that he seems almost unbelievable. But both he and Tom Doniphon are larger than life, and are opposite sides of the same coin. Valance *must* be supremely evil in order to threaten Tom Doniphon's goodness and righteousness in Ford's mythic version of the death of the West. Earlier in his career, Marvin had played villains with more subtlety and variety; here he is called on to swagger and leer with a feral intensity, to shout, bully and destroy with all possible viciousness. Marvin would later parody the look and some of the mannerisms of this role in *Cat Ballou*, for which he would win an Academy Award as Best Actor.

Interestingly, like *Citizen Kane* before it, *The Man Who Shot Liberty Valance* was not highly regarded upon its first release. Critics who were used to colorful widescreen sagas found the film starkly shot, curiously claustrophobic and melodramatic. It was years before a gradual re-evaluation took place and the film began to gain in stature. Today it is seen as an American classic, a permanent member in the pantheon of great western films, and though it isn't his final film, a fitting coda to John Ford's career.

Many westerns have explored the taming of the Old West and the death of the gunfighter. *The Man Who Shot Liberty Valance* encompasses these themes and more, expressing them with the passion and depth for which John Ford was renowned. It is a rich film, beautifully textured and nuanced, packed with colorful, engaging characters and filled with a deep appreciation of the struggle toward maturity. It is a high point in the careers of all who participated in its creation and a film of which they can and should be justifiably proud.

Donovan's Reef (1963)

CREDITS: Paramount. *Produced and Directed by* John Ford. *Screenplay by* Frank Nugent, James Edward Grant. *Story by* Edmund Beloin. *Music Scored by* Cyril Mockridge. *Conducted by* Irvin Talbot. *Orchestration*: Leo Shuken, Jack Hayes. *Director of Photography*: William H. Clothier. *Edited by* Otho Lovering. *Art Direction*: Hal Pereira, Eddie Imazu. *Set Decoration*: Sam Comer, Darrell Silvera. *Sound Recording by* Hugo Grenzbach, Charles Grenzbach. *Costumes*: Edith Head. *Makeup Supervision*: Wally Westmore, S.M.A. *Hair Style Supervision*: Nellie Manley, C.M.S. *Assistant Director*: Wingate Smith. *Special Photographic Effects*: Paul K. Lerpae, A.S.C. *Process Photography*: Farciot Edouart, A.S.C. Not Rated. Technicolor. *Technicolor Color Consultant*: Richard Mueller. Flat (1.33:1). 109 minutes. Released in July 1963. Currently available on VHS videotape. Previously available on laserdisc.

CAST: *Michael "Guns" Donovan*, John Wayne; *Aloysius "Boats" Gilhooley*, Lee Marvin; *Amelia Sarah Dedham*, Elizabeth Allen; *Dr. William Dedham*, Jack Warden; *Marquis Andre de Laage*, Cesar Romero; *Australian Naval Officer*, Dick Foran; *Miss Lafleur*, Dorothy Lamour; *Father Cluzeot*, Marcel Dalio; *Sergeant Menkowicz*, Mike Mazurki; *Leilani Dedham*, Jacqueline Malouf; *Sally Dedham*, Cherylene Lee; *Luki Dedham*, Tim Stafford; *Francis X. O'Brien*, Edgar Buchanan; *Mister Eu*, Jon Fong; *Sister Gabrielle*, Carmen Estrabeau; *Sister Matthew*, Yvonne Peattie; *James*, Ralph Volkie; *Captain Martin*, Frank Baker; *Servants*, June Y. Kim, Midori; *Naval Officer*, Ron Nyman; *Naval Lieutenant*, Patrick Wayne; *Festus*, Chuck Roberson; *Grand Uncle Sedley Atterbury*, Charles Seel; *Officer*, Cliff Lyons; *Mate*, Duke Green; *Lawyer*, King Lockwood; *Members of Family Counsel*, Mae Marsh, Sara Taft, Carl M. Leviness, Fred Jones, Scott Seaton, Major Sam Harris; *Native Girl at Pool*, Aissa Wayne.

Donovan's Reef is a film which defies categorization. It doesn't fit at all comfortably into John Ford's career path, especially after the dark drama of *The Man Who Shot Liberty Valance*. It is a typical example of South Pacific island comedy, filled with slapstick brawls and oafish behavior, and which hammers home its obvious moral points. For years, scholars and fans of John Ford's films have debated the relative values of *Donovan's Reef*, and today the debate continues.

The film takes place on the imaginary Hawaiian island of Haleakaloa. "Boats" Gilhooley (Lee Marvin) arrives on the island on December 7th, just in time for his annual joint birthday brawl with "Guns" Donovan (John Wayne). They beat up each other in Donovan's Reef, the local bar owned and run by Donovan. "Doc" Dedham (Jack Warden) is the third man in the trio of soldiers who fought on the island in World War II and remained there afterward, building a new life on the native soil. Their idyllic life is interrupted by the arrival of Dedham's grown daughter, Amelia (Elizabeth Allen), whom he has never seen.

Doc is on a medical trip to other islands when Amelia arrives from Boston, and his well-meaning friends decide to conceal Doc's current family—two daughters and a younger son—from Amelia, not knowing how she

"Guns" Donovan (John Wayne) and "Boats" Gilhooley (Lee Marvin) display the results of their annual birthday brawl in *Donovan's Reef*.

would react to them. Donovan adopts them as his own for the duration of Amelia's visit. Amelia makes a splash upon her arrival, instantly disliking Donovan and his friends. Gradually, she warms up to Donovan and his family, whom she immediately adores, and learns how to appreciate the slower pace of island living. Doc returns and spends time with his "new" eldest daughter, getting to know her and allowing her to get to know him.

Amelia gradually realizes that Donovan's three kids are not his at all, and when they are revealed to be Doc's, she is not surprised. She is stunned to find, however, that the oldest, Leilani (Jacqueline Malouf), is a princess (Doc had married Manulani, a Polynesian princess who died giving birth to their third child). Amelia gladly accepts the youngsters as her own brothers and sisters, then returns to Donovan and professes her love for him as he spanks her and imparts his bar to Gilhooley.

South Pacific island films are usually presented as "holidays"—they take viewers to exotic locales with beautiful native people; they depict a more leisurely, idyllic way of life; and they promote acceptance of other cultures and philosophies. *Donovan's Reef* certainly meets these parameters and adds a few more: it compares Boston society, unfavorably, to life in the island paradise; it demands attention to the welfare and needs of children; it shows the folly of those people who would bend the truth; and it mounts an entertaining battle of the sexes.

John Ford's film takes its 109 minutes to make and reinforce those points, some of which are so obvious that they simply do not need to be made in the first place. Ford's primary message seems to be one of acceptance. Leilani is crushed when she is asked to pose as Donovan's child, saying, "I understand. It is because I am not white." The familial coverup is ridiculous to start with and strains credulity every additional minute it lasts. When Amelia accepts her new sister at the end of the film, it is because she loves Leilani for who she is (though the fact that she is a true princess probably helps). This message is also undercut by the film's many jokes at the expense of its Oriental population, which seem cruel and out of place, though at least one of them is quite funny. There is a beauty and effectiveness in subtlety. Ford was able to use this to his advantage in many of his greatest films; unfortunately, it is absent here.

Donovan's Reef is a wildly uneven comedy with silly, superficial characters. It is a major disappointment from Ford, who directed the film, produced it himself, and wrote the script on the fly while filming progressed. The comedy ranges from slapstick to more slapstick, although there are a few truly funny moments which somehow managed to sneak into the finished product. However, performers Dorothy Lamour and Dick Foran waste their time and talent getting thrown into pools and having beer bottles smashed over their heads, respectively.

The film can be seen as a remake of Howard Hawks' *Hatari!*, made one year earlier. Ernest Callenbach, in *Film Quarterly*, pointed out that *Donovan's Reef* does contain the same basic structure as *Hatari!*, with John Wayne (aided by a comic friend) introducing a city girl to a life in natural surroundings and, "After a terminal crisis involving a good deal of dashing about in a jeep, he catches her and marries her." If so, *Hatari!* is clearly the superior picture because it is genuinely entertaining and funny and does not strain to force its moral platitudes upon the audience as does *Donovan's Reef*.

John Wayne is very physical in this film, driving his jeep at high speeds around the island and actually sprinting from place to place in several scenes. It is hard to believe that within two years he would have one lung removed in a major cancer operation. Wayne plays his role broadly, with little character definition, but the film doesn't suffer much from that decision. With John Wayne, in many films (including this one), what one sees is what one gets. Jack Warden does better with his role, though his character seems far too pious and serious to have remained friends for so long with Donovan and Gilhooley.

Elizabeth Allen is the surprise performer in the film. She does fit the stereotype of the staid Boston executive determined to eliminate her unknown father's interest from the shipping business she runs. But once she falls into the water upon her arrival at Haleakaloa, Amelia becomes surprisingly human. The water skiing sequence, which ends in Amelia challenging Donovan to a swimming race, is pivotal in demonstrating that Amelia is a real woman (intelligent, alluring, with a sense of humor and unafraid of a challenge) and a good match for Donovan. Allen is the only major cast member who truly gives a performance, and it is quite good.

Lee Marvin is right for his role as Gilhooley, but apart from the bout with Wayne at the beginning of the movie, he is totally wasted. Gilhooley is clearly a spectator in the affairs of the island and the chicanery involving Doc Dedham's children. It seems that he is only around to drink and fight people in the bar. Marvin is billed second in the credits, but his relative importance to the film is much lower. Some critics found Marvin's buffoonery overplayed, but that criticism can apply to most of the cast. In this case, Marvin is criminally underused. He doesn't have enough to work with here to create a character, and, apart from the opening fight with Wayne, he doesn't bother to try.

Donovan's Reef remains an enigma. The cast seems to have enjoyed their time in the South Pacific, and some of that enthusiasm and vitality is apparent in the film. But the movie itself is slapdash and far below the standards of quality usually applied to a Ford film. Perhaps for Ford, this was a "vacation" from his serious filmmaking. If so, audiences should be very glad that Ford only took a few "vacations" during his career.

The Killers (1964)
(aka *Ernest Hemingway's the Killers*)

CREDITS: Revue. *Distributed by* Universal. *Produced and Directed by* Donald Siegel. *Screenplay by* Gene L. Coon. (*Based on the story by* Ernest Hemingway). *Music Score*: Johnny (John) Williams. (*Opening Credit music taken from* "Touch of Evil," *by* Henry Mancini). *Song* "Too Little Time" *by* Henry Mancini, Don Raye; *sung by* Nancy Wilson. *Musical Supervision*: Stanley Wilson. *Director of Photography*: Richard L. Rawlings. *Film Editor*: Richard Belding. *Art Directors*: Frank Arrigo, George Chan. *Set Decorations*: John McCarthy, James S. Redd. *Sound*: David H. Moriarty. *Costumes by* Helen Colvig. *Make-Up*: Bud Westmore. *Hair Stylist*: Larry Germain. *Technical Advisor*: Hall Brock. *Dialogue Coach*: Scott Hale. *Editorial Department Head*: David J. O'Connell. *Assistant Director*: Milton Feldman. Not Rated. Eastmancolor. Flat (1.33:1). 93 minutes. Released in July 1964. Currently available on VHS videotape.

CAST: *Charlie Strom*, Lee Marvin; *Sheila Farr*, Angie Dickinson; *Johnny North*, John Cassavetes; *Jack Browning*, Ronald Reagan; *Lee*, Clu Gulager; *Earl Sylvester*, Claude Akins; *Mickey*, Norman Fell; *Miss Watson*, Virginia Christine; *Mail Truck Driver*, Don Haggerty; *George*, Robert Phillips; *Receptionist*, Kathleen O'Malley; *Gym Assistant*, Ted Jacques; *Mail Truck Guard*, Irvin Mosley; *Salesman*, Jimmy Joyce; *Maitre D'*, Davis Roberts; *Race Marshal*, Hall Brock; *Elderly Man*, Burt Mustin; *Instructor*, Peter Hobbs; *Porter*, John Copage; *Steward*, Tyler McVey; *Postal Clerk*, Seymour Cassel; *Hotel Clerk*, Scott Hale.

The Killers, which is loosely based on the famous Ernest Hemingway short story, was originally planned to be the first made-for-television movie. *Johnny North*, its original title, was supposed to be the premiere offering of an NBC program titled *Project 120*, an anthology of television movies. The best of these would also be distributed to theaters through MCA (Universal). Once the NBC brass saw *Johnny North*, however, they deemed it too violent for television, renamed it *The Killers*, and sent it straight to theatrical release. They also canceled the *Project 120* concept.

Like the original short story, *The Killers* focuses on the activities of two hit men. Charlie (Lee Marvin) and Lee (Clu Gulager) find former race driver Johnny North (John Cassavetes) teaching at a school for the blind. Johnny puts up no resistance, refusing to run, and dies passively. Charlie can't understand why a man would accept his own death and determines to find out why Johnny did. The two hit men track down people from Johnny's past (Claude Akins, Norman Fell), who, under heavy persuasion, indicate that Johnny was involved in a million-dollar holdup a few years previously.

The Killers

The trail of the missing money leads to Jack Browning (Ronald Reagan), the crime boss who engineered the holdup, and to Sheila Farr (Angie Dickinson), the woman with whom Johnny had fallen deeply in love, but who was also Jack Browning's girl. Charlie and Lee scare the story out of Sheila that Jack and she had double-crossed Johnny after the robbery and tried to kill him then. Charlie then understands and tells Sheila why Johnny had not tried to run. "The only man who's not afraid to die is the one who is already dead. You killed him four years ago."

Charlie and Lee realize that Jack Browning had lied to them, so they decide to visit him and keep the robbery loot for themselves. Jack ambushes them, killing Lee and wounding Charlie. Bleeding profusely, Charlie finds Jack and Sheila at Jack's house getting ready to leave town with the money. He coldly shoots Jack in the belly and then shoots Sheila as she tries to proclaim her innocence in the matter. Charlie, with the briefcase full of money, makes it as far as the front lawn before collapsing for the final time.

The Killers is a very uneven movie. The sections with Charlie and Lee tracking down Johnny North's past and pressuring the other characters to talk is stylishly done, with a real sense of menace. Occasional shots, such as the titled angle of the two hit men walking down a hallway in the school of the blind or, late in the film, the shot of Charlie on the floor, pointing his absurdly long gun with its silencer past the camera at Jack and Sheila, add to the odd ambiance of the film and its surreal quality of life-and-death bargaining. In addition, the mail truck robbery sequence works pretty well, partly because it is never fully explained beforehand.

The flashback sequences focusing on Johnny North's auto racing and his romantic pursuit of Sheila are far less effective. Far too much time is spent at one particular race, where Johnny North's racing career ends in a spectacular crash. This sequence was filmed

Charlie Strom (Lee Marvin) takes aim at his final target in *The Killers*.

at an actual race where a real racer wiped out and walked away. That determined which car Johnny would be seen driving in the early scenes. Unrealistic process photography then adds Johnny to the race in close-ups. The same poor blue-screen process is used in another sequence where Johnny and Sheila ride go-carts. As for the romance, watching two characters fall in love can be magical and enchanting—or tedious and boring. Here Angie Dickinson and John Cassavetes try too hard to make magic without enough of a script to sustain motivation, and the effect is numbing.

Director Don Siegel was in the running to direct the first version of the story back in 1946, but Warner Brothers refused to lend him out for the assignment. Eighteen years later Siegel got a second chance, agreeing to the project only when it was decided that the new version wouldn't be a copy of the first one in any way. As producer as well as director, Siegel was instrumental in the casting and writing of the film. It was he who, at the request of Universal head Lew Wasserman, finally secured Ronald Reagan for the role of crime kingpin Jack Browning.

Today *The Killers* is mainly known for being Ronald Reagan's final film, and the first one in which he ever played a real villain. Reagan was changing the focus of his life from film to politics and wasn't very interested in acting anymore, much less playing a gangster. He was prevailed upon by former agent Wasserman, then Don Siegel, and finally relented, though he often stated afterward that he wished he hadn't taken the role. Reagan garnered generally good reviews for his performance and was well paid, but he never liked the idea of the public seeing him as a murderous crime czar. The film certainly didn't hurt his political ambitions; just two years after its release he was elected Governor of California.

John Cassavetes took the role for the money (to finance his own filmmaking efforts), but had to be taught how to drive properly so it would look real on camera. He fits the role of race driver Johnny North well, and the film helped propel him to bigger and better projects, including another with Lee Marvin, *The Dirty Dozen*. Angie Dickinson also fits her role well, though she isn't as convincing in her double-crossing scenes as she should be. Also strong in smaller roles are Claude Akins and Norman Fell.

Don Siegel made sure that his two hit men, Charlie (Lee Marvin) and Lee (Clu Gulager), were poles apart in terms of character motivation and performance. Where Charlie is professionally calm and determined, Lee is impulsive, impudent and probably sadistic. Charlie is also an intellectual, wanting to know why someone would not run away from certain death. Lee doesn't care, but the money interests him. Together, the two men make an imposing, deadly team, for they get along well and use their differences to their mutual benefit.

Clu Gulager gives a scene-stealing, chomping-at-the-bit performance that at times distracts from the action but most often propels it forward. His high-level energy works in the film's favor, making Lee the unpredictable man the script intended. When he slugs Angie Dickinson, it does truly shock. Lee Marvin is just as formidable as the cobra-like Charlie, though with a much more measured personality. Marvin's interpretation of Charlie most closely fits with Ernest Hemingway's original vision. Marvin gets a chance to shine near the end of the film, once Charlie is shot. His final line, spoken to Sheila just before he shoots her, "Lady, I just haven't got the time," has become legendary.

Critics were fairly divided on the film's merits, though nearly all compared it rather unfavorably to the 1946 version with Burt Lancaster. Over time the film has gained appreciation for its realistic brutality and stylistic touches, much in the same way that John Boorman's film *Point Blank*, (also with Marvin) has, though to a far lesser degree.

On a more trivial note, though Johnny (later to become John) Williams composed the film's music score, the music behind the opening credit sequence is actually taken from two separate cuts in *Touch of Evil*, composed by Henry Mancini, also for Universal. Evidently Mancini's music must have been just right to set the movie's murderous tone.

The Killers gave Lee Marvin his first true solo starring role. It shouldn't be forgotten that it was intended to be a made-for-television movie, but it was a starring role nonetheless. Lee Marvin had finally, with the help of *M Squad*, been given the chance to make or break a film on his own, with his name at the top of the credits. It was Marvin's thirty-fifth film. And in it, he gave a strong, lethal, professional performance which proved to Hollywood and to audiences that he was ready for better roles and ready to deliver more action when he obtained them.

Cat Ballou (1965)

CREDITS: Columbia. *Directed by* Elliot Silverstein. *Produced by* Harold Hecht. *Associate Producer*: Mitch Lindemann. *Screenplay by* Walter Newman, Frank R. Pierson. *Based on a Novel by* Roy Chanslor. *Music by* (Frank) DeVol. *Songs by* Mack David, Jerry Livingston. *Director of Photography*: Jack Marta. *Film Editor*: Charles Nelson, A.C.E. *Art Director*: Malcolm Brown. *Set Decorator*: Richard Mansfield. *Sound*: Earl Snyder. *Miss Fonda's Gowns Designed by* Bill Thomas. *Make Up Supervisor*: Ben Lane, S.M.A. *Hair Styles by* Virginia Jones, C.M.S. *Second Unit Director*: Yakima Canutt. *Assistant Directors*: Lee Lukather, Ray Gosnell. *Choreographer*: Miriam Nelson. *Scene Supervisor*: Charles J. Rice. Not Rated. Eastman Color. Flat (1.33:1). 97 minutes. Released in May 1965. Currently available on VHS videotape and laserdisc.

CAST: *Catherine "Cat" Ballou*, Jane Fonda; *Kid Shelleen / Tim Strawn*, Lee Marvin; *Clay Boone*, Michael Callan; *Jed*, Dwayne Hickman; *Singer "The Sunrise Kid,"* Nat King Cole; *Singer "Professor Sam DeShaies,"* Stubby Kaye; *Jackson Two-Bears*, Tom Nardini; *Frankie Ballou*, John Marley; *Sir Harry Percival*, Reginald Denny; *Sheriff Cardigan*, Jay C. Flippen; *Butch Cassidy*, Arthur Hunnicutt; *Sheriff Maledon*, Bruce Cabot; *Accuser*, Burt Mustin; *Train Messenger*, Paul Gilbert; *Klem*, Robert Phillips; *James*, Charles Wagenheim; *Homer*, Duke Hobbie; *Hedda*, Ayllene Gibbons; *Train Engineer*, Everett L. Rohrer; *Train Conductor*, Harry Harvey, Sr.; *Honey Girl*, Hallene Hill; *Mabel Bentley*, Gail Bonney; *Frenchie*, Joseph Hamilton; *Singing Tart*, Dorothy Claire; *Hardcase*, Charles Horvath; *Armed Guard*, Chuck Roberson; *Gunslinger*, Ted White; *Valet*, Erik Sorenson; *Train Fireman*, Ivan L. Middleton; *Mrs. Parker*, Carol Veazie; *Bit Part*, Nick Cravat.

After his starring role in *The Killers*, Lee Marvin accepted a co-starring part with Jane Fonda in this western parody, in a role originally offered to Kirk Douglas. It was one of the smartest moves Marvin ever made because it reminded audiences that he could handle comedy as well as a pair of guns. To everyone's surprise, *Cat Ballou* was a huge success, bolstering the careers of both Fonda and Marvin, and resulting in Marvin's only Academy Award nomination—and win.

Catherine Ballou (Jane Fonda) is a mild-mannered young woman in Wolf City, Wyoming in 1894 who is waiting to be hanged. She is introduced by two singers (Nat King Cole and Stubby Kaye, acting as the film's Greek chorus), who sing "The Ballad of Cat Ballou," telling her story in flashback. Cat is traveling back to her father's ranch in Wyoming to become a local school teacher. On the train ride home, she unwittingly aids Jed (Dwayne Hickman) in rescuing his nephew Clay Boone (Michael Callan) from the law, winning Clay's affection by doing so.

When she arrives home, Cat is horrified to find the ranch run down and without cattle. Her father Frankie (John Marley) won't explain, but his one ranch hand, Jackson Two-Bears (Tom Nardini), tells Cat that a city conglomerate wants the ranch for its water rights and has been applying steady pressure on Frankie to sell. Cat is startled by Tim Strawn (Lee Marvin), a black-clad, silver-nosed man, prowling about the ranch, whom Frankie warns away. Jackson suggests that Cat hire a gunfighter, so she writes to legendary Kid Shelleen.

At a local dance, Cat is twirled around by her father and Jackson, then Clay and Jed, who accompany the Ballous home after an inevitable—and memorably funny—fight breaks out. Clay admits his basic cowardice but agrees to stay and help Cat protect her father. Kid Shelleen (Lee Marvin) arrives and proves that he can't even hit a barn door when sober. After a few drinks, however, Shelleen is a crack shot, full of bravado—until he hears about Strawn. The following day, surrounded by Clay, Jed and Jackson (while Shelleen sleeps it off), Frankie Ballou is shot down by

Tim Strawn, who is given an alibi by Wolf City's crooked sheriff (Jay C. Flippen). Cat tries to shoot Strawn but is stopped by her friends.

The Wolf City Development Corp. takes over the ranch, forcing Cat to relocate to Hole-In-The-Wall, the legendary hiding place of Wyoming outlaws. Cat decides to rob a payroll train, using one of Kid Shelleen's published memoirs as a plan. The robbery goes well and nets the group some $50,000. Clay professes his love for Cat and suggests that they go to St. Louis with the money, but she refuses. Tim Strawn appears and warns Cat to return the money, or else. Kid Shelleen, happy and confident because of the successful train robbery, begins preparations to face Strawn. With Jackson's help, Shelleen limbers up, practices his shooting, bathes and dresses for the occasion in a beautiful black dueling outfit. Shelleen finds Strawn in the town brothel, and the two men shoot it out.

Kid Shelleen returns, gleeful, to Hole-In-The-Wall and tells the rest of the gang how he was able to kill his evil brother. Instead of facing the resulting posse that is sure to hunt them down, Cat pays a visit to Sir Harry Percival (Reginald Denny) as a hooker named Trixie. Cat attempts to force him to sign a confession admitting to her father's murder, but Sir Harry refuses and is killed trying to take away her gun. Back in the present, Cat faces her hanging with head held high. She is rescued at the last possible moment by Jed, Clay and Jackson, who help her escape while Kid Shelleen delays the posse. Cat Ballou and her gang happily ride off into the sunset.

Cat Ballou is a western parody in the broadest sense. The film takes various western

Tim Strawn (Lee Marvin) and Kid Shelleen (Lee Marvin) face each other (in a trick photograph—note the building) in *Cat Ballou*.

stereotypes (the schoolmarm, the gunfighter, the faithful Indian sidekick) and joyously reconstructs them. Likewise, it toys with familiar conventions (the social dance, the barroom brawl, the posse chase, the train robbery), turning them inside out, looking for laughs by reversing their usual polarity. Even when played with mock seriousness, such as Kid Shelleen's elaborate preparations for battle, the deliberateness and over-emphasis of Shelleen's movements create a mood of giddy anticipation. The comedy contained within *Cat Ballou* is somewhat uneven, but the film deserves high marks for its ambitions, as well as its high rate of success.

The centerpiece of the film is Jane Fonda's relatively straight portrayal of Cat, which gives the film its emotional center and allows the rest of the cast to cavort. Except for some reaction shots and double takes, Fonda's seriousness in the title role provides the natural, realistic foundation for the film's comedic elements to play against. Therefore, the mugging of Michael Callan, deadpan witticisms of Tom Nardini and expansive body language of Lee Marvin seem even funnier. Fonda is completely winning in the role and beguiling to watch. She glows with star quality; this was the first film to truly tap it.

The warmest character in the film is Jackson Two-Bears, the Indian ranch hand who becomes Cat's best friend and confidant. Jackson has seen his share of injustice but reacts to each new setback with cynical wisdom and an upbeat sense of humor. Jackson's feelings for Cat are obvious but remain unrequited; it is to Tom Nardini's credit that this does not depress his character. Jackson becomes Kid Shelleen's personal valet, doling out Shelleen's rations of drink and helping to condition and dress the gunfighter, and he also has some of the film's funniest lines. The funniest sight gag in the film also belongs to Nardini when, during the fight at the dance, Jackson grabs a man by the hair—and the man's toupee comes off in his hands! Jackson is startled, then gives out an Indian whoop and throws it behind him to two women, who think it's a scalp and promptly faint.

While some reviewers didn't like the idea of Nat King Cole and Stubby Kaye as balladeers narrating the story from time to time with song, they keep the film moving along, and their primary song, "The Ballad of Cat Ballou," is eminently hummable. Not nearly as impressive are Michael Callan, Dwayne Hickman and John Marley. Callan is grating as Cat's lust-filled love interest, and his performance is not as finely honed as that of his co-stars. In his brief role, Hickman has little to do. John Marley's role is also small and he plays it one-dimensionally, in a loud voice.

Lee Marvin, for the first and only time in his film career, plays two roles: drunken gunfighter Kid Shelleen and silver-nosed gunfighter Tim Strawn. As Strawn, whose nose was bitten off in a fight, Marvin is wasted—it's a nothing part, requiring only a sense of menace and a silver nose guard. Kid Shelleen, however, is another matter. With a curly gray wig and dirty wardrobe, Marvin embodies the over-the-hill legend, employing his expert body language to convey the lack of motor skills Shelleen exhibits when fully soused. The real beauty of Marvin's performance comes as the film moves on, taking Kid Shelleen from his original drunken state to an almost childlike sense of wonder ("My plan?" he keeps asking), to the seriousness of a gunfighter facing death and back again to a drunken stupor. Marvin gives the role his all, bypassing subtlety in the name of comedy, dropping his pants, losing his balance, barking his dialogue and crossing his eyes for whatever laughs he can get. Marvin's performance is indeed nuanced, providing glimpses of Shelleen's true temperament and character beneath the mugging, but Shelleen is a role requiring an over-the-top sensibility, and Marvin doesn't back away from making himself look foolish when it is called for. Shelleen can also be seen as a spoof of Marvin's own larger-than-life role of Liberty Valance, filmed just three years earlier. In both films, he borders on the absurd, walking the fine line between outrageousness and ridiculousness. Marvin's is a good performance, but Oscar caliber?

Yes, according to critic Judith Crist. "Lee Marvin—who runs off with the picture and, if there is any justice in the contemporary Far West, an Oscar in his dual role..." *Newsweek* remarked, "But it is Marvin, the wooziest gun in the West, around whom director Elliot Silverstein and producer Harold Hecht have fashioned this splendid film, and every time he hitches up his belt, audiences will hold their sides laughing. He may be a peculiar top gun, but he is natural and assured as the top banana of the old frontier."

Even critics who didn't find the film very funny found Marvin's performance worth writing about. *Time* commented, "What's best about it [the film] is probably Lee Marvin. Dressed in snaky black, with a silver schnozz tied on where his nose used to be before 'it got bit off in a fight,' Marvin soberly parodies several hundred western badmen of yore, then surpasses himself as the dime-novel hero, Kid Shelleen." *Newsweek* reported that producer Harold Hecht was planning to make a sequel to *Cat Ballou* entitled *Kid Shelleen* and starring Lee Marvin—something which never came to pass. Six years later, ABC produced a television pilot based on the film starring Forrest Tucker and Jack Elam. It aired on September 5, 1971 and, like most other pilots based on popular films, promptly vanished into obscurity.

Newsweek also noted that, "There is some chatter around Hollywood about a possible Oscar for Lee Marvin next year." Marvin's chances for an Oscar were immensely improved by his second film role of the year, in *Ship of Fools*. This dramatic film provided a point-counterpoint comparison of Marvin's comedic and dramatic skills and ensured that Marvin would be remembered when award time came.

One other cast member won an award for his performance in *Cat Ballou*: Smoky, Kid Shelleen's gray horse. Smoky was honored with a Craven award for his acting—particularly the scene near the film's climax in which he, with front legs crossed, and Marvin are leaning against a brick building, looking hung over. That image is evidently a spoof of James Earle Fraser's famous statue of the tired Indian entitled "The End of the Trail," and has become the movie's most indelible image.

In January of 1966, the Academy Award nominations for 1965 were announced, and *Cat Ballou* received five nods: Best Screenplay (Based on Material from Another Medium), Best Song ("The Ballad of Cat Ballou"), Best Scoring of Music (Adaptation or Treatment), Best Film Editing—and Best Actor (Lee Marvin). Marvin's colleagues who were also nominated were Richard Burton for *The Spy Who Came In from the Cold*, Laurence Olivier for *Othello*, Rod Steiger for *The Pawnbroker* and Oskar Werner for *Ship of Fools*. Burton, who had received three previous nominations but had not won, seemed to be the favorite, while Steiger seemed to be the most deserving.

On the big night, April 18, 1966, it was neither Burton nor Steiger who accepted the Best Actor Academy Award. Nor was it Olivier or Werner. Lee Marvin, astonished, strode forward to the enthusiastic applause of his peers and received a little golden statue that represented respect and gratitude for his years of professionalism. There was little doubt that the Oscar was one of the Academy's infrequent "lifetime achievement" awards, given to somebody for their body of work rather than for one single performance. Marvin, still stunned that he had actually won, picked up the statue and said, "I think half of this belongs to a horse somewhere out in the Valley," making Smoky proud, though the horse never did get his half of the award.

The Academy Award was not the only honor bestowed upon Lee Marvin's dual-role performance. Marvin was chosen as Best Actor by the National Board of Review, won the Golden Globe for Best Actor—Musical/Comedy, won the British Academy Award for Best Actor, and was chosen Best Actor of the Berlin Film Festival. At the end of the decade, the Los Angeles Times conducted a survey of film favorites, and Lee Marvin's role in *Cat Ballou* was chosen by its readers as their favorite comedic performance of the 1960s.

Cat Ballou had not been a dream project for Marvin. Elliot Silverstein was the twenty-fifth director offered the picture, and Kirk Douglas (to his regret) had turned down the dual roles before they had been offered to

102 Cat Ballou

The classic image from *Cat Ballou*: Kid Shelleen (Lee Marvin) and his horse (Smoky), both seemingly soused.

Marvin. It had been a fast shoot with a lot of pressure from Columbia executives, who second-guessed many of Silverstein's choices, including the casting of Marvin. Jane Fonda remembers that, "I did not get to know Lee Marvin well. But there was one thing about Lee that really impressed and touched me at the young age I was when I made *Cat Ballou*. Being a young woman without much self esteem, I was easy to take advantage of. The producers had us working very, very long hours on a very low budget. One day Lee Marvin came to me and said, 'Look, Jane, we're the stars of this show. If we let them take advantage of us, they are also taking advantage of all the crew that are working on this film. We're the ones that have to stand up and say no, not just for the sake of ourselves, but for all the other folks working on this movie.' I think that speaks reams about the kind of person Lee Marvin was."

A true professional, Lee Marvin worked

Kid Shelleen (Lee Marvin) tries to hit the proverbial barn door—and misses—while watched by Jed (Dwayne Hickman), Jackson (Tom Nardini), Clay (Michael Callan), and Catherine and Frankie Ballou (Jane Fonda, John Marley).

hard on the set, whether behind or in front of the cameras. Legend has it that it took Marvin eight takes to shoot the scene where he can't hit the broad side of a barn. He played the first seven for comedy before going for poignancy in the eighth—and final—take. Once that take was printed, Marvin knew how to play Shelleen, and he went on to win Hollywood's highest accolades for his performance. The popular success of *Cat Ballou*, and the Oscar which Marvin won for his role(s) in the film, directly led to Marvin's greatest successes over the next few years. Marvin had finally been "discovered"—as a talented actor and as a box office draw—and from here on, he could—and did—write his own ticket.

Ship of Fools (1965)

CREDITS: Columbia. *Produced and Directed by* Stanley Kramer. *Screenplay by* Abby Mann. *Based upon the Novel by* Katherine Anne Porter. *Music by* Ernest Gold. *Songs by* Ernest Gold (music) and Jack Lloyd (lyrics). *Music Editor*: Maury Winetrobe. *Director of Photography*: Ernest Laszlo, A.S.C. *Film Editor*: Robert C. Jones. *Production Designer*: Robert Clatworthy. *Set Decorator*: Joseph Kish. *Sound*: James Z. Flaster. *Sound Effects*: James Richard. *Sound Supervisor*: Charles J. Rice. *Re-recorded by* Clem Portman. *Special Photographic Effects*: Albert Whitlock. *Process Photography*: Farciot Edouart, A.S.C. *Special Effects*: John Burke. *Costume Design by* Bill Thomas. *Costume Supervision*: Joe King. *Miss Leigh's Clothes by* Jean Louis. *Makeup Supervision by* Ben Lane, S.M.A. *Hair Styles by* Virginia Jones, C.M.S. *Production Supervision*: Ivan Volkman. *Construction Coordinator*: Bud Pine. *Camera Operator*: Richard Johnson. *Property Master*: Ernest Graber. *Company Grip*: Marty Kaschuk. *Chief Electrician*: Seldon White. *Script Supervisor*: Marshall Schlom. *Assistant Director*: John Veitch. Not Rated. Black and White. Flat (1.33:1). 148 minutes. Released in September 1965. Currently available on VHS videotape. Previously available on laserdisc.

CAST: *Mary Treadwell*, Vivien Leigh; *La Condesa*, Simone Signoret; *Rieber*, Jose Ferrer;

Bill Tenny, Lee Marvin; *Doctor Schumann*, Oskar Werner; *Jenny*, Elizabeth Ashley; *David*, George Segal; *Pepe*, Jose Greco; *Peter Glocken*, Michael Dunn; *Captain Thiele*, Charles Korvin; *Lowenthal*, Heinz Ruehmann; *Frau Hutten*, Lilia Skala; *Amparo*, Barbara Luna; *Lizzi*, Christine Schmidtmer; *Freytag*, Alf Kjellin; *Lieutenant Heubner*, Werner Klemperer; *Graf*, John Wengraf; *Frau Schmitt*, Olga Fabian; *Elsa*, Gila Golan; *Lutz*, Oscar Beregi; *Hutten*, Stanley Adams; *Frau Lutz*, Karen Verne; *Johann*, Charles de Vries; *Pastora*, Lydia Torea; *Fat Man*, Henry Calvin; *Carlos*, Paul Daniel; *Woodcarver*, David Renard; *Ric*, Rudy Carrella; *Rac*, Silvia Marino; *Guitarist*, Anthony Brand; *Religious Man*, Peter Mamakos; *Waiter*, Walter Friedel; *Second Officer*, Bert Rumsey; *Student*, Jon Alvar; *Headwaiter*, Charles H. Radilac; *Steward*, Steven Geray; *Spanish Dancers*, Justo Robles Quintero, Maribel DeCirez Garcia, Jose Santiago Martinez.

Marvin's second film appearance in 1965 was in Stanley Kramer's highly regarded all-star drama *Ship of Fools*, in which he was billed fourth, after previous Oscar winners Vivien Leigh, Simone Signoret and Jose Ferrer. Marvin had previously appeared in four films for the socially conscious producer-director; *Ship of Fools* would be their final project together.

Ship of Fools chronicles the intertwining paths of several passengers aboard a luxury liner as it journeys across the Atlantic in 1933. La Condesa (Simone Signoret) is a wealthy woman deported from Cuba for her political activities and facing prison in Spain. She is befriended by the ship's doctor (Oskar Werner), who takes more than a medical interest in her. Their poignant story is the most powerful in the film (and the lengthiest). Both stars were nominated for Oscars for their work.

While La Condesa and Dr. Schumann are falling in love, American artists Jenny (Elizabeth Ashley) and David (George Segal) are trying to define their mostly sexual relationship. An American widow, Mrs. Treadwell (Vivien Leigh), passes the time flirting and dancing with the ship's purser (Werner Klemperer). Bill Tenny (Lee Marvin), a retired baseball player, drinks and tries to bed Amparo (Barbara Luna), one of the Spanish dancers onboard. A dwarf named Karl Glocken (Michael Dunn) just tries to stay out of everybody's way.

Herr Rieber (Jose Ferrer) is a vocal German who espouses eradication of the Jews to anyone who will sit still and listen, and spends time wooing voluptuous blonde Lizzi (Christiane Schmidtmer). Rieber is forced to share a room with a Jew named Lowenthal (Heinz Ruehmann) and hates it. Another German passenger, Freytag (Alf Kjellin), is traveling back to Germany to find his Jewish wife, whom he had left. And in steerage are hundreds of Spanish migratory workers who had spent the last few years in Cuba.

There is no traditional plot to *Ship of Fools*, but rather the intertwining effects of each person on everyone else on the voyage. Clifton Fadiman reviewed the novel for the Book of the Month Club with these words: "As *Ship of Fools* cannot be said to have a plot in any conventional sense, these characters *are* the book. They are bound together only by the cobweb relationships spun during any brief ocean voyage. But Miss Porter has woven her web with such subtlety and economy that we are willing to forgo the attractions of mere suspense in favor of the more vibrant, almost eerie tension we feel when we are remorselessly drawn into a living world of the imagination."

The same is true for the film version. As the characters become more familiar, we not only identify with them, we empathize with them. We may not like them, for some of them are rather despicable, but we understand them, and the confined world of their ship is conducive for a desire to understand them. This effect is due both to the remarkable job which Abby Mann did in reducing a gargantuan book to a serviceable script and to the actors who imbue the characters with true individuality.

Producer-director Stanley Kramer specialized in films with social messages, and he focuses here on his most cherished virtue: tolerance. Where the book dwells on the racial and social differences between the passengers, the film points out that those differences, though they certainly exist, don't really mean much and shouldn't cause prejudice. Some of his message is delivered with humor or even irony, as when Glocken tells Lowenthal that he is the most German person he has ever met.

As with other Kramer projects, however, some critics found the underlying message of the film heavy-handed and preachy. The movie certainly has its moments when a soapbox is undoubtedly present, but the drama (and the moral) is usually delivered through the context of the characters, and thus is more palatable. The film (and book before it) are also meant as a civics lesson of public attitudes in 1932 regarding the rise to power of the Nazis and the casual disregard of that menace by virtually everyone. Even Lowenthal, ever the optimist, regards the Nazis as nothing more than a nuisance. "What shall they do," he asks Glocken, "kill us all?"

In order to attract audiences, Kramer filled his cast with international movie stars, beginning with Vivien Leigh as Mary Treadwell. In her final film, Leigh gives a cool, detached portrait of a lonely divorcee, displaying real emotion only twice: when she suddenly, momentarily cuts loose with a jitterbug when no one else is around to see it, and when she mauls Lee Marvin with her shoe after he drunkenly attacks her, then stops, embarrassed at mistaking her for the dancer he was after.

Simone Signoret received an Oscar nomination for her portrait of La Condesa, the woman deported from Cuba for her political activities. She is the most pathetic character, needing drugs from the doctor in order to sleep, but she is also the most vulnerable and the most charming. Oskar Werner, as the lonely doctor who warms up to La Condesa, was also nominated for an Oscar for his role. His struggle concerning La Condesa eventually causes his ailing heart to literally break, and his death is the one truly affecting emotional moment in the film.

The third Oscar-nominated performance comes from Michael Dunn as Glocken, who introduces the film (breaking the so-called fourth wall by speaking directly to the camera) and has a last word before the closing credits. Dunn serves as a truth-finder, asking the other characters how they feel about things and encouraging them to bare their souls. Heinz Ruehmann also should have received an Oscar nomination for his sly, knowing portrayal of Lowenthal, who puts up with prejudice with a sigh and loves his German music.

Jose Ferrer is incredibly energetic and loud as Rieber, while Charles Korvin is surprisingly quiet and thoughtful as the Captain. Opinion is divided on George Segal and Elizabeth Ashley as David and Jenny, the two most important characters in the book. Some critics found them shrill and shallow; however, those are the characters as written. In an autobiography, Ashley calls her work in the film terrible, but she is overreacting. Since most of the main characters are much older than David and Jenny, the young couple form an important counterpoint to the more mature passengers; the story presents various aspects of love—young and old—leaving the audience to divine whether David and Jenny should stay together.

The character of William Denny in the novel was "a young chemical engineer." For the film he became Bill Tenny, a washed-up baseball player who, in one of the movie's best scenes, explains to Glocken how he couldn't hit a curve ball over the outside corner. Bill Tenny is an ignorant bigot, one who insults various races and creeds without even realizing it, as opposed to the deliberate propaganda of Herr Rieber. He learns some tolerance due to bunking in the same room with David and Herr Glocken, but is rather an extraneous character on this voyage.

Lee Marvin underplays Tenny, preferring the more realistic mode to Jose Ferrer's more bombastic approach. Marvin also has to play dumb, because Bill Tenny isn't a very smart guy. He's slow on the uptake, and drinking impairs his thinking; this is the kind of role Marvin was familiar with. Marvin keeps his character charmless, making him the kind of man who drinks too much and talks too much to party guests who would rather not listen. This type of acting is risky because the audience may not identify with such roles, but most of the characters in this film are of this type, and Marvin proves that he can play one as well as anybody in the cast.

Ship of Fools was also important to Lee

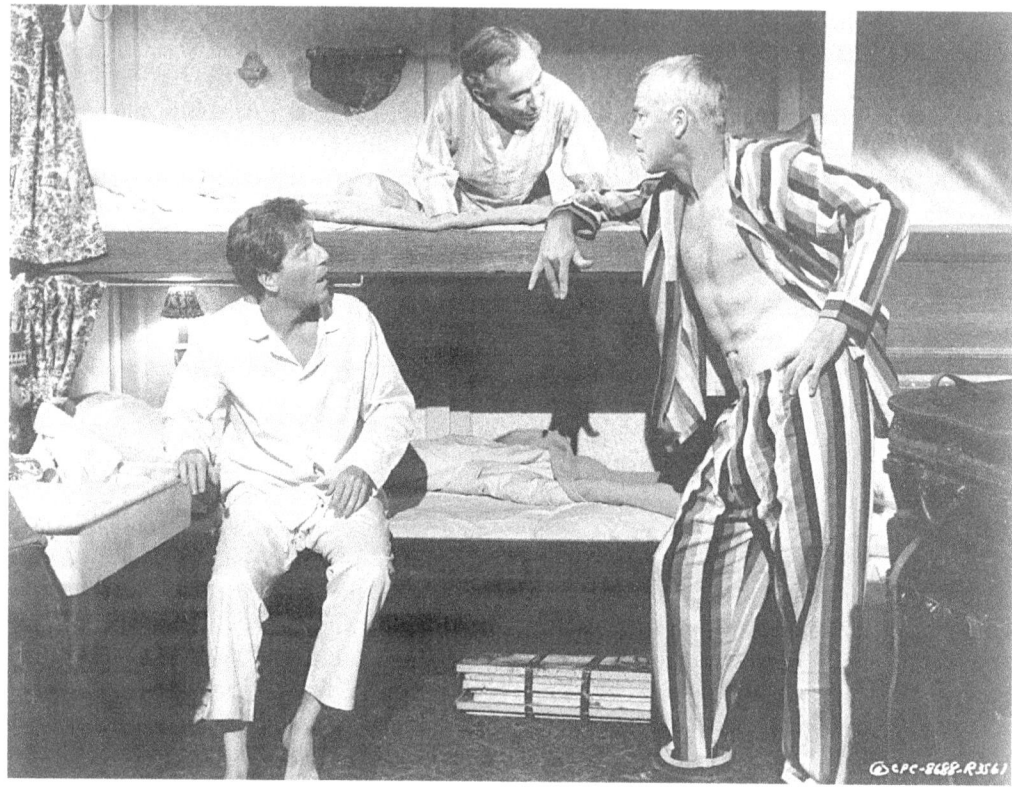

Cabinmates David (George Segal), Herr Glocken (Michael Dunn) and Bill Tenny (Lee Marvin) discuss life onboard the *Ship of Fools*.

Marvin for personal reasons; he met and fell for Barbara Luna's stand-in on the set, a young woman named Michelle Triola. They would spend the next five years together and the next decade afterward battling each other in the legal system when Michelle, as his common-law wife, sued Lee for what commonly became known as "palimony," asking for half of his earnings over that five-year period.

Apart from this future consideration, *Ship of Fools*, as a prestige picture, gave Marvin's career an extra dignity, showing the arthouse film audience who might not see Marvin's usual work that he was an actor worth watching. It certainly aided his Academy Award chances, garnering votes from people who might have shunned the lowbrow antics of *Cat Ballou* and helping to demonstrate his dramatic range. This film marked Lee Marvin not as a movie star, but as an *actor*.

The Professionals (1966)

CREDITS: Columbia. *Written for the Screen and Directed by* Richard Brooks. *Based on the novel* A Mule for the Marquesa *by* Frank O'Rourke. *Music by* Maurice Jarre. *Music Editor*: Maury Winetrobe. *Director of Photography*: Conrad Hall. *Film Editor*: Peter Zimner. *Art Director*: Edward S. Haworth. *Set Decorator*: Frank Tuttle. *Sound*: William Randall, Jr., Jack Haynes. *Sound Effects*: Del Harris, Kay Rose. *Sound Supervisor*: Charles J. Rice. *Wardrobe*: Jack Martell. *Hairdresser*: Jackie Bone. *Makeup*: Robert Schiffer. *Unit Production Manager*: Lee Lukather. *Special Effects*: Willis Cook. *Property Master*: Joseph LaBella. *Chief Electrician*: Harry Sundby. *Script Supervisor*: John Franco. *Assistant Director*: Tom Shaw. Through the courtesy of the U.S. Department of the Interior, the National Park Service, the Death Valley National Monument, the Nevada Department of Conservation and Natural Resources, and the Valley of Fire State Park. Not Rated. Technicolor. Panavision (2.35:1). 116 minutes. Released in October 1966. Currently available on VHS videotape and DVD. Previously available on laserdisc.

The Professionals

CAST: *Bill Dolworth*, Burt Lancaster; *Henry Rico Fardan*, Lee Marvin; *Hans Ehrengard*, Robert Ryan; *Jesus Raza*, Jack Palance; *Maria*, Claudia Cardinale; *J. W. Grant*, Ralph Bellamy; *Jake Sharp*, Woody Strode; *Ortega*, Joe De Santis; *Fierro*, Rafael Bertrand; *Padillia*, Jorge Martinez de Hoyos; *Chiquita*, Marie Gomez; *Revolutionaries*: Jose Chavez, Carlos Romero.

After *Cat Ballou* and *Ship of Fools*, Marvin turned once again to his forte: action-adventure. *The Professionals* proved to be Marvin's biggest success to date, a rousing western which made tons of money. Marvin portrayed the leader of the group, a role which he would repeat with even greater impact in *The Dirty Dozen* and other films throughout the remainder of his career.

The Professionals opens with quick introductions (during the credits) of its four main characters—weapons expert Henry Rico Fardan (Lee Marvin), scout and bowman Jake Sharp (Woody Strode), horseman Hans Ehrengard (Robert Ryan) and skirt-chasing demolitions expert Bill Dolworth (Burt Lancaster)—as they currently find themselves in the southwestern desert of the United States, circa 1917. Fardan, Sharp and Ehrengard each receive telegrams from millionaire J. W. Grant (Ralph Bellamy) requesting their presence for an unusual job interview. Grant explains that his young, beautiful wife Maria has been kidnapped by Mexican revolutionary Captain Jesus Raza, and that he wants them to bring her back for a fee of $10,000 each. Fardan, the unquestioned leader, doesn't argue; he merely asks for a dynamiter: Dolworth. Grant bails Dolworth out of jail, and the professionals prepare for their assignment.

A few days into Mexico, Dolworth is scouting ahead when he is captured by bandidos and hung upside down in a rugged pass. When the others rescue him, Dolworth is in his long underwear (for the second time in the film!) and a hair's breadth away from death.

Fardan (Lee Marvin) and Dolworth (Burt Lancaster) discuss the best ways to attack Raza's camp in *The Professionals*.

Once clothed again, Dolworth and Sharp rig the pass with dynamite to ensure their escape on their way back through in a few days. The group's first glimpse of Raza (Jack Palance) and his revolutionaries is from a ridge, as they watch Raza attack and overcome a Mexican government supply train. The captured government soldiers are lined up next to the train and executed by Raza, who follows Pancho Villa's belief that by killing prisoners he would not have to fight them another day. After the raid, Fardan and his men simply follow Raza back to his base camp and make their plans.

In a daring raid of their own, the professionals sneak into Raza's camp at night to rescue Maria (Claudia Cardinale). While Dolworth sets dynamite charges, Fardan moves in and removes the men guarding her. As Fardan and Dolworth watch, Maria is joined by Raza for some romance, which she encourages. Stunned, they realize that Grant had lied to them. They burst in, knock out both Raza and Maria, and carry her off to freedom. The group escapes in a train mining car as the camp explodes around them. Raza and his men follow and narrowly miss capturing Maria and her captors as they board the government train. Maria tries to escape, even offering herself to Dolworth as a bribe, but to no avail. She tells the men that she belongs to Raza, even though Grant forced her to marry him.

The professionals beat Raza to the rigged pass and blow it up before Raza and his revolutionaries can pass through. Dolworth stays behind to delay Raza and his forces while Fardan and the others escort Maria back to Grant. Dolworth battles Raza and former flame Chiquita (Maria Gomez) at the pass; both of the men are wounded, while Chiquita is killed and dies in Dolworth's arms. As the adventurers are delivering Maria to Grant, Dolworth rides up with an injured Raza in tow. Grant flies into a rage, orders Raza killed, which Dolworth prevents, and slaps Maria around when she pledges allegiance to Raza, her lifelong love. Fardan responds by sending Raza and Maria back to Mexico together, thereby kissing the money goodbye. While Grant fumes with rage, the professionals ride off into the sunset.

The Professionals quickly became the most popular western of the mid–1960s and one of the most profitable films of the year. It was a "sleeper," a film that wasn't predicted to do particularly well, but which struck a chord with the public and did exceptionally strong business. Part of the film's allure can be traced to two familiar elements: sex and violence. Two years before the MPAA's rating code was finally established, films like *Blow-Up*, *Who's Afraid of Virginia Woolf?* and *Alfie* were pushing the boundaries of screen sex, nudity and language. *The Professionals* was the first western to feature nudity (although it is a long-range view and tame by later standards) and Claudia Cardinale steamed up the screen in several sequences. The violence was rugged, and quite graphic in the sequence where Raza's revolutionaries attack the government troops on the train. This trend was decried by critics, yet undoubtedly helped bring bigger crowds into the theatres.

The Professionals works primarily because it is a tightly-written, pulse-pounding adventure which can be admired for its literacy, exquisite cinematography, exciting action sequences and aura of fun. Many films since have tried to emulate this success, but few are as downright fun and exciting as this one. One of the movie's greatest strengths is Conrad Hall's masterful widescreen cinematography, which brings the desolate desert landscape to forbidding life. *The Professionals* was shot at the Death Valley National Monument in California and the Valley of Fire State Park in Nevada, with most of the night action filmed during the day and shaded using photographic filters.

Writer-director Richard Brooks cast Marvin as the rugged leader of the group, leaving the other actors to craft juicy character parts out of their supporting roles. It is Burt Lancaster, who at 53 was still performing his own stuntwork, who steals the show. As Bill Dolworth, Lancaster uses his glib tongue, life-loving smile and fast feet to romance his way into trouble and dynamite his way out of it. Woody Strode is strong and stoic in his role, while Robert Ryan adds leathery vulnerability to the group as the horseman who hates to see animals suffer.

Claudia Cardinale is awe-inspiring as Maria. Her incredible oiled beauty gives credence to the price that J. W. Grant is willing to pay for her return. Cardinale had not ridden horses before appearing in this film; it was Lee Marvin who taught her to ride comfortably and realistically. The one actor with little to do is Jack Palance, who isn't even seen until the film's second half and has little dialogue to deliver until he and Burt Lancaster shoot it out late in the film.

Though Marvin has more screen time than anyone else save Lancaster, he has one of the quieter roles in this movie. His character makes most of the strategic decisions and participates in most of the action, but does so with wry humor and little fanfare. Some of Marvin's earliest scenes actually feature more of his back than his face. Yet his command, established at the beginning of the movie by Grant, is never questioned, and his succinct dialogue (which predates Clint Eastwood's sparse style) helps define the character as no-nonsense yet droll and intelligent.

Marvin's Henry Rico Fardan is also fairly nostalgic for the past, and surprisingly poetic. Early on, Grant displays an old newspaper photo of Fardan with Raza, and notes, "Your hair was darker then." Fardan smiles dryly and replies, "My heart was lighter then."

When Dolworth exclaims, "I'll be damned!" Fardan adds, "Most of us are." And most memorably, when Grant, at the film's climax, calls Fardan a bastard, Fardan politely answers him with, "In my case, an unfortunate accident of birth, but you, sir, are a self-made man."

Marvin's quiet authority is reinforced by his restraint. In many of his early thug roles, such as in *The Big Heat*, *The Wild One* or *The Man Who Shot Liberty Valance*, his characters were menacing due to their outlandish behavior and brutality. The image in *The Professionals*, cultivated by Marvin later in *The Dirty Dozen*, *Prime Cut* and others, is more like a coiled cobra, ready to strike but awaiting provocation to do so. Perhaps paradoxically, this professional is not only more lethal, but more threatening and sexually potent because of his restraint.

Fardan (Lee Marvin) takes deadly aim in *The Professionals*.

The Professionals gathered surprisingly mixed reviews, the most famous of which is Pauline Kael's observation in the *New Republic* that, "This 1966 action-western...has the expertise of a cold old whore with practiced hands and no thoughts of love." Kael, and several other critics, found the film manipulative, shallow and somewhat pretentious.

On the other hand, Joseph Morgenstern of *Newsweek* wrote, "Rare is the Western that can boast political insights, intricate motivations, applied philosophy and some literary grace in its dialogue. Rarer still is the Western, like *The Professionals*, that succeeds in spite of that. Richard Brooks, who wrote the screenplay, shoots high and often hits the clouds. Richard Brooks, who directed, fires away at stunning scenery, good faces and great action, and hits the bullseye almost every time."

Phil Hardy, in his *Western Film Encyclopedia*, noted that, "One of the most successful of recent westerns, *The Professionals* is a more complex film than its adventure plot might suggest. Brooks' script is eloquent but it is his integration of the action sequences into the flow of the film's perspective on the fast-changing West that makes the movie so successful."

Despite the critical mix, audiences went to the theater in droves to watch one of the most exciting western adventures ever put on film. The popularity and professionalism of the film was rewarded a few months later with Oscar nominations for Richard Brooks' exciting direction and literate screenplay and for Conrad Hall's exquisite photography. The film lost in all three categories to the historical drama *A Man for All Seasons*.

The popularity of *The Professionals* pushed Lee Marvin into the stratosphere of the biggest box-office stars in the world and proved that his Oscar for *Cat Ballou* was not a flash in the pan. His next project would eclipse even the most optimistic hopes for his career, as well as further fanning the flames of the debate about violence on the big screen.

The Dirty Dozen (1967)

CREDITS: Metro-Goldwyn-Mayer. *Directed by* Robert Aldrich. *Produced by* Kenneth Hyman. *Associate Producer*: Raymond Anzarut. *Written by* Lukas Heller and Nunnally Johnson. *From the Novel by* E. M. Nathanson. *Music by* (Frank) DeVol. *Songs*: "The Bramble Bush" *by* (Frank) DeVol, Mack David; "Einsam" *by* (Frank) DeVol, Sibylle Siegfried. *Director of Photography*: Edward Scaife, B.S.C. *Film Editor*: Michael Luciano, A.C.E. *Art Director*: W. E. Hutchinson. *Special Effects Supervisor*: Cliff Richardson. *Unit Production Manager*: Julian Mackintosh. *Continuity*: Angela Allen. *Sound Recording*: Franklin Milton, Claude Hitchcock. *Sound Editor*: John Paynor. *Makeup by* Ernest Gasser, Walter Schneiderman. *Assistant Director*: Bert Batt. *Camera Operators*: Alan McCabe, Tony Spratling. *Main Title Design*: Walter Blake. Not Rated. Metrocolor. Metroscope (1.66:1). 149 minutes. Released in June 1967. Currently available on VHS videotape, laserdisc and DVD.

CAST: *Major John Reisman*, Lee Marvin; *General Worden*, Ernest Borgnine; *Joseph Wladislaw*, Charles Bronson; *Robert Jefferson*, Jim Brown; *Victor Franko*, John Cassavetes; *Sergeant Clyde Bowren*, Richard Jaeckel; *Major Max Armbruster*, George Kennedy; *Pedro Jiminez*, Trini Lopez; *Captain Stuart Kinder*, Ralph Meeker; *Colonel Everett Dasher Breed*, Robert Ryan; *Archer Maggot*, Telly Savalas; *Vernon Pinkley*, Donald Sutherland; *Samson Posey*, Clint Walker; *General Denton*, Robert Webber; *Milo Vladek*, Tom Busby; *Glenn Gilpin*, Ben Carruthers; *Roscoe Lever*, Stuart Cooper; *Corporal Carl Morgan*, Robert Phillips; *Seth Sawyer*, Colin Maitland; *Tassos Bravos*, Al Mancini; *Private Arthur James Gardiner*, George Roubicek; *General Worden's Aide*, Thick Wilson; *German Officer's Girl*, Dora Reisser.

If there is one movie for which Lee Marvin will be remembered, *The Dirty Dozen* is the one. It is not the best acting Marvin ever did and not the best film in which Marvin was ever involved, but it was certainly the most popular. Based on a best-selling novel by E. M. Nathanson, the film was the biggest moneymaker of 1967. It also (with the help of his next film, *Point Blank*) made Lee Marvin the number one male box office star in America that year. The film led to many imitations (such as *The Devil's Brigade*) and, some twenty years later, three made-for-television sequels. Today the film is justly regarded as one of the classic action films of the 1960s.

The Dirty Dozen can be divided into three sections: the introduction of the prisoners and

Major John Reisman (Lee Marvin), chosen to lead *The Dirty Dozen*.

the formation of the Dirty Dozen, the training exercise which proves that the Dozen can operate as a team, and the climactic attack upon the chateau. The first section is the longest and most detailed, as Major John Reisman (Lee Marvin), a maverick officer who speaks his mind, is given an assignment he doesn't like at all: to train twelve military prisoners condemned to death or long prison sentences to act as a covert fighting force for a special behind-the-lines mission on D-day. Reisman argues with General Worden (Ernest Borgnine) that the prisoners must get clemency for the plan to work, and Worden reluctantly agrees—with a caveat that if any prisoners do escape or cause trouble, they must all return for execution of their original sentences.

The prisoners are worse than Reisman feared, but he gathers them and transports them to a remote area in Britain where they begin to build a camp. Helping Reisman keep the men in line is Sergeant Bowren (Richard Jaeckel) and a few other guards. The twelve prisoners are taught hand-to-hand combat, trained on weapons, put through grueling physical exercises, and watched carefully while they train for the mission and build the camp. At parachute training school, the Dozen learn to jump while Reisman tries to keep their mission secret from nosy Colonel Everett Dasher Breed (Robert Ryan).

The second section comes after Colonel Breed is humiliated and demands action against Reisman and the prisoners. General Worden agrees to test them in upcoming military maneuvers. If they can successfully capture Colonel Breed and his headquarters, they will not go back to prison. Using a detailed plan, the various skills of the men, and a great deal of subterfuge, the Dozen—without Reisman's help—are able to capture Colonel Breed and his entire staff, with General Worden as a witness.

Finally, the big mission: to attack a chateau where German officers are staying and wipe out as many as possible. The Dozen parachute into France and immediately incur one fatality, Jiminez (Trini Lopez), who doesn't survive the jump. They go over the plan again and go into action. Reisman and Joseph Wladislaw (Charles Bronson), the only person who speaks fluent German, walk into the chateau disguised as German officers. The rest of the men set up a perimeter and penetrate the chateau's upper floors. Archer Maggot (Telly Savalas) prematurely sets off the alarms when he murders a German woman and is gunned down by Robert Jefferson (Jim Brown), the black man he hates. The Germans take shelter in an underground cellar and are locked in by Reisman, who orders gasoline and grenades poured into their air vents.

German reinforcements begin to arrive and various firefights begin. One by one, the Dirty Dozen begin to die. Jefferson races from one open air vent to another, dropping live grenades; he almost makes it to the German half-track that hothead Victor Franko (John Cassavetes) has commandeered before he is shot down. As the chateau explodes, Reisman takes over and drives the half-track over a bridge to safety, but is shot in the process. An exuberant Victor Franko is shot and killed as the truck slowly drives away. In a military hospital, only Reisman, Sergeant Bowren and Joseph Wladislaw survive to fight another day.

The Dirty Dozen is a rip-roaring World War II action-adventure with a ridiculous premise that makes the film that much more fun. As Reisman puts it in the movie's second scene: "It [the plan to use prisoners] confirms a suspicion that I've had for some time now. That one of the officers in command of this operation is a raving lunatic." General Worden privately agrees with Reisman's assessment, and the view that authority is untrustworthy, stupid and deadly pervades the whole movie. That sentiment is what, above all the action and adventure, brought people into theaters in huge numbers. In 1967, as the Vietnam war raged on and civil strife took place all across America, such an anti-authoritarian sentiment was enormously popular, and people responded to it, even if they were unaware of it.

Like *M*A*S*H* three years later, *The Dirty Dozen* accurately reflected the social climate of the time while purporting to depict

112 The Dirty Dozen

Major Reisman (Lee Marvin) and his men escape from the chateau, blasting their way to freedom in *The Dirty Dozen*.

events of twenty-some years earlier. Thus, both films can, and perhaps should, be read as microcosms of the war in Vietnam, even though they are set in two completely different eras. Both films depict the utter chaos of battle, the needless human suffering, the often senseless acts by authority, the disregard for human life, and the courage of individuals, and *The Dirty Dozen* in particular does so in a film structure familiar enough to send the message clearly yet entertainingly. That isn't to say that the film is a social commentary, but rather that people responded to its view that the condemned prisoners, put together with a fixed purpose in mind, could work as well or better than any authoritative agency—and have more fun doing it.

The real reason that *The Dirty Dozen* was such a huge hit, and continues to be revered as a seminal action film, is that it *is* fun. Director Robert Aldrich plays with his improbable premise and plays down the inevitable demise of most of his cast, choosing instead to focus on the antics of the men who are reprieved from death or long prison stays. The men, though worked hard and trained hard, know that they are free, and they delight in their freedom. "Twelve rugged individualists," Reisman calls them, and one of the great things about the film is the way that these twelve individuals are trained to work and think as one unit—without sacrificing their individuality.

This is shown explicitly during the film's middle section, the training exercise when the Dozen must capture Colonel Breed's headquarters. Without Reisman's aid, the Dozen must trust each other and stick to the plan to make it work, yet each man remains his own distinct self, whether glorying in the subversive task at hand or worrying about the small details of the operation. This middle section is essential to the film because it gives the criminal prisoners real personalities and lets them express themselves; it allows them to prove that they are worth redemption. Aldrich directs it so skillfully that the underlying message is completely glossed over by the action and comedy of the sequence.

The prisoners ultimately give the film its personality. Though there are a dozen members of the Dirty Dozen, only seven of them stand out; the other five are just warm bodies. John Cassavetes earned an Oscar nomination for his role as volatile Victor Franko, the one prisoner who does make an escape attempt and is beaten up by the others for it. Franko is thoroughly selfish and defines "disciplinary problem," yet he is also a born leader and contributes vitally once he is converted to the cause. Cassavetes' intensity sets the screen ablaze at times, overpowering most of his costars. Donald Sutherland gives a strong early performance as Vernon Pinkley, the lanky goofball who makes the most of his opportunity to impersonate a general, and is the first of the Dozen to die at the hands of a Nazi at the chateau.

Charles Bronson, who also appeared in the male-oriented action classics *The Magnificent Seven* and *The Great Escape*, completes his 1960s action triumvirate as Joseph Wladislaw, the most dependable of the Dozen, one who Reisman learns to trust and value. Of all the prisoners, only Wladislaw lives through the attack on the chateau, only to be patly complimented by General Denton, leading to the film's final line: "Killing generals could get to be a habit with me." Clint Walker, a giant of a man, plays Samson Posey, who once killed a man with one blow. Walker creates a sincere portrayal of a simple man, and is the only prisoner who truly threatens Reisman (in the memorable scene when Reisman gives him a hunting knife and tells him to attack). Curiously, though Posey is most certainly killed at the chateau, his death is not seen.

Telly Savalas *is* Archer Maggot, the religious fanatic who claims to be God's tool of retribution. Maggot is truly creepy, the only prisoner that seems capable of fouling up the plan purposefully, yet Savalas also brings a sense of humor to the role. Trini Lopez plays Pedro Jiminez, the guitar-playing prisoner who sings "The Bramble Bush" in the film. According to the movie's preview trailer, Jiminez is "crawling with hate," a hilariously overstated characteristic. Jiminez is the least formidable of all the prisoners; he doesn't represent much of a threat to anyone. His big scene occurs when he can't crawl up the training rope until Reisman shoots it out from under him. Reportedly, Lopez was written out of the script for the final sequence when he demanded more money for his role—the result is that Jiminez dies, unseen, in the parachute jump into France.

The other important prisoner is Robert Jefferson, played by football star Jim Brown. Brown recalls, "I loved my part. I was one of the Dozen, a quiet leader and my own man, at a time when Hollywood wasn't giving those roles to blacks. *The Dirty Dozen* was an American classic, the most popular film I've ever done, and I've never had more fun making a movie. The male cast was incredible. I worked with some of the strongest, craziest guys in the business." Though his character name was changed from the novel's Napoleon White, the character remained the same: tough, patient, smart, ready and able to stand up for his beliefs.

Jefferson's run at the chateau, dropping grenades into each air shaft and hustling to the next, is one of the film's most exciting scenes. Jefferson's death, as he is cut down by a Nazi with a submachine gun, is *the* emotional moment of the film. It isn't just Reisman, Wladislaw and Franko urging him on, it's the audience; and when he doesn't make it, we realize for the first time that for any of these characters to make it back alive, it will take a miracle. With Jefferson's death, the fun film turns tragic, as we finally and fully understand how hard these men have worked for their freedom and how foolhardy an idea the whole operation really was. Twenty-six years later, Jefferson's death would be immortalized in the comedy *Sleepless in Seattle*, as Tom Hanks compares his emotional reaction to the combat scene with Rita Wilson's tearful reaction to *An Affair to Remember*.

Perhaps the film's finest performance is given by Richard Jaeckel as Sergeant Bowren, the glue that holds the Dirty Dozen together. Bowren is in charge of the prisoners when Reisman meets them at the Marston-Tyne Military Prison, and he tags along when Reisman transfers them out for their mission. Bowren is strong and efficient, keeping a tight rein on the prisoners, whom he is sure will try to escape or shoot Reisman in the head. He is the one who terms them "the Dirty Dozen," and he gradually begins to trust them, despite himself. Though he doesn't have to, Bowren accompanies the men on their mission and feels their deaths perhaps more keenly than anyone else. Jaeckel is great in the small role, immaculate and shiny-faced, brimming with energy and enthusiasm under the most dogged of circumstances.

The actors who play the Army officers who implement the plan—the establishment—are Ernest Borgnine, Robert Webber, George Kennedy, Ralph Meeker and Robert Ryan. Borgnine is in fine form as General Worden, sassy yet pragmatic, ready to follow orders but secretly questioning the sanity of those orders. Webber plays General Denton by the book, giving the standard lectures to Reisman and leaving little impression. George Kennedy is Max Armbruster, General Worden's aide, who comes up with the idea of including the Dozen in the military maneuvers and who accompanies the Dozen as an observer. Kennedy is fine in his small role, but had a much greater impact in his other 1967 film, *Cool Hand Luke*, for which he took home the Best Supporting Actor Oscar.

Ralph Meeker is Captain Stuart Kinder, the psychologist who warns Reisman of the danger to himself from the prisoners and who wants to weed out the worst. Meeker allows himself to condescend to the prisoners and at times looks foolish doing so, giving credence to the idea that the prisoners are smarter than the Army men guarding them. Robert Ryan plays Colonel Everett Dasher Breed as a spit-and-polish martinet, unwilling to give Reisman any slack at all. Breed considers it his duty to run Reisman out of the Army and tells him so. Ryan's character represents all that's wrong with the Army—arrogant, unable to think quickly, judgmental rather than open-minded, more interested in appearances than results. Ryan plays him as a vain, vengeful man who sees himself as an arbiter of justice. In this thankless role, Ryan delivers a professional performance. This was the third film Ryan had made with Marvin; they would team once more in Ryan's final movie, *The Iceman Cometh*.

In the preview trailer for *The Dirty Dozen*, Lee Marvin is quoted as saying that his role "is the best I've ever been asked to play." While that may or may not be true, it is probably his most memorable. Marvin, who had played many anti-establishment rebels during his twenty-five years in Hollywood, was now the head of the asylum, taking charge of a dozen criminals and crackpots and told to form them into a fighting unit. Major John Reisman rides the fence here; he is part of the Army (and to the prisoners represents their newest captor), but he is also a maverick officer who doesn't do things by the book and who must make the mission work well enough to save his own career, as well as his skin.

Marvin forcefully embodies John Reisman, using his brains to handle the men and his strength to keep himself a step ahead of them. Marvin comes across as the most fair and understanding of officers, if not the most tactful. Reisman allows his men to remain individuals, to have fun, and Marvin allows his costars to share the spotlight, preferring to play the role straight and true. There isn't a false note in Marvin's performance; he brings a necessary sense of truth and a commanding presence to the proceedings. In *The Professionals*, Marvin led quietly, giving costars Burt Lancaster, Woody Strode and Robert Ryan opportunities to shine on their own. Here, Marvin is the main man, and if he can't keep actors like John Cassavetes, Charles Bronson, Donald Sutherland and Telly Savalas in line, they would blow him off the screen. Marvin has no such trouble, handling each scene and challenge with aplomb.

The MPAA movie rating system went into effect in 1968, giving age recommendations based on the quotient of violence, sex, nudity and adult themes in each movie. The system was started because the mid–1960s saw such adult fare as *Who's Afraid of Virginia Woolf?*, *The Graduate*, *The Pawnbroker*, *Bonnie and Clyde*, *In Cold Blood* and *The Dirty Dozen* push the envelope of what could be considered fit fare for all ages. Many critics who liked *The Dirty Dozen* were nevertheless jolted by the amount of violence in the final half-hour of the film, particularly the scene where Reisman orders gasoline and grenades poured into the air vents of the air raid shelter where the German officers *and civilians* are hiding and blows them all to hell, reminding many of the horrors of the gas chambers at Auschwitz and other death camps.

Major Reisman (Lee Marvin), as he appears in the comic book version of the hit film *The Dirty Dozen*.

Director Aldrich countered those critics by asking whether "critics and audiences would see the parallel between Americans roasting Germans and certain German behavior patterns in the war. I wanted to make the point that violence is just as disagreeable when it comes from Americans as it does from Germans." According to Aldrich, the film's point is "to show the necessity for collective courage in circumstances that would make collective cowardice more likely, and to show that almost anybody can be redeemed if certain circumstances and pressures are sufficient."

Whether people watched *The Dirty Dozen* for its formidable entertainment value or saw in it an artistry or a social message is a moot point. The film was the biggest hit of the year, making Lee Marvin the biggest male star in America. Despite critics such as Bosley Crowther, who called it "an astonishingly wanton war film" and wrote that, "the intent of this loud picture is just to delight and stimulate the easily moved," the film won an audience and earned its status as an action classic. It was nominated for four Academy Awards: Supporting Actor (John Cassavetes), Film Editing, Sound, and Sound Effects, winning the Sound Effects award. *The Dirty Dozen* remains beloved by people today and will stand for generations as Lee Marvin's (and Robert Aldrich's) most popular triumph.

Point Blank (1967)

CREDITS: Metro-Goldwyn-Mayer. *Directed by* John Boorman. *Produced by* Judd Bernard, Robert Chartoff, Irwin Winkler. *Screenplay by* Alexander Jacobs, David Newhouse, Rafe Newhouse. *Based upon the Novel* The Hunter *by* Richard Stark. *Music*: Johnny Mandel. *Song* "Mighty Good Times" *by* Stu Gardner, *sung by* Stu Gardner Trio. *Director of Photography*: Philip H. Lathrop, A.S.C. *Film Editor*: Henry Berman. *Art Directors*: George W. Davis, Albert Brenner. *Set Decoration*: Henry Grace, Keogh Gleason. *Recording Supervisor*: Franklin Milton. *Make-up by* William Tuttle. *Hair Styles by* Sydney Guilaroff. *Assistant Director*: Al Jennings. *Unit Production Manager*: Edward Woehler. *Dialogue Coach*: Norman Stuart. *Special Visual Effects*: J. McMillan Johnson. *Production Associate*: Patricia Casey. *Assistant to Producer*: Rafe Newhouse. *Special Photographs for Production*: David Steen. *Color Consultant*: William Stair. Not Rated. Metrocolor. Panavision (2.35:1). 92 minutes. Released in September 1967. Currently available on VHS videotape and laserdisc.

CAST: *Walker*, Lee Marvin; *Chris*, Angie Dickinson; *Yost / Fairfax*, Keenan Wynn; *Brewster*, Carroll O'Connor; *Frederick Carter*, Lloyd Bochner; *Stegman*, Michael Strong; *Mal Reese*, John Vernon; *Lynne*, Sharon Acker; *Hired Gun*, James (B.) Sikking; *Waitress*, Sandra Warner; *Mrs. Carter*, Roberta Haynes; *First Citizen*, Kathleen Freeman; *Carter's Man*, Victor Creatore; *Car Salesman*, Lawrence Hauben; *Girl Customer*, Susan Holloway; *Penthouse Lobby Guards*, Sid Haig, Michael Bell; *Receptionist*, Priscilla Boyd; *Messenger*, John McMurtry; *Two Young Men in Apartment*, Ron Walters, George Stratton; *Carter's Secretary*, Nicole Rogell; *Reese's Guards*, Rico Cattani, Roland LaStarza; *Men*, Jerry Catron, Joe Mell; *Football Player*, Ted White; *Dancers*, Casey Brandon, Roseann Williams, Bonnie Dewberry, Carey Foster; *Waitress*, Karen Lee; *Guards*, Bill Hickman, Chuck Hicks; *Policeman*, Louis Whithill; *Bellhop*, Felix Silla; *Desk Clerk*, Andrew Orapeza.

While he was making *The Dirty Dozen* in London, Lee Marvin met with a young British director named John Boorman who had a project in mind for him. Marvin and Boorman bonded right away, and Marvin immediately agreed to make the project, an adaptation of Richard Stark's bleak novel *The Hunter*, his very next movie. Later, when MGM questioned whether Boorman had the proper credentials to direct a film with the number one male star in America, Marvin supported him, telling the nervous executives that he would not make the film with another director. The two men became lifelong friends, making *Hell in the Pacific* right after *Point Blank*, and almost collaborating on *Deliverance* four years later (Marvin eventually pulled out, feeling that he was too old for either of the major roles).

Point Blank is a movie about vengeance and greed. Walker (Lee Marvin) is asked by Mal Reese (John Vernon) to help with a simple robbery—to intercept a shipment of laundered mob money at Alcatraz island and steal it. During the robbery, however, Reese kills the two men delivering the money and then shoots Walker, leaving him in an open cell to die. Reese then claims Walker's wife Lynne (Sharon Acker), with whom he has been having an affair, as his woman. Somehow, Walker survives and makes it across the bay to San Francisco.

Some time later, fully healed, Walker returns to Alcatraz and meets Yost (Keenan Wynn), who has a plan that will give Walker the revenge (and robbery money) he thirsts for. Walker begins his rampage at home, shooting the empty bed which once held Reese. Lynne is now a drug addict and commits suicide without revealing where Reese has gone. Lynne's sister Chris (Angie Dickinson) is more helpful, allowing herself to be used as bait to catch Mal Reese in his penthouse apartment with his pants down. Reese falls to his death, giving Chris great satisfaction but leaving Walker without the robbery money he feels he is owed.

Walker follows the money trail to Frederick Carter (Lloyd Bochner), who, under a great deal of pressure, agrees to pay off the angry man. Instead, he sets up a trap for Walker, using a hit man (James B. Sikking). Walker predicts the trap, forces Carter to take his place, and watches as Carter and an accomplice are gunned down. Next is Brewster (Carroll O'Connor), the mob's number two man, who readily agrees to Walker's demands and arranges for the payoff at

Walker (Lee Marvin) returns home looking for revenge and the stolen money he believes belongs to him in *Point Blank*.

Alcatraz. Brewster, with Walker watching from the shadows, meets the money delivery and is killed by the hit man, who is also hiding. Yost, identifying himself as Fairfax, the top man in the organization, calls out to Walker to join him, but Walker declines to come out into the open, leaving the money untouched.

Point Blank is one man's search for the source of his unhappiness, presented in an almost hallucinatory manner. Walker's search, which takes him beyond mere revenge, is revealed in a series of stylish sequences that cause one to question the reality of each new situation or development. As pointed out by critic David Thomson, *Point Blank* can also be read as Walker's death-dream as he succumbs in the Alcatraz prison cell; this could explain why Walker, between his destructive purges, seems almost lifeless and doesn't care what happens to him. It would also explain why he leaves the money he's worked so hard to get in the final scene: If he dies, he has no need of the cash. Finally, it would take care of a major plot point—how did Walker ever get off of Alcatraz island, especially after being shot?

Whether Walker is imagining his revenge or actually carries it out is immaterial to the film. Director Boorman's purpose is to tell a suspenseful, action-packed story with every cinematic means at his disposal. *Point Blank* challenges traditional thrillers, at least in terms of narrative structure, scene construction and focus on style rather than the substance of conventional plotting and characterization. His film is much more of a visceral experience than most others. Years before it became trendy to do so, Boorman was making innovative use of sound, music and sound effects as important character elements, mood enhancers and scene transitions, surrounding his viewers with as much sound (or silence) as he felt was warranted.

If *Point Blank* has a fatal flaw, it must be its expansive stylishness. Boorman's style does overwhelm the picture, causing various audience reactions. Some people and critics find his technical wizardry dazzling, reading various meanings into the dream-like imagery, or simply respond to the brute force of the film. Others view such relentless distortion distastefully, not being able to relate to it or looking for something more familiar. *Point Blank* is not an avant-garde experiment, but it is highly stylized, much in the manner of Brian DePalma's films of the early 1980s, which were exaggerations of Hitchcock's films, featuring contorted, extended camera movements amid swirling orchestral music.

Character motivation in *Point Blank* is most basic. Greed and survival are the only motivations for its characters, with greed usually the primary characteristic. The film takes the position that every character is jaded and corrupt, that no one is immune to the need for money. And when greed and survival are not enough (or too much), death is the only answer. Boorman populates his nihilistic view with startling images, many of them sexual, to depict man's (and woman's) most base instincts. The sex in the film is not pretty Hollywood sex—it's rough, mean, violent gratification with no trace of romance. When Chris allows Reese to seduce her while Walker sneaks into the penthouse, it's almost rape; when Chris beds Walker later on, it's violent foreplay followed by basic human need.

The cast takes on this ugliness with enthusiasm. Hollywood heavy John Vernon made his film debut here, playing Mal Reese as an unrepentant, power-hungry thug, and made an indelible impression doing so. Keenan Wynn, Carroll O'Connor and Lloyd Bochner play their syndicate roles as consummate businessmen, looking for the most profitable angle to every situation and hoping to get ahead by casually eliminating each other. James B. Sikking portrays his hit man in the same way that Lee Marvin played his in *The Killers*—intelligently, with enough sense to know a setup when he sees one. Sharon Acker is bland as Walker's suicidal wife, but there's not much to the part.

Angie Dickinson gives her all to her role as Chris, the sister of despondent Lynne. After Lynne kills herself, revenge for her sister's senseless death drives Chris the same way it drives Walker. That's why they end up together after causing Mal Reese's plunge from his penthouse; their vengeance has bonded them. Dickinson is stunning, whether letting Reese paw her or beating herself breathless against Walker's chest. Her vitality is in direct contrast to Walker's lifelessness, and he seems to draw energy from her to keep himself going. Dickinson's film career is very spotty, and while she ably decorates most of her films, *Point Blank* gives her a real opportunity to light up the screen, and she does.

Walker is an ideal role for Lee Marvin because it allows him to exhibit his physical prowess as a killer, but minimizes his emotional connection to the audience. Walker is alive when preparing to avenge his wife's death and when nearing the money he wants so badly, but dead at most other periods, particularly when Lynne or Chris is trying to talk to him. Marvin expresses Walker's brutal instincts superlatively, and simply closes down when Walker isolates himself. While the role itself is somewhat unwieldy, Marvin fills it to a tee. Like the Terminator twenty years later, Walker is an inhuman killing machine.

While *Point Blank* was ahead of its time in 1967, time has since passed it by, leaving the film as a dated relic of the 1960s Los Angeles scene. Its relevancy and attitude are still contemporary, but its style and setting give it an unavoidable "time capsule" aura. War films and westerns seem to avoid this problem, but social documents such as *Point Blank*, *The Graduate* and *Divorce American Style*, to name three disparate 1967 films, have all lost some of their charm and power because the social context explored in each of them was so fleeting.

Lee Marvin's decision to make *Point Blank* after *The Dirty Dozen* was a fateful one. Marvin had always liked to freelance and never tied himself to any one studio. He looked for projects which interested him as an actor rather than for their box-office potential or the size of the leading role. While *Point Blank* was much admired by the critics, it was only a modest success and did not further his popularity in the way that *The Dirty Dozen* had.

Marvin did not like to repeat himself; he tried not to take roles which he felt were retreads of earlier roles. For instance, he turned down *The Wild Bunch* because he felt it covered much the same territory as *The Professionals* had. In this case, however, his judgment led him to play a hit man for the second time in four years. Indeed, Marvin's role in *Point Blank* can be seen as an extension of his role in *The Killers*, and is in truth not dissimilar. His popularity might have continued to grow had he chosen his next few projects more carefully. *Point Blank* did not hurt Marvin's career, but it didn't help it much either, and the later *Hell in the Pacific*, also directed by Boorman, was so non-commercial as to be invisible.

Sergeant Ryker (1968)

CREDITS: Roncom Films/Universal. *Directed by* Buzz Kulik. *Produced by* Frank Telford. *Associate Producers*: Joel Rogosin, Jo Swerling, Jr. *Screenplay by* Seeleg Lester, William D. Gordon. *Story by* Seeleg Lester. *Music by* Johnny (John) Williams. *Music Supervision by* Stanley Wilson. *Director of Photography*: Walter Strenge, A.S.C. *Film Editor*: Robert B. Warwick, A.C.E. *Art Director*: John J. Lloyd. *Set Decorations*: John McCarthy, Robert C. Bradfield. *Sound*: Waldon O. Watson, William Lynch. *Makeup*: Bud Westmore. *Hair Stylist*: Larry Germain. Not Rated. Pathe Color. Flat (1.33:1). 86 minutes. Filmed in 1963 as "The Case Against Paul Ryker" for *Kraft Suspense Theatre*. Released in February 1968. Currently available on VHS videotape.

CAST: *Sergeant Paul William Ryker*, Lee Marvin; *Captain David Young*, Bradford Dillman; *Major Frank Whitaker*, Peter Graves; *Ann Ryker*, Vera Miles; *General Amos Bailey*, Lloyd Nolan; *Captain Leonard Appleton*, Murray Hamilton; *Sergeant Max Winkler*, Norman Fell; *Colonel Arthur Merriam*, Walter Brooke; *President of the Court-Martial*, Francis DeSales; *Corporal Jenks*, Don Marshall; *Major Kitchener*, Charles Aidman.

Back in 1963 Lee Marvin had starred in a two-part episode of NBC's new hour-long anthology series, the *Kraft Suspense Theatre*. "The Case Against Paul Ryker" had aired on October 10th and 17th of 1963 as *Kraft*'s premiere episode and garnered good reviews and ratings. Five years later, after Marvin's 1965 Oscar and his climb to the top of the money-making stars list, Universal Studios decided to edit the two-part episode into a releasable feature film to further capitalize on Marvin's success.

Sergeant Ryker takes place during the Korean War in 1951 and stars Marvin as the title character, Sergeant Paul William Ryker, who has been tried and convicted of treason—for collaborating with the North Koreans—and sentenced to death. His wife Ann (Vera Miles) arrives in Tokyo, Japan and persuades prosecuting attorney Captain David Young

120 Sergeant Ryker

(Bradford Dillman) to investigate the case on his own, despite orders to the contrary from his boss, Major Frank Whitaker (Peter Graves).

In Seoul, South Korea, Young and Ann persuade Sergeant Max Winkler (Norman Fell) to help locate the personal belongings of Colonel Chambers, the officer who Ryker claims sent him on a secret mission in North Korea but was killed before Ryker's return. Later, during a confrontation with General Bailey (Lloyd Nolan) and Whitaker, Young puts forth his case to have Ryker's imminent execution at least delayed. General Bailey listens to Young's evidence, including the discovery that Colonel Chambers' body was not in its grave, and grants Ryker not only a stay of execution but a new trial, and this time appoints Captain Young as Ryker's *defense* lawyer. Whitaker vows to prosecute the case himself.

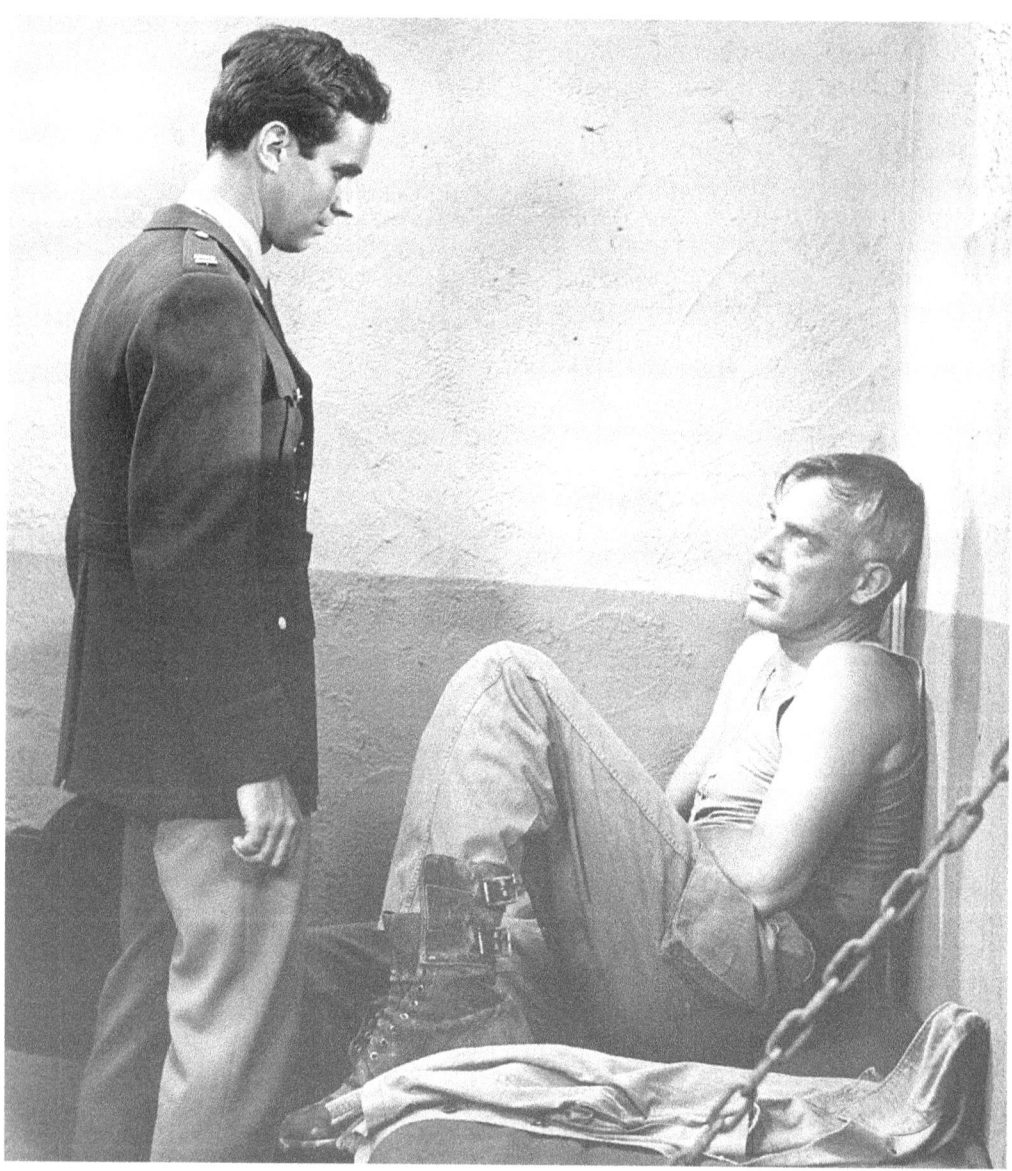

Captain David Young (Bradford Dillman) tries to persuade Sergeant Paul Ryker (Lee Marvin) to tell him the truth in *Sergeant Ryker*.

It is late at night when Young drops in on Ann Ryker to give her the good news; the conversation turns personal as Ann confesses that she loves him more than her husband. As they kiss, General Bailey enters and orders Young to be court-martialed as well, after the new Ryker trial is concluded.

The trial begins. Witnesses support the Army's position that Ryker had defected to the North Koreans and was returning as a North Korean spy. Flashbacks show some of Ryker's initial interrogation by Captain Appleton (Murray Hamilton) and Young's discovery of Colonel Chambers' empty coffin. Two surprise witnesses testify that Ryker knew a current North Korean general when they attended college together back in the States and that Ryker helped that current general interrogate American P.O.W.s while he was in North Korea.

Young puts Ryker on the stand. Under Whitaker's accusatory cross-examination, Ryker loses his temper. When all hope seems lost, Sergeant Winkler tells Young that he also had a secret assignment from Colonel Chambers, who was concerned about an information leak in his department. The next day, with General Bailey present, Young recalls Sergeant Winkler, who tells of his secret assignment to check on a Korean woman whom Captain Appleton has been seeing. Captain Appleton testifies that he has been keeping company and drinking with this woman; Young then notes that the lady in question has just asked for political asylum at the Soviet embassy. The defense rests and Sergeant Paul William Ryker is acquitted of treason. After the trial, Ann tells Young that Ryker will never be fully believed—despite the acquittal—and that she must stay with him. General Bailey congratulates Young on plugging the information leak and saving the life of a war hero.

Sergeant Ryker is similar in subject to Marvin's earlier film *The Rack*, which starred Paul Newman as the accused and which also had its origins as a television play. Both films examine dark issues of war—treason and collaboration—although *Ryker* is more of a legal drama of military justice than *The Rack*'s psychological exploration of a soldier under duress. The issue of American soldiers collaborating with the North Koreans and Chinese during the Korean War was a new and disturbing concept to Americans. While *The Rack* dramatized one soldier's plight, *Sergeant Ryker* focused on the legal and military implications of a soldier's alleged collaboration.

The film offers a fascinating glimpse of military justice. It is very even-handed, depicting the shortcomings of the military court-martial system as well as the search for truth. The character of General Bailey, in particular, is representative of such justice: tough, no-nonsense, but ultimately fair and willing to consider all the facts. And like the court-martials in *The Caine Mutiny* and *The Rack*, *Sergeant Ryker*'s also focuses on the defense of someone who is accused of a crime so heinous that just finding him an attorney is a challenge.

The acting is superior throughout, with honors going to Bradford Dillman as Captain Young, the lawyer who sticks to his principles even though he feels that his client deserves whatever he gets. Dillman doesn't overact; he simply lets himself become the character, and every emotion and feeling we see rings true. Peter Graves and Lloyd Nolan are stalwart as the military brass, while Norman Fell and Murray Hamilton make the most of their supporting roles. Vera Miles is also strong and believable, though her role has some clichés and poor dialogue to overcome.

Lee Marvin does well in a surprisingly small role as the sullen title character; ironically, despite the fact that the feature was released to capitalize on Marvin's popularity, some of his original scenes were cut from the finished film! Marvin's relatively few remaining scenes are confined to the brig or the courtroom. While Marvin does register as the distraught officer, there is no middle ground in his performance. He's either resigned to his fate, believing that nothing can save him, or boiling with emotion, particularly anger, at his situation. His most telling line begins spitefully and ends with a dark pride as he tells the trial judges that, "They [the North Koreans] believed me. They made me a major!"

The editing of the film from the original two-part episode is haphazard and sloppy. Instead of the straightforward chronological approach originally taken, the film starts in the middle of the story and then uses flashbacks to fill in the gaps. The first half is full of gaffes because the location has been changed to Tokyo instead of Seoul. Some dialogue is lost, including General Bailey's decision not to prosecute Young at the end of Ryker's second trial! The worst editing occurs when Young and Ann are traveling to Seoul and are followed, and then fired upon, by a mysterious motorcyclist. In the TV version, his presence is questioned and has some importance; in the film, however, he is scared away by added stock footage of jets attacking a road convoy, never to be referred to again.

Still, *Sergeant Ryker* is an interesting, well-acted film which still holds up as a fine courtroom drama and study of military procedure. It was distributed by Universal in March 1968, but did little business, despite poster art which depicts Marvin in brutal action, very reminiscent of the artwork for *The Dirty Dozen*. However, this just isn't the case; *Sergeant Ryker* is not an action film.

Howard Thompson of the *New York Times* commented on the film's television origins and gave it a favorable review, noting that, "Mr. Marvin and Mr. Dillman are fierce and fine, with firm support from Murray Hamilton, Peter Graves, Norman Fell and that old pro, Lloyd Nolan, who couldn't give a bad performance if he tried."

"The Case Against Paul Ryker," the original NBC *Kraft Suspense Theatre* program, is available for viewing at certain locations across the country, such as Chicago's Museum of Broadcast Communications. It is well worth seeing, and is superior to the film version.

Three years after "The Case Against Paul Ryker" aired on NBC, a television show debuted on ABC entitled *Court Martial*, starring Bradford Dillman as Captain David Young and Peter Graves as Major Frank Whitaker. The setting of the show was changed from the Korean War to World War II, but the format was essentially the same: The Judge Advocate General's lawyers travel across Europe collecting evidence, then go to trial. *Court Martial* lasted for twenty-six episodes during the 1966 season, though some of them never aired in America. Lee Marvin took no part.

Hell in the Pacific (1968)

CREDITS: Selmur and 20th Century–Fox. *Directed by* John Boorman. *Produced by* Reuben Bercovitch. *Executive Producers*: Selig J. Seligman, Henry G. Saperstein. *Screenplay by* Alexander Jacobs, Eric Bercovici. *Story by* Reuben Bercovitch. *Music*: Lalo Schifrin. *Music Editor*: James Henrikson. *Director of Photography*: Conrad Hall, A.S.C. *Film Editor*: Thomas Stanford. *Art Directors*: Anthony D. G. Pratt, Masao Yamazaki. *Set Decorator*: Makoto Kikuchi. *Sound Recording*: Tooru Sakata. *Rerecording Supervisor*: Clem Portman. *Sound Effects by* Frank E. Warner. *Makeup*: Shigeo Kobayashi. *Production Managers*: Lloyd E. Anderson, Harry F. Hogan, Isao Zeniya. *Property Masters*: Frank A. Wade, Kesataka Sato. *Script Supervisor*: John Franco. *Camera Operator*: Jordan Cronenweth. *Key Grip*: Arthur Brooker. *Lighting*: Harry Sundby. *Communications*: Bert Hallberg. *Special Effects*: Joe Zomar, Kunishige Tanaka. *Assistant Director*: Yoichi Matsue. *Production Assistant*: B.C. (Doc) Wylie. *Assistant Editor*: Neil Travis. *Technical Adviser*: Masaaki Asukai. *Technical Assistance by* Trissen Enterprise S. A. Tokyo. Rated G. Technicolor. Panavision (2.35:1). 103 minutes. Released in November 1968. Currently available on VHS videotape and laserdisc.

CAST: *American Soldier*, Lee Marvin; *Japanese Soldier*, Toshiro Mifune.

Lee Marvin liked working with director John Boorman on *Point Blank* so much that he agreed to work with Boorman on his next project, originally entitled *The Enemy*. Not only would this film be a rigorous, physical location shoot, but it would force Marvin to face his own memories of combat in the South Pacific during World War II.

There isn't any conventional plot to *Hell in the Pacific*. An American soldier (Lee Marvin) in a lifeboat lands on a South Pacific island and finds a Japanese soldier (Toshiro Mifune) already there. They chase each other around the island, scaring one another away

An American soldier (Lee Marvin) and a Japanese soldier (Toshiro Mifune) engage in a war of their own in *Hell in the Pacific*.

from their own meager stores. They taunt, plant traps for, and eventually capture one another, but neither man can bring himself to kill the other. Each man takes turns as master of the other, and then slave. Eventually, they form a primitive communication and begin to work together for survival. At certain points, they even become close.

The two men build a raft and successfully launch it. They drift across the sea for endless days, finally landing at another island, where they find a bombed-out military fort. The men shave, put on new clothes, cut their hair, smoke and drink a bit. They laugh together, happy to be alive. Pictures of slaughtered Japanese soldiers in a *Life* magazine split the two apart, however, as they begin to argue about the war and the existence of God. The two men, still enemies but unable to harm each other, walk away from each other just before the fort is bombed into rubble and they (presumably) die.

Hell in the Pacific is an existential two-character drama, an allegory about the futility of war and an examination of human nature under extreme conditions. It is mostly successful in conveying the ideas that people need to work together to survive, that people are mostly the same no matter what their nationalities or political views, and that the human need for companionship can, on a personal level, transcend the condition of war. It is convincing in its argument that if people are forced to bond together to survive, even without a common form of communication, they will.

Director Boorman uses some intriguing devices to tell his story. First, Lee Marvin only speaks English and Toshiro Mifune only speaks Japanese. To widen the chasm of communication between them for the audience, no subtitles are used for either language. This is not only the most realistic way to film the story, but the most meaningful, forcing the actors as well as the audience to focus on what the other actor is trying to express. Another highlight is Conrad Hall's exquisite widescreen photography. Hall, who also photographed *The Professionals, Cool Hand Luke, In Cold Blood* and *Butch Cassidy and the Sundance Kid* was the top cinematographer of the mid- and late 1960s, and he gives *Hell in the Pacific* his personal touch.

The film benefits from its authentic South Pacific location. It was filmed on Palau, in the Caroline Islands of Micronesia, over a four-month period. The jungle and beach settings are as real as can be, and the two actors did all of their own stunts. Boorman strove for authenticity regarding every detail of the environment, every conflict between the two men, every vestige of human nature. And, as far as he could, he succeeded.

The one area in which the film doesn't succeed is in regards to the characters. Even though Marvin and Mifune are very good, their roles are not individual characters; they are nationalistic stereotypes. They don't even have names. They are representatives, not people, and in that sense, Boorman is not being authentic. National archetypes fit Boorman's use of the film as allegory, but that same utilization hurts the film as narrative because the audience has little identification with the characters except for nationality and personality. And in this film, with so little dialogue and no real communication between the two combatants, there is not much individual personality shown by either actor. They are too busy representing.

Both actors represent very well, however. Lee Marvin was a natural choice for the role of the American and gives the character an earthy, elemental quality. Even better is Toshiro Mifune, who took the role to show the world what kind of people the Japanese really are. He took pains to make his character a model soldier, refusing to shame the character in any way. Even so, he brings a sense of humor and a thorough understanding of human nature to the role, and ultimately gains more audience empathy than does Lee Marvin, perhaps due to overcoming the difficulty of communication.

The film has one major flaw which isn't John Boorman's responsibility—the ending. It is understandable when the two men walk away from each other at the end, not being able to come to an understanding. But then, seconds later, they are both presumably killed by shelling that seems to come from nowhere (although it is heard coming closer in the background during the scene). This nihilistic ending does not fit the film's message at all and does not add one single shred of meaning. It was a terrible decision, evidently made because there wasn't enough violence in the movie up until then. Boorman's original ending, which allows the two men to go their separate ways, is much more realistic, though still somewhat unsatisfying, and is included on the laserdisc version of the film as an alternate ending.

Filming *Hell in the Pacific* brought Lee Marvin back to the South Pacific for the first time in twenty-three years. It rekindled his interest in the area, for he soon afterward took up deep sea fishing and began to travel more extensively than he had previously. It also brought back memories of the campaigns he had fought at Kwajalein, Eniwetok and Saipan. Physically, it was an extremely grueling shoot; over the course of four months, a very fit Marvin lost twenty pounds. But mentally reliving the past and remembering all of the people he had known who hadn't lived through the war was tougher.

On June 18, 1944, after having fought on twenty-one separate islands in the South Pacific over a twenty-two month period, Private First Class Lee Marvin was, as he put it, "shot in the ass" during the battle of Saipan. Upon returning to the United States, Marvin spent the next thirteen months in military hospitals recuperating from his wound.

According to John Boorman, "Reliving that period of his life provoked a kind of crisis in him. The producers wanted him to kill Mifune in the end. And perhaps that's also what the public wanted. But I refused. Everything that Lee was—his violence, his killer's instinct—made him want to kill Mifune. The fact that we were able to film that [non-violent] ending was a kind of catharsis for Marvin. He said to me: 'I'm sick of killing people to gratify millions of spectators. From now on they can kill each other.'" Further backing up Marvin's stand is his own take on the movie: "The story is about two men who *can't* kill each other."

Hell in the Pacific was released briefly in November of 1968 and received a wider exposure in March of 1969. Though it garnered some favorable notices from critics who responded to its authentic realism or its allegorical message, it never found much of an audience. Because of its two-character structure, lack of dialogue and defeatist ending, it is not a commercially viable film. For an audience, watching a two-character drama can be exasperating, especially when those two characters cannot even communicate with each other. Add an ending that defeats the purpose of the film, and the result is a movie that few people will bother to watch. Unfortunately, few did.

Paint Your Wagon (1969)

CREDITS: Paramount. *Directed by* Joshua Logan. *Produced by* Alan Jay Lerner. *Associate Producer*: Tom Shaw. *Screenplay and Lyrics by* Alan Jay Lerner. *Adaptation by* Paddy Chayevsky. *Music by* Frederick Loewe. *Music for Additional Songs by* Andre Previn. *Based upon the Musical Play* Paint Your Wagon. *Presented on the Stage by* Cheryl Crawford. *Choral Arrangements and Music Assistant to the Producer*: Joseph J. Lilley. *Orchestral Music Scored and Conducted by* Nelson Riddle. *Choral Music Conducted by* Roger Wagner. *Songs* (by Lerner/Loewe): "I'm on My Way," "I Still See Elisa," "I Talk to the Trees," "Hand Me Down That Can o' Beans," "Whoop-Ti-Ay," "They Call the Wind Maria," "There's a Coach Comin' In," "Wand'rin' Star." *Songs* (by Lerner/Previn): "Best Things," "The Gospel of No-Name City," "A Million Miles Away Behind the Door," "The First Thing You Know," "Gold Fever." *Director of Photography*: William A. Fraker, A.S.C. *Film Editor*: Robert C. Jones. *Art Director*: Carl Braunger. *Set Decorator*: James I. Berkey. *Sound Mixer*: William Randall. *Stereophonic Rerecording Engineer*: Fred Hynes. *Costumes and Production Design by* John Truscott. *Costume Coordinator*: Anne Laune. *Costume Supervisor*: Bill Jobe. *Makeup*: Frank McCoy. *Hairdresser*: Vivian Zavitz. *Special Effects*: Maurice Ayers, Larry Hampton. *Camera Operator*: David Walsh. *Camera Assistant*: Bob Byrne. *Gaffer*: Joe Smith. *Key Grip*: Tom May. *Property*: Bob Eaton. *Production Managers*: Carl Beringer, Fred LeMoine. *First Assistant Director*: Jack Roe. *Script Supervisor*: Marshall Wolins. *Dialogue Coach*: Joseph Curtis. *Production Coordinator*: Gene Levy. *Titles Designed by* David Stone Martin. *Assistant to the Producer*: Jonas Halperin. *Second Unit Direction*: Tom Shaw, Fred LeMoine. *Second Unit Photography*: Loyal Griggs. *Aerial Photography*: Nelson Tyler. *Choreography for* "Gold Fever" *and* "Best Things:" Jack Baker. *First Assistant Director, Second Unit*: Al Murphy. Rated M (later PG). Technicolor. Panavision (2.35:1). 166 minutes. Released in October 1969. Currently available on VHS videotape and laserdisc.

CAST: *Ben Rumson*, Lee Marvin; *Pardner*, Clint Eastwood; *Elizabeth*, Jean Seberg; *Mad Jack Duncan*, Ray Walston; *Rotten Luck Willie*, Harve Presnell; *Horton Fenty*, Tom Ligon; *Parson*, Alan Dexter; *Joe Mooney*, Terry Jenkins; *Mrs. Fenty*, Paula Trueman; *Steve Bull*, H. B. Haggerty; *Heywood Holbrook*, Ben Baker; *Horace Tabor*, William O'Connell; *Foster*, Geoffrey Norman; *Atwell*, Robert Easton; *Mr. Fenty*, Alan Baxter; *Schermerhorn*, Karl Bruck; *Jacob Woodling*, John Mitchum; *Sarah Woodling*, Sue Casey; *Indian*, Eddie Little Sky; *Higgins*, Harvey Parry; *Wong*, H. W. Gim; *Frock-Coated Man*, William Mims; *Hennessey*, Roy Jenson; *Clendennon*, Pat Hawley; The Nitty Gritty Dirt Band.

In perhaps the biggest blunder of his career, Lee Marvin turned down a project with buddy Sam Peckinpah in order to make this big-budget musical. Marvin was wooed to *Paint Your Wagon* personally by producer-lyricist Alan Jay Lerner and then paid a cool million dollars for his efforts on the film. *Paint Your Wagon* was one of the last of Hollywood's big-budget musicals, and though it is not as bad a film as its legend suggests, it certainly exemplifies Hollywood excess at its worst. The film that Marvin passed on with Sam Peckinpah was a western for Warner Brothers titled *The Wild Bunch*.

Paint Your Wagon takes place during the California gold rush of 1849–50 as thousands of men headed west to find what they thought was certain wealth. One of them is Ben Rumson (Lee Marvin), a bearded, bear-like, workhorse of a man who likes his whiskey and loves his gold. He saves the life of a man who becomes his "Pardner" (Clint Eastwood), and together they stake one of the richest claims of what quickly becomes No-Name City. Pardner is a quiet, reserved man who takes long walks and sings to the trees.

Their lives become complicated in a hurry when a Mormon stops in town and agrees to sell one of his two wives. In a drunken stupor, Ben buys beautiful Elizabeth (Jean Seberg) and marries her. Elizabeth is a dignified woman, and she persuades Ben to treat her kindly and build her a cabin. When Ben's jealousy begins to threaten the marriage, he arranges, with some other men, to hijack a wagon of prostitutes bound for another town. While Ben is gone, Elizabeth falls for Pardner, a fact which Ben discerns as soon as he returns. To everyone's surprise, Elizabeth doesn't want to give up either man, so she, in essence, marries both of them.

This situation works for a long while, until a family rescued during a nearby snowstorm boards at the cabin, causing Elizabeth to rethink her morality and to temporarily evict Ben. Meanwhile, the gold supply is beginning to run low, so Ben, Pardner and Mad Jack Duncan (Ray Walston) devise a plan to dig underneath the town's stores and collect the gold dust that has dropped through the floor boards of each building. In a raucous finale, Elizabeth dumps both husbands, and the entire town literally collapses as the buildings fall into the tunnels dug beneath the streets. Ben leaves the ruins of No-Name City behind as Pardner stays with Elizabeth to build a new life.

On Broadway, *Paint Your Wagon* ran for 289 performances—a respectable, if not overwhelming, run. For the film, producer-lyricist

During the destruction of No Name City, Ben Rumson (Lee Marvin) finds himself and a friend travelling down the creek without a paddle.

Alan Jay Lerner cut some of his own (and Frederick Loewe's) songs and hired Andre Previn (with Loewe's approval) to write music to his new lyrics. The play's narrative, of a prospector and his daughter who finds love in the wilderness, was also altered by Paddy Chayevsky to make it more cinematic. Despite this massive retooling, the film still has many flaws—it's an hour too long, half of the songs are easily forgettable, the supporting characters have little to do but sing, the choreography is non-existent, and the main story isn't exactly compelling. Then there's the casting.

Alan Jay Lerner wanted Lee Marvin to play Ben Rumson, and offered the actor so much money that he got his man. But *Paint Your Wagon* is a musical, and Marvin proves that he isn't a singer, particularly on the song "Best Things." Marvin has only two solos—"The First Thing You Know" and "Wand'rin' Star," though he joins in on several of the other songs as well. The latter song is Marvin's one musical highlight, a melodic trail song with a nice easy rhythm, fit to his low, rumbling voice (which co-star Seberg once referred to as "rain gurgling down a rusty pipe"). "Wand'rin' Star" is one of the film's few memorable musical moments and unexpectedly became a huge #1 hit in Britain, giving Lee Marvin his one and only gold record.

Joseph Morgenstern of *Newsweek* had particular praise for Marvin's rendition of the song, while, surprisingly, sidestepping the issue of Marvin's voice: "Marvin does the tune in a gallant croak, accompanied by a vast, pretentious chorus. It's all to his advantage to be musical underdog, but the real reason for his brief success is that he does the thing straight. He watches as he wanders. For once his eyes seem to be seeing things. Throughout the movie he has rolled them in lechery, raised them in mock piety, squinted them in suspicion. Now, for a few marvelous, silent moments, he uses them to see with, and to release that inner energy without which actors, and whole movies, are dead weight." He couldn't be more right.

Another actor who couldn't pass up the chance to sing on-screen was Clint Eastwood, who was anxious to break away from the tight-lipped mythic action figures he had been playing. Eastwood, an accomplished pianist, had sung on his *Rawhide* television show and had even released an album years earlier. He was not a bad choice for the role of Pardner, but his voice does seem "light and thin" (Pauline Kael's words) compared to that of Harve Presnell, the only real singer in the cast. Eastwood's four songs are "I Still See Elisa," "I Talk to the Trees," "Gold Fever," and "Best Things." As good as the song is, it is disconcerting to watch the man who later played Dirty Harry walking alone in the forest singing "I Talk to the Trees."

Jean Seberg was chosen for the film for her dramatic talents and beauty, but she still has to lip-sync the movie's weakest song, "A Million Miles Away Behind the Door"; Seberg's singing is dubbed by Rita Gordon. Fourth-billed Ray Walston has absolutely nothing to do, heard only occasionally singing a line or two in "Best Things." The entire cast, other than Harve Presnell, seems completely musically misused. Hollywood had cast non-singers in musicals before, most notably in *Camelot*, but critics and audiences had found the trend wanting. Why make a musical if your main stars can't sing credibly? If *Paint Your Wagon* had been a low-key project, it might have come and gone without much notice, but this was not to be.

Paint Your Wagon became legendary before its own release for the incredible problems the cast and crew experienced on location in Baker, Oregon. Paramount paid nearly $500,000 for road improvements when rain washed out the only road to the set. Hundreds of hippies who had been hired as extras eventually banded into a self-styled union, demanding more pay and doggie bags of food to take back to their non-working friends. It rained heavily during Oregon's dry season. Trees were imported from Los Angeles to fill in a set that looked "barren." Daily helicopter trips to the set for cast, crew and occasional visitors helped boost production costs, and the budget for the film spiraled from $9 million up to the $20 million level, making it, at that time, one of the most expensive films ever made.

Paint Your Wagon

Ben Rumson (Lee Marvin) breaks into song in *Paint Your Wagon*.

First-time producer Alan Jay Lerner undermined veteran director Joshua Logan's directorial efforts without thinking twice. After the first week of shooting, the *Los Angeles Times* reported that Logan would be replaced by Richard Brooks. Logan found that he was locked into his contract and, under great stress, continued to direct, with no enthusiasm, for the next five months. In post-production, Lerner took over the editing from Logan and fashioned the film in his own way, ignoring his director's wishes.

The result is an overblown musical adventure of polyandry and greed, punctuated with a few memorable sequences. The pace and editing of the "There's a Coach Comin' In" sequence perfectly matches the song's rousing melody and is easily the most impressive musical segment in the film. Likewise, Harve Presnell's rendition of the plaintive "They Call The Wind Maria" stands out (even though the song is staged without wind of any sort). And Lee Marvin's bullfrog rendition of "Wand'rin' Star" is, in its own way, unforgettable. But the rest of the film is below par.

With this performance Marvin began to parody himself on-screen, making every gesture overly theatrical, contorting his face into as many shapes as it would go to elicit laughs from the audience. His buffoonery was kept to a minimum during the songs, but it increased during the lulls between the musical numbers. Eastwood rarely expresses any emotion other than the steely grimness of a man caught in a trap. Seberg gives the film a helping of sexuality and dignity, but falters when virtue and morality raise their heads late in the story.

The film received mostly unfavorable notices, but audiences were curious enough to make it a modest hit which eventually came close to breaking even. While many reviews focused on the struggles behind the scenes, occasional reviews actually targeted the problems of the actual film. Most took aim at the screenplay, some at the music, some at the performers. One of the more incisive came from *Cue* magazine, which noted that, "the vigorous choreography many remember (from the original stage play) is reduced to clomping around in the mud." This comment not only applies to the choreography but to the project as a whole.

Paint Your Wagon, in its way, did change movie history. It taught Paramount and the other studios that big wasn't always better, that location shooting was sometimes too expensive to justify, and that blockbuster musicals, particularly with non-singers as leads, were nearing extinction. It taught Clint Eastwood to take charge of his own career, which he did by spending more of his time and effort on his production company, Malpaso. It became a legendary debacle, epitomizing the worst of Hollywood's wasteful ways.

The movie isn't very good, but it isn't that bad, either. There is some comedy along the way and, if one is in the right mood, the story can be touching or compelling. And it does present audiences with the one and only chance to see screen greats Lee Marvin and Clint Eastwood actually sing. But they do their best, and if it weren't for this movie, their dubious singing talents might have remained undiscovered.

Monte Walsh (1970)

CREDITS: Cinema Center/National General. *Directed by* William A. Fraker. *Produced by* Hal Landers, Bobby Roberts. *Screenplay by* Lukas Heller, David Zelag Goodman. *Based upon the Novel by* Jack Schaefer. *Music Composed and Conducted by* John Barry. *Song* "The Good Times Are Comin'" *by* John Barry, Hal David; *sung by* Mama Cass. *Director of Photography*: David M. Walsh. *Film Editors*: Richard Brockway, Robert L. Wolfe, A.C.E., Raymond Daniels, Gene Fowler, Jr., A.C.E. *Production Designed by* Albert Brenner. *Supervising Sound Editor*: Jack Finlay. *Supervising Music Editor*: Gene Feldman. *Art Director*: Jack Roe. *Unit Production Managers*: Bill Finnegan, Chris Seiter. *Camera Operator*: John Hussey. *Camera Assistant*: Bobby Byrne. *Set Decorator*: Phil Abramson. *Sound*: Jerry Kosloff. *Music Produced by* Phil Ramone. *Properties by* Richard Rubin. *Makeup*: Emile LaVigne. *Hair Stylist*: Dione Taylor. *Script Supervisor*: John Franco. *Women's Costumer*: Patricia Norris. *Men's Costumer*: Alan Levine. *Special Effects*: George Peckham. *Gaffer*: Joe Smith. *Key Grip*: Tom May. *Second Assistant Director*: Al Murphy. *Assistant Film Editor*: John Sheridan. *Casting by* Lynn Stalmaster. Rated GP (later PG). Technicolor. Panavision (2.35:1). 108 minutes. Released in October 1970. Currently available on VHS videotape.

CAST: *Monte Walsh*, Lee Marvin; *Martine Bernard*, Jeanne Moreau; *Chet Rollins*, Jack Palance; *Shorty Austin*, Mitchell Ryan; *Cal Brennan*, Jim Davis; *Sonny Jacobs*, John Hudkins; *Sunfish Perkins*, Ray Guth; *Petey Williams*, John McKee; *Dally Johnson*, Michael Conrad; *Sugar Wyman*, Tom Heaton; *Hal Henderson*, G. D. Spradlin; *Skimpy Eagans*, Ted Gehring; *Jumpin' Joe Joslin*, Bo Hopkins; *Fightin' Joe Hooker*, John McLiam; *Rufus Brady*, Matt Clark; *Powder Kent*, Billy Green Bush; *Mary Eagle*, Allyn Ann McLerie; *Doctor*, Charles Tyner; *Colonel Wilson*, Eric Christmas; *Marshal*, Leroy Johnson; *Farmer*, John Carter; *Card Cheat*, Jack Colvin; *J Cowboys*, Richard Farnsworth, Fred Waugh, Blackie Escalante; *Bartenders*, William Graeff, Jr., Frank Green; *Farm Boys*, Billy Fraker, Kurtis Roberts; *Old Man*, Guy Wilkerson; *Saloon Proprietor*, Roy Barcroft.

Following the over-the-top entertainment of *Paint Your Wagon*, Lee Marvin chose to make a small, quiet, elegiac western, one which would showcase the acting merits (rather than the more popular, violent sides) of himself and costar Jack Palance. Based upon the respected western novel by the author of *Shane*, Jack Schaefer, *Monte Walsh* covers some of the same territory, exploring the role of morality in a country where men are forced by circumstances to make difficult choices with serious consequences. As with *The Man Who Shot Liberty Valance*, *Monte Walsh* takes place beneath the setting sun of the old West.

After spending the winter away from the ranch where they are employed, Monte Walsh (Lee Marvin) and saddle pal Chet Rollins (Jack Palance) return to the tiny town of Harmony to find that the ranch has been sold and that they are out of work. Both men are hired at another ranch, which is being run for an

Eastern conglomerate by Cal Brennan (Jim Davis). Among the other ranch hands is Shorty Austin (Mitchell Ryan), a bronco buster with a short temper, whom Monte and Chet befriend. Monte spends his extra time with sometime hooker Martine Bernard (Jeanne Moreau), whom he calls "Countess." Chet has his eye on "the hardware widow," Mary Eagle (Allyn Ann McLerie).

The ranch owners force Brennan to release some of the ranch hands; Brennan chooses the three youngest: Shorty, Sugar Wyman (Tom Heaton) and Rufus Brady (Matt Clark). Some time later, Shorty shoots a man who has drawn his gun on Rufus in the rain, not realizing that the man is a U. S. marshal, and unaware that Rufus and Sugar had robbed a bank. The three men, now outlaws, ride off. Chet and Mary Eagle marry, and Chet begins work at the hardware store, depriving Monte of his riding pal and best friend. Monte discovers that Shorty and Rufus have been rustling cattle from Brennan's ranch, and Monte warns them to stop. Rufus draws on him and Monte shoots him down.

Chet's wedding causes Monte to consider the same arrangement with Martine, but in spite of her enthusiasm he delays the action. Melancholy, Monte happens to find the horse that Shorty couldn't tame and decides to do the job himself. Unfortunately for the town of Charleyville, the gray horse doesn't want to be broken and destroys several buildings, inside and out, before he submits to Monte's will. The horse's owner, Colonel Wilson (Eric Christmas), offers Monte a lucrative job riding in his Wild West show as "Texas Jack Butler," but after considering the offer, Monte refuses. "I ain't spitting on my whole life," he decides.

Shorty and another man visit Chet's hardware store to ask for money, and when Chet refuses and tells him to turn himself in, Shorty kills his old friend. Monte tracks Shorty to Sugar, who tells him that Martine is sick. Monte arrives in Charleyville after Martine, who had suffered from tuberculosis, dies. He spends some time with her before being called out by Shorty. Monte follows Shorty to a stockyard, where the two men stalk each other in the shadows. Finally, after being wounded in the shoulder, Monte shoots and kills his former friend. "I broke the gray [horse]," Monte tells him. At film's end, Monte is leading and talking to his horse, looking for something to do, someplace to go, some reason to live. He keeps moving on.

William A. Fraker had been a noted cinematographer before *Monte Walsh*, his first directing assignment. Somewhat strangely, Fraker refrains from using the usual panoramic vistas that often frequent western sagas. Instead, he uses medium and close-up shots. These are effective much of the time, particularly late in the film when the characters are especially wistful or sad. On the other hand, Fraker also uses them during a barroom fracas and a bunkhouse brawl, which dramatically weakens the effect of the action. The nicest cinematography occurs during the mustang roundup, in a scene which recalls some classic westerns of the past.

Monte Walsh is a melancholy, powerful western that depicts in no uncertain terms the poverty of frontier life and the immense toll such existence extracts from the people who endure it. It is one of the most realistic, authentic westerns ever made; its characters are not heroes or villains—just people who somehow find themselves at odds with each other. Perhaps its greatest strength is that it rarely becomes maudlin, melodramatic or depressing; the emotions it displays (and inspires) are real because they are firmly rooted in truth. And the truth, as in all great movies, begins with the characters.

The male characters in *Monte Walsh* are all just regular guys, but the script, just as the novel, gives them firm identities, and the actors breathe fascinating life into them. Chet Rollins is perhaps the most memorable because Jack Palance, usually cast as a villain, does a wonderful job as the smiling, happy cowhand. Playing a genuinely nice person, Palance was a revelation to audiences accustomed to seeing him kill without conscience for two decades. In his film debut, Mitchell Ryan is excellent as Shorty, the bronco buster who unwittingly becomes an outlaw and who

Monte Walsh (Lee Marvin) watches Shorty Austin take target practice.

cannot bring himself to prevent his fate, despite the cost to his friends. The cast also includes top supporting actors Matt Clark, Jim Davis, G. D. Spradlin, Ted Gehring, Billy Green Bush, Charles Tyner, Richard Farnsworth and old-time cowboy star Roy Barcroft.

But *Monte Walsh* is Lee Marvin's movie, and Marvin has never given a more vulnerable, human performance than he gives here. Vincent Canby of the *New York Times* found Marvin to be "professionally cute, given to comic mannerisms...," and some other critics concurred, but this criticism applies much more forcefully to the movies he was to do for American International Pictures six years later. Here, perhaps for the first time, Marvin allows himself to show his unprotected side and to display deep, honest human emotion. One does not think of gentleness and tenderness when thinking of Lee Marvin, but both of those characteristics are important and effective aspects of Monte's character. Marvin had always been a charismatic performer and a good actor, but in *Monte Walsh* he goes beyond his talent and reaches the heart of his character, and the result can be seen in his eyes. Within this film is perhaps the single greatest film performance Lee Marvin ever gave.

Marvin may have been inspired by the presence of Jeanne Moreau, with whom he had an affair during filming. At the time, Moreau was widely quoted as saying, "Lee Marvin is more male than anyone I have ever acted with. He is the greatest man's man I have ever met and that includes all the European stars I have worked with." High praise indeed from one of the world's most beautiful and talented actresses.

Monte Walsh received mixed reviews from critics, but most audiences who sought it out liked it. It was not the success hoped for, and Marvin himself later admitted that he was disappointed in the film as a whole, though it was one of his favorite projects. It is a flawed work from a first-time director, and its somber tone does seem to prevent audiences from rediscovering it, but it is quite effective and, perhaps most importantly, contains marvelous performances by Lee Marvin and Jack Palance.

Pocket Money (1972)

CREDITS: First Artists/National General. *Distributed by* Warner Bros. *Directed by* Stuart Rosenberg. *Produced by* John Foreman. *Screenplay by* Terry Malick. *Based on the Novel* Jim Kane *by* J.P.S. Brown. *Adaptation by* John Gay. *Musical Score by* Alex North. *Song* "Pocket Money" *Written and Performed by* Carole King. *Director of Photography*: Laszlo Kovacs. *Edited by* Bob Wyman. *Art Direction*: Tambi Larson. *Set Decorator*: Darrell Silvera. *Sound*: Lawrence Jost, Bud Grenzbath. *Sound Effects by* Edit-Rite, Inc. *Costumes*: Jim Linn. *Men's Hair Consultant*: Jim Markham. *Hair Stylist*: Jane Shugrue. *Makeup*: Richard Cobos. *Associate Producer*: Frank Caffey. *Technical Advisor and Second Unit Director*: James Arnett. *Production Manager*: Arthur S. Newman, Jr. *Assistant Director*: Mickey McCardle. *Script Supervisor*: John Franco. *Production Representative*: Hank Moonjean. *Casting by* Lynn Stalmaster. *Locations by* Cinemobile. Rated GP (later PG). Technicolor. Flat (1.33:1). 102 minutes. Released in April 1972. Currently available on VHS videotape.

CAST: *Jim Kane*, Paul Newman; *Leonard*, Lee Marvin; *Bill Garrett*, Strother Martin; *Stretch Russell*, Wayne Rogers; *Juan*, Hector Elizondo; *Adelita*, Christine Belford; *Ex-wife*, Kelly Jean Peters; *Chavarin*, Gregg (Gregory) Sierra; *Uncle Herb*, Fred Graham; *American Prisoner*, Matt Clark; *Ministerio Publico*, Claudio Mirando; *Don Tomas*, R. Camargo; *Border Patrolman*, Wynn Pearce; *Rustler*, G. Escandon; *Vasquero*, D. Herrera; *Almara*, John Verros; *Stunt Doubles*, Mickey Gilbert, R. Loney; *Neiblas*, E. Baca; *Filling Station Attendant*, N. Roman; *Foreman*, R. Manning; *Workman*, Terry Malick; *Bit Parts*, Richard Farnsworth, W. Sanders, A. Sandoval, J. Bailey, G. Payne, B. Stout, F. Garcia, P. Johnson, E. Jarvis, J.P. Carranza, P. Avenetti, R. Westberg, D. Starr, F. Soto, P. Espinosa, B. Cutterr, J. Martinez, L. Armando, Jr., Poupee Bocar, D. Hudkins, R. Gainter, J. Alfasa, P. Regas, R. Montoyo, L. Dominguez, R. Romero.

In 1969 Paul Newman teamed up with Sidney Poitier and Barbra Streisand to form a production company which they called First Artists. It was a throwback, an attempt to duplicate the success of United Artists, which had been formed in 1919 by Mary Pickford, Douglas Fairbanks, Charlie Chaplin and D.W. Griffith, and which is still producing films today. First Artists was joined in 1971 by Steve McQueen and in 1972 by Dustin Hoffman. Their company officially went into business when *Pocket Money* began filming in April of 1971. *Pocket Money* was First Artists' premiere offering, and thus was highly anticipated.

Based on the novel *Jim Kane*, and originally using that title during filming, *Pocket Money* is a comedy-drama which tells the meandering story of two modern-day cowboys, Jim Kane (Paul Newman) and Leonard (Lee Marvin), as they try to make a little money and tackle a small cattle drive in Mexico. Jim is a little dim, trusting in first impressions, interpreting comments from people literally. When he buys horses without having them tested and then loses them to disease and quarantine, he is forced to take on another job to pay his outstanding bills.

After some consideration, Jim takes an offer from shady businessman Bill Garrett (Strother Martin) to round up some rodeo cattle down in Mexico. Jim looks up a friend named Leonard (Lee Marvin) to assist him, and they go to Mexico and begin purchasing cattle. Jim overspends his expenses, has a run-in with a Mexican (Gregory Sierra) and lands in jail for a time. Plans change and Jim is told that the cattle need to be transported to Chihuahua. Jim objects, believing that they will be quarantined, but Stretch Russell (Wayne Rogers), Garrett's associate, tells him it's all fixed up—no quarantine will occur.

Jim and Leonard (still in his dark suit, gloves and chaps) drive the cattle across country to Chihuahua, where they are put in quarantine. Stretch refuses to pay Jim's expenses, so Leonard follows him to Garrett. The two men bully Garrett for the money, but he holds out and eventually they give up. Jim and Leonard wander down to the train station and wait for the next train out of town.

There isn't much plot in *Pocket Money* and what there is isn't very compelling. This movie, like *Eight Iron Men*, *Ship of Fools* and *Hell in the Pacific*, is completely character-driven. Unfortunately, unlike those other films, *Pocket Money* doesn't have the compelling characters to keep viewer interest high. For instance, Jim meets a woman named Adelita

(Christine Belford) at a barbecue, and they have one scene where they talk about his ex-wife and look at the beautiful sunset together. It is obvious that they like each other...but she is never mentioned or seen in the film again.

The movie is full of such vignettes which do help illustrate character but don't move the film forward at all. It is professionally made—photographed by Laszlo Kovacs and featuring an Alex North score—but it is almost wholly without drama. Slice-of-life movies only work well when there is some underlying meaning to the narrative, some defined point to the proceedings. *Pocket Money* seems pointless and thus rather boring.

Pocket Money is a comedy, and there are a few chuckles along the way, due solely to the actors' immersion into character and their reactions to absurd situations. Neither actor is afraid to let himself look foolish if that is what the script requires. Paul Newman does a nice job as Jim Kane, but his intellect and sensitivity in previous roles make him the wrong actor for this role. We keep waiting for him to come to his senses and straighten out his character's life.

Lee Marvin is also quite convincing as Leonard, though he really has little to do. Leonard is also the closest which Lee Marvin ever came to playing himself on-screen in a fictional role. Marvin is completely casual, though dressed in a dark suit throughout, and he uses his personal mannerisms—pointing his finger like a gun, making strange noises with his mouth—in this film as in no other. The style of the film is so naturalistic that Marvin's nonchalance and laid-back passivity seem completely at home.

The character of Leonard is almost whimsical. He accepts what comes without question, just trying to keep a little ahead of

Leonard (Lee Marvin) and Jim Kane (Paul Newman) transport their cattle by railroad in *Pocket Money*.

the game. Leonard is a dreamer, cooking up schemes to try to make some money. At one point, he asks Jim what he thinks of the idea of colored salt, which might keep people from putting too much on their food. Marvin's best scene occurs at the end of the cattle drive, when Jim is paying the Mexicans who helped them. Leonard stands up and gives them a pep talk, thanking them and assuring them that if he ever returns, he will hire them again, even though he doesn't know any of their names. Leonard is an amiable guy, bearing no grudges or anger against anyone, just looking to enjoy his life.

Unfortunately for First Artists, that's not what people wanted to see. With both stars playing against type and the seeming disappearance of a plot, *Pocket Money* was a critical and box-office failure. There were some critics who appreciated the film for what it was, but they were vastly outnumbered by critics and audiences who found it dull to the point of tedium and certainly not very funny.

Prime Cut (1972)
(aka *Kansas City Prime*)

CREDITS: Cinema Center/National General. *Directed by* Michael Ritchie. *Produced by* Joe Wizan. *Executive Producer*: Kenneth L. Evans. *Written by* Robert Dillon. *Music by* Lalo Schifrin. *Director of Photography*: Gene Polito. *Edited by* Carl Pingitore. *Art Director*: Bill Malley. *Set Decorator*: James Payne. *Sound Mixer*: Barry Thomas. *Dubbing Mixer*: Joel Moss. *Sound Effects Editor*: Jack Finlay. *Costumes by* Patricia Norris. *Men's Wardrobe by* Ray Summers. *Makeup by* Ken Chase, Emile LaVigne. *Hairstylist*: Salley Bailey. *Gaffer*: Clifford C. Hitchinson. *Key Grip*: Charles Renaud. *Casting*: Hoyt Bowers. *Unit Production Manager*: David Salven. *Assistant Director*: Michael Daves. *Script Supervisor*: Charlsie Bryant. *Production Assistant*: Betty Gumm. *Location Consultant*: Les Kimber. *Title Design*: Don Record. *Special Effects*: Logan Frazee. *Still Photographer*: Orlando Suero. *Property Master*: Allan Levine. *Assistant Property Master*: Terry Lewis. *Assistant Film Editor*: Herb Steinore. *Associate Producer*: Mickey Borofsky. Rated R. Technicolor. Panavision (2.35:1). 91 minutes. Released in June 1972. Not currently available on home video. Previously available on VHS videotape.

CAST: *Nick Devlin*, Lee Marvin; *Mary Ann*, Gene Hackman; *Clarabelle*, Angel Tompkins; *Weenie*, Gregory Walcott; *Poppy*, Sissy Spacek; *Violet*, Janit Baldwin; *Shay*, William Morey; *Delaney*, Clint Ellison; *Shaughnessy*, Howard Platt; *O'Brien*, Les Lannom; *Jake*, Eddie Egan.

Lee Marvin's second 1972 release was a crime melodrama entitled *Prime Cut*. It is a strange and often repellent gangster film, one of many which were made in the wake of *The Godfather*. Though Marvin's screen persona was tough and brutal, he actually appeared in few R-rated films, of which this was the first. Most of his career took place before the Motion Picture Association of America (MPAA) began its voluntary rating system in 1968, and afterward, surprisingly, only about one-third of his films were violent enough to be termed "restricted."

Prime Cut's opening sequence takes place in a slaughterhouse, as Weenie (Gregory Walcott) personally handles a special order between chopping-block credits. By the end of the production line, it is evident that the wieners he has produced contain a great deal of human protein. Weenie then sends the package to Chicago where mob boss Jake (Eddie Egan) realizes that the wieners contain the remains of one of his men. He hires a tough enforcer, Nick Devlin (Lee Marvin), to go to Kansas City and get Jake's share of the slaughterhouse's profits as well as some measure of revenge.

Jake picks three men and a driver (William Morey, Clint Ellison, Les Lannom and Howard Platt) to aid Devlin, and the five drive to Kansas City. They arrive at a large Kansas farm where "Mary Ann's Meats" are produced, and Devlin insists that Mary Ann (Gene Hackman) pay up. Mary Ann promises to pay the next day at a local fair. He then shows Devlin his side business—auctioning off drugged, nude young girls as slaves—and introduces Poppy (Sissy Spacek) and Violet (Janit Baldwin). Devlin picks up Poppy and carries her out to his limousine, taking her "on account."

At the Jayhawker fair the next day, Devlin meets former flame Clarabelle (Angel Tompkins), who is now married to Mary Ann.

Devlin gets down to business and demands payment; Mary Ann gives him a box filled with animal entrails. Violet causes a diversion, and Devlin and Poppy race into the crowd, escaping into the wheat fields surrounding the fair; but then they are menaced by a grain reaper that threatens to cut them into ribbons. Devlin's men arrive and drive their limo into the twirling reaper blades. They survive, though the limousine doesn't.

Devlin stops in to see Clarabelle at her houseboat home. He declines her sexual advances, realizing that she has set up the war between Mary Ann and the Chicago mob, and angrily sends her boat sailing down the Missouri river. While he is gone, Mary Ann's men attack and wound one of Devlin's men, kidnap Poppy, and leave Violet to be gang-raped. Devlin and his two remaining men break out the big guns and approach Mary Ann's farm through a sunflower field. Only Devlin emerges unscathed from the ensuing gun battle, so he goes on to face Mary Ann and Weenie alone.

He commandeers a semi-trailer and crashes through the gate and into a large greenhouse. Devlin shoots it out with Mary Ann and his gang in the livestock barn. Mary Ann is shot and drops, still alive, into a hog pen; Weenie is killed. Devlin finds Poppy and leaves Mary Ann to die. Devlin, his two injured men, and Poppy and Violet stop at the orphanage where Mary Ann raised the girls that he sold. Poppy slugs the woman who runs the place as the girls scamper out and romp about in the afternoon sunshine.

Prime Cut is a stylish, slickly-made, fast-paced gangster melodrama that was made to cash in on the success of *The Godfather*. By transplanting the action from the big city to America's rural heartland, the film tries to provide a fresh perspective on gangster violence and a novel setting for its shoot-em-ups. Most of Mary Ann's gun-toting guards are blond-haired, blue-eyed, corn-fed country boys in overalls, one of whom impales Devlin's limo with a pitchfork. There is a strange,

Nick Devlin (Lee Marvin) makes his move against Mary Ann's mob in *Prime Cut*.

almost surreal quality to the shootout in the sunflower field, and the almost silent grain reaper chase scene is surprisingly effective. One of the film's nicest aspects is its widescreen photography, which thoughtfully frames the destructive actions of greedy men against the whispering beauty of the rolling hills.

However, *Prime Cut* is also a tawdry, tasteless, unsavory melodrama with few likable or honorable characters, using a story that borders on the preposterous and which features plenty of nudity and violence. Mary Ann introduces his side business to Devlin by saying, "Cow flesh, girl flesh, it's all the same to me." The most repellent scene occurs when Devlin finds Violet after she's been gang-raped, clutching the nickels that each of the men paid her for the privilege. If the film has a saving grace, it would have to be its black humor. Though the slaughterhouse setting is certainly gruesome, it does provide the characters, particularly Weenie, with some satirical moments.

The movie's chief point of interest remains its cast. Sissy Spacek made her film debut as Poppy, whom Devlin rescues from a life of white slavery. She is winsome and simple in the part, displaying some acting talent as well as her body. The casting surprise is Gene Hackman as Mary Ann (the name is never explained). He had won an Oscar the year before for *The French Connection*, and evidently chose this role for its character rather than its dignity. He's a flamboyant villain and matches up well against Marvin. Hackman and Gregory Walcott are quite convincing as brothers, as well.

Lee Marvin plays Nick Devlin with an air of cool detachment. He is a thorough professional: deadly with or without weapons, nattily attired, socially charming, amoral, resorting to violence only when provoked. His ulterior motives involving Poppy may be questionable, yet he treats her with respect and never touches her. He also treats his assigned men with respect, even agreeing to meet one's mother before the trip to Kansas City. *Prime Cut* does provide Lee Marvin with one of his most archetypal roles.

Prime Cut was blasted by those critics who bothered to pay any attention to it. Richard Schickel in *Life* "...found this movie repulsive. Not because of its brutality but because of the self-consciously beautiful way director Michael Ritchie shoots and edits it—hypocrisy through technique." Vincent Canby of the *New York Times* detailed the film's "...very uneven quality..." and called it "...somewhat sick-making and essentially silly...."

Jay Cocks of *Time* was also unimpressed: "...*Prime Cut* was obviously intended to be a tough, surreal gangster film in the *Point Blank* mold, a kind of jazzy allegory about brutality and dehumanization. *Point Blank*, however, had John Boorman directing Lee Marvin. *Prime Cut* has only Lee Marvin and a director who must have taken a very long lunch hour. Against all odds, Marvin summons up a measure of dignity. Hackman looks abashed." Cocks also described newcomer Sissy Spacek as "...a young and resplendently unpromising actress..."

Interestingly, the movie those critics hated may not have been the one that Michael Ritchie intended to direct. Reportedly, Ritchie's first cut of the film played in Minneapolis briefly and is far more impressive. However, no verification of such a version could be made for this book.

Director Ritchie not only had to compete against other gangster films but against imself as well. Two weeks before *Prime Cut* was released, his other 1972 feature, *The Candidate*, opened. *The Candidate*, with Robert Redford as an appealing political newcomer, garnered excellent reviews and did strong business. When *Prime Cut* came out it was compared unfavorably with Ritchie's other—much better—film, and it performed very poorly. Today *Prime Cut* is remembered chiefly for its high-powered cast and stylized heartland-of-America violence.

Emperor of the North (1973) (aka *Emperor of the North Pole*)

CREDITS: Inter-Hemisphere and 20th Century–Fox. *Directed by* Robert Aldrich. *Produced by* Stan Hough. *Executive Producer*: Kenneth Hyman. *Written by* Christopher Knopf.

Music: Frank DeVol. *Song* "A Man and a Train" *by* Frank DeVol, Hal David;41 *sung by* Marty Robbins. *Director of Photography*: Joseph Biroc, A.S.C. *Film Editor*: Michael Luciano, A.C.E. *Associate Editors*: Roland Gross, A.C.E., Frank Capacchione. *Art Director*: Jack Martin Smith. *Set Decorator*: Rafael Bretton. *Sound Mixer*: Richard Overton. *Sound Rerecorder*: Theodore Soderberg. *Wardrobe*: Ed Wynigear. *Makeup*: William Turner. *Construction Coordinator*: John La Salandra. *Dialogue Supervision*: Robert Sherman. *Script Supervisor*: Howard Hohler. *Property Master*: Yonacio Sepulveda. *Second Unit Director*: Michael D. Moore. *Unit Production Manager*: Saul Wurtzel. *Assistant Director*: Malcolm Harding. *Second Assistant Directors*: Barry Steinberg, Larry Powell. *Casting*: Jack Baur. *Special Effects*: Henry Millar, Jr. *Visual Effects*: L. D. Abbott, A.S.C. *Sound Effects*: Edward Rossi, William Hartman, Don Isaacs, Don Walden. *Dubb Dialogue Editor*, Godfrey Marks. *Camera Operators*: Joe Jackman, Ken Peach, Jr. *Title Design*: Walter Blake. Rated PG. Color by DeLuxe. Widescreen (1.85:1). Originally 132 minutes. Video version 118 minutes. Released in May 1973 as *Emperor of the North Pole*, later reissued as *Emperor of the North*. Currently available on VHS videotape. Previously available on import laserdisc.

CAST: *A No. 1*, Lee Marvin; *Shack*, Ernest Borgnine; *Cigaret*, Keith Carradine; *Cracker*, Charles Tyner; *Hogger*, Malcolm Atterbury; *Coaly*, Harry Caesar; *Policeman*, Simon Oakland; *Yardman's Helper*, Hal Baylor; *Yardlet*, Matt Clark; *Gray Cat*, Elisha Cook; *Dinger*, Joe Di Reda; *Smile*, Liam Dunn; *Girl in Water*, Diane Dye; *Conductor*, Robert Foulk; *Fakir*, James Goodwin; *Preacher*, Ray Guth; *Grease Tail*, Sid Haig; *Pokey Stiff*, Karl Lukas; *Yard Clerk*, Edward McNally; *Stew Bum*, John Steadman; *Yardman*, Vic Tayback; *Groundhog*, Dave Willock.

Emperor of the North was supposed to be directed by Sam Peckinpah, but the director, who had worked for three years to bring it to fruition, had the project taken away from him. The script was then offered to Robert Aldrich, who hired the actor Peckinpah had always wanted for the role of the world's toughest hobo—Lee Marvin. Peckinpah had worked with Marvin in the early 1960s on television, but they had never made a film together; Marvin had been offered the lead in Peckinpah's *The Wild Bunch*, but he turned it down (in part for the big paycheck of *Paint Your Wagon*). Aldrich was happy to work again with one of his favorite actors; he knew exactly what to expect from Marvin and knew what he could coax out of him.

Emperor of the North sets up a symbolic conflict between legendary vagabond A No. 1 (Lee Marvin) and train conductor Shack (Ernest Borgnine), who refuses to let any hobo, for any reason, ride the rails on his No. 19 train. On the way into Portland, Oregon, A No. 1 and a younger derelict who calls himself Cigaret (Keith Carradine) travel in a boxcar, locked inside by sadistic Shack. A No. 1 starts a fire and crashes out before the train reaches the Portland station, forcing quick work by the railroad men to keep the fire from spreading. Cigaret is caught and claims that he was the only man there, and that he rode the train all the way in, disputing Shack's record.

Before Shack's train leaves Portland, A No. 1 announces that he will ride No. 19 all the way to Eugene, Oregon. Bets are made and interest runs high as Shack begins his run at high speed so that no hobos will be able to jump onboard. A No. 1 changes the switches up the line, however, forcing the train to stop, reverse and pull onto a siding just before an express train speeds by in the other direction. Both A No. 1 and Cigaret board the freight, and Shack sees them. He uses a metal pin on a rope to dislodge the men from underneath the train, laughing as they tumble away from the train, down a slope.

A No. 1 shows Cigaret how to grease the tracks so that a passing passenger train is forced to stop. They climb on top and ride the train to a hobo encampment near Salem, where they eat, attend a revival meeting and get some rest. As No. 19 pulls out of Salem, A No. 1 and Cigaret board it again. Shack again uses the pin and rope, and because Cigaret refuses to help him, A No. 1 kicks the emergency break to end the beating, killing one train man and injuring the other three, including Shack. As the train starts forward, Shack moves in to kill Cigaret. A No. 1 challenges him, and the two titans fight with 2 x 4s, chains and hammers on an empty boxcar. A No. 1 finally knocks Shack off of the train,

138 Emperor of the North

The king of the hobos, A No. 1 (Lee Marvin), carries his dinner with him in *Emperor of the North.*

plot, for he becomes A No. 1's pupil—the ignorant hobo who doesn't know the rules, customs or traditions. What A No. 1 teaches Cigaret, he teaches the audience. Unfortunately, Cigaret is also an arrogant, lying young punk with whom the audience can never feel empathy. As played by Keith Carradine, Cigaret has the dream but not the drive. He hasn't paid his dues and doesn't intend to. When Cigaret gets his comeuppance at the end of the film as A No. 1 happily throws him off the train into a river, it is a vast relief. Carradine has the attitude for the part but does not have the integrity which would have made the character work.

Integrity, of a sort, drives Shack and makes his quest for hobo-less train rides seem almost reasonable. He's a sadistic brute, but his obsession revolves around duty to his job. Why he is so violently against free riders is never quite explained, however, and this works against the character. Ernest Borgnine is not subtle in his performance; he's all bulging eyes, roaring voice and crashing fists, larger than life in a mythic role.

If anything, Lee Marvin underplays *his* mythic role as A No. 1, king of the hobos. Why he is "A No. 1" is never explained, nor is his purpose in riding No. 19 to Eugene, other than to defy Shack. All of these characters seem to have no past or future lives—only the violent here and now. *Emperor of the North* is minimalist filmmaking at its peak; no other reality or sense of time exists outside the film's simple schedule. Marvin is excessively dignified as A No. 1, travelling in a soiled suit and exuding dignity even when carrying a stolen chicken. Marvin is commanding, despite having little dialogue. As a king should, he has a stately posture and countenance that demand attention. Marvin also has fun with the role, pushing the limits of absurdity while teasing a cop with a turkey and enjoying the revival meeting for somewhat less than honorable reasons.

Marvin preferred the original title of the film. "If you're 'Emperor of the North Pole,' that means you're an emperor of nothing, and 'Emperor of the North' doesn't say that to me," he stated. The film was released as

then throws Cigaret off for good measure. He alone is "Emperor of the North."

The film's opening prologue describes how important trains are to the hobos of the country, but the film itself never deals with that issue. Instead, it pits one sadistic train conductor against one very determined hobo, who is accompanied by a young hobo whom he must instruct in the ways of bumdom. Thus, the film's symbolism is minimized and the conflict becomes one of personality. Between the personalities of Ernest Borgnine, Keith Carradine and Lee Marvin, there is no question which one will emerge victorious.

The character of Cigaret is crucial to the

Emperor of the North Pole in May of 1973, but pulled out of release due to poor business. It was thought that audiences were expecting some kind of Arctic adventure, so the name was shortened to *Emperor of the North*. Business remained poor, surprising director Robert Aldrich and the many critics who recommended the film.

Critics did like the movie. Vincent Canby of the *New York Times* called it "a fine, elaborately staged action melodrama" and noted that, "the suspense of the film is unrelenting and the performances first-rate." Most other critics agreed, but audiences just never connected with the film—under either title.

The movie was filmed on location in Oregon, utilizing the Oregon Pacific and Eastern Railroad. The excellent cinematography was contributed by Joseph Biroc, making the forested vistas exceptionally beautiful and the No. 19 train a bona fide member of the cast. The film's one truly awful aspect is the song "A Man and a Train," warbled by Marty Robbins over the opening credits. "A man's not a train, and a train's not a man, for a man can do things a train never can." In spite of the song, the film is a thoughtful (if perhaps underdeveloped) exploration of human conflict. And despite Robert Aldrich's expertise, one wonders what the resulting film would have been in the hands of Peckinpah, then at the peak of his directorial powers.

The Iceman Cometh (1973)

CREDITS: American Film Theatre. *Director*: John Frankenheimer. *Producer*: Ely Landau. *Executive Producer*: Edward Lewis. *Play by* Eugene O'Neill. *Director of Photography*: Ralph Woolsey, A.S.C. *Film Editor*: Harold F. Kress, A.C.E. *Production Design*: Jack Martin Smith. *Costume Consultant*: Dorothy Jeakins. *Production Supervisor*: Irving Temaner. *For The American Film Theatre*: Henry T. Weinstein. *Casting*: Lynn Stalmaster. *Text Editor*: Thomas Quinn Curtiss. *Assistant Directors*: Kurt Neumann, Barry Steinberg. *Camera Operators*: Chris Schwiebert, Richard W. Johnson. *Set Decorator*: Raphael Bretton. *Wardrobe*: Ed Wynigear. *Makeup*: Emile LaVigne, Tom Tuttle. *Script Supervisor*: Karen Wookey. *Assistant Film Editor*: William DeNicholas. *Hairdresser*: Pat Abbott. *Sound Mixer*: Glen Anderson. *Gaffer*: George Holmes. *Re-Recording Mixer*: Theodore Soderberg. *Key Grip*: Andy Nelhams. *AFI Story Consultant*: Edward Anhalt. *Production Associate*: Les Landau. *Stills by* Orlando. *Property Master*: Bob McLaughlin. *Production Assistants*: Bob Graham, Linda Solomon. Rated PG. Eastman Color. Panavision (1.85:1). 239 minutes. Also released in a 101 minute version. Released in October 1973. Not currently available on home video.

CAST: *Teddy Hickey*, Lee Marvin; *Harry Hope*, Fredric March; *Larry Slade*, Robert Ryan; *Don Parritt*, Jeff Bridges; *Willie Oban*, Bradford Dillman; *Hugo*, Sorrell Booke; *Margie*, Hildy Brooks; *Pearl*, Nancy Juno Dawson; *Cora*, Evans Evans; *Cecil Lewis (The Captain)*, Martyn Green; *Joe Mott*, Moses Gunn; *Pat McGloin*, Clifton James; *Jimmy Tomorrow*, John McLiam; *Chuck Morelo*, Stephen Pearlman; *Rocky Pioggi*, Tom Pedi; *Piet Wetjoen (The General)*, George Voskovec; *Detective Lieb*, Don McGovern; *Detective Moran*, Bart Burns.

In 1973, Lee Marvin accepted the most challenging acting role of his career when he signed on to film the screen adaptation of Eugene O'Neill's *The Iceman Cometh*. John Frankenheimer's task was to film, as realistically as possible, O'Neill's tragicomic play, and to do so he rounded up a powerhouse cast, including Marvin, Fredric March, Robert Ryan, Jeff Bridges, Bradford Dillman and Moses Gunn. The finished four-hour film was shown on public television first, then released to theaters, which unfortunately prohibited it from Academy Awards consideration. A truncated 101-minute version was also released.

The Iceman Cometh is set solely in Harry Hope's New York bar in the summer of 1912. Harry (Fredric March) hasn't set foot outside of the bar since his wife died some twenty years earlier, and most of the regulars at the bar seem similarly rooted to the place. There's Larry Slade (Robert Ryan), a former anarchist who acts as the bar's philosopher; Hugo (Sorrell Booke), another anarchist who awakens for bursts of oratory before settling back into a troubled sleep; Willie Oban (Bradford Dillman), a lawyer unable to cope with the judicial system; and Joe Mott (Moses Gunn), a black man who wants to be accepted in the white world.

Other regulars include The Captain (Martyn Green) and The General (George Voskovec), two officers who fought on the opposite sides of the Boer War now spending time trading war stories, and three hookers (Hildy Brooks, Nancy Juno Dawson, Evans Evans) who call themselves tarts and enjoy maddening the bartender, Rocky (Tom Pedi), by referring to him as their pimp. Joining them is newcomer Don Parritt (Jeff Bridges), a young man who seeks out Larry because Larry had known he and his mother in the anarchist movement. Parritt tries repeatedly to talk to Larry, but the older man rebuffs him. These characters and more are all waiting for the arrival of Hickey (Lee Marvin), a hardware salesman who stops by the bar twice a year and regales them with jokes, gags and tales of his wife and the Iceman.

On this visit, however, Hickey is different. He is a new man—on the wagon and full of inner peace. He challenges each of the barflies to look intently at their own lives, to reject the "pipe dreams" which keep them tied to the bar, and to start their lives over again. Hickey succeeds in ruining Harry Hope's birthday party with his lecturing and fuels antagonism in everyone who listens to him. Nevertheless, the next day each and every soul leaves the bar to begin their lives anew, if only to get away from the badgering of Hickey. Harry Hope himself even ventures outside for the first time in twenty years.

By nightfall, every one of the regulars returns, courage spent, ready to face the fact that the bar is their necessary refuge from the world, and Hickey be damned. Hickey is aghast, unable to understand why his friends cannot respond to his advice and wisdom. So he tells them (in a long monologue) that he finally found peace by ending his unhappy marriage by killing his wife. Hickey's act of kindness ended her suffering and his guilt, providing him with psychological freedom. Two detectives arrive in time to hear Hickey's story and take him away to certain death. The barflies decide that Hickey was deranged and celebrate his capture—and Harry Hope's birthday—by getting uproariously drunk.

All except for Larry Slade and Don Parritt. Slade insists that Parritt pay for his betrayal of his own mother and the anarchist movement, and that the best way for him to pay penance is suicide. Larry sits by himself, waiting darkly until Parritt throws himself off of the fire escape outside. He alone is left to ruminate over Hickey's talk about pipe dreams and self-denial. Larry is unable to join in the celebration, knowing that he is the one person that Hickey reached, the only one to understand that illusions can be fatal.

The Iceman Cometh is an ambitious and mostly successful film. Eugene O'Neill's long play is about as uncinematic as it can be, staged in one location with little movement and virtually no action. Director John Frankenheimer uses fluid camera movement to move from character to character, light and shadow as mood and character enhancements, and dialogue as emotional action. To his credit, the film smoothly recreates the pungent atmosphere of a New York City bar, circa 1912, and the characters are brought as vividly to life as one could have hoped. On the other hand, Frankenheimer is unable to completely eliminate the staginess of the piece; it does drag from time to time, and one element in particular—O'Neill's references to the anarchist movement—are completely out of date and mean absolutely nothing to modern moviegoers.

Most of all, *The Iceman Cometh* is a character study, examining how each of a group of people react to Hickey's demand that they reevaluate their lives and start again. Most of the people involved are fraught with poignancy, unable to conquer their personal demons and afraid to try. A few of the characters, such as Hugo (and to a lesser extent, Willie Oban), are cartoonish to the point of exasperation. Others, such as the General and the Captain, Joe Mott, Pat McGloin and Jimmy Tomorrow, represent points of view more than actual human beings. The three tarts and Rocky form their own little island of vice and virtue in Harry's bar. The real meat of the play deals with Hickey, Larry Slade and Don Parritt, and to a lesser extent, Harry Hope.

Harry Hope is at the crux of the film; it is his bar and he lets all these do-nothings hang around just to keep him company, as long as they stay quiet. His "pipe dream" is to leave the bar for the first time in twenty years and walk around the block. Eventually, he makes it outside, but scampers back quickly, frightened, and spends the rest of the movie complaining about how Hickey has done something to take away the power of the booze. As played by Fredric March, Harry is geriatric, running his bar as if it were his own old folks' home stocked with liquor. It was March's last performance, and he was very sick during filming, unable to rehearse or work for long periods of time. Unfortunately, March's frailty makes Harry Hope seem weaker than he is meant to be.

The darkest side of the play focuses on Larry Slade and his refusal to do anything for Don Parritt, the son of a woman he knew—and perhaps once loved—in "the movement." Larry believes himself to be outside the realm of human contact, a commentator on all things within view or thought. Parritt's arrival involves Larry *personally* in life again, and Larry is unwilling to experience true life again. One of the play's major themes is that each character has his or her own dirty little secrets which must finally be faced; Parritt's involves betraying the anarchist movement and (perhaps) inadvertently sacrificing his mother by doing so. Larry, who may or may not have committed a similar act long ago, finally impresses upon Parritt that the only way out—to save his own soul, to become a martyr for his mother, to pay for his sins—is suicide. The final few minutes of the film, when Larry sits, aching, waiting for Parritt to kill himself and knowing he could stop the act, is taut with tension. Parritt's death only ensures that Larry will continue to live in his own personal hell for the rest of his days.

Though Hickey makes his challenge for personal betterment to everyone in the bar, it is meant as a particular challenge to Larry Slade. Hickey and Larry are the protagonists of the film, each trying to reason with the other and convert the other to his manner of thinking. In this version of the play, Larry, not Hickey or Harry Hope, becomes the primary focal character. Larry rejects the philosophies of both Hickey and Don Parritt, yet both men force Larry to re-evaluate his own life, and he finds it wanting. Robert Ryan, who was making his fourth film with Lee Marvin, turned out to be the perfect choice to play an imperfect man.

As Larry, Robert Ryan gives the performance of his lifetime, one which was awarded the Best Actor of the Year citation by the National Board of Review. *Time* wrote that, "The movie belongs most securely to Robert Ryan, and it is an eloquent memorial to his talent going. ...It would be easy to sentimentalize his performance. But such a gesture would diminish its greatness. With the kind of power and intensity that is seldom risked, much less realized, it has its own pride and stature."

Variety concurred: "The late Robert Ryan [he died of cancer soon after filming was completed] is amazing. He has enlarged the role of Larry, too frequently played as a glib, whining cynic, and invested him with something close to heroism. The doomed, detached anarchist is less a copout in this interpretation than one fearful of exercising a huge power to affect other lives. His strength and dignity have almost created a new Larry." Pauline Kael wrote that, "Ryan is so subtle he seems to have penetrated to the mystery of O'Neill's gaunt grandeur—to the artist's egotism and that Catholic Cassandra's pride in tragedy which goes along with the fond pity for the foolish clowns lapping up their booze."

While Robert Ryan garnered lavish and deserved praise for his final acting job, Lee Marvin struggled with decidedly mixed reviews for his sincere performance. The general consensus was that Frankenheimer should have hired Jason Robards, Jr., for the part he had immortalized on Broadway. Which is, of course, why Frankenheimer refused to consider Robards. Frankenheimer states that, "I made one provision: I wouldn't do it with Jason Robards. I'd worked with Jason. He's a wonderful actor and a friend of mine, but Jason had done it so often on stage that the idea of directing him in *The Iceman Cometh* was very unexciting." Frankenheimer wanted Marlon Brando, Gene Hackman or Lee Marvin. Brando refused and Hackman was not approached because Marvin called the director and wanted the part.

The part that Marvin wanted and received is one for which not everyone thinks he was right. Bradford Dillman, who plays Willie Oban in the film, believes that *The Iceman Cometh* is "...a brilliant film with a fatal flaw at its center, the casting of the leading role. Perhaps because he was a box-office draw at the time, or for whatever reason, the part of Hickey was given to Lee Marvin. Now, Marvin was a first-rate heavy; no man was better at conveying hostility. But Hickey's entrance is set up by the derelicts' yearning for his arrival because he's such a card, so many laughs. Lee Marvin was as many laughs as a knuckle sandwich. Jason Robards, who played the part at the Circle in the Square *was* Hickey, right down to his spats. Had he been awarded the role, *Iceman* might have been a motion picture classic."

Dillman misses the point that Hickey is *not* a card on this visit, and because of his new-found peace of mind, he isn't supposed to provide a barrel of laughs. Nevertheless, many critics agreed with Dillman's assessment, noting that Marvin wasn't right temperamentally to play Hickey. Nora Sayre wrote in the *New York Times*: "As one character says, Hickey has 'the fixed idea of the insane,' and Marvin does convey that. However, his Hickey seems deliberately charmless—although the play demands a maniac spellcaster. Marvin's performance is just too rationally earthbound for a part that needs the touch of a magician." Pauline Kael dissected Marvin's performance this way: "Hickey, with his edgy, untrustworthy affability, is a part for a certain kind of actor, and Lee Marvin isn't it. Marvin has a jokester's flair for vocal tricks and flip gestures...Here it's a matter not just of his not being up to it but of his being all wrong for it."

But not everyone felt that Marvin was a disappointment in the role. "The director has provoked an astonishingly good performance from Lee Marvin," wrote *Boxoffice*. Charles

Hickey (Lee Marvin) reminisces while the three tarts who call Harry Hope's bar home listen raptly, in *The Iceman Cometh*.

Champlin of the *Los Angeles Times* wrote, "He was wonderful in *Cat Ballou*, but I think *Iceman Cometh* was Lee Marvin's finest hour," and director Frankenheimer agreed with him, calling the film the finest he'd ever directed. Marvin received some of his best notices for *The Iceman Cometh* and felt good about his performance, realizing that some people would never accept anyone but Jason Robards, Jr., in the role.

Marvin *is* good—he's very good. He uses his natural sales techniques to sell the other characters his notion of personal redemption, utilizing his vocal strength and expressive gestures to keep attention from wandering. Despite Dillman's reflection that Marvin is as funny as a knuckle sandwich, the film's pace does pick up when Hickey arrives, and his haranguing of the barflies keeps things moving. Marvin also shows a keen sense of timing, knowing just when to deliver a throwaway line, when to emphasize a point with a handclap, or when to keep quiet and let someone else have the spotlight for a few moments.

Marvin truly shows his acting chops near the end of the film, during the long monologue when he explains how he found his peace of mind. As Hickey talks of his marriage to the most wonderful of women and how devastating purity and faith can be to a sinner, his character truly comes alive. Once the audience understands that his wife's death is inevitable, Hickey becomes hateful, pitiable, certifiable and tragically human all at once, and Lee Marvin delivers his monologue with such alternating force and gentleness that it becomes mesmerizing. Here at last, Marvin is able to strip a character down to its bare bones, searing the flesh away with hot blasts of human truth, to expose the moral skeleton beneath, and it's a terrifying sight, just as Eugene O'Neill had intended.

Perhaps Lee Marvin wasn't the perfect choice for the role of Hickey; perhaps John Frankenheimer missed his opportunity to create a truly great film. But anyone who views the film will see that Lee Marvin was indeed an *actor*, capable of much more than the action-packed films which Hollywood continued to offer him. Marvin took his trade seriously and wasn't afraid of the challenge of an *Iceman Cometh*, a *Monte Walsh* or a *Hell in the Pacific*. He delighted in risky parts, roles that defied conventional characterization, and worked as hard as he could to successfully fulfill them. In some ways *The Iceman Cometh* is the best film work Lee Marvin ever did and the pinnacle of his long and illustrious film career.

The Spikes Gang (1974)

CREDITS: Mirisch Corporation. *Distributed by* United Artists. *Directed by* Richard Fleischer. *Produced by* Walter Mirisch. *Screenplay by* Irving Ravetch, Harriet Frank, Jr. *Based on the Novel The Bank Robber by* Giles Tippette. *Music by* Fred Karlin. *Music Editor*: George Brand. *Director of Photography*: Brian West, B.S.C. *Film Editors*: Ralph E. Winters, Frank J. Urioste. *Art Director*: Julio Molina. *Set Decorator*: Antonio Mateos. *Production Supervisor*: Tom Pevsner. *Camera Operator*: Neil Gemmell. *Sound*: George Stephenson. *Sound Editor*: Frank Wagner. *Re-recording*: Jack R. Woltz. *Special Effects*: Antonio Parra. *Production Manager*: Jose Maria Rodriguez. *First Assistant Director*: Tony Tarruella. *Script Supervisor*: Isabel Mula. *Make Up*: Mariano Garcia Rey. *Wardrobe*: Agustin Jiminez. *Gaffer*: Ricardo Arenas Arino. *Grip*: Carlos Esteban Adrada. *Unit Manager*: Francisco Ruiz. Rated PG. Color by DeLuxe. Flat (1.33:1). 96 minutes. Released in May 1974. Not currently available on home video.

CAST: *Harry Spikes*, Lee Marvin; *Wilson Young*, Gary Grimes; *Les Richter*, Ron Howard; *Tod Mayhew*, Charlie Martin Smith; *Kid White*, Arthur Hunnicutt; *Jack Basset*, Noah Beery; *Abel Young*, Marc Smith; *Cowboy*, Don Fellows; *Billy*, Elliott Sullivan; *Posse Leader*, Ralph Brown; *Gillis*, Bill Curran; *Doctor*, Ricardo Palacios; *Sheriff*, David Thomson; *Bank Teller*, Bert Conway; *Pawnbroker*, Adolfo Thous; *Morton*, Allen E. Russell; *Mrs. Young*, Frances O'Flynn.

After *The Iceman Cometh*, Lee Marvin decided to return to the Old West for his next project, *The Spikes Gang*. The film provided him with another well-written character to play—gentleman bank robber Harry Spikes. Based on Giles Tippette's novel *The Bank Robber*, *The Spikes Gang* gives Marvin a character into which he could sink his teeth and imbue with his own brand of courtly charm.

The Spikes Gang

At the beginning of *The Spikes Gang*, three teenagers—Will (Gary Grimes), Les (Ron Howard) and Tod (Charlie Martin Smith)—happen across a bloody body lying in the sagebrush. The body is that of Harry Spikes (Lee Marvin), a wounded bank robber who asks the boys to hide him and take care of him until he gets well enough to move on. They do, lying to the law about seeing him and nursing him back to health. When Harry does leave, the boys feel empty; taking care of him has been the most exciting episode in their young lives. Led by Will, the boys decide to leave their unfulfilling home lives behind and look for adventure.

Some time later, very hungry, the trio follow Harry's example and hold up a bank. In the process, they shoot a Senator to death and lose the money. They flee to Mexico and are jailed for petty thievery. Harry Spikes happens by and bails them out, then feeds, cleans and clothes them, thereby returning the favor they had done him. He moves on again, leaving the boys to fend for themselves. They get menial jobs digging outhouse holes, cutting beef and washing dishes, but cannot seem to get ahead. Harry finds them once again and rescues them from their lives of drudgery, taking them on as partners. He teaches them the fine arts of casing banks, making getaway plans and shooting straight, even providing nearsighted Tod with a pair of glasses.

Despite fine planning, their big bank robbery turns disastrous, leaving Tod mortally wounded and Will slightly hurt. Harry advises the boys to leave Tod behind, but Will and Les cannot do that. Harry bids the boys adieu, leaving them alone again. Tod dies and is buried by his remorseful friends. Will sneaks away from Les to deliver a letter Tod had written to his family. When he returns he finds Les mortally wounded, ambushed by two bounty hunters. Les dies in Will's arms. Will avenges Les' death by killing the first

Will (Gary Grimes), Les (Ron Howard) and Harry Spikes (Lee Marvin) watch nearsighted Tod (Charles Martin Smith) practice his shooting in *The Spikes Gang*.

bounty hunter, then goes after the second: Harry Spikes.

Will confronts Harry in Harry's rundown hotel room and gives his former friend a fighting chance. They shoot each other, with Harry receiving the worst of it. He dies on the floor. Will stumbles out and makes it to the train station before dying of his wounds.

The Spikes Gang does have some worthwhile aspects besides the excellent character work performed by Lee Marvin. It features good chemistry and performances by its trio of teenagers, Gary Grimes, Ron Howard and Charlie Martin Smith. It is their story and they tell it well. In addition, it depicts a very faithful, realistic account of the harshness and drabness of the Old West. Westerns have a tendency to romanticize the conquering of the frontier, to mythicize the larger than life people who tamed the wilds. There's none of that here. The West is seen as a dry, dusty, unforgiving place where the people are subjected to boring, backbreaking work just to survive. This realism is more accurate than that of other westerns, though perhaps not quite as entertaining.

The film is also unashamedly nihilistic, which keeps in character with its sense of truth-telling, but works against its likability. Virtually every major character takes action or makes mistakes which lead to their own destruction, leaving the viewer with the feeling that the Old West is not only a heartless place without pity but represents a time and place where mere survival is almost impossible. To its credit, everyone pays for their actions, but it doesn't make the film a pleasant one to watch.

One noted weakness of the film is that it was photographed in Spain, and often doesn't seem as authentic as films shot in the Southwest United States. It might also have benefited from a widescreen process; the film seems more suited to television than to a big screen.

The greatest asset of *The Spikes Gang* is the performance of Lee Marvin as Harry Spikes. This is another of Marvin's restrained, intelligent acting jobs, with plenty of room for comic notes along the way. Harry Spikes is a teacher for the trio of youths who adore him, dispensing common sense and wisdom to them without condescension. He also takes pains to ensure that they learn how to enjoy the small details of life, even while describing the difficulties of their chosen profession. He is forced into his role as bounty hunter by circumstance, and does not enjoy it.

Marvin's Spikes is a wily old fox and a marvelously charming one. His engaging performance, as noted by the many critics who disliked the film, is reason enough to see it, and proof, once again, that Lee Marvin could, and did, give performances strong enough to save otherwise weak films. Though *The Spikes Gang*, often noted as an unofficial follow-up to 1972's *Bad Company*, failed both critically and commercially, Lee Marvin was not held responsible for its failure. The film isn't as bad as its reputation suggests, and does boast one of Marvin's more interesting character interpretations.

The Klansman (1974) (aka *The Burning Cross and KKK*)

CREDITS: Paramount. *Directed by* Terence Young. *Produced by* William Alexander. *Executive Producers*: Howard Effron, Bill Shiffrin. *Associate Producers*: Joe Ingber, Michael Marcovsky, Rosemary Christenson, Peter A. Rodis, Alvin Bojar, Jerry Levy, Daniel K. Sobol. *Screenplay by* Millard Kaufman, Samuel Fuller. *Based upon the Novel by* William Bradford Huie. *Music by* Dale O. Warren, Stu Gardner. *Arranged and Conducted by* Dale O. Warren. *Supervised by* Larry Shaw, Forest Hamilton *in association with* The Stax Organization. *Song* "The Good Christian People" *by* Mack Rice, Bettye Crutcher; *sung by* The Staple Singers. *Additional Music by* Mack Rice, Bettye Crutcher. *Director of Photography*: Lloyd Ahern, A.S.C. *Supervising Cameraman*: Aldo Tonti. *Production Supervisor*: Emmett Emerson. *Production Designer*: John S. Poplin. *Film Editor*: Gene Milford. *Assistant to the Producer*: Michael Ingber. Rated R. Technicolor. Flat (1.33:1). 112 minutes. Released in November 1974. Released on videotape as *The Burning Cross* (at 91 minutes) and *KKK*. Currently available on VHS videotape.

CAST: *Sheriff Bascomb*, Lee Marvin; *Breck Stancill*, Richard Burton; *Deputy Butt Cut Bates*,

Cameron Mitchell; *Loretta Sykes*, Lola Falana; *Trixie*, Luciana Paluzzi; *Mayor Hardy*, David Huddleston; *Nancy Poteet*, Linda Evans; *Garth*, O. J. Simpson; *Mr. Shaneyfelt*, Ed Call; *Vernon Hodo*, John Alderson; *Flagg*, David Ladd; *Taggart*, John Pearce; *Hector*, Vic Perrin; *Willy Washington*, Spence Wil-Dee; *Alan Bascomb*, Wendell Wellman; *Bobby Poteet*, Hoke Howell; *Johnson*, Virgil Frye; *Reverend Josh Franklin*, Robert Porter, *Reverend Alverson*, Lee De Broux; *Associated Press Reporter*, Charles Briggs; *New York Times Reporter*, Morgan Upton; *Mrs. Shaneyfelt*, Eve Christopher; *Mrs. Bascomb*, Susan Brown; *Charles Peck*, Gary Catus; *Jim Hodo*, Scott E. Lane; *Annie*, Jo Ann Cowell; *Doctor*, Bert Williams; *Lightning Rod*, Larry Williams; *Mary Anne*, Jeanie Bell.

With the sudden, surprising popularity of *Shaft*, *Superfly* and other so-called "blaxploitation" pictures in the early 1970s, the time seemed right to film William Huie's novel of racial tensions in a Southern town, *The Klansman*. Paramount Pictures decided to make it a big-name project, recruiting Lee Marvin, Richard Burton, Cameron Mitchell, Linda Evans, Lola Falana and, in his film debut, football star O. J. Simpson. The studio did not, however, count on the myriad of problems that plagued the project, both behind and in front of the cameras.

The Klansman takes place in imaginary Atoka County, Alabama, where whites and blacks maintain an uneasy peace. That peace is disrupted when beautiful white Nancy Poteet (Linda Evans) is raped and states that it was a black man who raped her. Sheriff "Big Track" Bascomb (Lee Marvin) quickly takes into custody the man most likely to have done it, before the local Ku Klux Klan members, led by his own deputy, Butt Cut Bates (Cameron Mitchell), can lynch the man themselves. Feeling cheated, the Klan members find and chase down an unarmed black man, castrate him and then blow his head off, as his friend Garth (O. J. Simpson) watches from a safe distance after barely escaping the vigilantes himself.

Wealthy landowner Breck Stancill (Richard Burton), who lets poor black families stay on his mountain rent-free, welcomes Loretta Sykes (Lola Falana) back into town. Loretta is returning from college in Chicago and is now looking for something to do with her life. Tensions escalate as two religious civil-rights leaders (Robert Porter, Gary Catus) arrive in town to set up a weekend demonstration and look to Loretta for help, angering the KKK. Meanwhile, Garth begins hunting down the men who killed his friend one at a time and killing them very publicly.

As his racist friends die, Butt Cut takes matters into his own hands, teaching Loretta the power of the law by savagely raping her. Nancy Poteet is chased out of church by bigots and stays with Stancil, who sleeps with her to make her feel socially acceptable once again. At the demonstration, Garth kills another Klansman, this time on national television. Nancy Poteet leaves town, causing a fight between Stancil and Butt Cut in which the deputy is knocked senseless by Stancil's lethal judo-chopping hands. Humiliated, Butt Cut leads the KKK to attack Stancil's mountain.

Sheriff Bascomb, perhaps a KKK member himself, tries to stop the assault, but the hooded men burn down the poor black people's shacks and come after him with guns blazing. Joined by his son, Bascomb shoots several of the Klan, while Garth sneaks up on them from the rear and eliminates more. Stancil shoots one man, but then lets himself be killed rather than cause any more violence. Loretta picks up his gun and doesn't hesitate to shoot. Bascomb confronts Garth but doesn't stop him from continuing his killing spree. Butt Cut is shot by Bascomb, but before dying is able to shoot the sheriff in the back. Bascomb dies in his son's arms. Loretta surveys the carnage and burns down Stancil's "hanging tree," where his grandfather had been hanged some fifty years earlier.

The Klansman may not be the worst film Lee Marvin made, but it's certainly the most abominable. *The Klansman* purports to be socially responsible, building a case that racism leads beyond prejudice to violence and death, but the film wallows in its own filth, depicting that very prejudice, violence and death with relish. Almost everything in the film seems exploitive and degrading, not only to blacks but to women as well. There are three

Sheriff Big Track Bascomb (Lee Marvin) of Atoka County, Alabama, in *The Klansman*.

rapes—one to open the film (which is treated cavalierly), Nancy Poteet's mostly unseen attack, and Butt Cut's violent, brutal, bloody rape of Loretta which makes one sick from having seen it.

While the original intentions of the filmmakers may have been honorable—to present racism as honestly and accurately as possible—the realism soon turns to melodrama, and any honorable point there may have been soon drowns in blood. Except for Sheriff Bascomb, who is a man walking a tightrope, there isn't any balance to any of the characters: the Klansmen are all one-dimensional bigots, the black people are all oppressed and exploited. The other main character, Breck Stancil, is a righteous idiot, unable to understand what his own actions precipitate.

If the film weren't so nasty, it might be entertaining on a trash level, especially since the murder trial of O. J. Simpson. Certain images eerily predict the future, such as when Garth emerges from the back seat of Stancil's Ford Bronco and holds a gun to Stancil's head and lectures him about racism, or at the climax, when Bascomb holds a gun to Garth's head as Garth executes another Klan member, then just lets him walk away to freedom. Such images change the experience from watching a bad movie to watching something far more tasteless but perhaps more ironic and reflective of reality than the filmmakers ever intended.

Over time, several writers and directors were attached to the project, of which maverick director Samuel Fuller was the most noted. Some of Fuller's script remains, but virtually none of his artistry. No stranger to controversy, Fuller might have handled the subject with his trademark blunt honesty and directness, but it would certainly have been a better movie than this mess. Part of the blame must go to the script, and part of it to the hard-drinking star of the show, Richard Burton.

During the production, Richard Burton, who was badly miscast as Southerner Breck Stancil, drank so heavily that he had to film many of his scenes, particularly early in the film, sitting or lying down because he didn't have the strength to stand up. Burton's skin is sallow, his speech occasionally slurs and at times he even appears incoherent. The judo scene wherein he demolishes Butt Cut borders on the ludicrous because earlier in the film he could barely move. It was during this time that he broke up, again, with wife Elizabeth Taylor, which didn't help. Immediately after filming was completed, Burton, reportedly near death, was hospitalized and spent weeks recovering from the binges to which he had subjected himself.

On the other hand, Lee Marvin was trying to keep Burton from overdoing it and trying to give the film some kind of dignity. Instead of overacting, Marvin settles into the part of Sheriff Big Track Bascomb with the easy grace of John Wayne in many of his older roles, imbuing the part with a quiet authority. Marvin's Bascomb is understanding, commanding and has the best interests of the town at heart, even when he makes mistakes (such as forcing Loretta to lie about the identity of her rapist). He doesn't court trouble, but doesn't back away from it either.

Marvin's performance could be transplanted to an Old West or New York City setting and he would serve as an effective lawman in either case. Interestingly, the only other times he played lawmen in the movies, other than bit parts as M.P.s, were as the comic policeman in *Gorilla at Large* and as the Mountie goaded into action in *Death Hunt*. Of course, he had played Detective Frank Ballinger for three years on *M Squad*, but Marvin seemed to favor the other side of the law when it came to his big-screen roles. Marvin is certainly the best thing about this film, which has become, because of its insane combination of casting, overly-ripe dialogue, racial melodrama and post-murder trial O. J. Simpson eeriness, something of a campy cult favorite—as well as an embarrassment to many of the people involved.

The Meanest Men in the West (1976)

CREDITS: Universal. *Directed by* Samuel Fuller, Charles S. Dubin. *Produced by* Charles Marquis

Warren, Joel Rogosin. *Associate Producer*: David Levinson. *Written by* Ed Waters, Samuel Fuller. *Music*: Hal Mooney. *Directors of Photography*: Lionel Lindon, A.S.C., Enzo A. Martinelli, Alric Eden. *Film Editors*: Gene Palmer, A.C.E., Jean-Jacques Berthelot. *Art Director*: George Patrick. *Set Decorations*: John McCarthy, Glen L. Daniels, James M. Walters, Sr. *Sound*: Frank H. Wilkinson, William A. Russell. *Unit Production Managers*: Abby Singer, Frank Arrigo. *Assistant Directors*: George Bisk, Lou Watt. *Make-Up*: Bud Westmore, Leo Lotito. *Hair Stylists*: Larry Germain, Florence Bush. *Color Coordinator*: Robert Brower. *Color Consultant*: Alex Quiroga. Not Rated. Technicolor. Flat (1.33:1). 92 minutes. Released in March 1976. Currently available on VHS videotape and DVD.

CAST: *Judge Garth*, Lee J. Cobb; *Harge Talbot, Jr.*, Charles Bronson; *Martin Kalig*, Lee Marvin; *Eva Talbot*, Miriam Colon; *The Virginian*, James Drury; *Quinn*, Albert Salmi; *Preble*, Don Mitchell; *Elizabeth*, Sara Lane; *Arnie Doud*, Charles Grodin; *Keeler*, Brad Weston; *Bassett*, Ross Hagen; *Shorty*, Gary Clarke; *Harge Talbot, Sr.*, Michael Conrad; *Sharkey*, Warren Kemmerling; *Cord*, Michael Mikler; *Eddie*, Jan Stine; *Young Kalig*, Lance Kerwin; *Sarah Ann*, Betty Beaird; *Doctor*, Regis Cordio; *Aunt Myrtle*, Bonnie Bartlett; *Mungo*, Ron Soble; *Trampas*, Doug McClure.

The Meanest Men in the West is the second film starring Lee Marvin which was edited into a feature from a television source. Unlike *Sergeant Ryker*, however, which was put together from a two-part television special and isn't radically different from its source, this film was actually compiled from two episodes of the television series *The Virginian*, made several years apart, and mixes stories from the two episodes into one. One of *The Virginian* episodes featured Lee Marvin, while the other featured Charles Bronson. A prologue explaining that Marvin's and Bronson's characters are actually brothers was filmed in 1976 to link the episodes and make the movie more cohesive.

The film begins with that prologue. Harge Talbot (Michael Conrad), has a difficult choice to make: save his pregnant wife or his unborn son. Either way, the other will die. Talbot chooses the son, and his stepson, Kalig (Lance Kerwin), never forgives him for sending his mother to her death. Harge catches Kalig stealing his hidden savings, and rather than face another beating, Kalig kills the elder Talbot, takes his baby brother Harge, Jr., to be raised at an aunt's home, and strikes out on his own.

Years later, Kalig (Lee Marvin) is a hardened criminal and planning the kidnapping of the prosperous judge who had previously sent him to jail. Meanwhile, his brother Harge (Charles Bronson) is also involved in a kidnapping. He blames the Virginian (James Drury) for a robbery gone bad in which some of his men were killed, and arranges for the Virginian's friend Elizabeth (Sara Lane) to be kidnapped. Elizabeth will be used as a midwife to aid Harge's wife Eva (Miriam Colon) in childbirth, and will ensure that the Virginian will be captured.

Kalig and his men (whom he inherits by killing another outlaw leader) kidnap Judge Garth (Lee J. Cobb) and demand $100,000 ransom. The Virginian delivers the ransom, but Kalig holds onto the Judge as a hostage to ensure his escape. The Virginian tells Trampas (Doug McClure) and Shorty (Gary Clarke) to follow Kalig's gang but to resist attacking, fearing for Judge Garth's safety. Then he rides to Harge's home to determine why Elizabeth was forcibly taken there, and is taken hostage himself. Harge resists killing the Virginian until his wife gives birth, despite the wishes of his own men.

After Harge's son is born, Harge and his men celebrate, allowing the Virginian and Elizabeth to escape. The Virginian is followed by Harge's gang but is able to prove that he had not betrayed Harge in the previous robbery—only Harge's brother Kalig could have informed the authorities beforehand. Harge, his men and the Virginian all converge at the spot where Kalig is holding the Judge and attack. Kalig is killed by his brother, the Judge is freed, and everyone else goes their own way.

The genesis for this film are the two original *Virginian* episodes. *It Tolls for Thee* is the episode which tells how Martin Kalig (no relation to Harge Talbot) kidnaps Judge Garth for revenge. The Virginian, Trampas and

The artwork used to advertise *The Meanest Men in the West*.

Shorty trail Kalig and rescue the Judge before Kalig can kill him. Kalig is wounded, but remains alive and is in custody at episode's end. The other episode chronicles Harge Talbot's quest for revenge after his gang had been ambushed by the law during a holdup. As in the movie, eventually Harge discovers the Virginian's innocence and kills the man responsible for informing the authorities. At no time in the series, however, did these episodes have anything to do with each other, except for the *Virginian*'s regular cast.

The Meanest Men in the West is edited from these two episodes, and the result is one of the worst films in which Lee Marvin ever appeared. Since the episodes were filmed a few years apart to begin with, and the prologue was added (shot on video) more than a decade later, there is absolutely no conformity or continuity between the segments. The finished product is a pastiche of various film grains, color and sound levels, making the movie seem completely amateurish and poorly produced.

The worst aspect is the tenuous connection which binds Harge and Kalig together as brothers. The two men are never in the same frame as each other, though cross-cutting does give the illusion that they are in the same scene. The climactic gunfight in which Kalig is killed originally showed Kalig shot by the Virginian or Trampas; in the film, Harge is seen drawing his gun and Kalig is seen to be shot, inferring that Harge shot Kalig. It happens so quickly that a good view of the situation is never provided, nor is it meant to be, because the obvious trickery of the scene would be revealed. This use of re-editing after the fact is pathetic and almost criminal in intent. It certainly has nothing whatsoever to do with the original television show.

The original *Virginian* shows, which each filled ninety minutes, are entertaining and often thoughtful explorations of life in the Old West. *It Tolls for Thee* has a subplot involving Judge Garth's abhorrence of violence which is only inferred in the film, and is recommended as far and away the better version of this story. None of the actors or crew of the original *Virginian* shows had anything to do with this abomination; it was created by executives at Universal who wanted their studio to cash in somehow on the popularity of Lee Marvin and Charles Bronson and who obtained the necessary rights to the original shows to desecrate them. The film disappeared from theaters within a few weeks, as moviegoers were not fooled by its misleading advertising campaign, and was completely forgotten until resurrected in the age of video. This is one title which should have remained buried.

The Great Scout and Cathouse Thursday (1976) (aka *Wildcat*)

CREDITS: 1976. American International. *Directed by* Don Taylor. *Produced by* Jules Bock, David Korda. *Executive Producer*: Samuel Z. Arkoff. *Associate Producer*: Richard Shapiro. *Written by* Richard Shapiro. *Music by* John Cameron. *Music Editor*: Ken Johnson. *Director of Photography*: Alex Phillips, Jr. *Film Editor*: Sheldon Kahn. *Production Designer*: Jack Martin Smith. *Set Decorator*: Enrique Esteves. *Stunt Coordinator*: Jerry Gatlin. *Wardrobe Designer*: Rene Conley. *Makeup*: John Inzerella. *First Assistant Director*: Brad Aronson. *Camera Operator*: Carlos Montano. *Sound Mixer*: Manuel Topete. *Script Supervisor*: Jose Luis Ortega. *Property Master*: Graham Sumner. *Publicity*: Julian Myers. *Production Accountant*: John C. Sargeant, G.F.P.H. *Sound Effects Editors*: Bernard Pincus, Norman Schwartz, Greg Dillon. *Assistant Editors*: Bob Hernandez, Nicholas Korda. *Production Coordinator*: Roz Catania. *Production Secretary*: Patricia Cartas. *Production Executives*: Robert A. Kantor, Peter Buchanan. *Production Supervisor*: Joseph Lenzi. *Production Executive for* AIP: Harry Templeton. *In Charge of Post Production*: Salvatore Billitteri. *Production Services*: Galloping Film Productions. *Production Management by* International Producing Associates. *Locations by* Cinemobile Systems. *Production Finance Executive*: Andy Birmingham. *Sound by* Ryder Sound Services, Inc. *Music Recorded by* The Music Centre, UK. *Title Design*: Phill Norman. *Opticals by* Cinefx. Rated PG. Technicolor. Flat (1.33:1). 102 minutes. Released in June 1976. Currently available on VHS videotape.

CAST: *Sam Longwood*, Lee Marvin; *Joe Knox*, Oliver Reed; *Jack Colby*, Robert Culp; *Nancy Sue*, Elizabeth Ashley; *Billy*, Strother Martin; *Mike*, Sylvia Miles; *Thursday*, Kay Lenz; *Vishniac*, Howard Platt; *Trainer*, Jac Zacha; *Friday*, Phaedra; *Saturday*, Leticia Robles; *Holidays*, Luz Maria Pena; *Monday*, Erika Carlson; *Tuesday*, C. C. Charity; *Wednesday*, Ana Verdugo.

For his first true comedy since *Cat Ballou*, Lee Marvin turned to small American International Pictures, home of the "low-budget quickie," and returned to the Old West. But unlike *Cat Ballou*, his Oscar-winning triumph eleven years earlier which had parodied the western genre's customs and stereotypes, *The Great Scout and Cathouse Thursday* (also known as *Wildcat*) finds its humor mainly below the belt and in the outhouse.

Sam Longwood, the great scout of the title (Lee Marvin), and Billy (Strother Martin) are roguish con men in the Old West,

Sam Longwood (Lee Marvin), the Great Scout of *The Great Scout and Cathouse Thursday*.

currently working a con involving a defanged rattlesnake. When Sam spots Jack Colby (Robert Culp), a former partner who stole their $4,000 gold prospecting profits fifteen years earlier, he plots revenge.

Sam's other partner, half-Indian Joe Knox (Oliver Reed!), is busy hijacking a paddywagon full of prostitutes, each of whom he names for days of the week. He plans to infect them with his gonorrhea and set them loose upon an unsuspecting white man's world. He gives up his plan in order to help Sam and sends the women away, but one stays behind, hiding. Sam and Joe Knox visit Jack Colby and demand their money, plus interest, totaling $60,000. Colby writes them a check but then double-crosses them, sending them away empty-handed and soaking wet for the trouble of bothering him.

Sam, Joe Knox and Billy head for the town of Serenity. On the way, they discover the hiding hooker, Thursday (Kay Lenz), who goes on to destroy their wagon after taking it for a joyride. In Serenity, Thursday is spotted by Mike the madam (Sylvia Miles), who starts shooting and chases Thursday and her consorts through the hotel, restaurant and local buildings. They escape only after passing through Mike's cathouse, where topless women turn Sam cross-eyed. That night Sam and Joe Knox spring into action, kidnapping Colby's unfaithful wife Nancy Sue (Elizabeth Ashley). Sam is horrified to find that Nancy Sue, his former love, has been sleeping around and cursing like a bandit. Thursday and Nancy Sue share an instant dislike and jealousy which Thursday fuels by waking up the following morning next to Sam. She professes her love for him, but Sam is not ready to settle down.

Sam demands $60,000 ransom for Nancy Sue, but Colby refuses to pay. After fifteen years, Colby has had more than enough of Nancy Sue's infidelity. When she hears of Colby's refusal to pay, Nancy Sue blows a gasket, then plots revenge. The revenge takes place at the boxing match in Serenity. Posing as beer vendors, Sam and Joe Knox steal the portable box office. Colby, Mike the Madam and a posse follow, but the group gets away with the money after Thursday surrenders herself so that her friends can escape. Sam turns back, unable to leave her behind, and challenges Colby to a fight, with the winner to receive all of the money. The two men beat the tar out of each other, and knock out Mike the Madam and Nancy Sue as well, but the last man standing is Colby. As he triumphantly drives back to town, Colby finds that he has been tricked; the money has been switched by Sam, who rides off with Billy, Joe Knox, Nancy Sue, the money and his girl Thursday.

Most of the humor in *The Great Scout and Cathouse Thursday* is of the lewd variety, despite its PG rating. Some of it is funny, but jokes and sexual innuendo about whores, the clap, penis size, age difference and rape get old quickly. Unfortunately, the film also tries for moments of poignancy using some of the same subjects, which is even worse than the humor. The script tries to tell a ribald story using conservative characters, and the result is a mess. The rest of the humor in the film is slapstick, leading to routine physical gags and two boring chase scenes.

One curious aspect of the film regards the political discussions which take place. Several times, the ongoing presidential race between William H. Taft and William Jennings Bryan is discussed by the main characters, who take their party affiliations very seriously; the discussions seem downright odd within the comedic framework of the film.

Acting honors in this movie go to Robert Culp, who is affably charming as crooked Jack Colby, a man who will do anything for money and power, and to Oliver Reed, the British actor who is somehow excellent as wacky Indian Joe Knox. Reed overplays the role at first, but as the film progresses his distinctive voice and even temperament create a truly individual and memorable character. The women are less effective, with Elizabeth Ashley nailing her character while Kay Lenz does the best she can with hers.

Lee Marvin is wasted. His role as the fictional great scout and Indian fighter Sam Longwood is ill-conceived and rather stupid. If he was such a great scout, why couldn't he find Jack Colby for fifteen years? Too often Marvin has to play straight man to the supporting characters and is unable or unwilling to define Sam Lockwood on his own. Other than one terrific speech in which Sam vows that he'll never settle down with a woman or a dog, Marvin mugs his way through this role. His appearance is grizzled and, at the boxing match (wearing a red and white uniform and a round vendor's hat with a flag on it) becomes ridiculous.

The film was in and out of theaters so quickly that few critics even bothered to review it. Those who did were not impressed. Audiences stayed away and the film quickly disappeared into oblivion. Lee Marvin usually shied away from straight comedies, and this film proves the wisdom of that philosophy.

Shout at the Devil (1976)

CREDITS: American International. *Directed by* Peter Hunt. *Produced by* Michael Klinger. *Associate Producer*: Robert Sterne. *Asssitant Producer*: Tony Klinger. *Producers Associates*: Neville Meyer, Denis Bieber. *Screenplay by* Stanley Price, Alastair Reid, Wilbur Smith. *Based upon the Book by* Wilbur Smith. *Music Composed and Conducted by* Maurice Jarre. *Director of Photography*: Michael Reed, B.S.C. *Editor*: Michael Duthie. *Assistant Director*: Frank Ernst. *Camera Operator*:

154 Shout at the Devil

Alec Mills. *Production Designer*: Syd Cain. *Continuity*: Joan Davis. *Makeup*: Paul Engelen. *Wardrobe*: Philippe Pickford. *Hairdresser*: Mike Jones. *Casting*: Irene Lamb. *Gaffer*: Frank Heeney. *Props*: Terry Wells. *Grip*: Jim Kane. *Sound by* John Mitchell. *Dubbing Editor*: Nick Stevens. *Dubbing Recordist*: Bill Rowe. *Fighting Sequences*: Nick Turvey. *Models and Special Effects*: Derek Meddings. *Stunt and Fight Arranger*: Les Crawford. *Aerial Photography*: Ken Eddy. *Process Work by* Theo Nischwitz. *Production Accountant*: Denton Scott. *Production Secretary*: Vicki Deason. *Liaison*: Linda Allen. *Sound Recording*: E.M.I Studios. *Equipment and Servicing by* Samuelson's. *Electrical Services*: Mole-Richardson. *Costumes by* Caledonian Costumes. *Publicity*: Geoff Freeman, Fred Hift Associates. *Stills*: George Whitear. *Second Unit Director*: John Glen. *Second Unit Cameraman*: Alan Hume. *Second Unit Camera Operator*: Jim Devis. *Africa Crew—Art Director*: Ernie Archer. *Production Manager*: Brian Burgess. *Location Manager*: Dusty Symonds. *Construction*: Dick Frift. *Set Dresser*: Vernon Dixon. *Malta Crew—Art Director*: Bob Laing. *Production Manager*: Stuart Freeman. *Construction*: Leon Davis. *Set Dresser*: Hugh Scaife. *Special Facilities*: Paul Auellino. Rated PG. Technicolor. Panavision (2.35:1). 128 minutes. Released in November 1976. Currently available on VHS videotape. Previously available on laserdisc.

CAST: *Flynn O'Flynn*, Lee Marvin; *Sebastian*, Roger Moore; *Rosa O'Flynn*, Barbara Parkins; *Fleischer*, Rene Kolldehoff; *Mohammed*, Ian Holm; *Von Kleine*, Karl Michael Vogler; *Kyller*, Horst Janson; *Braun*, Gernot Endemann; *Mr. Smythe*, Maurice Denham; *Mrs. Smythe*, Jean Kent; *Cynthia*, Heather Wright; *Captain Joyce*, Bernard Horsfall; *Captain Henry*, Robert Lang; *Admiral Howe*, Peter Copley; *Lieutenant Phipps*, Murray Melvin; *Mackintosh*, Geoff Davidson; *French Pilot*, Gerard Paquis; *El Keb*, George Coulouris; *Mr. Raji*, Renu Setna; *Bit Part*, Simon Sabela.

Shout at the Devil was Lee Marvin's second venture for American International Pictures in 1976. It is a far more ambitious film than *The Great Scout and Cathouse Thursday*, serious in tone and based on an historical incident, though the story and characters which surround the incident are completely imaginary. For this big-budget action-adventure project, American International pulled out all the stops, hiring many people who had worked on the James Bond series of films, including Roger Moore, former editors Peter Hunt and John Glen (now working as directors), miniatures man Derek Meddings and even title designer Maurice Binder. The hope was to make a James Bond-style historical adventure.

Flynn O'Flynn (Lee Marvin) is an Irish ivory poacher in Zanzibar, 1913, who persuades expatriate Englishman Sebastian (Roger Moore) to aid him on one of his illegal runs into Tanganyika, currently under German rule. The raid is cut short by the sudden appearance of German district commissioner Fleischer (Rene Kolldehoff), who kills most of Flynn's raiding party and chases the rest, by boat, into the Indian Ocean. A German warship, the *Blucher*, runs down Flynn's boat, but Captain Von Kleine (Karl Michael Vogler) refuses to shoot the survivors as Fleischer wishes, leaving them adrift among the wreckage. Flynn, Sebastian and Flynn's mute manservant Mohammed (Ian Holm) survive, eventually drifting onto the East African shore.

Flynn transports Sebastian, who has contracted malaria, back to Flynn's plantation in Mozambique, where his estranged daughter Rosa (Barbara Parkins) nurses Sebastian back to health. Sebastian and Rosa fall in love, leading to a comic fight between the two men. Sebastian and Rosa are soon married and eventually have a baby. In the meantime, Germany has declared war on Britain and its holdings, giving Fleischer the opportunity for revenge. German troops attack Flynn's plantation while Flynn and Sebastian are away on an expedition to steal German tax money, and, as the plantation burns, Rosa's baby is thrown into the fire.

Upon returning, Sebastian and Flynn find Rosa determined to kill Fleischer, and the three swear vengeance. The British Navy contacts Flynn, asking if he could find the *Blucher*, which has been sinking British ships, but was damaged and is under repairs somewhere along the coast. Flynn and his followers find Fleischer and disrupt his efforts to transport heavy metal plate across country, leading to a delay of the ship's repairs. A

French pilot and his biplane arrive, and eagle-eyed Sebastian is sent aloft to find the *Blucher*. Though camouflaged, the *Blucher* is found, but the biplane is shot and barely makes it back to Flynn's camp before crashing, killing the French pilot.

The final attack on the *Blucher* takes place as Sebastian, disguised as an African worker, smuggles a bomb aboard the ship. He plants the device in the ammunition hold, then discovers that Rosa has been taken prisoner onboard the ship. Flynn and Sebastian make a bold rescue attempt, with Flynn holding off the Germans as Sebastian and Rosa swim to safety. Mortally wounded, Flynn dies just before the *Blucher* explodes. Fleischer also survives, jumping off the ship before the explosion, but is shot to death by Sebastian, ending the cycle of vengeance.

Shout at the Devil is an entertaining but overblown outdoor saga with dollops of humor amid a curiously brutal atmosphere. Though rated PG, the film is extremely violent, depicting the almost joyous mass murder of Africans by Fleischer, the nonchalant poaching of elephants (all staged—no animals were hurt) by Flynn and Sebastian, and the horrifying death of Rosa and Sebastian's baby. Dozens of people are shot during this movie, yet the film attempts to maintain its buoyant sense of adventure throughout. Times were different before the first World War, but the idea of killing either man or beast for fun should never have been considered entertaining.

Though American International's resources were certainly smaller than that of other studios, the film's production values are strong. Location filming in Africa and Malta provided authenticity, and the widescreen Panavision cinematography gives the movie the expansive look and stature of classic grand-scale adventures. The bitterness between the British and the Germans is expressed adroitly and, as always, the Germans make the best movie villains, efficient and deadly.

Sebastian (Roger Moore), Rosa O'Flynn (Barbara Parkins) and Flynn O'Flynn (Lee Marvin) are the protagonists of *Shout at the Devil*.

What the movie lacks is good drama. There is a lot of plot (too much, according to the *New York Times*) but not enough character interaction to stimulate it. The various characters seem strong and recognizable as individuals, but they are merely pawns to be moved on the chessboard of the story. Sebastian in particular is cruelly taken advantage of, forced to do many things against his will; things that just don't make sense. After the death of her baby, Rosa becomes one-dimensional, seeking vengeance above all else and becoming rather dull as a result. The only character which continually surprises and doesn't fall prey to formula is mute Mohammed (having had his throat cut some years before), played superbly by British actor Ian Holm. Mohammed was not mute in the original novel, but the alteration works well here, giving the character much more dimension.

Roger Moore is well cast as Sebastian, trying to expand his acting beyond the James Bond image. He is appropriately heroic and understanding, befuddled or smart, as the scenario demands. Yet Moore doesn't command the screen—he hangs back to let Lee Marvin take center stage. That's exactly what Marvin does. This is a film, much like *Cat Ballou* and *Paint Your Wagon*, in which Marvin is called upon to overact, to make his appearance and dialogue as flamboyant as possible. Unfortunately, that's not always a good thing. "And Lee Marvin, who does toughness well enough, is insufferable when he is trying to be the comic Irishman. His doubletakes come like delayed mail," commented Richard Eder in the *New York Times*.

As he had proven earlier in the year, Lee Marvin was not only capable of overacting a part for effect, he could throw himself into it with gusto. Though he does not appear as foolish as he had in *The Great Scout and Cathouse Thursday*, Marvin's bushy beard and sideburns only serve, as they did in *Paint Your Wagon*, as a reminder to the audience that he is supposed to be *funny* in this role. Marvin's exaggerated body language and louder than normal vocal range indicate that he isn't taking the proceedings very seriously, thereby undermining the intended effect. While Marvin is entertaining to watch as he mugs, his performance actually hurts the movie, which is one of the few times that that occurs.

Though it was American International's biggest film project, *Shout at the Devil* was a critical and commercial disappointment, failing to lure the James Bond audience and doing nothing for the careers of its participants. It was to be the last film Lee Marvin was to make for some three years, as he devoted himself to home life with his second wife, Pamela, and the outdoor activities which he loved. In addition, Marvin attempted to live normally through the infamous Michele Triola "palimony" lawsuit which, after almost a decade, finally went to trial in 1979. The judge declared Lee Marvin not guilty on all counts, but awarded Triola $104,000 for "rehabilitation purposes," a point which was later overturned. Though totally exonerated of any penalty in the case, Marvin had become more famous for this unsightly social entanglement than for any movie role.

Avalanche Express (1979)

CREDITS: Lorimar and 20th Century–Fox. *Produced and Directed by* Mark Robson. *Associate Producer*: Lynn Guthrie. *Screenplay by* Abraham Polonsky. *Based on the Novel by* Colin Forbes. *Music Composed and Conducted by* Allyn Ferguson. *Music Editor*: Ken Johnson. *Music Coordinator*: Bodie Chandler. *Director of Photography*: Jack Cardiff (uncredited). *Film Editor*: Garth Craven, Dorothy Spencer (uncredited). *Production Designer*: Fred Tuch. *Unit Production Manager*: Harry Caplan. *Costume Designer*: Mickey Shirrard. *Makeup*: Rudiger, Ado Von Sperl. *Set Decorators*: Elke Etzold, Travis Nixon. *Supervisors of Special Effects*: John Dykstra, Bruce Logan. *Special Effects*: Kit West. *Assistants—Special Effects*: Peter Dawson, Jeff Clifford. *Sound Effects by* Fred Brown, M.P.S.E., Michele Sharp Brown, M.P.S.E., Caryl Wickman. *Art Director for Miniatures*: Ed Graves. *Assistant Film Editors*: Ken Morrisey, Veronica Manchot. *Sound Mixer*: George Stevenson. *Re-recording Mixers*: Wayne Artman, Tom Beckert, Michael Jiron. *Boom Operator*: Charles McFadden. *Camera Operator*: Alec Mills. *Assistant Camera Operators*: John Cardiff, Miki Thomas. *Clapper / Loader*: Michael Waldleitner. *Gaffer*: Frank Heeney.

Grip: Chunky Huse. *Property Master*: Sam Gordon. *Property Buyer*: Eberhard Schwartz. *Wardrobe Mistress*: Friedl Schroeder. *Wardrobe Man*: Anton Eder. *Assistant Director*: Weiland Liebske. *Second Assistant Director*: Don French. *Bavaria Production Executive*: Willy Egger. *Production Supervisors*: Rudi Geiger, Karl Schaffer. *Script Supervisors*: Angela Allen, Trudy Von Trotha, Betty Chaplin. *Production Secretaries*: Veronika Daisenberger, Elke Busch, Pam Hauser. *Publicist*: Vic Heutschy. *Production Accountant*: Elizabeth Yanoska. *Production Controller*: Bea Blondell. *Casting*: Renate Arbes. *Location Manager*: Jack English. *Production Consultants*: Anthony Foutz, Rospo Pallenberg. *Still Photographer*: Barry Peake.

Boat Battle Sequence—Directed by Alan Gibbs. *Director of Photography*: Howard Anderson, II. *Special Effects*: Ross Hahn. *Stunt Coordination*: Tom Lupo. *Property Master*: Ralph Aubert.

Special Photographic and Miniature Effects by Apogee. *Assistant Director*: Gerald Walsh. *Second Assistant Director*: John Pare. *Assistant—Special Effects*: Bill Nipper. *Camera Operator*: Roger Smith. *First Assistant Cameraman*: E. T. Bowen. *Effects Production Manager*: Robert Shepherd. *Grips*: Jerry Deats, Richard Deats. *Gaffer*: Brink Brydon. *Special Effects Gaffer*: Richard Helmer. *Chief Model Maker*: Grant McCune. *Model Construction Crew*: David Scott, Jon Erland, David Beasley, David Sosalla, John Ramsey. *Cine Technician*: Richard Alexander. *Production Coordinator*: Cass McCune.

Marine Sequences and Facilities by Motion Picture Marine. *Title Design by* Burke Mattsson. Rated PG. Color by DeLuxe. Panavision (2:35:1). 88 minutes. Released in October 1979. Currently available on VHS videotape.

CAST: *Colonel Harry Wargrave*, Lee Marvin; *General Marenkov*, Robert Shaw; *Elsa Lang*, Linda Evans; *Colonel Bunin*, Maximilian Schell; *Leroy*, Joe Namath; *Scholten*, Horst Buchholz; *Haller*, Mike Connors; *Molinari*, Claudio Cassinelli; *Helga Mann*, Kristina Nel; *Geiger*, David Hess; *Muehler*, Gunter Meissner; *Olga*, Sylvia Langova; *Sedov*, Cyril Shaps; *Zannbin*, Vladets Shebal; *Neckerman*, Arthur Brauss; *Philip John*, Sky Dumont; *Prachko*, Richard Marner; *Comissar (Maxim Gorky)*, Arnold Drummond; *Alfredo*, Paul Glawion; *Bernardo*, Dan Van Husen; *First Policeman*, Rainer Steffen; *Second Policeman*, Dieter Groest; *Dutch Customs Man*, Hans Jurgen Luethen; *Swiss Officer*, Maximilian Wolters; *Adjutant of Molinari*, Guido Hoegel; *First Signal Man*, Rudolf Waldemar Brem; *Second Signal Man*, Erland Erlandson; *Engineer*, Walter Kraus; *Security Agent*, Osman Ragheb.

Lee Marvin's return to the silver screen after a three-year absence (due in some part to the legal demands of his palimony trial) came in *Avalanche Express*, a lightweight espionage suspense-thriller boasting a strong cast of familiar faces. It followed other films which also used moving trains as claustrophobic venues of death (*Murder on the Orient Express*, *The Cassandra Crossing*, etc.) in that particular mini-genre.

Avalanche Express, as its title implies, takes place mostly on a train—the Atlantic Express—travelling through the snowbound landscapes of Italy, Switzerland and West Germany en route to Rotterdam in The Netherlands. Aboard the train are various American and European security personnel who are trying to protect defecting Russian General Marenkov (Robert Shaw), who is defecting in order to stop Project Winter Harvest, an insidious plan to use deep cover Russian agents in Europe to employ biological weapons against the West, put into motion by his deputy, Bunin (Maximilian Schell). By using himself as a target on the train, Marenkov hopes to force Bunin to "awaken" the deep cover agents in Europe and utilize them as assassins to keep Marenkov from successfully defecting.

Orchestrating Marenkov's escape on the train are American security agents Harry Wargrave (Lee Marvin), his boss, Haller (Mike Connors); former lover, agent Elsa Lang (Linda Evans); and fellow agent Leroy (Joe Namath), along with some Europeans. Once en route, the train is attacked three times. The first attack, by armed gunmen and women, exposes a mole in the security forces which Wargrave suspected and addresses. The second attack is the title disaster, an avalanche. Featuring miniature effects supervised by *Star Wars* wizard John Dykstra, the train rushes toward the safety of a mountain

158 *Avalanche Express*

Colonel Harry Wargrave (Lee Marvin), Elsa Lang (Linda Evans) and Haller (Mike Connors) are the American agents who witness and escape a gigantic avalance in *Avalanche Express*.

tunnel while a huge avalanche cascades toward it from above. Meanwhile, Wargrave and Elsa begin to re-establish their relationship.

The third attack involves a rogue European terrorist unit called the Geiger group, whom Bunin personally recruits for an armed assault. At this attack, Leroy and the entire Geiger group are killed, and Marenkov and the security team leave the train to follow Bunin on his marine escape route. Adapting the guise of the terrorist group, Wargrave and his remaining team steal a Dutch Coast Guard cruiser and attack the Russian freighter which is transporting Bunin safely back to Russia. They blow it up, ending the crisis and the movie.

Avalanche Express is a total failure on almost every level. As a suspense-thriller, it is neither suspenseful nor thrilling. As an espionage film, it is ludicrous, beginning with the target-on-train plot and continuing by the numbers until its abrupt conclusion. Its characters are cardboard, its vaunted special effects are ordinary and obvious, its dialogue is sometimes dreadful and, worst of all, it's often boring. Unfortunately, *Avalanche Express* was the final film of director Mark Robson and actor Robert Shaw, both of whom died of heart attacks soon after filming was completed. In fact, most of Shaw's dialogue in the film was dubbed in later by a mimic, and it shows.

As with most failures, most of the blame must rest with the script. Based on a clever thriller by Colin Forbes, Abraham Polonsky's screenplay is pedestrian, placing the focus on a rickety plot rather than strong characters with whom audience members can identify. Polonsky's characters are paper-thin (note that most have just a last name, a sure sign of trouble) and speak inanities and clichés to the audience rather than true dialogue with each other. Even charismatic performers such as Marvin, Shaw, Connors, Evans and Schell can do little with a poor script, and director Robson further compounds the problem by utilizing unwise tricks, such as speeded-up action during a brief fight and obvious model work involving the train.

The biggest problem with the script involves the use of the train. In the novel, a huge blizzard covering most of Europe forced the Americans to use the only escape route available—namely, the train. In the movie, it barely snows. Instead, Wargrave suggests using the train and themselves as bait to flush out the Russian sleeper agents. Due to budget restraints, the filmmakers decided not to attempt to recreate the blizzard conditions described in the book. The result is that, because of Marenkov's importance, the basic idea of using the train instead of flying out of Europe seems incredibly foolish.

Espionage thrillers are not actor-friendly. Most films of this ilk require their characters to support their intricate plots (rather than the other way around) and use dialogue as the key means to keep the audience informed as to what is going on (rather than reveal character traits and/or emotion). *Avalanche Express* is a case in point. The characters move around cautiously, eyes glancing sideways, then have a quick chat and explain things to each other. This monotony is interrupted by an occasional gunfight or fistfight, and then it's back to grinding out the plot.

Critics eviscerated the film upon its release. Vincent Canby of the *New York Times* noted that, "As junk movie melodramas go, *Avalanche Express* is of a not-quite-all-star tackiness that should make [producer] Sir Lew Grade furious with envy. *Avalanche Express* hasn't any wit, but it has a few laughs, such as the sight of Mr. Namath reacting when one actor delivers some startling information to another actor. Apparently told to do something, Joe looks hurt and surprised, as if no one wanted his autograph."

The supporting cast includes such European actors as Maximilian Schell, Horst Buchholz and Claudio Cassinelli, as well as Americans Mike Connors and Joe Namath, so it would appear as if the producers were trying to ensure overseas sales of the film by making the cast as international as possible.

Lee Marvin's return to the silver screen after his sensation-making palimony trial was, by all accounts, a huge disappointment. He looks tired and wan, not up to the physical challenges of the role and not very interested in the dull proceedings. His tender moments with Linda Evans aren't convincing, and his supposed death early in the film is far too obvious to be believable. Marvin certainly has the intelligence for an espionage role, as he demonstrated four years later in *Gorky Park*. However, this role doesn't challenge him, and he, in essence, sleepwalks through it.

Interestingly, however, Lee Marvin *is* mentioned in the novel. In a sequence when Elsa Lang is disguising General Marenkov, she says, "Well, you may not be Gregory Peck, but you could pass as Lee Marvin if you were taller." Markenkov responds, "He's a villain—like me." Ultimately, of course, Robert Shaw became Marenkov and Marvin took the more commanding role of Harry Wargrave. Both actors probably wished they had stayed at home instead.

The Big Red One (1980)

CREDITS: Lorimar/United Artists. *Distributed by* Warner Bros. *Written and Directed by* Samuel Fuller. *Produced by* Gene Corman. *Music Composed and Conducted by* Dana Kaproff. *Music Supervision*: Bodie Chandler. *Music Editor*: Gene Feldman. *Director of Photography*: Adam Greenberg. *Supervising Editor*: David Bretherton, A.C.E. *Edited by* Martin Tubor. *Art Director*: Peter Jamison. *Second Unit Director*: Lewis Teague. *Sound Editor*: Jack A. Finlay. *Assistant Editor*: Erica Flaum. *Sound Mixer*: Cyril Collick. *Re-recording Mixers*: William L. McCaughey, C.A.S., Robert L. Harman, C.A.S., David Dockendorf, C.A.S. *Unit Production Manager*: Peter Cornberg. *Assistant Director*: Arne L. Schmidt. *Second Assistant Director*: Todd Corman. *Casting*: Barbara Miller. *Key Grip*: Jim Dunn. *Best Boy*: Albert Karnas. *Gaffer*: Mel Maxwell. *Property Master*: William Hankins. *Special Effects*: Kit West, Peter Dawson, Jeff Clifford. *Location Auditor*: Elizabeth Yanoska. *Unit Publicist*: Vic Heutschy. *Gunsmith*: Alan Weisman. *Production Assistant*: Craig Corman. *Script Supervisor*: Lynn Aber. *Second Unit Continuity*: Lori Steiner. *Casting in France*: Edith Cottrell. *Horse Stunt Coordinator*: Roy Street. *Makeup and Hairstylist*: Blanche Shuler. *Still Photographer*: Laurel Moore. *Israeli Production Manager*: Rony Yacov. *Titles by* MGM. *Recorded in* Dolby Stereo. Rated PG. Metrocolor. Widescreen (1.85:1). 113 minutes. Released in July 1980. Currently available on VHS videotape, laserdisc, and DVD.

CAST: *The Sergeant*, Lee Marvin; *Griff*, Mark Hamill; *Zab*, Robert Carradine; *Vinci*, Bobby DiCicco; *Johnson*, Kelly Ward; *Schroeder*, Siegfried Rauch; *Walloon*, Stephane Audran; *Ronsonnet*, Serge Marquand; *General / Captain*, Charles Macaulay; *Broban*, Alain Doutey; *Vichy Colonel*, Maurice Marsac; *Dog Face POW*, Colin Gilbert; *Shep*, Joseph Clark; *Lemchek*, Ken Campbell; *Switolski*, Doug Werner; *Kaiser*, Perry Lang; *Smitty*, Howard Delman; *Madame Marbaise*, Marthe Villalonga; *Woman in Sicilian Village*, Giovanna Galetti; *The Hun*, Gregori Buimistre; *German Male Nurse*, Shimon Barr; *Sicilian Boy*, Matteo Zoffoli; *German Field Marshal*, Avraham Ronai; *Pregnant Frenchwoman*, Galit Rotman.

After a long, self-imposed exile from filmmaking, maverick director Samuel Fuller finally made the movie which had been fermenting in the back of his mind for three decades. Based upon his own wartime experiences, *The Big Red One* (which refers to the insignia of the First Infantry Division) was originally planned to star John Wayne years previously, but, like so many other Fuller projects, the independent producer-director's deal fell through before filming began. Fuller kept the concept alive and in the late 1970s was finally able to realize his dream, though as with all of his other projects, his budget was constrained and his shooting schedule was tight.

The Big Red One is narrated by Zab (Robert Carradine), a young World War II soldier who is based upon Fuller himself. Zab is a writer, prone to colorful phrases and (like Fuller) never without a cigar. On a troop ship to a North African beach in November of 1942, Zab and his fellow "wet nurses" are introduced. His buddies are Griff (Mark Hamill), Vinci (Bobby DiCicco) and Johnson (Kelly Ward), all of whom are about to face their first combat. They are led by the nameless Sergeant (Lee Marvin), seeing action in his second world war.

French forces are holding the North African beach, and they fire upon the American soldiers as they land. After a brief battle, the French surrender, then join the Americans as loyal friends. Griff refrains from shooting anyone in the skirmish and begins to wonder if he may be a coward. At the Kasserine Pass in North Africa, the First Infantry Division is vastly outnumbered and only survives by hiding in the rocky terrain and fleeing after the German tanks have passed. The Sergeant is wounded trying to stop the soldiers from running from the battle, but recuperates quickly and joins the only four remaining members of his squadron—Zab, Griff, Vinci and Johnson—in Tunis.

In Sicily in July of 1943, the Sergeant and his Four Horsemen, as they are now known, fight their way ashore again and are assigned to find a large German gun that has somehow remained hidden. The Sergeant makes a deal with a local boy to transport his dead mother to a graveyard and bury her if he will pinpoint the gun's location. The boy leads the squad to a hillside building housing a tank. The squad disposes of the tank and its crew, thereby freeing the captive Sicilian women who were giving the area its disguise. The women cook the men of the First Infantry Division a celebratory dinner.

Seven months later, the squad prepares for D-day. At Omaha Beach, Griff is forced to face his fear: He must carry a "Bangalore Relay" (fifty feet of tubing with TNT at one end) and blow a hole in the German defenses—or die trying. Griff succeeds, and the infantrymen rush through. Later, Zab encounters a soldier reading one of his published books, and is justifiably proud. The next test for the soldiers comes when a group of German soldiers play possum around a half-destroyed tank, hoping to catch an American platoon unaware and at close range. The Sergeant discovers the ruse and is able to save most of his men before the inevitable firefight begins. Immediately afterward, Johnson is forced to use his limited medical experience to deliver a Frenchwoman's baby—inside the German tank.

In September of 1944, the infantry is assigned to infiltrate an insane asylum in Belgium and rescue a woman named Walloon (Stephane Audran), who has a plan for killing the Germans who have assumed control. The men watch, astounded, as Walloon dances around with a doll, seemingly crazy, adroitly cutting the throats of the Nazis she circles. The inevitable firefight occurs and some of the inmates join in—one man starts shooting everybody and yells, "I am one of you! I am sane!"—and has to be killed. In Germany three months later, another firefight takes place in a misty forest, and more men are killed by an unseen enemy.

The squad is sent into Czechoslovakia in May of 1945 to liberate a concentration camp. Griff finally finds an outlet for his emotion as he pumps bullet after bullet into a Nazi machine-gunner who had cornered him. The Sergeant finds a small boy and tries to comfort him, but the boy is too weak to eat or drink. Touched by the boy's plight, the Sergeant carries him outside and spends some time with him before the boy quietly dies while riding on the Sergeant's shoulders. Later, the Sergeant knifes a wandering German soldier, discovering to his horror that the war has just ended (the film had begun with a black-and-white scene paralleling this one,

The Sergeant (Lee Marvin) and his Four Horsemen—Johnson (Kelly Ward), Vinci (Bobby DiCicco), Zab (Robert Carradine) and Griff (Mark Hamill) safely storm a North African beach in *The Big Red One*.

in which the Sergeant kills a Hun who had tried to surrender to him). Now he's done it again, but this German soldier still lives, and the Sergeant and his Four Horsemen do everything they can to make sure he survives. Zab finishes the film's narration noting that, "Surviving is the only glory in war."

Samuel Fuller had spent World War II as an infantryman and been involved with, or had heard of, the true stories behind the vignettes contained within this film. After the war, he had made a name for himself as an independent writer-director of westerns, crime melodramas and, most importantly, gritty, hard-hitting war films (such as *Fixed Bayonets*, *The Steel Helmet* and *Merrill's Marauders*) which chilled viewers with their authenticity. However, Fuller did not get along with studio executives and was continually fighting for the right to make his pictures *his* way. Thus, Fuller remained a "B" movie director, admired as an auteur in France but scorned for his bluntness in America.

The Big Red One was Fuller's vindication, proving that he could make an exciting film within the studio conditions he disliked. While his budget was still limited, Fuller was given carte blanche to create the definitive dogface film that he had always dreamed of making. As if realizing he would never get the chance again, Fuller stuffed every idea he could think of into the project, attempting to link the experience of war with life inside an insane asylum, and depicting with joy the lunacy of delivering a new life into the world from within a German tank—a machine of death. Fuller sometimes strains for the irony which he cherishes, but unlike the routine "war is hell" message of many war dramas, Fuller truly has comments to make about battle.

Fuller's wartime canvas is a big one, stretching over three years of action and battlefields as variant as North Africa, Sicily and Normandy. The director doesn't focus on the historical events which took place, however; he is much more interested in how his Four Horsemen reacted to each strange, new situation. Some of the scenes are terrifyingly real, with death close at hand, while others are punctuated with humor to display the folly of war. Fuller's film does not attempt, like many, to analyze the historical events and actions of World War II in terms of strategy and importance. He wants viewers to know how it *feels* to be in the arid North African desert, outnumbered and facing Panzer patrols. He wants viewers to *see* the bloody devastation on Omaha Beach and to *listen*, along with each numbered soldier, for his turn to die.

Samuel Fuller was largely successful in bringing his vision of the war to the screen, but not totally so. One factor which works against him is the film's budget. As authentic as the film looks, it does lack the sheer number of people, especially in the D-day sequence, needed to make the film awe-inspiring. It is hard to ignore the fact that in this film's version of the war, only several dozen soldiers take part. Another problem is that the Sergeant and the Four Horsemen do not seem special or smart enough, individually or as a group, to deserve to live through the war while virtually every other American soldier with whom they come in contact is eventually killed. Realistically, at least two of the five men should have died or been wounded, which could have added to the film's emotional impact. As it is, the characters seem somehow—unnaturally—immortal.

Ultimately, Fuller's vision is too wide-ranging to be truly effective. Memorable scenes abound, such as the German troops pretending to be dead and waiting to ambush the Americans, the insane asylum sequence, the scene between the Sergeant and the boy he finds in the concentration camp, Griff's death-defying crawl forward on Omaha Beach, and the cave sequence in North Africa. Those sequences work well here, and probably would in any traditional war movie. But when they are edited together, one after another, taking these characters from one tight spot into another, the work as a whole becomes numbing and tends to lose some of its power.

The Four Horsemen also never make much of an impression. Griff has to battle his own fear, Vinci doesn't like jokes about his Italian ancestry and Johnson has some

The Sergeant (Lee Marvin) prepares to fire a flare.

medical experience. That is as detailed as their history ever gets, and the actors, besides shooting and running, don't have much to do. Mark Hamill, in particular, does not make much of a mark, though he is billed second because of his *Star Wars* fame. The only one of the four who matters is Zab. Robert Carradine is, in essence, playing Sam Fuller, and does so with smiling, crinkled eyes and a cigar wedged into the corner of his mouth. He is the only one of the quartet who really registers, because he is the only one with a real character to play, and the director made sure that he got it right.

Because the movie's point is to depict the actual horror, humor and drudgery of the war, it must focus on the young soldiers who must learn to adapt to it, characters with whom the audience can identify. However, the Sergeant's character is the key. His experience keeps the youngsters alive. He learns to trust his soldiers, allows them to perform and gives them the slack they need to keep their individuality. He leads firmly, by example, using his brains to overcome the obstacles facing the First Infantry Division. For the Four Horsemen, their sergeant is the one constant on which they can depend.

In the film's first half, Lee Marvin fills the prototypical sergeant role admirably, and he comes alive in the second half, as the character gains dimension and focus. This occurs on Omaha Beach, when he reminds Griff to keep moving forward by shooting the helmet next to him, and during the attempted ambush, when he recognizes the trap, silently kills the three Germans inside the tank, and tries to walk his platoon away from the ambush without incident. Marvin shows the most emotion during the film's wildest scene, as the Sergeant and Johnson deliver the Frenchwoman's baby inside that same tank.

Marvin knows when to underplay as well, and his finest moments come at the liberation of the concentration camp, when the Sergeant, with almost no dialogue, comforts the dying young boy to the best of his ability. Indeed, the film's most emotional moment occurs as the Sergeant gently puts the boy on his shoulders to carry him, and the boy slumps lifelessly to one side. Marvin keeps his face set as he realizes the boy has died, yet his eyes fill with sadness. Zab notes that the Sergeant continues to carry the boy for a half-hour after his death, adding to the tragic poignancy of the scene.

Marvin is a perfect fit for the role of the Sergeant, more human than John Wayne would have been in the role, but no less tough. Critics lauded the film and Marvin's strong performance in it, noting that his star power was intact after years of bombs and inactivity. As a result, Marvin again became "bankable" and was offered much better scripts than in the previous half-decade. Samuel Fuller returned to moviemaking, though mostly as an actor. As the years go by, *The Big Red One* has gained in stature as an incisive portrait of what the war was really like, particularly as shown from the perspective of the common soldier.

It is perhaps too uneven and wild to stand up to the more traditional classics of war, and cannot match the virtuosity of films like *The Longest Day* or *Saving Private Ryan*, but it does qualify as the most personal and truthful of war chronicles.

Death Hunt (1981)

CREDITS: Golden Harvest and 20th Century–Fox. *Directed by* Peter Hunt. *Produced by* Murray Shostak. *Executive Producers*: Albert S. Ruddy, Raymond Chow. *Associate Producer*: Robert Baylis. *Written by* Michael Grais, Mark Victor. *Music by* Jerrold Immel. *Music Editors*: James Henrickson, Michael Tronick. *Song* "For You" *by* Al Dubin (lyrics), Joe Burke (music). *Director of Photography*: James Devis. *Edited by* Allan Jacobs, John F. Burnett, A.C.E. *Assistant Editors*: William Jacobs, Mario Leone. *Apprentice Editor*: Cathy Rose. *Dialogue Editor*: Carl Mahakian. *Production Designer*: Ted Haworth. *Set Decorator*: Bob Benton. *Set Designer*: Tom Doherty. *Costume Designer*: Olga Dimitrov. *Make-up*: Bill Morgan. *Hairstylist*: Paul LeBlanc. *Stunt Coordinator*: Alex Green. *Special Effects*: Tom Fischer, John Thomas. *Casting by* Reuben Cannon & Associates. *Production Supervisor*: Andre Morgan. *Unit Production Manager*: Les Kimber. *First Assistant Director*: Frank Ernst. *Second Assistant Director*: David MacLeod. *Director of Photography—Second Unit*: Richard Leiterman. *Camera Operator*: Rod Parkhurst. *Script Supervisor*: Pam Carlton. *Sound Design by* New Creative Sound. *Sound Recordist*: Richard Lightstone. *Re-recording Mixers*: Robert K. Litt, David J. Kimball, Elliot Tyson. *Title Design by* Phill Norman. *Assistant to the Producer*: Margo Baxley. Rated R. Technicolor. Panavision (2.35:1). 96 minutes. Released in May 1981. Currently available on VHS videotape. Previously available on laserdisc.

CAST: *Albert Johnson*, Charles Bronson; *Sergeant Edgar Millen*, Lee Marvin; *Alvin Adams*, Andrew Stevens; *Sundog*, Carl Weathers; *Hazel*, Ed Lauter; *Pilot Hank Tucker*, Scott Hylands; *Vanessa*, Angie Dickinson; *Bill Luce*, Henry Beckman; *Ned Warren*, William Sanderson; *Hawkeye*, Jon Cedar; *Hurley*, James O'Connell; *Lewis*, Len Lesser; *Beeler*, Dick Davalos; *Clarence*, Maury Chaykin; *Deak DeClerque*, August Schellenberg; *Trappers*, Dennis Wallace, James McIntyre, Rayford Barnes; *Charlie Rat*, Maurice Kowaleski; *News Reporter*, Sean McCann; *W. W. Douglas*, Steve O. Z. Finkel;

Jimmy Tom, Denis La Croix; *Indian Woman*, Tantoo Martin; *Buffalo Woman*, Amy Marie George.

Death Hunt, believe it or not, is the only film in Lee Marvin's career in which he portrays a true-life character. Out of sixty movies, there is not a single fact-based biography or ripped-from-the-headlines docudrama (though *The Delta Force* comes close). While *The Raid* and, to a lesser degree, *Pillars of the Sky* are based on true episodes of American history, only *Death Hunt*, an action-adventure film, tells its true story featuring the actual historical figures who were involved. Marvin had played several historical figures on television but had, for various reasons, turned down opportunities to play them in films such as *Patton*.

The film is set in the Canadian Yukon Territory in November of 1931, as trapper Albert Johnson (Charles Bronson) returns to civilization from the Canadian wild. Johnson stops a vicious dogfight and beats one of the dogs' owners, Hazel (Ed Lauter), belatedly giving him $200 for the badly mangled white dog and taking it with him. Hazel vows vengeance against the trapper and goes to town to force Canadian Mountie Sergeant Edgar Millen (Lee Marvin) to retrieve the dog and prosecute Johnson for theft. A new Mountie named Alvin Adams (Andrew Stevens) also arrives in town at the same time and is aghast at what he considers Millen's disregard of duty (much like Ensign Keith felt about Captain DeVriess in *The Caine Mutiny*).

Sergeant Millen only takes action after Hazel and his friends attack Johnson on their own, leading to the death of one of the men and of the dog. Millen, accompanied by a posse of a dozen trappers, almost talks Johnson into returning to town, but one of the men starts shooting and the bloodbath begins. Johnson kills several men before escaping into the wilderness when his cabin is destroyed by dynamite. Millen is forced to leave his paramour Vanessa (Angie Dickinson) and civilization behind while he, along with fellow Mounties Adams and Sundog (Carl Weathers), Hazel, and two other men, track down the now famous killer, Albert Johnson, who is heading north toward Alaska and freedom.

Millen and his men are followed by prospectors and trappers who want to cash in on the $1000 bounty put on Johnson's head, as well as a pilot who tries to shoot Johnson from the air. When attacked by the plane, Johnson shoots it out of the sky, but not before it inadvertently kills Sundog. Johnson also kills Hazel, and is aided by trapper Bill Luce (Henry Beckman), who, as a "mad trapper," kills two other men in Millen's party for the gold in their mouths. Millen and Adams close in, as does Bill Luce, and Johnson is able to use Bill as a decoy in order to escape. Bill's faceless body, killed ostensibly by Adams, serves as proof of Johnson's death, though both Millen and Adams watch as Johnson—the victim of justice—crosses the mountain range into the safety of Alaska.

Death Hunt has a few things in its favor, beginning with its beautiful Panavision cinematography which captures the stark serenity of its scenic setting. The location filming (in Alberta, Canada) is authentic, and the costuming in particular is noteworthy. The film is also very well cast and acted, making the picture more effective than it really has any right to be, because it remains, ultimately, a disappointing action-adventure.

The script is far too black-and-white for this colorful story, failing to provide the men who want to kill Albert Johnson with adequate motivation. Johnson is so obviously a victim of justice that there is no doubt he will ultimately prevail. Similarly, Hazel and his cohorts are so obviously bloodthirsty and stupid that there is no doubt regarding their final fate. Only Millen and his Mounties, caught in the middle of the situation, provide any drama. If the script had made Johnson even remotely guilty of something for which he should be pursued, the film would have been more effective. Likewise, Johnson proves himself so lethal during the first skirmish, and even more so at the second, that any trapper who comes after him again seems brainless. It just isn't believable.

What does work is the film's final half-hour. As word of Johnson's escape spreads, people bored by their own difficult lives follow the story enthusiastically, betting for or against the trapper with abandon. The $1000 reward for Johnson's capture appeals to the greed in all of the prospectors and trappers, causing them to put themselves in peril for a quick payoff, just as they are already doing by living in the Yukon wilderness. The scenes involving the pilot are also effective, pitting the skills of Millen and his traditional methods in competition with forces of the future—the airplane and its machine gun. Thematically, the ending works well as Millen recommends ending the bloodshed (by letting Johnson escape) but allows Alvin Adams to make the final decision, thus forcing him into a position of maturity and responsibility.

Charles Bronson is commendable as Albert Johnson. Strong, cautious and mostly silent, Bronson knows the value of underplaying and employs the technique well. Johnson is an enigmatic figure, only revealing his real nature to the dog which he nurses back to health. Andrew Stevens is properly militaristic as the new Mountie on the block, and his introduction to Millen's regimen of poker, alcohol and women before duty provides much of the film's comedy. Carl Weathers is relaxed and entertaining as Sundog, whose real name—George Washington Lincoln Brown—tickles Millen's funny bone. In a small role, Angie Dickinson brightens things up as Vanessa, though Vanessa's very presence in the Yukon defies logic.

As Sergeant Edgar Millen, Lee Marvin draws upon his lifetime of experience to portray a semi-alcoholic, womanizing, profane Mountie who constantly derides authority and who would rather play solitaire than do his job. Nevertheless, once he is spurred into action, Millen becomes a professional, taking steps to safeguard the men assigned to him and making every reasonable attempt to prevent further bloodshed. It is an ultra-realistic portrayal of a complex, very human, being. Marvin clearly enjoys himself in the early scenes, taking delight in showing Mountie Alvin Adams the seamier side of Yukon life; and in the later scenes, he is athletic and focused, proving why Millen is so highly regarded in the Mounties.

Death Hunt (a terrible title; the film was originally called *Arctic Rampage*) was at one time to be directed by Robert Aldrich, and one wonders what might have resulted had Aldrich, a master of the action-adventure genre, actually directed the film. While Peter Hunt captures the spirit of the piece, the chase

Sergeant Edgar Millen (Lee Marvin), a Royal Canadian Mountie, braves the freezing conditions of northern Canada on a mission to track down a man he knows to be innocent.

is too one-sided to be truly effective drama. Perhaps Aldrich would have balanced the battle between Millen and Johnson in some way, or given it his special brand of symbolic understanding. As it is, *Death Hunt* is always interesting, sometimes exciting, but often disappointing. It, like *The Killers*, *Point Blank* and *The Big Red One* before it, are decent films which had the potential for greatness but were not able to reach that standard.

Gorky Park (1983)

CREDITS: Orion. *Directed by* Michael Apted. *Produced by* Gene Kirkwood, Howard W. Koch, Jr. *Executive Producer*: Bob Larson. *Associate Producers*: Efrem Harkham, Uri Harkham. *Screenplay by* Dennis Potter. *Based upon the Novel by* Martin Cruz Smith. *Music Composed by* James Horner. *Music Editor*: George Brand. *Director of Photography*: Ralf D. Bode, A.S.C. *Film Editor*: Dennis Virkler. *Assistant Editor*: Mary McGlone. *Production Designer*: Paul Sylbert. *Costume Designer*: Richard Bruno. *Costume Supervisor*: Sue Wain. *Set Decorator*: Michael Seirton. *Makeup*: Alan Boyle, Ken Lintott. *Hair Stylist*: Tricia Cameron. *Stunt Coordinator*: David Ellis. *Casting by* Mary Selway. *Property Master*: Brian Humphrey. *First Assistant Director*: Dan Kolsrud. *Second Assistant Directors*: Peter Waller, Lauri Torhonen, Anders Hedin. *Third Assistant Directors*: Chris Thompson, Henrik Von Sydow, Pirjo Hokkanen. *Camera Operator*: Peter MacDonald. *Sound Mixer*: Simon Kaye. *Re-recording Mixers*: Robert J. Litt, C.A.S., Elliot Tyson, C.A.S., Rick Kline, C.A.S. *Orchestrations*: Greig McRitchie. *Music Scoring Mixer*: Dan Wallin. *Supervising Sound Editor*: Michael Hilkene. *Sound Editing*: Echo Film Services, David Elliott, Fred Judkins, John Kline, Russ Tinsley, Christopher T. Welch. *Production Manager*: Redmond Morris. *Unit Manager*: Juhani Jotuni. *Script Supervisor*: Mary Holdsworth. *Reconstruction by* Eoin Sprott Studio. *Assisted by* Michael Miles, Polly Wood Holland, Cathy Colby Grauer. *Cadavers by* Carl Fullerton Company. *Assisted by* Neal Martz, David Smith. *Gaffer*: Martin Evans. *Best Boy*: Ray Meehan. *Press Agent*: Howard Brandy. *Still Photographer*: Frank Connor. *Assistant to Mr. Koch and Mr. Kirkwood*: Michelle Papier. *Assistant to Mr. Apted*: Ann Pollack. *Production Associates*: Bradley Clayton, Barry Rosenbush. *Production Assistant*: Jennie Raglan. *Location Manager*: Alan Grabelsky. *Assistant Location Managers*: Toiva Lehmusvirta, Asko Partanen, Guy Travers, Susanne Ruben. *Secretary to Mr. Apted*: Andrea Fontaine. *Production Secretaries*: Dena Vincent, Heidi Nyberg, Tusse Nilsson. *New York Casting*: Bonnie Timmermann. *Focus Puller*: John Campbell. *Clapper Loader*: Eamonn O'Keefe. *Camera Grip*: Frank Batt. *Boom Operator*: David Sutton. *Sound Maintenance*: Taffy Haines. *Assistant Art Directors*: Peter Childs, Vesa Tapola. *Design Coordinator*: Jeanette D'Ambrosio. *Set Designer's Assistant*: Kjell Eriksson. *Set Dressing Buyer*: Jim Erikson. *Drapery*: Sean Casey. *Standby Props*: Dave Reilly, Barry Arnold, Brian Camby, Lars Logard, Pertti Kuusela. *Set Dressing Props*: Lee Benson, Dennis Simmonds, Gordon Phillips, Bob Douglas, Lari Lunkka, Fredrika Berghult. *Wardrobe Assistants*: Paddy Sharkey, Pat Williamson, Marjatta Nissinen, Juha Tuura. *Construction Managers*: Jack Carter, Lee Apsey. *Standby Carpenter*: Dave Williamson. *Standby Painter*: Derek Dackombe. *Standby Stagehand*: John Cope. *Standby Rigger*: James Crockett. *Electricians*: George Parish, Alan Williams, David Moroni, Brian Sullivan, Alan Grosch, Jari Heino, Kari Kekkonen, Teld Lindahl, Ulf Bjork. *Makeup Assistant*: Eija-Leena Lehmuskallio. *Comptroller*: Fred Wallach. *Production Accountant*: Jim Franklyn. *Accounting Assistants*: Ellen Kolsrud, Anneli Brummer, Heli Hanninen. *Production Runner*: Lotti Fogde. *Special Effects*: Candy Flannagan, Paul Stewart, Alan Whibley. *Drivers*: Bob Freeman, Dave Bruyea, Nick Perry. *Transport Manager*: Tero Porlamo. *Picture Car Coordinator*: Timo Nasman. *Crowd Casting*: Katri Ruotsalainen. *Catering*: Rafael Garcia. *Editing Apprentice*: Peter Lonsdale. *Uniforms by* Peruzzi. *Technical Advisor*: Anatoly Davydov. *Title and Optical Effects by* Movie Magic. *Processing by* Technicolor London. *Prints by* DeLuxe. *Arriflex Cameras by* Joe Dutton. *Lighting and Grip Equipment by* Lee Electric. *Financial Services*: Howard R. Schuster. Rated R. Technicolor. Panavision (2.35:1). 130 minutes. Released in December 1983. Currently available on VHS videotape. Previously available on laserdisc.

CAST: *Arkady Renko*, William Hurt; *Jack Osborne*, Lee Marvin; *William Kirwill*, Brian Dennehy; *Iamskoy*, Ian Bannen; *Irina*, Joanna Pacula; *Pasha*, Michael Elphick; *Anton*, Richard Griffiths; *Pribluda*, Rikki Fulton; *General*, Alexander Knox; *Golodkin*, Alexei Sayle; *Professor Andreev*, Ian McDiarmid; *KGB Agent Rurik*, Niall O'Brien; *Levin*, Henry Woolf; *Natasha*, Tusse Silberg; *Fet*, Patrick Field; *James Kirwill*, Jukka Hirvikangas; *Valerya Davidova*, Marjatta

Nissinen; *Kostia Borodin*, Hekki Leppanen; *Director*, Lauri Torhonen; *Babuska*, Elsa Salamaa; *KGB Agent Nicky*, Anatoly Davydov; *Shadowers*, Lasse Lindberg and Jussi Parvianen; *Russian Tea Band*, Black Pearls; *Rock & Roll Band*, Bad Sign.

Gorky Park was one of the big Christmas movies of 1983. Based on a huge best-selling thriller by Martin Cruz Smith and starring hot new star William Hurt, the film was highly anticipated. It was Lee Marvin's biggest movie since *The Big Red One* three years earlier, and proved that he was still not only an actor to be reckoned with but could still play an adversary with inimitable style.

Militia policeman Arkady Renko (William Hurt) is called to a murder scene in Gorky Park in Moscow, where three bodies have been found, all shot in the chest and butchered—they have no faces or fingertips. Renko, leery of the case, tries to pass it on to the KGB, but is told by his boss, Iamskoy (Ian Bannen), to follow it, no matter where it may lead. Piece by piece, Renko and his partner Pasha (Michael Elphick) reconstruct the murder of the three friends, but they lack suspects and a motive. Renko interviews Irina Amasova (Joanna Pacula), whose figure skates were found on the dead woman. When he sees her with Jack Osborne (Lee Marvin), a wealthy, powerful American businessman, he is sure that they are both somehow involved.

Another American named William Kirwill (Brian Dennehy) also becomes involved, jumping Renko at one point and later saving his life. Kirwill is sure that one of the bodies in the snow was his brother James, and that he was trying to help smuggle the other two out of Russia. Renko and Kirwill form an uneasy alliance, trading information and leads to each other and rescuing Irina from a KGB attack after she goes to see Osborne. Irina and Renko are drawn to each other, but she cannot bring herself to fully trust him. Renko and Pasha find the lead they are looking for, but then Pasha is killed. Kirwill provides the final piece of the puzzle, discovering that Osborne had hired the three to make a religious chest to help him smuggle six sables out of Russia. Renko restages the murders for Irina, forcing her to confirm what he already knows.

As Renko and Kirwill prepare to wrap up the case, they discover that Osborne has yet

Moscow detective Arkady Renko (William Hurt) watches as his boss, Iamskoy (Ian Bannen), cordially greets American businessman Jack Osborne (Lee Marvin) in *Gorky Park*.

another ally, Iamskoy, who had wanted to put enough pressure on Osborne to get better terms for his end of the deal. Renko confronts Iamskoy, who admits everything, then tries to wrestle away Renko's gun. Iamskoy is killed, and Renko winds up in the hands of the KGB. To his surprise, Renko finds himself in Stockholm with orders to kill Osborne, who wants to make a trade. Renko is astonished to find Irina, who tells him that Osborne has a total of twelve sables, not just six. Osborne will trade the six that are known, secretly keeping the other six and smuggling them to America. Renko agrees to Osborne's trade terms and lets Kirwill know about the setup.

When the trade occurs the following day, Kirwill is found, gutted, by Osborne, who calmly shoots the KGB agents. Renko and Osborne stalk each other around the sable pens before Osborne is shot repeatedly by Irina, avenging the deaths of her three friends in Gorky Park. Irina goes to New York, as she believed her friends had done, and Renko, after freeing the sables into the wilds of Stockholm, goes back to Moscow to further serve the State.

Gorky Park was a complex police procedural thriller as a book, and, happily, most of the assets of the book are also assets in the movie. While domestic police procedurals are common, the foreign setting and inter-agency intrigue work in this film's favor to keep up viewer interest. Watching Renko, Pasha and Kirwill piece together the events that led up to the three deaths is compelling, made even more so by the constant danger that they are exposed to from the KGB. The film also does a sound job of moving the scale from the intimate details of the murder investigation to the bigger picture of the international ramifications involving Jack Osborne and the sables.

The details of the film are also authentic, from showing Renko waiting in a long Moscow line to buy bread, to the piecemeal gun which Kirwill smuggles into Russia, to the intricate reconstruction of the murdered people's faces by Professor Andreev for Renko's benefit. As in the novel, it is the small, relatively insignificant details of the story which, over time, make it real and true. It is attention to detail which ultimately makes or breaks criminal cases, and director Michael Apted and screenwriter Dennis Potter deserve a lot of credit for taking the time to include as many of those details as they have.

Critical opinion was evenly divided on the film. While many critics found it engrossing and intriguing, another group found the film dull and tedious. The central performance of William Hurt seemed to be the dividing line; if critics accepted him, they liked the movie, and vice versa. Bruce Williamson of *Playboy* wrote, "...this is one hell of a movie—the sharpest, most provocative edge-of-your-seat thriller in the past decade or so," while Dave Kehr in the *Chicago Reader* called it "...a lumpy thriller" and was generally disappointed with the result. Williamson found Hurt perfect to play Renko, but Kehr wrote that, "...he's all technique and no presence." The film was a modest hit for Orion not the blockbuster for which they had hoped, but one which made money.

William Hurt's portrayal of Renko is the key to the entire movie, and he makes it work from the first scene. His plodding, methodical, modest manner belies the obvious intelligence in his face and makes the character more likable. While the part does not have the emotional baggage that was included in the novel, Hurt still conveys Renko's inner longings for comradeship, respect, truth and a sense of order about things. Caution seems to be part of Renko's face, ingrained by years of paranoia and occasional setbacks. As he falls for Irina, the progression from slight interest in to worry for, from simple concern to emotional attachment, is not only there to see but is also combined with the knowledge that she may make or break his case and therefore must be handled carefully.

Such complexity also applies to Jack Osborne, the American sable dealer with whom Renko plays a deadly game of cat-and-mouse. As portrayed by Lee Marvin, Osborne is a businessman of the upper class, to be treated with courtesy and respect. Marvin plays the role coolly as a cobra, ready to strike if necessary but preferring to dominate his foes by his formidable wits. Near the end of the movie, Osborne holds off the KGB and Renko with a high powered rifle—which he shoots accurately *from the hip*—displaying the kind of cool machismo not seen in movies since the heyday of the western.

Osborne even gives Renko a timetable to stop him from leaving the country, thus challenging the policeman to a personal confrontation which he is confident he will win. Marvin is just right in the morally ambiguous role; he demands respect for his power and intelligence even while using them in murderous ways. William Hurt commented that, "he acted the hell out of his scenes. He acted better than I did. Instead of trying to beat him, which was of course not my job, I wanted to let this person teach me…And he did, on so many levels you wouldn't believe."

Joanna Pacula was a veteran of many Polish stage productions and had made more than ten films in Poland before being "introduced" to American audiences as Irina in *Gorky Park*. Brian Dennehy, who, like Lee Marvin, made many of his early film appearances as a heavy, gives his role of William Kirwill a strong physical presence and a savvy streetwise intelligence. Most of the lead Russian roles are filled by Britishers—Ian Bannen, Michael Elphick, Richard Griffiths and Alexander Knox—who use their natural British accents for their roles, which led to a curious critical reaction.

Many critics who wrote about the film attacked it for its use of accents. Though set in Russia, the Russian characters (except for Irina) speak with British accents, while the two Americans keep their American accents. Critics eviscerated the film, and particularly William Hurt, for this decision, apparently forgetting that such actors as James Mason, Richard Burton and Robert Shaw had done precisely the same thing to great effect in years gone by. The use of British accents, while not authentic, is still *foreign* to most American ears, and the more precise, clipped speech patterns of the dialect serve the story well. Hurt, who had spent a year studying drama in Britain, has no trouble with his accent and did not deserve the harsh criticism which he received for it.

Lee Marvin was to make two more movies and one made-for-television film, but *Gorky Park* represented his last, best work on the screen. His Jack Osborne not only gives Arkady Renko a formidable foe, but his elegant, professional style helps elevate the film to another level. Though Marvin was 59 years old at the time, he seems at least ten years younger, still more than able to handle himself with guns or women, fully in control and comfortably in command. *Gorky Park* is Lee Marvin's last great film appearance.

Dog Day (1984) (aka *Canicule*)

CREDITS: Swanie-TopI-TFI-Cinetele and UGC. *Directed by* Yves Boisset. *Produced by* Norbert Saada. *Screenplay by* Jean Herman (Vautrin), Michel Audiard, Dominique Roulet, Serge Korbe, Yves Boisset. *Based on a novel by* Jean Vautrin. *Music by* Francis Lai. *Conducted by* Christian Gaubert. *Director of Photography*: Jean Boffety. *Edited by* Albert Jurgenson, Nadine Muse. *Set Designer*: Jacques Dugied. *Sound*: Jean-Louis Ducarme. *Mixer*: Joel Belldent. *Production Manager*: Guy Azzi. *Production Assistants*: Marc Angelo, Alain Baudy, Paul Barzman, Jacqueline Gaveau, Pericles Prokopiadis, Thomas Korber. *Executive Assistants*: Jean Guillaume, Hubert Barbin, Jean Cherlian, Patrick Loiseau. *Administration Assistants*: Villes Villiers, Monique Colotte. *Assistant Cameramen*: Michel Deloire, Christian Vivier, Laurent Machuer, Victor Rodrigue. *Assistant Sound Editors*: Joel Riant, Gerard Manneveau. *Sound Effects*: Daniel Couteau. *Assistant Set Decorators*: Chantal Giuliani, Andre Piltant, Marc Lirola, Dominique LeMaire. *Special Effects*: Georges Demetreau, Pierre Foury. *Assistant Editors*: Chantal Pernecker, Martine Fleury, Anna Bertona. *Costume Designers*: Rosine Lan, Sylvie Nabrin, Cecile Rocheman. *Make-up and Hair Stylists*: Joel Lavau, Gill Robillard, Isabelle Arnal. *Publicity Manager*: Josee Benabent-Loiseau. *Costumes, Weapons*: Collection of Jean-Charles Maratier, MAC-TAC France, Heli-Union S.A., Caliop Helicoptere S.A. *Sound Recording Music*: Emmanuel Guiot. *Studio*: Palais Des Congres. *Record Distributor*: W.E.A. Filipacchi. *Mixing*: Paris Studio Cinema. *Stunts Coordinator*: Remy Julienne.

Strip-tease by Chantal. Filmed in the city of Orleans, France. Rated R. Fujicolor. Dolby Stereo. Panavision (2.35:1). 101 minutes. Released in 1984. Currently available on VHS videotape.

CAST: *Jimmy Cobb*, Lee Marvin; *Jessica*, Miou-Miou; *Socrate*, Jean Carmet; *Horace*, Victor Lanoux; *Chim*, David Bennent; *Segolene*, Bernadette Lafont; *Torontopoulos*, Jean-Pierre Kalfon; *Lily*, Grace De Capitani; *Noemie Blue*, Tina Louise; *Le Barrec*, Jean-Claude Dreyfus; *Marceau*, Henri Guybet; *Snake*, Pierre Clementi; *Gusta*, Muni; *Maggy*, Juliette Mills; *Rojinski*, Julien Bukowski; *Julio*, Jean-Roger Milo; *Doudou Cadillac*, Joseph Momo; *with* Myriam Salvoldi, Inger Ekdom, Lillemour Jonsson, Jean Cherlian, Mohamed Bekhtaoui, Chrystel.

Most major American actors make their way to Europe at one time or another in their careers to make one or more European films. Sometimes, as Clint Eastwood proved with his three "spaghetti westerns," such a move can make the actor an international star and lead to much bigger and better roles upon the actor's return to Hollywood. For some actors, a stint in Europe can be a reawakening of dormant acting instincts, brought back to life by the different rhythms, pacing, styles and approaches of European films. And for some actors, as Lee Marvin discovered for himself, making a European movie can be a mistake best forgotten.

Dog Day takes place in France, depicting the aftermath of an armored car robbery gone bad. Only Jimmy Cobb (Lee Marvin) escapes from the robbery shoot-out with the police, and he has a bag full of money. Cobb makes his way through golden fields to a farm compound where he hides, after burying the money in a field for safekeeping. Unfortunately for Cobb, the people who run this particular farm comprise a collection of the most greedy, perverse, depraved, pathetic human beings imaginable, and Cobb is ill-equipped to survive in their midst.

Cobb is discovered by Jessica (Miou-Miou), who agrees to protect him if he will kill her husband Horace (Victor Lanoux), whom she can't stand to have touching her. Before Cobb can act, he is discovered and taken prisoner by Horace and his brother Socrate (Jean Carmet). The men, who want the robbery loot, hide Cobb from the police, who place an officer at the farm to watch for the fugitive. Meanwhile, the cash has been dug up by Jessica's son Chim (David Bennent) and stashed in another field. One of the farm workers later finds the money the kid has buried and puts it in his car.

At night, Horace goes on a killing spree, murdering the policeman staying at the farm and two women camping nearby. Horace returns to the farm and is killed by Jessica. Cobb gets loose and takes over, helping Jessica hide her husband's body. Cobb arranges for his own escape the next day and sends Jessica to make contact with his girlfriend Noemie Blue (Tina Louise). Jessica contacts Noemie, then seduces and executes a detective who has followed her to Noemie.

Cobb makes his escape from the farm in a tractor but can't find the money where he buried it. A police helicopter spots him, and Cobb, wounded, flees to a barn, where the boy Chim holds him prisoner, wanting to take credit for capturing—and killing—the gangster. When the police shoot into the barn, Cobb grabs the kid's shotgun and shoots himself, depriving Chim of his imagined glory. Jessica arrives at the barn among a media circus interviewing the boy, who is taking credit anyway. She walks away into the rain with her boy Chim, now free from the influence of the hated Horace and somehow better for knowing Jimmy Cobb.

Dog Day is the sleaziest, stupidest, most horrific film in which Lee Marvin ever appeared. In its depiction of human depravity it even surpasses *The Klansman*, which is certainly Marvin's most tasteless American movie. Ultimately, *Dog Day* must be seen as the worst of Marvin's films because the actor is utterly wasted in the movie. Marvin is certainly a natural choice to play the American gangster who masterminds an armored car robbery, but that aspect of the film is almost insignificant. Marvin the actor has absolutely *nothing* to do during the rest of the movie until the moment he finally blows his own head off, ending the madness. At least in *The Klansman* Marvin portrayed a character and gave that film its only dignity.

The focus of *Dog Day* is on the depraved family who take Cobb prisoner. The members of Horace's family belong in a horror movie. They dream of murder, rape and revenge, and Cobb's arrival pushes them into action. Once their instinct for greed is aroused, they think nothing of betraying or killing each other for Cobb's loot. Somehow Cobb's arrival gives Jessica the courage, or freedom, to take her life into her own hands, murder her husband, seduce and then execute a detective, and become her own woman. The ending, with Jessica and son Chim leaving the farm in the cleansing rain for a better life is so upbeat it is preposterous. The utter pointlessness of this movie is staggering.

While *Dog Day* did play in France (under its original title, *Canicule*), it was barely released at all in the United States. Lee Marvin looks haggard and old in this movie, much more so than in *Gorky Park*, filmed the previous year. (Perhaps that's why the box artwork for the *Dog Day* video release bypasses the film completely and features a photo of Marvin in *Gorky Park* as its main selling point). For the first time, Marvin seems too old to be playing cops and robbers on-screen, and it comes as a relief when, at the film's climax, he purposefully kills himself. This sad excuse of a movie represents the lowest point of Lee Marvin's mostly memorable career. Unfortunately, his next project, the first made-for-television sequel to his biggest hit, *The Dirty Dozen*, was only a small step up from this calamity.

The Dirty Dozen: Next Mission (1985)

CREDITS: MGM. *Directed by* Andrew V. McLaglen. *Produced by* Harry R. Sherman. *Associate Producer*: Frederick Muller. *Written by* Michael Kane. *Based upon Certain Characters from the Screenplay by* Nunnally Johnson, Lukas Heller. *Derived from the Novel by* E. M. Nathanson. *Music by* Richard Harvey. *Director of Photography*: John Stanier, G.B.C.T. *Film Editor*: Alan Strachan. *Production Designer*: Peter Mullins. *Art Director*: Bill Alexander. *Set Decorator*: Robin Tarsnane. *Sound Editor*: Don Deacon. *Production Sound Mixer*: Paul LeMare. *Re-recording Mixer*: Milan Bor. *Costume Designer*: Betsy Heimann. *Make-up Artist*: Jane Royle. *Hairstylist*: Stevie Hall. *Property Master*: Brian Payne. *Special Effects Supervisor*: Dave Beavis. *U. S. Casting by* Joseph D'Agosta. *U. K. Casting by* Allan Foenander. *Airplanes by* Aces High, Ltd. *Sound Recording—Bavaria*: Atlelier, G.M.B.H. *Music Recording*: Angel Recording Studios, Ltd. *Production Supervision*: Steven P. Saeta. *Executive in Charge of Production*: Ted Zachary. Not Rated. Made for Television. Technicolor. Flat (1.33:1). 100 minutes. Televised in 1985. Currently available on VHS videotape.

CAST: *Major John Reisman*, Lee Marvin; *General Worden*, Ernest Borgnine; *Louie Valentine*, Ken Wahl; *Tommy Wells*, Larry Wilcox; *Sam Sixkiller*, Sonny Landham; *Sergeant Clyde Bowren*, Richard Jaeckel; *General Dietrich*, Wolf Kahler; *Arlen Driggers*, Ricco Ross; *Conrad E. Perkins*, Gavan O'Herlihy; *Otto Deutsch*, Stephen Hattersley; *Robert E. Wright*, Rolf Saxon; *Didier LeClair*, Jay Benedict; *Baxley*, Michael John Paliotti; *Reynolds*, Paul Herzberg; *Sanders*, Jeff Harding; *Anderson*, Sam Douglas; *Gary Rosen*, Russell Sommers; *Adolf Hitler*, Richael Sheard; *Colonel*, Bruce Boa; *Field Marshal Meisterlein*, John Malcolm; *German General*, Morgan Sheppard; *Schmid*, Crispin De Nys; *General Pierre Fontaine*, Denis Holmes; *General Bulldog Bardsley*, Alan Barry; *General Trent Tucker*, Don Fellows.

Eighteen years after the original *Dirty Dozen*, MGM decided to return to World War II, using the same formula for a plot and as many of the same actors as would agree to come back for this made-for-television movie. Lee Marvin, Ernest Borgnine and Richard Jaeckel agreed to reprise their roles as the Army officers behind the so-called "Next Mission," while a whole new squad of prisoners was recruited, mostly from the ranks of television actors of the 1980s.

The "Next Mission" takes place in 1944, as Major Reisman (Lee Marvin) is again told by General Worden (Ernest Borgnine) to choose twelve prisoners sentenced to death or long terms for a behind-the-lines mission to kill German General Dietrich (Wolf Kahler), who is believed to be planning an assassination attempt at Adolf Hitler. Reisman returns to Marston-Tyne prison (in a long shot lifted directly from the first film!) and reunites with

Only a few months after his first mission, but somehow almost twenty years older, Major John Reisman (Lee Marvin) leads another suicide raid in *The Dirty Dozen: Next Mission*.

Sergeant Clyde Bowren (Richard Jaeckel), who helps introduce him to the prisoners and then train them.

With their objective firmly in mind, the Dozen practice assaulting the train on which General Dietrich will be travelling. The prisoners make no secret of their hatred for Reisman, but are forced to comply with his orders. When the operation timetable is moved up, they fly into occupied France in German uniforms, fight their way off of the air field, and miss the train. The prisoners rebel, refusing to make new plans to kill the general, preferring to go free in occupied France. Reisman baits them back by telling them the German train is a "treasure train," and that they can have anything they can find on it once the general is eliminated.

Somehow the Dozen are parachuted (without any training) to a location where the train will stop. It is heavily guarded, and a surprise guest—Adolf Hitler himself—arrives. The sharpshooter of the Dozen wants to kill Hitler, but Reisman insists that Dietrich remain the target. Finally, Dietrich is killed, spraying blood onto Hitler, and the Dozen try to escape the wrath of the Nazis. Following a firefight in which most of the prisoners are killed, the remaining Americans steal the plane in which Hitler had arrived and fly it to England, landing in a field just beyond the White Cliffs of Dover. The only survivors are Reisman and three of his dozen, one of whom is injured.

The original *Dirty Dozen* was an entertaining action-adventure with a preposterous plot—and compared to its sequel, it is a Shakespearean masterpiece. *The Dirty Dozen: Next Mission* is a total ripoff, with virtually no redeeming qualities. It lifts complete scenes and speeches from the original (but slightly paraphrased so they won't take up quite as much time). Reisman and Worden have the same arguments about the prisoners' fate as they did in the first film, with almost the same exact wording. Reisman's warnings to his men are also the same, with a word or two substituted here and there. Unfortunately, here they are delivered woodenly and without feeling or enthusiasm.

Of course, the fact that Reisman, Worden and Bowren have aged almost *twenty years* in the few months between the original and next mission is never brought up or explained. Nor is it ever questioned how once the Dozen miss the German train the first time—in *occupied* France—they find the means and are suddenly able to *parachute* to its new location—without any training—and land like butterflies. The parachuting sequence is included only because the first film contained one, and this movie wants to imitate the other as closely as possible to ensure its familiarity to audiences.

Nor is the twisted logic behind the idea that Hitler must not be killed very convincing. The Allied command evidently wants Hitler to stay in command because he's so inept, and is afraid that the war could drag on indefinitely if he were killed. Such an idea is hogwash. The only real intrigue in the *Next Mission* comes when Hitler arrives at the train and the men want, rightly, to kill him. At that point, the perspective changes to a philosophical one, and a difficult choice must be made, one that could conceivably change history. However, since Hitler's history is already known, this too becomes a moot point.

The film is sluggishly directed by Andrew V. McLaglen, an action veteran who seems content just to repeat many of the images (descending ropes instead of climbing them, two prisoners stopping one from escaping, learning the assault plan by numbers) from the first film. It is lackluster and uninspired direction, matched by the routine, often silly, script by Michael Kane, which is far too derivative and underdeveloped. Besides the actual plot, the only twist here is that the prisoners are bent on escaping—or at least leaving Reisman behind while they scatter across the French countryside—and Reisman is forced to make up the story of the "treasure train," though that turns out to be true.

Unlike the original, in which the prisoners gave the film its personality, here the prisoners are strictly by-the-numbers cardboard cutouts, acted routinely primarily by television actors (Ken Wahl, Larry Wilcox) and unknowns. What character development there is takes place with all the familiarity and obviousness which make most television movies inherently inferior to feature films. Example: Valentine (Ken Wahl) is bigoted and baits black Arlen Driggers (Ricco Ross) at every opportunity. Yet, on the plane ride home at the end, Driggers dies of wounds received during the escape and Valentine, out of the blue, comforts him and says, "He was okay."

Perhaps the most depressing aspect of this sad film is the performance of Lee Marvin, who looks old and tired and obviously doesn't want to be there. This is the only sequel with which Marvin was ever involved and was a huge mistake for the actor. Marvin shows none of the fire that John Reisman had in the first film; he was obviously content to play pretend and cash his paycheck. To be fair, Marvin wasn't in the best of health at the time, and shooting the film in cold, dank Bavaria didn't help. But Marvin appears more pathetic than commanding, and proves that he should have retired after he made *Gorky Park*.

MGM milked the *Dirty Dozen* cash cow for two additional television movies, both starring Telly Savalas and Borgnine (and both reportedly better than this film), then based a short-lived television series on the concept. Lee Marvin was unwilling and unable to take part in any further *Dirty Dozen* efforts.

The Delta Force (1986)

CREDITS: Cannon. *Directed by* Menahem Golan. *Produced by* Menahem Golan, Yoram Globus. *Associate Producer*: Rony Yacov. *Written by* James Bruner, Menahem Golan. *Music by* Alan Silvestri. *Director of Photography*: David Gurfinkel. *Film Editor*: Alain Jakubowicz. *Production Designer*: Lucisano Spadoni. *Production Supervisor*: Itzhak Kol. *Production Manager*: Doy Maoz. *Second Unit Director*: Carlos Gil. *Second Unit Photography*: Hans Khules, Jr. *Set Designer*: Leonardo Coen Cagli. *Set Decorator*: Ladi Wilheim. *Special Effects*: John Gant. *Stunt Coordinator*: Don Pike. *Unit Production Manager*: Zion Chen. *Costumes by* Tami Mor. *First Assistant Director*: Tony Brandt. *Second Assistant Directors*: Mike Katzin, Michael Engel. *Third Assistant Director*: Haim Rinsky. *Casting—Los Angeles*: Robert MacDonald, Perry Bullington. *Casting—Israel*: Tova Cypin. *Camera Operator*: Danny Sheneor. *Focus Pullers*: Mickey Benyamini, Avi Koren. *Camera Assistants*: Rami Siman Tov, Danny Schneider, Benny Mali. *Still Photographer*: Yoni Hamenachem. *Sound Mixer*: Eli Yarkoni. *Boom Operator*: Yosi Yarkoni. *Set Dresser*: David Varod. *Assistant Set Dressers*: Eli Fishboim, Haim Kor, Avital Van Der Veden, Yosi Gino. *Key Grip*: Shimon Sabach. *Best Boys*: Avi Avrahami, David Saranga. *Grips*: Micha Sabach, Ephraim Aiami, Reuven Aiami, David Alrobi. *Gaffers*: Abraham Leibman, Danny Ben Menahem. *Electricians*: Franco Naim, Moshe Alon, Rud Van Der Veden, Michael Inbari, Shlomo Brenner, Avital Elati. *Assistant Electricians*: Avichai Honig, Rami Levi. *Art Department Coordinator*: Zvika Hen. *Sketch Artist*: Jean Peyre. *Standby Painter*: Salvatore Saito. *Draughtsmen*: Edna Lavi, Yehuda Ako. *Art Department Buyer*: Eli Zion. *Property Master*: Batia Grafka. *Property Assistants*: Carol Yanovachanski, Arie Weiss, Yosi Zilber, Shimon Cohen. *Armourer*: Pini Klavir. *Assistant Armourer*: Yitseak Barel. *Wardrobe Mistress*: Rina Mor. *Wardrobe Assistants*: Zmira Herscovitz, Pam Ayli, Shimon Elimelech, Hilary Ross, Chris Oren, Naomi Golan. *Key Makeup Artist*: Vitorio Biseo. *Makeup Artists*: Zivit Yakir, Esty Kariv. *Makeup Assistants*: Limor Bar Oz, Michaela Lavi. *Hair Stylists*: Tami Levy, Patgrice Morieres. *Location Managers*: Avner Peled, Raz Chen. *Production Coordinator*: Naomi Mayberg. *Production Coordinators—Los Angeles*: Alan Gershenfeld, Jim Taylor. *Production Secretaries*: Charlotte Rose, Edna Rosen, Sharon Kahn. *Script Supervisor*: Vivalda Vigorelli. *Crowd Casting*: Zeev Zigler. *Unit Publicist*: Sophie Kahn. *Production Accountant*: Naomi Kol. *Production Auditor*: Shneor Ratskovski. *Production Auditor—Los Angeles*: Lisa Howard. *Paymaster*: Aaron Marcus. *Army Consultant*: Jim Monaghan. *Army Liaison*: Giora Oren. *Aviation Consultant*: Yoel Saraf. *Construction Manager*: Arie Ben Yishai. *Transport Captains*: Sam Rubi, Meir Sigura. *Mechanics*: Israel Hatooka, Moshe Salem. *Action Vehicles*: Doron Mizrachi. *Special Effects*: Chris Gant, Ian Biggs, Chris Corbould, Neil Corbould, Yoram Pollack, Andy Williams. *Special Effects Assistants*: Yoram Zargary, Alan Reuven, Shemesh Yaron. *Unit Doctors*: Dr. Zeev Weiss, Dr. Shmuel Beck. *Dialogue Coaches—Arabic*: Jahashan Tarid, Shoshana Linyado. *Security Officer*: Chanan Adaki.

Second Unit. First Assistant Director: Avner Oshalimi. *Second Assistant Director*: Avi Mograbi. *Third Assistant Director*: Shauli Gorodeski. *Camera Operator*: Arik Bernstein. *Focus Pullers*:

Mark Brower, Offer Frant. *Camera Assistants*: Micha Lozone, Genan Jakubowicz. *Still Photographer*: Shlomo Avidan. *Sound Mixer*: Danny Natovitz. *Boom Operator*: David Liss. *Key Grip*: Shmuel Levy. *Best Boy*: Yehuda Tatarko. *Grips*: Moshe Flechter, Amonon Nuriani. *Assistant Grip*: Michael Ooshmi. *Electricians*: Haim Flechter, Michael Greenbaum, Victor Lepelman. *Assistant Electricians*: Steve Cameron, Gil Florman, Yosef Benari. *Assistant Set Dressers*: Moshe Magnezi, Yosef Eyni, Zeev Aloni, Avi Tannenbaum. *Property Master*: Caesar Alava. *Property Assistant*: Miguel Merkin. *Assistant Armourer*: Pesach. *Wardrobe*: Mica Saban, Zion Tubi. *Makeup Artists*: Hannah Ezra, Charles Biderman. *Hair Stylist*: Haim Adut. *Location Manager*: Danny Kedem. *Script Supervisor*: Janette Nae. *Transportation Captain*: Moki Ben Hamo.

Post Production Supervisor: Michael R. Sloan. *First Assistant Editors*: Kobi Dagan, Dory Lubliner, Anne Couk. *Second Assistant Editors*: Iris Dagan, Elinoah Hardy, Anat Kenet, Omer Tal, Robert Baird, Albert Gasser, Craig Weintraub, Tony Wakefield. *Third Assistant Editors*: Hadara Oren, Smador Cohen. *Supervising Sound Editor*: Jerry Ross. *Sound Effects Editors*: Ed Callahan, Alan Hartz, Martin Maryska, Dave Bartlett, J. W. Compare, Richard King, Fred Wasser. *Supervising Dialogue Editor*: George Berndt. *Dialogue Editors*: Victor Grodecki, David Lebrun, Tom Fucci, Andy Patterson, Ruth Schell. *ADR Editors*: Tracey Smith, Cliff Latimer. *Supervising Foley Editor*: Craig Smith. *Foley Editors*: Lee Dragu, Baird Bryant, Mark Eiges, Keith Critchlow. *Assistant Sound Editors*: Sue Mazzei, Peter Friedberg, Ralph, Stuart, Ron Bartlett, Marian Wilde, Justine Vacco, Gilberto Costa Nunes, Stephanie Ng, Denise Cochran, Jessica Callahan, Ann Ducommon, Oscar Mitt. *Additional Sound Services*: Gomillion Studios. *Foley by* Taj Soundworks. *Re-recording*: Todd-AO. *Re-recording Mixers*: Christopher Jenkins, Gary Alexander, Larry Stensvold. *Title Design*: Wenden K. Baldwin, Kyle O'Feere. *Main Titles and Opticals*: Freeze Frame. *Music Supervisor*: Paula Erickson. *Music Editor*: Tom Carlin. *Scoring Mixer*: Dennis S. Sands. *Audio Programming*: David Bifano. *All Music Written and Performed on* The Synclavier Digital Music System; New England Digital. *New England Digital*: Brad Naples, Sydney Alonso, Cameron Jones, David Nichtern, Warren Weinberg.

Special Thanks to Anheuser-Busch, Inc., Brigade Quartermasters, Ltd., Chenowth Racing Products, Inc., Dugit T.A. Underwater Equipment, Gargoyles Sunglasses. Rated R. Color. Dolby Stereo. Widescreen (1.85:1). 125 minutes. Released in February 1986. Currently available on VHS videotape. Previously available on laserdisc.

CAST: *Major Scott McCoy*, Chuck Norris; *Colonel Nick Alexander*, Lee Marvin; *Ben Kaplan*, Martin Balsam; *Harry Goldman*, Joey Bishop; *Abdul*, Robert Forster; *Sylvia Goldman*, Lainie Kazan; *Father O'Malley*, George Kennedy; *Ingrid*, Hanna Schygulla; *Deborah Levine*, Susan Strasberg; *Captain Campbell*, Bo Svenson; *General Woodbridge*, Robert Vaughn; *Edie Kaplan*, Shelley Winters; *Sister Mary*, Kim Delaney; *Pete Peterson*, William Wallace; *Bobby*, Steve James; *Tom Hale*, Charles Floye; *Mustafa*, David Menahem; *David Rosovsky*, Yehuda Efroni; *Robert Levine*, Jerry Lazarus; *Father Nicholas*, Shai K. Ophir; *Doctor Jack*, Gerry Weinstock; *Dave Hoskins*, Marvin Freedman; *Jim Montgomery*, Bob Levit; *Tina*, Chelli Goldberg; *Lesley*, Chris Ellia; *Ellen Levine*, Natalie Roth; *Ted Bilicki*, Jerry Hyman; *Rosalee Bilicki*, Gael Lehrer; *Jay Bilicki*, Hank Leninger; *Ed*, Howard Jackson; *Andy*, Eric Norris; *Sister Ann*, Zipora Peled; *Mike Fraser*, Aaron Kaplan; *Sally Fraser*, Caroline Langford; *Jaffer*, Avi Loziah; *George Berri*, Uri Gavriel; *Peter*, Panos Nicolaou; *Bartender*, Elki Jacobs; *Isaam*, Menahem Eini; *Raffi Amir*, Assaf Doyan; *Lebanese Minister*, Jack Cohen; *Salim*, Adiv Gahshan; *Samir*, Haim Sirafi; *TV Reporter*, Mosco Alkalai; *Journalist*, Larry Price; *ATW Girl*, Susan Ophir; *ATW Agent*, Jack Messinger; *Female TV Announcer*, Janet Harshman; *Israeli Commandos*, Ezra Kafri, Danny Freedman; *Captain Ross*, Richard Salano; *Pete's Assistant*, Andy Shulman; *Delta Pilot*, Joe Sapel; *American Ambassador in Algiers*, Richard Peterson; *American Ambassador in Tel Aviv*, Eugene Klein; *Controller in Algeria*, Albert Amar; *Officer with George*, Ben Ami Shmueli; *Terrorist in Plane*, Moti Shirin; *Amai Sergeant*, Itzik Aloni; *Gate Guard*, Boaz Ofri; *Passport Inspector*, Albert Iluz; *Information Agent El Al*, Osnat Vishinski; *Male TV Announcer*, David Leshnik; *Stunt Players*, John Epstein, Gary Pike, Mike DeLuna, B. J. Davis, Greg Gault, B. J. Worth, Albert Vaknin.

Lee Marvin appeared on the silver screen for the final time in this torn-from-the-headlines action melodrama which was loosely based on an airline hijacking that occurred the year before the film's release. This is not a retelling of TWA Flight 847's fate, although the film does "borrow" several actions which occurred during that incident. The more realistic, less important half of the film depicts the situation on the hijacked airliner, while the less realistic, more important, action-packed half depicts the rescue efforts of the Delta Force.

Colonel Nick Alexander (Lee Marvin) commands the elite Delta Force, a U.S. commando unit trained to combat international terrorists and who specializes in hostage rescue operations. His right-hand officer is Major McCoy (Chuck Norris), and in the opening scene they are participants in—and witness to—the aborted attempt to rescue the hostages from Iran in 1980. Five years later, the Delta Force is given another chance when ATW (instead of TWA) Flight 282 is hijacked. As the Delta Force prepares to fly to Beirut, Major McCoy, who had retired in disgust after the Iranian debacle, arrives to help just as Col. Alexander had expected.

Terrorist Abdul (Robert Forster) seizes control of Flight 282 soon after its takeoff from Athens and diverts its destination from Rome to Beirut. In Beirut, the plane, full of American tourists, secretly takes on additional terrorists before being flown to Algiers. The Delta Force arrives in Algiers just before Flight 282 and prepares an assault. The terrorists release all of the female and underage hostages, but force most of the men to remain. Just as the assault is to begin, Col. Alexander discovers from brave stewardess Ingrid (Hanna Schygulla) that far more terrorists are aboard than had been known. Alexander calls off the assault, alarming the terrorists in the process, and as the jet takes off again, Abdul murders a passenger and drops his body to the tarmac.

The jet lands in Beirut for the second time, and two groups of hostages—one of Jewish men, the other of Navy servicemen—are dispersed to hideouts along Beirut's Mediterranean coast, while others are kept on the plane along with the airliner's crew. The Delta Force, with some guidance, moves in from the sea and surrounds the hideouts, then

Colonel Nick Alexander (Lee Marvin, right) leads his Delta Force team against terrorists who have hijacked a jetliner in *The Delta Force*.

attacks quickly and rescues the men while eliminating dozens of terrorists. The next day, while Major McCoy is personally tracking down and terminating Abdul, the Delta Force transports the hostages to the airport, overpowers the terrorists guarding the jet, and prepares for takeoff. McCoy joins them at the very last moment, blasting more terrorists before being hauled aboard as the jet speeds down the runway. In Israel, the men are reunited with their wives and families, and the Delta Force begins the long flight home.

There are two distinct portions of this film, which never truly balance. One of them is onboard the hijacked airliner, as terrorist Abdul makes life hell for his captives. The scenes set on the jet are played for authenticity and suspense, with claustrophobia and violence adding to their harrowing effectiveness. Abdul is played with ferocious intensity by Robert Forster, who handily gives the best performance in the film. The actors and actresses who play the passengers also take their roles seriously, but because those actors are familiar Hollywood veterans Martin Balsam, Shelley Winters, Lainie Kazan, Joey Bishop, George Kennedy, Susan Strasberg and others, the seriousness of the situation is diminished amidst the *Airport*-style all-star tackiness. Nevertheless, this half of the film is the more worthwhile effort.

Perhaps more exciting, but far more ridiculous, are the scenes involving the vaunted Delta Force. Led by iron horse Lee Marvin, but personified by tough Chuck Norris, the Delta Force is viewed as an outfit underused by Army brass but overpowering once unleashed. While the Force itself is underused in the film, the same cannot be said for its kickboxing leader, Chuck Norris. Major McCoy seems to be the only man able to handle the situation, whether reconnoitering the hostage hideout, beating the tar out of Abdul and then killing him with a rocket launched from his motorcycle, or clearing the runway of bad guys for the escaping jet with the same machine gun-equipped motorcycle. Norris' physical prowess is exceptional, but his charisma is somewhat lacking, and he is obviously far too individualistic to ever fit into the Delta Force team profile.

The biggest fault of the film is its unrelenting jingoism. While the hijacking scenes are treated seriously and suspensefully, the rescue scenes are almost cartoonish in their absurd simplicity and pandering attitude. *The Delta Force* is meant to appeal on a very basic level to Americans' patriotic outrage at terrorist attacks on American people and property. It oversimplifies a complicated international situation and advocates action which, no matter how exciting and enjoyable to watch, in reality would probably lead to armed conflict and further death. It provides simple, easy-to-understand-and-appreciate answers to questions which cannot be so easily answered. And while such escapist entertainment may be satisfying to watch, it is not responsible filmmaking.

Lee Marvin has far too little to do, but at least he is more animated here than in his previous two film appearances. Colonel Nick Alexander is a tailor-made role for Marvin, though a relatively empty one. Marvin leads with authority, and his command is never questioned; though with Norris on the scene, any leadership is extraneous. Alexander and McCoy share a bond as the best of the good guys, and Marvin and Norris make that bond work onscreen, showing each other a great deal of respect.

Robert Vaughn remembers that Marvin was weak during filming of *The Delta Force*. In fact, Marvin was exhausted, and confided to his wife soon after his return home that he had not expected to leave Israel (where much of the filming occurred) alive. Marvin, whose health had slowly deteriorated over the years due to his excessive drinking and smoking (not to mention the ignominy and stress of the "palimony" case), had slowed his acting work, and this was to be his final feature film. Marvin was offered the role of Colonel Nick Alexander again for *The Delta Force II*, but he was unable to accept the role due to his declining health.

After filming *The Delta Force*, Marvin was interviewed for a television special honoring Spencer Tracy entitled *The Spencer Tracy Legacy: A Tribute by Katharine Hepburn*. He then narrated a short film for the U. S.

Marine Corps called *Combat Leadership: The Ultimate Challenge*. It was to be the last film work Marvin would complete.

A combination of the flu, asthma and years of smoking led to respiratory problems that eventually caused Lee Marvin's heart to give out. Marvin died in Tucson, Arizona, on August 29, 1987. He was survived by his second wife, Pamela, three daughters—Claudia, Courtenay and Cynthia—and a son, Christopher. He was buried in Arlington National Cemetery in Arlington, Virginia.

Lee Marvin left behind a legacy of sixty feature film appearances and scores of television appearances by which to remember him.

Documentaries, Short Films and Stage Plays

Beginning in the 1960s, as Lee Marvin became famous worldwide, demand for his presence and talents increased, and he became involved with a number of documentaries as narrator, interviewee or guest star. The following is a list of those non-feature films in which Lee Marvin is known to have appeared or taken part, listed in chronological order.

Our Time in Hell (1966)

The History of the U.S. Marine Corps in World War II. A Film by Laurence E. Mascott. Narrated by Lee Marvin. 60 minutes.

This documentary of the actions of the U.S. Marine Corps during World War II is narrated by Lee Marvin, himself a veteran of many of the battles described in the film, though his personal details are never discussed. The video imagery is genuine footage of the Marine Corps at that time, filmed at each of the island battlefields during and after the fighting took place.

Tonite, Let's All Make Love in London (1967)

A Film by Peter Whitehead. With Pink Floyd, Julie Christie, Mick Jagger, Michael Caine, Lee Marvin, Vashti, Edna O'Brien, Alan Aldridge, David Hockney, The Small Faces, Chris Farlowe, Alan Ginsberg, The Marquess of Kensington, Twice as Much, Andrew Loog Oldham, Vanessa Redgrave, Eric Burdon and the Animals. 70 minutes.

This impressionistic (no narrative) look at swinging London in 1967 features the earliest video recordings of Pink Floyd (playing "Interstellar Overdrive") and interviews of various pop icons of the time, including Michael Caine, Julie Christie, Mick Jagger and Lee Marvin. Marvin is filmed in his World War II *Dirty Dozen* uniform and talks briefly about the advantages of minicars and miniskirts.

Samuel Fuller and The Big Red One (1979)

A Film by Thijs Ockersen. With Robert Carradine, Bobby DiCicco, Samuel Fuller, Mark Hamill, Lee Marvin, Kelly Ward.

This Dutch documentary features behind-the-scenes footage of Samuel Fuller directing his film *The Big Red One* and includes interviews with the major cast members.

The Spencer Tracy Legacy: A Tribute by Katharine Hepburn (1987)

Directed by David Heeley. With Katharine Hepburn, Joan Bennett, Garson Kanin, Stanley Kramer, Angela Lansbury, Joseph L. Mankiewicz, Lee Marvin, Sidney Poitier, Burt Reynolds, Mickey Rooney, Frank Sinatra, John Sturges, Elizabeth Taylor, Susie Tracy, Robert Wagner, Richard Widmark, Joanne Woodward. 90 minutes.

This documentary is narrated by Katharine Hepburn as she muses over the film career of her great friend and love Spencer Tracy. Tracy's costars reminisce about working with him; Lee Marvin remembers him from *Bad Day at Black Rock*. Hepburn concludes by reading aloud a letter she wrote to Tracy after his death.

Lee Marvin: A Personal Portrait by John Boorman (1998)

Directed by John Boorman. A remembrance of his favorite star by director Boorman, who made *Point Blank* and *Hell in the Pacific* with Marvin. 55 minutes.

Lee Marvin also appeared in occasional short films, usually promotional advertisements for his feature film work—such as *The Rock* (for *Point Blank*). He also made one short film, *Combat Leadership: The Ultimate Challenge*, for the U.S. Marine Corps shortly before his death.

Marvin had also appeared on stage before and during his first few movie roles. His list of stage play appearances, according to wife Pamela, includes *The Affairs of Anatole*, *Billy Budd*, *The Hasty Heart*, *Home of the Brave*, *John Loves Mary*, *The Male Animal*, *Our Town*, *Roadside*, *So's Your Uncle Dudley*, *A Streetcar Named Desire*, *Ten Nights in a Barroom*, *Three's a Family*, *Thunder Rock*, *The Vinegar Tree*, *Whistler's Mother* and *Years Ago*.

Television Appearances

M Squad

In 1957 Lee Marvin made the move from feature films to episodic television. MCA television made Marvin an offer he couldn't refuse—ownership of 50% of the show—if he would star as Chicago plainclothes detective Lieutenant Frank Ballinger. MCA wanted a rougher, tougher version of *Dragnet* and designed the show around Lee Marvin, the star who it was felt best exemplified the grittier side of the law. Marvin reportedly turned down the offer twice before accepting, but he finally relented and *M Squad* made him a household name after six years and thirty film roles that hadn't.

The early and mid–1950s granted great opportunities to actors on television. Classic dramas were being written by Paddy Chayevsky, Rod Serling, Reginald Rose, Robert Alan Arthur, Richard Maibaum, George Roy Hill, Horton Foote, Arthur Hailey, Roald Dahl, Blake Edwards, Dale Wasserman and dozens of others, and many of those dramas were performed *live* each week. Situation comedies had attained national popularity, and westerns, crime dramas and medical shows were dominating the network schedules. Actors such as Lee Marvin moved back and forth between film and television work with none of the stigma that separates the two formats today. Indeed, most viewers couldn't have told the difference between the two anyway, because most television shows were actually *filmed* at that time.

By the late 1950s, however, the Golden Age of Television had passed, and companies that advertised on television began to demand input and control based on the large amounts of money they were providing to support the programming. Two things immediately happened: production costs and schedules were tightened to save money and increase profits, and quality was significantly diminished. Producers no longer had the freedom to mount expensive or controversial projects, and advertisers began to veto projects they deemed inappropriate or non-commercial. Television programming began its long, sad descent to the most common denominator.

The first symptom of this malaise was imitation. Successful shows had always inspired imitation, but never to such an extent. The popularity of westerns, for instance, increased throughout the mid-fifties, peaking in 1958 with *37 separate episodic series* as each network tried to fill its schedule with profitable oaters. Within a few years only a handful were left standing, most notably *Gunsmoke*, *The Big Valley* and *Bonanza*. Crime dramas went through the same cycle, as each broadcast network attempted to repeat the success of *Dragnet*. Several crime-based series did become successful, all around the same time (in the late 1950s): *Perry Mason*, *The Untouchables*, *Peter Gunn*, *The Naked City*—and *M Squad*.

Lee Marvin's first television series is set in Chicago, though most of the filming took place on the studio lot in California. The "M Squad" (the M really doesn't stand for anything in particular) is a special detail of the Chicago police force, the one which deals with all of the cases too tough for the regular cops, usually involving murder, kidnapping or armed robbery. This division of plainclothes detectives consists of men working alone, on call 24 hours a day and with little or no personal lives, who are expected to put their lives on the line to benefit public citizens whenever necessary. In short, their job is to tackle everything the more staid, laid-back California cops in *Dragnet* could not, or would not, touch.

Marvin portrays Lieutenant Frank Ballinger and provides voice-over narration for the show, partly to emulate Jack Webb's successful *Dragnet* formula, and partly because *M Squad* was filmed so quickly that sound recording on location was impossible and all dialogue and sound effects had to be dubbed in afterwards. Ballinger is a hard-nosed cop, blunt and direct, only interested in rooting out the truth of his current investigation. He is patient and respectful with civilians, less so with criminal suspects, and becomes downright mean to gangsters and obviously guilty killers. Ballinger has a sharp intuition and is able to notice character traits or logic gaps that others miss; he often relies on his instincts, although he is sometimes slow to act on them.

Lt. Ballinger works his cases alone but checks in once or twice per show with Captain Grey (Paul Newlan) for new leads and advice. Occasionally, Captain Grey will accompany Ballinger into the field, backing up his number one detective or rescuing him at the last possible moment. Ballinger and Grey have a quiet, professional relationship, with little joking or comeraderie. Each man has a job to do and each wants to get on with it.

This direct approach illustrates exactly how the show works. Each episode has a compact crime story to tell, and it wastes no time telling it. Each of the 117 episodes usually devote about half of their time to the criminals and their crime, and the other half to Ballinger's efforts to stop them. A typical episode would feature a criminal act right after the opening logo and theme song, Ballinger's introduction to the case, the criminal's reaction to his or her crime and efforts to cover it up, Ballinger tracking down a lead, the criminal beginning to get worried and preparing to take further action, Ballinger finding the key piece of evidence, the criminal making a move, and Ballinger thwarting the crime, capturing or killing the criminal in the nick of time.

Formulaic, to be sure. *M Squad*, like *Dragnet* and a spate of crime dramas before and since, follows a simple formula and delivers the expected goods. Audiences know what to expect and when to expect it, and find satisfaction in the familiarity of the formula and the ultimate triumph of good over evil, of justice over criminality. As Lee Marvin once noted himself in a *TV Guide* interview, "Cliche? It's a great word—always used deprecatingly. I'm for the cliche—when it's well done. Some of the greatest stories were pure cliche, like *Shane*, for instance. It proved that if you do the cliche well, you'll *kill* your audience. They will be dumbfounded with its greatness."

However, over time Marvin became disenchanted with the entire process of filming *M Squad*, primarily because of what he considered to be its sometimes poor quality. As the show moved into its second and third seasons, Marvin looked for ways to get out of the series—and he also, concurrently, looked for ways to improve it. As part owner of the show, Marvin was happy with its profitability but wanted to improve the quality, especially to stop using the scripts which had been rejected by *Dragnet* and other police shows. As an actor, Marvin was fed up with long shooting schedules, short rehearsal and pre-production periods, scripts he considered inferior, and the total lack of free time. Marvin had become a television star, and he didn't like it very much.

For the most part, Marvin was right about the quality of the scripts he was given. By its third season, *M Squad* had taken to repeating plots from *itself*, used two seasons previously. At that time, a half-hour show such as *M Squad* would film 39 episodes per season, then pick the 12 or 13 best for summer reruns. Marvin, again in *TV Guide*, commented, "Then comes summer and you're trying to find 13 shows out of 39 that will make good reruns. I know that Jack Webb, who is a great perfectionist, has the same problem. He had two he really liked, four fair ones and seven

184 *Television Appearances*

Lieutenant Frank Ballinger (Lee Marvin) examines an empty safe on the episode of *M Squad*.

naah! I must say I know the feeling. There are some *M Squads* I'm not exactly proud of."

Yet while the show is definitely dated in many ways (some good, some bad), it holds up well because of its straightforward storytelling and direct approach to the always timely battle between right and wrong. Its voice-over narration is not as pedantic nor as unintentionally humorous as Jack Webb's in *Dragnet*. Its criminal cases are much more exciting than that of *Dragnet*, whose detectives had to deal with lots of day-to-day petty crime. Due to the Chicago locale and a lot of night sequences, its settings have much more atmosphere than *Dragnet*'s Los Angeles daytime scenes. Is *M Squad* a better show than *Dragnet*? In some ways, yes, though because *M Squad* was a syndicated show (not a network original) and has not been seen in most major markets in many years, it has been largely forgotten. *Dragnet* is certainly the more classic show of the two, simply due to its visibility.

One of the best features of *M Squad* was its music. Marvin and his producers wanted the Chicago show to have its own brand of music—namely, jazz. Stanley Wilson and Benny Carter were hired to provide a jazzy background to the hot action on-screen. After the first season, Count Basie wrote and recorded a new title tune, which became an instant hit, popular enough to inspire an album of *M Squad* music. While *Peter Gunn* and other shows would continue to use contemporary jazz as background to the actions of their characters, *M Squad* was, if not the first, certainly one of the first to prove the validity of the concept.

Thirty years later the show itself and Count Basie's music would be the inspiration for David and Jerry Zucker, Jim Abrahams and Pat Proft, who loosely based their short television series *Police Squad* and *Naked Gun* movie trilogy upon it. Leslie Nielsen's deadpan acting and narration, the abrupt, clipped editing style, and Ira Newborn's wild music score are all descendents from, parodies of, and homages to, crime shows of the late 1950s, primarily *M Squad* and, of course, *Dragnet*.

M Squad is still in syndication at various points around the country and is well worth watching. The 37 first season shows do not feature Count Basie's theme song, and so are easy to tell apart from the final 80 episodes, two of which were never aired during the show's original run on NBC. Guest stars on *M Squad* included such future television and film stars as Burt Reynolds, Leonard Nimoy, James Coburn, Tom Laughlin and Charles Bronson, as well as familiar character actors Morris Ankrum, Les Tremayne, Mike Mazurki and many others. Though Lee Marvin soon grew tired of the show's hectic pace and rather routine script quality, *M Squad* made him more famous than all of his movie roles had up to that time, and also made him rich.

M Squad Episodes

First Season (1957–1958)
37 episodes plus 2 unaired episodes

1. "The Golden Look"
September 20, 1957. *Guest Stars*: Bruce Gordon, Morris Ankrum, Henry Brandon, Ann Barton.
Ballinger tracks down a robbery suspect involved in a hit-and-run accident.

2. "Watchdog"
September 27, 1957. *Guest Stars*: Peggy Webber, Harlan Warde, Carol Hill, Gail Kobe.
Ballinger is forced to find a burglar bitten by a guard dog with rabies.

3. "Neighborhood Killer"
October 4, 1957. *Guest Stars*: Grant Richards, Don Kennedy, Robert Patten.
Ballinger goes after a jewelry thief who killed a Chicago policeman.

4. "Pete Loves Mary"
October 11, 1957. *Guest Stars*: Steve Wilcowski, Bobby Driscoll.
Ballinger tries to stop a killer who has just broken out of jail.

5. "Face of Evil"
October 18, 1957. *Guest Stars*: Werner Klemperer, Kevin Hogan, Maggie Stewart.
Ballinger investigates the murders of four women who lived within a two-mile area.

6. "Street of Fear"
November 1, 1957. *Guest Stars*: Barbara Turner, Lawrence Dobkin, Pamela Duncan, Morris Ankrum.
Ballinger poses as a furniture salesman to catch a ring of diamond smugglers.

7. "The Matinee Trade"
November 8, 1957. *Guest Stars*: Anthony Lawrence, Robert Burton, Natalie Norwick, Evelyn Scott.
Ballinger investigates a policeman accused of taking payoffs from gamblers.

8. "The Hard Case"
November 15, 1957. *Guest Stars*: Ray Foster, Howard Negley, George Mathews, William Murphy.
Ballinger goes to prison to find out whether an inmate's accusations are true.

9. "Killer in Town"
November 22, 1957. *Guest Stars*: Lee Larr, Russ Conway, Gail Kobe, John Hiestand, Roy Glenn.
Ballinger tracks a murder suspect who is also suspected in the death of a cop.

10. "Diamond Hard"
November 29, 1957. *Guest Stars*: William Phipps, Mike Ragan, Angie Dickinson, John Halloran.
Ballinger poses as a safecracker to keep a young woman from a life of crime.

11. "The Alibi Witness"
December 6, 1957. *Guest Stars*: Edward Binns, Will J. Wright.
Ballinger investigates an ex-convict's alibi who denies the ex-con's story.

12. "The Specialists"
December 13, 1957. *Guest Stars*: Dave Barry, Douglas Evans, Jan Arvan, Kem Dibbs, Richard Devon.
Ballinger discovers that three businessmen annually plan a perfect crime.

13. "Family Portrait"
December 20, 1957. *Guest Stars*: Jacques Aubuchon, Christine White, Raymond Bailey, Ron Hayes.
Ballinger goes after a mob kingpin implicated in a policeman's murder.

14. "The Palace Guard"
December 27, 1957. *Guest Stars*: Whit Bissell, Alix Talton, Noreen Arnold.
Ballinger is assigned to protect a mobster, and has trouble keeping the man alive.

15. "The Slow Trap"
January 3, 1958. *Guest Stars*: Robert Roark, Jacqueline Holt, Lyle Talbot, George E. Stone.
Ballinger tries to find out whether a bonded messenger staged his own robbery.

16. "The Cover Up"
January 10, 1958. *Guest Stars*: Willard Parker, Jeanne Cooper, Dan Tobin, Paul Langton.
Ballinger's murder investigation centers on a State attorney and a rival lawyer.

17. "Blue Indigo"
January 17, 1958. *Guest Stars*: Bethel Leslie, Nico Minardos, Jo Gilbert, Lillian Buyeff.
Ballinger must think differently to catch a killer who murders to music.

18. "The Long Ride" (aka "End of the Line")
January 24, 1958. *Guest Stars*: Joe Maross, Nancy Hale, Benny Baker, Tiger Farara, Ann Morrison.
Ballinger is overpowered by a prisoner while escorting him back to Chicago.

19. "Shakedown"
January 31, 1958. *Guest Stars*: Katharine Bard, Dean Harens, June Dayton, Duncan McLeod.
Ballinger tries to protect a dry-cleaner who refuses to pay "protection" money.

20. "Dolly's Bar"
February 7, 1958. *Guest Stars*: Janice Rule, Claire Carleton, Michael Bachus, Fredd Wayne.
Ballinger doesn't think an actress killed the columnist who was blackmailing her.

21. "Lovers' Lane Killing"
February 14, 1958. *Guest Stars*: Kent Smith, Ruta Lee, John Doucette, Angela Greene.
Ballinger investigates a murder in which a witness holds the key to the truth.

22. "The Frightened Wife"
February 21, 1958. *Guest Stars*: Marian Seldes, Whitney Blake, Esther Dale, Herbert Rudley.
Ballinger doesn't believe the murder confession of a missing businessman's wife.

23. "The Black Mermaid"
February 28, 1958. *Guest Stars*: Biff Elliott, Marcia Henderson, Arthur Hanson, Harry Bartell.
Ballinger infiltrates a robbery gang as a gunman, but they get wise to him.

24. "Man in Hiding"
March 7, 1958. *Guest Stars*: Alan Baxter, Willard Thompson, John Hoyt, June Vincent.
Ballinger is called upon to discover the true identity of a boy's school teacher.

25. "The Chicago Bluebeard"
March 14, 1958. *Guest Stars*: Vaughn Taylor, Bart Burns, Amzie Strickland, Mary Adams.
Ballinger tracks a murderer who meets his victims through a lonely hearts club.

26. "Girl Lost"
March 21, 1958. *Guest Stars*: Bill Williams, Maggie Mahoney, Myron Healey, Vera Marshe.
Ballinger tries to uncover the past of an amnesia victim threatened by criminals.

27. "Hideout"
March 28, 1958. *Guest Stars*: Stacy Graham, Jack Elam, Dick Miller, DeForest Kelley, Paul Comi.
Ballinger talks his way into a robber's hideout hoping to stave off violence.

28. "The 26 Girl"
April 11, 1958. *Guest Stars*: Diane Brewster, Simon Scott, Ellen Parker, Ward Wood.
Ballinger investigates a missing persons report linked to a murder victim.

29. "Fight"
April 18, 1958. *Guest Stars*: Charles Bronson, Judith Ames, Leonard Bell, Rusty Lane.
Ballinger questions why a boxer has had three attempts made on his life.

30. "Guilty Alibi"
April 25, 1958. *Guest Stars*: Ross Elliott, Brook Byron, Meg Wyllie, Viola Harris.
Ballinger distrusts a businessman who confesses to a hit-and-run accident.

31. "The Healer"
May 2, 1958. *Guest Stars*: Gloria Talbott, Robert Carson, Sarah Selby, Dayton Lummis.
Ballinger goes to a psychic healer—undercover—as a patient.

32. "Day of Terror"
May 9, 1958. *Guest Stars*: Fay Baker, Tom Pittman, Barbara Benson, Jess Kirkpatrick.
Ballinger tries to protect a couple from extortion perpetrated by a crooked adoption agency.

33. "Twenty-dollar Plates"
May 16, 1958. *Guest Stars*: Lynn Bernay, Logan Field, Joel Smith.
Ballinger tracks a counterfeiter using plates made some twenty years earlier.

34. "The Case of the Double Face"
May 23, 1958. *Guest Stars*: Jim Davis, Kristine Miller, Antony Eustrel, William Flaherty.
Ballinger finds that a robbery suspect has a double who is taking advantage of him.

35. "The System"
May 30, 1958. *Guest Stars*: Tol Avery, Rose Marie, Ted de Corsia, Gregg Martell, Ann Doran.
Ballinger sets his sights on Chicago's biggest gambling syndicate.

36. "The Woman from Paris"
June 6, 1958. *Guest Stars*: Paula Raymond, Philip Ober, Gine De Bard, Russ Bender.
Ballinger scrutinizes the apparent suicide of a tourist from Paris.

37. "Accusation"
June 13, 1958. *Guest Stars*: Fay Spain, Larry Blake, Dan Riss.
Ballinger investigates an industrialist's suicide, which he suspects is murder.

38. "A Shot in the Dark"
Unaired episode. *Guest Stars*: Karin Booth, Raymond Greenleaf, Clarke Gordon, John Beradino.
Ballinger searches Chicago for a sniper who wounds random victims.

39. "A Debt of Honor"
Unaired episode. *Guest Stars*: William Phipps, Nesdon Booth, Robert Clarke, Judy Bamber.
Ballinger protects a State attorney who is being hunted by a mobster.
Note: This episode has the opening credit sequence from the second and third seasons. It is unclear where it fits into the *M Squad* listing, so it was placed here.

Second Season (1958–1959)
39 episodes

40. "More Deadly"
September 19, 1958. *Guest Stars*: Ruta Lee, Voorhies J. Ardoin, Dorothea Lord, Paul Maxwell.
Ballinger doesn't believe the version of a robbery told by a pretty store clerk.

41. "Dead or Alive"
September 26, 1958. *Guest Stars*: Tom Pittman, Judi Meredith, Michael Pataki, Ralph Gamble.
Ballinger battles a newspaper reporter who doesn't agree with his methods.

42. "The Missing Claimant"
October 3, 1958. *Guest Stars*: Rebecca Welles, Harry Lauter, Joan Vohs, Theodore Newton.
Ballinger searches for a missing heir, suspecting he has been killed.

43. "The Refugee"
October 10, 1958. *Guest Stars*: Mark Neiman, Judith Braun, Jean Del Val, Ben Morris, Don Nagel.
Ballinger poses as an immigrant to assist a family threatened by gangsters.

44. "The Trap"
October 24, 1958. *Guest Stars*: Robert Fuller, Betty Lynn, Virginia Gregg.
Ballinger tries to find a young man suspected of robbing a pawn shop.

45. "Force of Habit"
October 31, 1958. *Guest Stars*: Maggie Mahoney, Rosco Ates, Patricia Huston, Robert Knapp.
Ballinger believes a safecracker presumed dead is alive and working at his trade.

46. "The Phantom Raiders"
November 7, 1958. *Guest Stars*: Yvette Vickers, Ed Nelson, John Brinkley, Nicky Blair, Dean Casey.
Ballinger dons cycle gear to catch a pair of masked holdup men using motorcycles.

47. "Merits of the Case"
November 14, 1958. *Guest Stars*: Paula Raymond, John Hoyt, Francis DeSales, Hugh Lawrence.
Ballinger doesn't agree that a woman killed an attorney who defended her husband.

48. "The Big Kill"
November 21, 1958. *Guest Stars*: Nelson Olmsted, Frank Thomas, Sr., Martha Rivers.
Ballinger searches for enough evidence to arrest a bank robbery suspect.

49. "The Sitters"
November 28, 1958. *Guest Stars*: Mary Webster, Robert Roark, Grant Richards, James Gavin.
Ballinger believes a baseball player is mixed up with a bookie ring.

50. "The Executioner"
December 5, 1958. *Guest Stars*: Herschel Bernardi, Dan Barton, Nan Leslie, Mary Munday.
Ballinger investigates a waiter's claim that a policeman tried to kill him.

51. "The Widows"
December 12, 1958. *Guest Stars*: Herb Ellis, John Goddard, Jeanne Vaughn, Joel Ashley, Jean Wood.
Ballinger finds that seemingly unrelated murder victims were all heavily insured.

52. "Contraband"
December 19, 1958. *Guest Stars*: Ross

Martin, Marti Stevens, King Calder, Bill Card, Thom Carney.

Ballinger suspects that a smuggling ring is using foreign cars for their operation.

53. "Prescription for Murder"
December 26, 1958. *Guest Stars*: George Neise, Helen Mowery, John Duke, John Berardino.

Ballinger tries to find the kidnapped wife of a surgeon so he will operate.

54. "The Teacher"
January 2, 1959. *Guest Stars*: Tom Laughlin, Burt Reynolds, Sue George, Mark Douglas.

Ballinger attempts to round up a teenage gang at a trade school.

55. "The Third Shadow"
January 9, 1959. *Guest Stars*: Monica Lewis, Tony Travis, Al Shelly, Amy Fields, Ted Thorpe.

Ballinger tries to clear a policeman accused of taking money during a holdup.

56. "One Man's Life"
January 22, 1959. *Guest Stars*: Stephen Chase, Robert H. Harris, Mark Roberts, June Vincent.

Ballinger investigates a condemned man's past to determine if he is truly guilty.

57. "The Jumper"
January 30, 1959. *Guest Stars*: Don Reardon, Ward Wood, Patricia Manning, John Goddard.

Ballinger races to stop a suicide attempt by clearing the man's name.

58. "The Last Act"
February 6, 1959. *Guest Stars*: Elaine Edwards, Donald Buka, Stewart Bradley, James Bannon.

Ballinger is assigned to protect a musical-comedy star when her life is threatened.

59. "Mugger Murder"
February 13, 1959. *Guest Stars*: Grace Raynor, Bern Hoffman, Jaclynne Greene, James Chandler.

Ballinger acts as a decoy in order to stop a series of violent muggings.

60. "The Star Witness"
February 20, 1959. *Guest Stars*: Virginia Vincent, Paul Picerni, Terry Becker, Sid Clute.

Ballinger suspects that a murder witness is more involved in a crime than was thought.

61. "The Take-Over"
February 27, 1959. *Guest Stars*: Joan O'Brien, Kem Dibbs, Murvyn Vye.

Ballinger tries to stop two rival gangs from beginning a full-scale gang war.

62. "Voluntary Surrender"
March 6, 1959. *Guest Stars*: Bert Remsen, Mary Adams, Mary Treen.

Ballinger doesn't believe a thief, thinking that the man is covering up a murder.

63. "Death Threat"
March 13, 1959. *Guest Stars*: Paul Burke, Jacqueline Mayo, Len Lesser, Sondra Rodgers.

Ballinger and two witnesses are threatened by the convict they sent to prison.

64. "The Harpies"
March 20, 1959. *Guest Stars*: Betsy Jones-Moreland, Gail Kobe, Beatrice Kay, Luana Anders.

Ballinger uncovers an unorthodox mother-daughter robbery team.

65. "The Vanishing Lady"
April 3, 1959. *Guest Stars*: William Hudson, Mary Scott, John Eldredge, Pat McCaffrie.

Ballinger tries to protect a witness who is being stalked by a murderer.

66. "The Crush Out"
April 10, 1959. *Guest Stars*: James Chandler, Tyler McVey, William Phipps.

Ballinger and a Senator are taken prisoner during a prison riot.

67. "The Firemakers"
April 17, 1959. *Guest Stars*: Leonard Nimoy, James Coburn, Georgine Darcy, Milton Frome.

Ballinger searches for an arsonist, and is aided by the man's son.

68. "The Terror of Dark Street"
April 24, 1959. *Guest Stars*: Jocelyn Brando, Carleton G. Young, Barbara Drew.

Ballinger questions why a murdered man's wife seems so unconcerned about it.

69. "Robbers' Roost"
May 1, 1959. *Guest Stars*: Mark Douglas, Robert E. Griffin, Howard McLeod, Evelyn Scott.

Ballinger investigates the hideout of a gang of teenage bank robbers.

70. "The Baited Hook"
May 8, 1959. *Guest Stars*: Vic Perrin, Laurie Carroll, Buddy Lester.

Ballinger attempts to help a man and daughter cope with murder threats.

71. "Model in the Lake"
May 15, 1959. *Guest Stars*: Whitney Blake, Charles Shelander, Richard Garland.

Ballinger discovers soapy water in the lungs of a model presumed drowned.

72. "The Outsider"
May 22, 1959. *Guest Stars*: Joyce Meadows, William Tregoe, Michael Garth, Nancy Valentine.

Ballinger looks for the person responsible for diluting a diabetic's insulin supply.

73. "High School Bride"
May 29, 1959. *Guest Stars*: Jimmy Murphy, Deanna Ross, Marian Ross, William Edmondson.

Ballinger searches for a young bride who disappeared during her honeymoon.

74. "The Dangerous Game"
June 5, 1959. *Guest Stars*: Jonathan Hale, Kasey Rogers, Max Dommar, House Peters, Jr.

Ballinger tries to rescue hostages taken during a robbery in a fur store.

75. "The Platter Pirates"
June 12, 1959. *Guest Stars*: Bruce Hayes, Tommy Farrell, Gale Robbins, Lou Krugman.

Ballinger tracks down the racketeers responsible for murdering a disc jockey.

76. "Mr. Grims's Rabbits"
June 19, 1959. *Guest Stars*: Tim Graham, Carole Mathews, Ralph Clanton.

Ballinger searches for a murderer and the smuggled fur missing from the victim.

77. "Decoy in White"
June 26, 1959. *Guest Stars*: Mike Road, Mike Mazurki, Judy Bamber, James Flavin.

Ballinger trails a money-laundering lawyer.

78. "Death Is a Clock"
July 3, 1959. *Guest Stars*: Douglas Henderson, Madlyn Rhue, Stacy Harris.

Ballinger tries to help an amnesiac convict recall his crime prior to his execution.

Third Season (1959–1960)
39 episodes

79. "Ghost Town"
September 4, 1959. *Guest Stars*: Alan Marshal, John Shaner, Sally Todd, Bill Baldwin, Sid Melton.

Ballinger races to save a kidnapped girl when her kidnapper is killed.

80. "Ten Minutes to Doomsday"
September 11, 1959. *Guest Stars*: James Bell, Ann Morrison, Ross Elliott, Francis De Sales.

Ballinger searches for a judge thought to be the target of a mad bomber.

81. "The European Plan"
September 25, 1959. *Guest Stars*: Paul Burke, Gail Bonney, Lili Kardell, Frank Albertson.

Ballinger tries to clear a young foreign maid accused of murder.

82. "Sunday Punch" (aka "Hand Made Murder")
October 2, 1959. *Guest Stars*: Barry Kelley, Robert Knapp, Joe Kaiser, Hugh Lawrence.

Ballinger investigates a murder in which the neighbor seems the most likely suspect.

83. "Jeopardy by Fire"
October 9, 1959. *Guest Stars*: William Keene, Marc Lawrence, Harlan Warde, Penny Edwards.

Ballinger searches for an arsonist among five suspects that have been assembled.

84. "Murder in C Sharp Minor"
October 16, 1959. *Guest Stars*: Lawrence

Dobkin, Harry Jackson, Howard McNear, Peter Leeds.

Ballinger investigates a murder in which a saxophone was the murder weapon.

85. "The Human Bond"
October 23, 1959. *Guest Stars*: Carolyn Craig, Don Orek, Roy Barcroft, Grant Richards.

Ballinger begins the search for a missing teenager with his uncooperative parents.

86. "Mama's Boy"
October 30, 1959. *Guest Stars*: William Allyn, John Beradino, Katherine Warren, Joseph Vitale.

Ballinger investigates the murder of a motel clerk but lacks a clear motive.

87. "Shred of Doubt"
November 6, 1959. *Guest Stars*: Don Dubbins, Peter Adams, Kendrick Huxham, Henry Hunter.

Ballinger tries to tie the murder of a woman to her drug-dealing husband.

88. "Death by Adoption"
November 20, 1959. *Guest Stars*: David Leland, Rayford Barnes, Gail Kobe, Bill Quinn.

Ballinger exposes a blackmailer who claims an adopted girl is his own.

89. "Another Face, Another Life"
November 27, 1959. *Guest Stars*: James Douglas, Barbara Stuart, Jay Novello, John Archer.

Ballinger investigates the murder of a publicist who was blackmailing celebrities.

90. "Voice from the Grave"
December 4, 1959. *Guest Stars*: Harry Conklin, Robert Karnes.

Ballinger protects the wife of a trucker who was to testify against the mob.

91. "The Upset"
December 11, 1959. *Guest Stars*: Richard Newton, Adam Williams, John McKee, Barbara Knudsen.

Ballinger and another detective are taken prisoner by the man they are questioning.

92. "One of Our Armored Cars Is Missing"
December 18, 1959. *Guest Stars*: Laurie Mitchell, Richard Carlyle, Joe Haworth, Joyce Meadows.

Ballinger searches for a delivery van with a stolen armored car inside.

93. "The Ivy League Bank Robbers"
December 25, 1959. *Guest Stars*: Ron Star, Danny Niles.

Ballinger chases three collegiate bank robbers after they injure innocent bystanders.

94. "The Twisted Way"
January 1, 1960. *Guest Stars*: Charles Cooper, Joanna Barnes, Walter McCoy, Ed Parker.

Ballinger looks for the lie in an accused liquor store robber's alibi.

95. "The Man Who Went Straight"
January 8, 1960. *Guest Stars*: Harry Bartell, Charles Victor, Harry Landers, Don Kohler.

Ballinger tries to help an ex-con go straight after the man gives him important tips.

96. "The Second-Best Killer"
January 15, 1960. *Guest Stars*: Ray Stricklyn, Penny Santon, Aline Towne, Ralph Joseph Votrian.

Ballinger faces public pressure to find the killer of a local Chicago hero.

97. "Pitched Battle at Blue Bell Acres"
January 22, 1960. *Guest Stars*: John Dennis, Frank Richards, George Keymas, Jack Mather.

Ballinger recruits major firepower to combat bank robbers who use a bazooka.

98. "The Man Who Lost His Brain"
February 2, 1960. *Guest Stars*: Vinton Hayworth, Fred Coby, Vince Williams.

Ballinger delivers the ransom for a stolen computer, hoping to catch the thieves.

99. "The Man with Frank's Face"
February 9, 1960. *Guest Stars*: Greta Thyssen, Herb Ellis, Robert Bailey.

Ballinger poses as his double, a European racketeer starting an American gang.

100. "Burglar's Nightmare"
February 16, 1960. *Guest Stars*: Robert Armstrong, John Goddard, Jim Oberlin, Connie Hines.
Ballinger tracks down two burglars once the safecracker of their group is identified.

101. "Needle in the Haystack"
February 23, 1960. *Guest Stars*: H. M. Wynant, Kip King, Marc Caveli.
Ballinger faces vengeance from an escaped killer who has vowed to kill him.

102. "Race to Death"
March 1, 1960. *Guest Stars*: Don O'Kelly, J. Pat O'Malley, Mary Munday, Diana Crawford.
Ballinger looks into the suspicious death of a stock car driver.

103. "The Velvet Stakeout"
March 8, 1960. *Guest Stars*: Whitney Blake, Malcolm Atterbury, Vic Adams, Oliver McGowan.
Ballinger moves into a murdered lawyer's home to search for evidence.

104. "Anything for Joe"
March 15, 1960. *Guest Stars*: Joseph Corey, John Shaner, Jody Warner, Charles Tannen.
Ballinger believes that a confessed thief is covering up for his brother.

105. "A Kid Up There"
March 22, 1960. *Guest Stars*: Al Ruscio, Bert Freed, Connie Gilchrist, Jimmy Baird.
Ballinger tries to determine whether a suspect has taken a hostage.

106. "Diary of a Bomber"
March 29, 1960. *Guest Stars*: Debbie Megowan, Maggie McCarter, Robert Carricart, Mark Neimar.
Ballinger links the discovery of a homemade bomb to threats made to a visiting prince.

107. "Let There Be Light"
April 5, 1960. *Guest Stars*: Les Tremayne, K. T. Stevens, Garry Walberg, Frank Killmond.
Ballinger searches for an opthalmic surgeon who disappeared during an operation.

108. "A Gun for Mother's Day"
April 12, 1960. *Guest Stars*: Frances Morris, Jeremy Slate, Ed Nelson.
Ballinger tracks a woman who springs her son from jail and commits robberies.

109. "The Man with the Ice"
April 19, 1960. *Guest Stars*: Stan Irwin, Jean Willes, Joe Flynn, Linda Lawson, Al Hodge.
Ballinger poses as a fence from Detroit to infiltrate a gang of jewel robbers.

110. "Dead Parrots Don't Talk"
May 3, 1960. *Guest Stars*: Bobbi Byrnes, Robert Ellis, Forrest Taylor, Arthur Batanides.
Ballinger searches for a burglar bitten by a parrot—with a transmittable disease.

111. "A Grenade for a Summer's Evening"
May 10, 1960. *Guest Stars*: Wesley Lau, Jeanne Cooper, Adam Becker.
Ballinger looks for a motive in a fatal incident involving a hand grenade.

112. "Two Days for Willy"
May 17, 1960. *Guest Stars*: Alan Hale, Harry Lauter, Peggy Webber, Mark Tapscott.
Ballinger races to find an important witness before the man is gunned down.

113. "Badge for a Coward"
May 24, 1960. *Guest Stars*: Edward Kemmer, Leonard Nimoy, Pat McCaffrie, Ruta Lee.
Ballinger investigates accusations of cowardice leveled at a fellow policeman.

114. "The Closed Season" (aka "Open Season")
May 31, 1960. *Guest Stars*: Dennis Patrick, Herbert Rudley, Paula Raymond, Chet Stratton.
Ballinger suspects that a bandleader is being framed for murder by his manager.

115. "Fire in the Sky"
June 7, 1960. *Guest Stars*: Richard Deacon, Tom Monroe, Frank Wilcox, Jerry O'Sullivan.
Ballinger helps Federal officials investigate the explosion of an airliner.

116. "The Tiger's Cage"
June 14, 1960. *Guest Stars*: Dan Riss, Don Barry, Regina Gleason, Alan Reed.

Ballinger looks for the robber of a circus who used clown makeup as a disguise.

117. "The Bad Apple"
June 28, 1960. *Guest Stars*: June Blair, Baily Harper, Pitt Herbert.

Ballinger thinks a daring daytime jewel robbery was an inside job.

Lawbreaker

Lee Marvin's second television series aired in the 1963-1964 season as a syndicated show. In its fall preview that year, *TV Guide* described the show this way: "*Lawbreaker*, starring Lee Marvin, features true crime stories filmed on the scene where they occurred and, whenever possible, with the real principals and with the cooperation of the local police. Marvin will appear as himself in the role of commentator—'a sort of involved Edward R. Murrow' is how he describes his role."

This half-hour series allowed each episode to focus on one particular crime, and featured interviews with the people involved, dramatizations of the crime itself, and commentary by Marvin on the development and outcome of each case. This should sound familiar, because the same concept was used twenty-five years later in the television shows *America's Most Wanted* and *Unsolved Mysteries*, among others. In 1963, however, it was a groundbreaking idea.

Lawbreaker was not very successful, lasting one season of twenty-six episodes. Once the show was established, each episode focused on a crime in a particular city, and the episodes were named for the city featured in that particular story.

Lee Marvin was host and narrator, hired because of his successful run as Chicago detective Frank Ballinger in *M Squad* a few years earlier. It was thought that his presence in a series about true-life crime would guarantee viewers, but the show did not play on a major network (it was instead syndicated to local networks thoughout the country, and aired whenever the local stations chose) and so never really had a chance to become successful. Marvin returned to the big screen, virtually abandoning television following the failure of this show.

Lee Marvin, as himself, on the television series *Lawbreaker*, where he served as host and narrator.

Lawbreaker Episodes
(1963-1964)
26 episodes

1. Pilot episode September 15, 1963
2. "Queen Anne Case" September 22, 1963
3. "James Meriwether Story" September 29, 1963
4. "Iannarelli Robbery & Kidnapping" October 6, 1963
5. "Dallas Story" October 13, 1963
6. "New Orleans Story" October 20, 1963
7. "Pittsburgh Story" October 27, 1963
8. "Indianapolis Story" November 3, 1963
9. "Cincinnati Story" November 10, 1963
10. "Detroit Story" November 17, 1963
11. "Hartford Story" November 24, 1963
12. "Boston Story" December 8, 1963
13. "Chicago A Story" December 15, 1963
14. "Houston Story" December 29, 1963
15. "Greenburgh Story" January 5, 1964
16. "Providence Story" January 19, 1964
17. "Baltimore Story" January 26, 1964
18. A. "Minneapolis Story, Part One" February 2, 1964
18. B. "Minneapolis Story, Part Two" February 9, 1964
19. "Rochester Story" February 16, 1964
20. "Philadelphia B Story" February 23, 1964
21. "Buffalo Story" March 1, 1964
22. "Culver City Story" March 8, 1964
23. "Burbank Story" March 15, 1964
24. "Long Beach Story" March 29, 1964
25. "Denver Story" April 5, 1964
26. "Milwaukee Story" April 12, 1964

Other Television Episodes

Counterpoint "The Witness"
1951. *Starring* Edwin Max, Vera Marsche, Lee Marvin, Robert Karnes, William Schallert, Vernon Dent, Jack Laird, James Dundee, Ilse Mader, Ruth Stevens. 30 minutes.

Thief Edwin Max completes a jewel robbery but returns to the scene to eliminate a possible witness. Lee Marvin plays Sergeant Krone, the detective assigned to the case.

Dragnet (NBC) "The Big Cast"
February 7, 1952. *Starring* Jack Webb, Ben Alexander. *Guest Starring* Lee Marvin. 30 minutes.

Rebound (ABC) "The Mine"
February 29, 1952. *Starring* Lee Marvin. 30 minutes.

According to Alex McNeil in his book *Total Television*, "Lee Marvin played his first major TV dramatic role in one [this] episode."

Easy Chair Theatre "Sound in the Night"
February 16, 1953. *Starring* Lee Marvin.

The Doctor (NBC) "The Runaways"
June 21, 1953. *Hosted by* Warner Anderson. *Starring* Lee Marvin. 30 minutes.

A postman and his wife are made curious by the mysterious comings and goings of their young boarder.

The Motorola TV Hour (ABC) "Outlaw's Reckoning"
November 3, 1953 *Starring* Eddie Albert, Wallace Ford, Lee Marvin. 60 minutes.

Pepsi Cola Playhouse (ABC) "Open Season"
March 19, 1954 *Starring* Dennis Morgan, Gordon James, Douglas Montgomery, Lee Marvin. 60 minutes.

A jealous husband invites several men on a hunting trip, including the man he suspects of being his wife's lover.

TV Soundstage (NBC) "The Psychophonic Nurse"
June 25, 1954. *Starring* Lee Marvin, Joanne Davis. 30 minutes.

An inventor creates a mechanical nurse for his infant, then wonders about the wisdom of such an invention.

Center Stage (ABC) "The Day Before Atlanta"
September 7, 1954. *Starring* Luther Adler, Joan Loring, Lee Marvin. 60 minutes.

The relationship between a Union soldier and a Southern girl becomes a microcosm for the conflict during the Civil War.

G. E. Theater (CBS) "Mr. Death and the Red Headed Woman"
November 28, 1954. *Hosted by* Ronald Reagan. *Starring* Eva Marie Saint, Lee Marvin. 30 minutes.

When her boyfriend is shot in a card game, Eva Marie Saint pleads with Lee Marvin, as Mr. Death, to save his life.

The Medic (**NBC**) "White Is the Color"
January 17, 1955. *Starring* Richard Boone as Dr Konrad Styner. *Guest Starring* Beverly Garland, Lee Marvin, Jeff York, Lillian Buyeff. 30 minutes.

Dr. Styner has a difficult task: keep a pregnant woman with leukemia alive long enough to safely deliver her baby. Lee Marvin is the woman's husband, who has to tell her the heartbreaking news and support her as she faces death. This is the premiere episode of *The Medic*, a dramatic medical anthology starring Richard Boone.

G. E. Theater (**CBS**) "The Martyr"
January 23, 1955. *Hosted by* Ronald Reagan. *Starring* Ronald Reagan, Brian Aherne, J. M. Kerrigan, Lee Marvin. 30 minutes.

This tale of the Irish Civil War stars Reagan as a leader of the Irish Free Staters who is captured, sentenced to death, and then offers to supply information in exchange for his life.

TV Reader's Digest (**ABC**) "How Charlie Faust Won a Pennant for the Giants"
April 11, 1955. *Starring* Lee Marvin, Alan Reed. 30 minutes.

Fantasy about a baseball pitcher who wins the pennant for the New York Giants without ever pitching the ball.

Fireside Theater (**NBC**) "The Little Guy"
September 27, 1955. *Hosted by* Jane Wyman. *Starring* Dane Clark, Lee Marvin. 30 minutes.

Dane Clark is a big man in the neighborhood, casually giving out advice to anyone and everyone who will listen.

Studio One (**CBS**) "Shakedown Cruise"
November 7, 1955. *Starring* Richard Kiley, Lee Marvin, George Mathews, Don Gordon, Frances Perkins. 60 minutes.

The crew of a nuclear submarine must contend with a limited air supply and mounting fear when a disaster occurs during a training cruise. Richard Kiley is the captain, contemplating a transfer before the disaster; Lee Marvin is the executive officer who desperately wants a command of his own. Each of them reacts to the situation in a different way, showing that even the most rigorous training is no substitute for experience. Directed by Franklin J. Schaffner.

Climax (**CBS**) "Bail Out at 43,000"
December 29, 1955. *Hosted by* William Lundigan. *Starring* Charlton Heston, Richard Boone, Nancy (Reagan) Davis, Lee Marvin. 60 minutes.

Three pilots—Heston, Boone and Marvin—must test the ejector seats on a high-altitude jet bomber. Each pilot reacts to the situation differently. Later made into a 1957 film starring John Payne. Directed by John Frankenheimer.

Kraft Television Theatre (**NBC**) "The Fool Killer"
March 7, 1956. *Starring* Malcolm Broderick, Karl Swensen, Arthur Tell, Tommy Halloran, Jane Rose, Larry Gates, Audra Lindley, Cavada Humphrey, Lee Marvin. 60 minutes.

Malcolm Broderick is a boy who runs away from home and meets various colorful characters on the road. He is taken in by kindly couple Karl Swensen and Audra Lindley, who run a store and had always wanted a son, and menaced by amnesiac hobo Lee Marvin, who eventually comes after the boy's surrogate family with an ax. Marvin dies falling off a roof and the boy remains with his new, adoptive family. Later made into a 1965 film starring Edward Albert and Anthony Perkins.

Front Row Center (**CBS**) "Dinner Date"
March 18, 1956. *Hosted by* Robert Sterling. *Starring* Lee Marvin, Peggy Webster, Richard Jaeckel, Whitfield Connor, Jeanne Cooper, Janet Stewart, Peter Votrian, Lillian Buyeff. 60 minutes.

Secretary Peggy Webster asks a man to pose as her boyfriend, but the man (Lee Marvin) turns out to be a homicidal maniac.

G. E. Theater (**CBS**) "The Doctors of Pawnee Kill"
January 27, 1957. *Hosted by* Ronald Reagan. *Starring* Lee Marvin, Kevin McCarthy, Margaret Hayes, Jean Howell, Dorothy Adams, Ted deCorsia, Don Devlin. 30 minutes.

Two brothers, Marvin and McCarthy, disagree how to rid a small frontier town of its various outlaws.

U. S. Steel Hour (CBS) "Shadow of Evil"

February 27, 1957. *Starring* Lee Marvin, Jack Cassidy, Shirley Jones, Russell Collins, Michael Strong, Fred Stewart, Joseph Sullivan. 60 minutes.

When a western sheriff, Marvin, kills a young man, the man's sister, Jones, attempts to clear his name.

G. E. Theater (CBS) "All I Survey"

February 2, 1958. *Hosted by* Ronald Reagan. *Starring* Joanne Dru, Lee Marvin. 30 minutes.

A woman (Joanne Dru) finds it difficult to stay true to her invalid husband when a friend offers her a life of luxury.

Climax (CBS) "The Time of the Hanging"

May 22, 1958. *Hosted by* William Lundigan. *Starring* Lee Marvin, William Shatner, Marsha Hunt, Harry Townes, John Litel. 60 minutes.

A westerner (Lee Marvin) takes Sheriff Townes and his wife hostage in order to save his brother (William Shatner) from being hanged.

Schlitz Playhouse of the Stars (CBS) "A Fistful of Love"

January 2, 1959. *Starring* Lee Marvin, Stanley Adams, Buddy Lester, Barbara Stuart, Herb Ellis, Art Lewis, Morris Erby, Joseph Mell. 30 minutes.

A veteran boxer (Lee Marvin) is slow to recover after a particularly brutal beating.

Desilu Playhouse (CBS) "Man in Orbit"

May 11, 1959. *Hosted by* Desi Arnaz. *Starring* Lee Marvin, E. G. Marshall, Peggy McCay, Martin Balsam, Robert F. Simon. 60 minutes.

The first man to be sent into space (Lee Marvin) is confused by the hostility of one of the scientists who is preparing him for his momentous journey.

G. E. Theater (CBS) "The Last Reunion"

September 27, 1959. *Hosted by* Ronald Reagan. *Starring* Lee Marvin, Simon Scott, Patricia Donohue. 30 minutes.

A veteran (Lee Marvin) returns from a war and finds himself unable to cope.

Sunday Showcase (NBC) "The American"

March 27, 1960. *Starring* Lee Marvin, Steven Hill, Frank Overton, Milton Selzer, Thomas Carlin, Frank Corsaro. 60 minutes.

This biopic follows the postwar life of Ira Hayes (Lee Marvin), one of the men who raised the American flag at Iwo Jima and returned to the States a hero, a fate he felt he didn't deserve. Directed by John Frankenheimer.

G. E. Theater (CBS) "Don't You Remember?"

May 8, 1960. *Hosted by* Ronald Reagan. *Starring* Simone Signoret and Lee Marvin. 30 minutes.

A desk clerk (Lee Marvin) is intrigued by a woman (Simone Signoret) who checks in to his fleabag hotel. To his surprise, she invites him to her room, where she confronts him with a loaded gun.

Wagon Train (NBC) "The Jose Morales Story"

October 26, 1960. *Starring* Ward Bond, Robert Horton, Terry Wilson, FrankMcGrath. *Guest Starring* Lee Marvin, Lon Chaney, Jr., Clark Howat, Aline Towne, Charles Herbert, Stevan Darrell, Gregg Palmer. 60 minutes.

Mexican bandit Jose Morales (Lee Marvin) gives three wagons crossing Sioux territory a lot of trouble.

The Americans (NBC) "Reconaissance"

March 6, 1961. *Starring* Richard Davalos, Darryl Hickman. *Guest Starring* Lee Marvin, Don Megowan, Diane Jergens, Brad Weston. 60 minutes.

Two brothers on the opposite sides during the Civil War are surprised to see each other at Harpers Ferry.

Wagon Train (NBC) "The Christopher Hale Story"

March 15, 1961. *Starring* Robert Horton, Frank McGrath, Terry Wilson. *Guest Starring* Lee Marvin, John McIntire, L. Q. Jones, Nancy Rennick, Claire Carleton, Wesley Lau, Charles Horvath, Red Morgan. 60 minutes.

Other Episodes 197

In *The Joke's on Me*, Lee Marvin starred (as a malicious comic) with Kathleen Hughes and Bud Abbott.

The company that owns the wagon train hires Lee Marvin to take over as wagon master, but his violent ways don't sit well with retired wagon master John McIntire. With the departure of Ward Bond, John McIntire took over as lead actor of this series in this episode.

Checkmate (CBS) "**Jungle Castle**"

April 1, 1961. *Starring* Anthony George, Doug McClure, Sebastian Cabot. *Guest Starring* Lee Marvin, Patricia Donohue, Denver Pyle, John Sutton, Raymond Greenleaf, Myrna Fahey. 60 minutes.

Lee Marvin calls on old friend (Sebastian Cabot) to help him figure out who is trying to kill him—his wife, his mistress, or his mistress' father, all of whom are currently staying in Marvin's Malaysian jungle home.

G. E. Theater (CBS) "**The Joke's on Me**"

April 16, 1961, *Hosted by* Ronald Reagan. *Starring* Lee Marvin, Bud Abbott, Mala Powers. 30 minutes.

Theatrical agent Bud Abbott tries to patch things up between his star comic (Lee Marvin) and his wife (Mala Powers).

The Untouchables (ABC) "**The Nick Acropolis Story**"

June 1, 1961. *Starring* Robert Stack, Paul Picerni, Nicholas Georgiade, Steve London. *Narrated by* Walter Winchell. *Guest Starring* Lee Marvin, Bruce Gordon, Constance Ford, Johnny Seven, Lindsay Workman, Leonard Stone. 60 minutes.

The Untouchables wiretap a bookmaking gang's telephone and witness one of the bookies being shot.

Alcoa Premiere (ABC) "**People Need People**"

October 10, 1961. *Starring* Lee Marvin, James Gregory, Arthur Kennedy, Katherine Squire, Jocelyn Brando, Marion Ross, John Alderman, Paul Comi, Russ Conway, David Faulkner, Joey Forman, Wesley Gale, Jordan Gerler, John Lassell, Ralph Reed, Bert Remsen, Paul Sand, Keir Dullea. *Emmy Nomination-Best Actor* Lee Marvin. 60 minutes.

Korean war veteran Marvin is one of a group of patients at a mental hospital who are put in an experimental ten-day program with no restrictions. The patients learn to band together and support each other. Marvin finally faces his feelings for his "dishwater" mother and womanizing father and his hellish time isolated in a foxhole during a long battle. Arthur Kennedy, as real-life therapist Dr. Wilmer, helps him understand how his feelings have become all twisted up in his mind and affected his marriage to Ross.

Marvin received his only Emmy nomination for this performance, but lost to Peter Falk, who starred in "The Price of Tomatoes" on the Dick Powell Theatre show. "People Need People" was also Emmy-nominated for its writing, direction and for Program Achievement—Drama (Best Drama). It lost all of these nominations to *The Defenders*.

Dr. Harry Wilmer served as technical advisor on this show and befriended Lee Marvin, beginning a relationship that would last until Marvin's death in 1987.

The Investigators (CBS) "**The Oracle**"

October 12, 1961. *Starring* James Franciscus, James Philbrook, Mary Murphy. *Guest Starring* Lee Marvin, Audrey Dalton. 60 minutes.

A cultist named Nostradamus (Lee Marvin) is persuading wealthy women to cash in their insurance policies and contribute to his group.

The Twilight Zone (CBS) "**The Grave**"

October 27, 1961. *Hosted by* Rod Serling. *Starring* Lee Marvin, Strother Martin, James Best, Lee Van Cleef, Stafford Repp, Ellen Willard, William Challee, Larry Johns, Richard Geary. 30 minutes.

Lee Marvin is a gunman in the Old West who is dared into visiting the grave of a man who vowed to reach up and grab him if he ever came near. Marvin takes the dare and plunges his knife into the grave to prove he was there, inadvertently pinning his coat to the ground when doing so. When he cannot rise, Marvin believes the dead man's vow has come true and dies of shock on the spot.

Route 66 (CBS) "**Mon Petit Chou**"

November 24, 1961. *Starring* Martin Milner, George Maharis. *Guest Starring* Lee Marvin, Macha Meril. 60 minutes.

Martin Milner takes a liking to Macha Meril, but her agent (Lee Marvin) doesn't want her to get involved with him.

Ben Casey (ABC) "A Story to Be Told Softly"
January 22, 1962. *Starring* Vince Edwards, Sam Jaffe, Harry Landers, Bettye Ackerman, Jeanne Bates. *Guest Starring* Lee Marvin, Jean Hagen, Jan Harrison, Marianne Stewart, Tony Maxwell. 60 minutes.

A husband and wife (Lee Marvin and Jean Hagen) separate over the issue of how to take care of their mentally retarded son.

The Untouchables (ABC) "Element of Danger"
March 22, 1962. *Starring* Robert Stack, Paul Picerni, Nicholas Georgiade, Abel Fernandez. *Narrated by* Walter Winchell. *Guest Starring* Lee Marvin, Victory Jory, Hugh Sanders, Paul Dubov, Sandra Warner, Howard Culver, Eve Cotton, Al Ruscio. 60 minutes.

Criminal Lee Marvin likes to live dangerously—gunning down a G-man who tracks down his cache of opium and giving the police false information about it; threatening to kill his boss (Victor Jory); personally setting a trap for Eliot Ness; taking a hostage in police headquarters; and facing up to four armed adversaries alone. Ness trails the vengeful Marvin to the source of the opium and watches Jory's drug empire explode in flames.

Bonanza (NBC) "The Crucible"
April 8, 1962. *Starring* Lorne Greene, Dan Blocker, Pernell Roberts, Michael Landon. *Guest Starring* Lee Marvin, Howard Ledig, Barry Cahill, Peter Kane, William Edmonson, Roy Barcroft, Paul Barselow. 60 minutes.

Adam Cartwright (Pernell Roberts) is robbed by two men in the mountains and left to die. While his brothers search for him, Cartwright finds Marvin, who is trying to mine a cave for gold. Marvin forces Cartwright to dig, taunting him all the while. Nevertheless, near death, Cartwright is found by his brothers trying to save Marvin's life.

Dr. Kildare (NBC) "One for the Road"
April 12, 1962. *Starring* Richard Chamberlain. *Guest Starring* Lee Marvin, Paul Carr, Maxine Stuart, Ralph Clanton. 60 minutes.

Dr. Kildare is chosen as an assistant at an experimental clinic for alcoholics run by Lee Marvin.

Dupont Show of the Month (NBC) "The Richest Man in Bogota"
August 5, 1962. *Starring* Lee Marvin, Miriam Colon, Richard Eastham, Eugene Iglesias, Dan Frazer, John W. Morley. 60 minutes.

A Colombian (Lee Marvin) wins a geiger counter that leads him to the Country of the Blind.

The Virginian (NBC) "It Tolls for Thee"
November 21, 1962. *Starring* Lee J. Cobb, James Drury, Doug McClure, Gary Clarke, Pippa Scott, Roberta Shore, Randy Boone. *Guest Starring* Lee Marvin, Albert Salmi, Ron Soble. 90 minutes.

Ex-con Kalig (Lee Marvin) and his gang kidnap Judge Garth (Lee J. Cobb) and demand an exorbitant ransom. After the Virginian (James Drury) pays it, Kalig keeps the Judge as hostage to ensure his gang's safe escape. At a river crossing, a desperate rescue attempt is made, the Judge is freed, and Kalig is captured. This episode and another were later combined and edited into a feature film, *The Meanest Men in the West*. Written and directed by Samuel Fuller.

The Untouchables (ABC) "A Fist of Five"
December 4, 1962. *Starring* Robert Stack, Paul Picerni, Nicholas Georgiade, Abel Fernandez. *Narrated by* Walter Winchell. *Guest Starring* Lee Marvin, Frank de Kova, Phyllis Coates, Ric Roman, Tom Brown, Roy Thinnes, James Caan, Mark Allen, Whitney Armstrong, Marianna Hill, Frank Wilcox, Jim O'Hara, Breena Howard. 60 minutes.

Policeman Lee Marvin is suspended for his violent arrests, so he decides to kidnap a local gangster for a reward, and persuades his four brothers (James Caan, Roy Thinnes, Mark Allen, Whitney Armstrong) to help.

200 *Television Appearances*

Sam Peckinpah directed Lee Marvin and Keenan Wynn in *The Losers*, a comedic adventure set in the Old West.

The gangsters refuse to pay, things turn violent, and the five brothers are literally torn apart by their actions. Directed by Ida Lupino.

Dick Powell Theater (NBC) "**The Losers**"
January 15, 1963. *Hosted by* Robert Mitchum. *Starring* Lee Marvin, Keenan Wynn, Rosemary Clooney, Russ Brown. 60 minutes.

Marvin and Wynn are two con-artists in the Old West looking for a new lamb to fleece. Directed by Sam Peckinpah. The characters of Dave Blassingame and Burgundy Smith are from *The Westerner*, an earlier series starring Brian Keith which Peckinpah created. There was talk of turning *The Losers* into a television series, but reportedly Lee Marvin's salary demand was high enough to cause the deal to fall through.

Dick Powell Theater (NBC) "**Epilogue**"
April 2, 1963. *Hosted by* Pat Boone. *Starring* Lee Marvin, Ricardo Montalban, Claude Akins, Patricia Breslin, Robert Crawford, Jr. 60 minutes.

At a reunion, an ex-Marine (Lee Marvin) confides to his former captain (Ricardo Montalban) that he has been murdering acquitted criminals to keep his training useful.

Combat (ABC) "**The Bridge at Chalons**"
September 17, 1963. *Starring* Vic Morrow, Conlan Carter. *Guest Starring* Lee Marvin, Lee Krieger, Rance Howard. 60 minutes.

Two demolition experts are assigned to help blow up the Chalons bridge.

The Twilight Zone (CBS) "**Steel**"
October 4, 1963. *Hosted by* Rod Serling. *Starring* Lee Marvin, Joe Mantell, Chuck Hicks, Tipp McClure, Marritt Bohn, Frank London, and Larry Barton. 30 minutes.

Lee Marvin and Joe Mantell are down-on-their-luck boxing promoters, and Tipp McClure is their broken-down boxing robot, Battling Maxo. When Maxo is unable to fight, Marvin disguises himself as Maxo and takes a beating in the ring. Because of his efforts, they are able to leave town with enough money to repair Maxo for their next fight. Writer Richard Matheson, a frequent contributor to *The Twilight Zone*, called this his favorite episode.

Kraft Suspense Theatre (NBC) "**The Case Against Paul Ryker**"
October 10 & 17, 1963. *Starring* Lee Marvin, Vera Miles, Bradford Dillman, Murray Hamilton, Peter Graves, Lloyd Nolan and Norman Fell. 120 minutes.

Lee Marvin is an American sergeant charged with treason during the Korean War and sentenced to death. His wife, Vera Miles, convinces prosecuting attorney Bradford Dillman to investigate further, which leads to a second court-martial, with Dillman this time serving as Marvin's defense lawyer. Dillman eventually finds that Marvin's story about pretending to be a defector in order to plug a security leak is true, and gets him acquitted.

This two-part story was later edited down to the 86-minute feature *Sergeant Ryker* in 1968. This original version is more smoothly edited than the feature film, is easier to follow, and makes more sense. In 1965 Bradford Dillman and Peter Graves reprised their roles in the television show *Court Martial*, although the series' setting was changed to World War II.

The Great Adventure (CBS) "**Six Wagons to the Sea**"
October 18, 1963. *Starring* Lee Marvin, Gene Lyons, Ellen Madison, Arthur Batanides, Richard X. Slattery, Walter Koenig, Al Ruscio. *Narrated by* Van Heflin. 60 minutes.

A raisin grower in 1907 (Lee Marvin), angered by exorbitant railroad freight prices, decides to transport his crop by horse instead.

Dr. Kildare (NBC) "**The Sound of a Faraway Hill**"
October 29, 1964. *Starring* Richard Chamberlain, Raymond Massey, Jean Inness, Steven Bell. *Guest Starring* Lee Marvin, John Megna, David Sheiner. 60 minutes.

Hospitalized baseball star Lee Marvin tries to inject some life into a fellow patient resigned to death.

Bob Hope Chrysler Theatre (NBC) "The Loving Cup"
January 29, 1965. *Starring* Polly Bergen, Lee Marvin, Patrick O'Neal. 60 minutes.

A yachtsman with an immediate need for cash contacts a wealthy sportsman, despite that sportsman's past history with his wife.

Variety Shows and Interviews

Ernie Ford Show (NBC)
October 24, 1957

Tonight Show (NBC)
September 21, 1958

Bob Hope Special
April 5, 1971

Bob Hope Christmas Special
December 9, 1971

All-Star Tribute to John Wayne
November 26, 1976

John Denver in Australia
February 16, 1978

Tomorrow Coast to Coast
May 8, 1981

Bob Hope Laughs with the Movie Awards
May 3, 1982

Bob Hope's Hilarious, Unrehearsed Antics of the Stars
September 28, 1984

Bibliography

This bibliography is designed to help the reader locate sources pertaining to the individual films. Films are listed chronologically as in the main text, with relevant sources listed alphabetically under each film title. Following the sources for the films are sources for documentaries, short films and stage plays; *M Squad*; *Lawbreaker*; and other television episodes. At the end of the bibliography are miscellaneous sources on Lee Marvin, sources discussing the palimony suit, and a listing of obituaries.

You're in the Navy Now (1951) (aka *U.S.S. Teakettle*)

Boxoffice February 24, 1951
Call Bureau Cast Service listing April 1, 1951
Commonweal page 544 March 9, 1951 Philip T. Hartung
Cue March 3, 1951
The Films of Gary Cooper pages 227-228 (1970, Citadel) Homer Dickens
Hollywood Citizen-News April 12, 1951 Ann Helming
Hollywood Reporter February 23, 1951
Library Journal pages 720, 719 April 15, 1951 Edith H. Crowell
Los Angeles Daily News April 12, 1951 David Bongard
Los Angeles Examiner April 12, 1951 Dorothy Manners
Los Angeles Times April 12, 1951 Philip K. Scheuer
The Motion Picture Guide page 3989 (1985, Cinebooks) Jay Robert Nash and Stanley Ralph Ross
Motion Picture Herald February 24, 1951 Red Kann
New Republic page 23 March 12, 1951 Robert Hatch
New York Times February 24, 1951 Bosley Crowther
New York Times March 4, 1951 Bosley Crowther
New Yorker page 101 March 10, 1951 John McCarten
Newsweek page 86 March 5, 1951
Saturday Review page 31 April 7, 1951 Richard Griffith
Tidings April 13, 1951 W.H.M.
Time pages 98, 100 March 12, 1951
Variety February 23, 1951

Teresa (1951)

Fred Zinnemann: A Life in the Movies pages 86-95 (1992, Scribners) Fred Zinnemann
The Lost Films of the Fifties pages 40-42 (1988, Citadel) Douglas Brode
The Motion Picture Guide page 3312 (1985, Cinebooks) Jay Robert Nash and Stanley Ralph Ross
New York Times March 25, 1951 Fred Zinnemann
New York Times April 6, 1951 Bosley Crowther
New York Times April 15, 1951 Bosley Crowther
Newsweek page 86 April 9, 1951
Oscar A to Z pages 859-860 (1995, Doubleday) Charles Matthews
Time pages 103, 104 April 9, 1951

Hong Kong (1951) (aka *Bombs Over China*)

The Films of Ronald Reagan pages 186-189 (1980, Citadel) Tony Thomas
Hollywood Reporter November 15, 1951
Los Angeles Daily News March 13, 1952 Howard McClay
Los Angeles Times March 13, 1952 Philip K. Scheuer
The Motion Picture Guide page 1265 (1985, Cinebooks) Jay Robert Nash and Stanley Ralph Ross
New York Times April 5, 1952 Howard H. Thompson
Newsweek page 110 May 19, 1952
Variety November 13, 1951
Variety November 14, 1951 Brog.

We're Not Married (1952)

Christian Century page 935 August 13, 1952
The Films of Marilyn Monroe pages 72-75 (1964, Citadel) Michael Conway and Mark Ricci
Life 69-70, 72 July 28, 1952
The Motion Picture Guide W-Z pages 3770-3771 (1985, Cinebooks) Jay Robert Nash and Stanley Ralph Ross
New York Times July 12, 1952 Bosley Crowther
New Yorker pages 70-71 July 19, 1952 John McCarten
Newsweek page 88 July 21, 1952
Saturday Review page 26 July 26, 1952 Arthur Knight
Theatre Arts pages 72-73 September, 1952 Robert Hatch
Time pages 72, 74 July 28, 1952

Diplomatic Courier (1952)

Boxoffice June 14, 1952
Call Bureau Cast Service listing December 31, 1951
Commonweal page 291 June 27, 1952 Philip T. Hartung
Cue June 14, 1952
Hollywood Citizen-News July 26, 1952 Lowell E. Redelings
Hollywood Citizen-News July 30, 1952 Lowell E. Redelings
Hollywood Reporter June 10, 1952
Library Journal page 1071 June 15, 1952 Earle F. Walbridge
Los Angeles Daily News July 26, 1952 Howard McClay
Los Angeles Examiner July 26, 1952 Ruth Waterbury
Los Angeles Times July 4, 1952
Los Angeles Times July 26, 1952 Philip K. Scheuer
The Motion Picture Guide page 661 (1985, Cinebooks) Jay Robert Nash and Stanley Ralph Ross
New York Times June 14, 1952 Bosley Crowther
Newsweek page 103 June 30, 1952
Spectator June 20, 1952
Theatre Arts pages 35, 88 August, 1952 Robert Hatch
Time pages 59-60 June 30, 1952
Variety June 10, 1952 Whit.
Variety June 11, 1952 Brog.
Variety August 27, 1952

The Duel at Silver Creek (1952)

Boxoffice July 19, 1952
Call Bureau Cast Service listing October 1, 1952
The Films & Career of Audie Murphy pages 44-46 (1996, Empire) Sue Gossett
Hollywood Citizen-News August 4, 1952 Lowell E. Redelings
Hollywood Reporter July 11, 1952
Los Angeles Daily News August 4, 1952 Howard McClay
Los Angeles Times August 4, 1952 Philip K. Scheuer
Mirror August 4, 1952 Tom Coffey
The Motion Picture Guide page 725 (1985, Cinebooks) Jay Robert Nash and Stanley Ralph Ross
Motion Picture Herald July 12, 1952 V.C.
New York Times August 2, 1952 Howard H. Thompson
Newsweek page 84 August 4, 1952
The Overlook Western Encyclopedia page 214 (1994, Overlook) Phil Hardy
Saturday Review page 26 July 26, 1952 Arthur Knight
Siegel Film, A pages 137-144 (1993, Faber and Faber) Don Siegel
Theatre Arts page 34 August, 1952 Robert Hatch
Variety July 11, 1952 Whit.
Variety July 16, 1952 Brog.

Hangman's Knot (1952)

Boxoffice November 1, 1952
Call Bureau Cast Service listing July 1, 1952
Cue December 13, 1952
Hollywood Citizen-News November 27, 1952 Lowell E. Redelings
Hollywood Reporter October 29, 1952
Los Angeles Times November 28, 1952
The Motion Picture Guide page 1149 (1985, Cinebooks) Jay Robert Nash and Stanley Ralph Ross
New York Times December 11, 1952 A. H. Weiler
Newsweek page 72 December 22, 1952
The Overlook Western Encyclopedia pages 214-215 (1994, Overlook) Phil Hardy
Randolph Scott: A Film Biography pages 129, 134 (1994, Empire) Jefferson Brim Crow III
Variety October 29, 1952 Brog.
Variety July 29, 1953

Eight Iron Men (1952)

Boxoffice October 25, 1952
Call Bureau Cast Service listing May 1, 1952
Catholic World page 144 November, 1952 Robert Kass
Christian Century page 1391 November 26, 1952
Commonweal page 425 January 30, 1953 Philip T. Hartung
Cue January 10, 1953
Films in Review page 472 November, 1952

Hollywood Citizen-News December 11, 1952 Lowell E. Redelings
Hollywood Reporter October 22, 1952
Los Angeles Daily News December 11, 1952 Howard McClay
Los Angeles Examiner December 11, 1952 Lynn Bowers
Los Angeles Times December 11, 1952 Philip K. Scheuer
A Mad, Mad, Mad, Mad World pages 97-99 (1997, Harcourt Brace) Stanley Kramer with Thomas M. Coffey
The Motion Picture Guide pages 750-751 (1985, Cinebooks) Jay Robert Nash and Stanley Ralph Ross
Motion Picture Herald October 25, 1952 A. S. Fishman
New York Times January 2, 1953 Bosley Crowther
New York Times January 11, 1953 Bosley Crowther
Newsweek page 60 January 5, 1953
Stanley Kramer: Film Maker pages 123-129 (1978, Samuel French) Donald Spoto
Theatre Arts page 84 December, 1952 Robert Hatch
Time page 104 December 8, 1952
Variety October 22, 1952 Brog.
War Movies page 84 (1987, Facts On File) Brock Garland

Seminole (1953)

Commonweal page 52 April 17, 1953 Philip T. Hartung
The Films of Anthony Quinn pages 132-133 (1975, Citadel) Alvin H. Marill
The Motion Picture Guide S pages 2817-2818 (1985, Cinebooks) Jay Robert Nash and Stanley Ralph Ross
Newsweek pages 108, 110 March 23, 1953
The Overlook Western Encyclopedia page 227 (1994, Overlook) Phil Hardy
Time page 104 February 23, 1953

The Glory Brigade (1953)

America page 526 August 29, 1953 Moira Walsh
Call Bureau Cast Service Cast listing March 1, 1953
Hollywood Citizen-News September 26, 1952
Los Angeles Daily News August 1, 1953 Roy Ringer
Los Angeles Times August 1, 1953 John L. Scott
The Motion Picture Guide E-G page 1038 (1985, Cinebooks) Jay Robert Nash and Stanley Ralph Ross
Motion Picture Herald May 16, 1953 V.C.
New York Times August 15, 1953 Howard H. Thompson

The Swashbucklers page 458 (1976, Rainbow) James Robert Parish and Don E. Stanke
Variety May 13, 1953 Brog.
War Movies page 105 (1987, Facts On File) Brock Garland

Down Among the Sheltering Palms (1953)

The Hollywood Musical page 334 (1981, Crown) Clive Hirschhorn
The Motion Picture Guide C-D page 704 (1985, Cinebooks) Jay Robert Nash and Stanley Ralph Ross
New York Times June 13, 1953 Howard H. Thompson

The Stranger Wore a Gun (1953)

The Motion Picture Guide S page 3164 (1985, Cinebooks) Jay Robert Nash and Stanley Ralph Ross
New York Times July 30, 1953 A. H. Weiler
Newsweek August 24, 1953
The Overlook Western Encyclopedia page 228 (1994, Overlook) Phil Hardy
Randolph Scott: A Film Biography page 134 (1994, Empire) Jefferson Brim Crow III

The Big Heat (1953)

America page 59 November 7, 1953 Moira Walsh
The Best Video Films page 183 (1984, Warner) Editors of Video Movies Magazine
The Big Heat (1992, BFI Publishing) Colin McArthur
Catholic World page 63 October, 1953 Robert Kass
Chicago Reader Internet Archive Review (1997) Don Druker
Cult Movies 2 pages 22-25 (1983, Delta) Danny Peary
Film Noir pages 41-42 (1995, McFarland) Michael L. Stephens
The Films of the Fifties pages 88-90 (1976, Citadel) Douglas Brode
The 500 Best American Films to Buy, Rent or Videotape page 46 (1985, Pocket)
Fritz Lang pages 329-337 (1976, Da Capo) Lotte Eisner
Fritz Lang: The Nature of the Beast pages 403-407 (1997, St. Martin's) Patrick McGilligan
The Great Gangster Pictures pages 35-36 (1976, Scarecrow) James Robert Parish and Michael R. Pitts

206 *Bibliography*

Guide for the Film Fanatic page 52 (1986, Fireside) Danny Peary
Library Journal page 1677 October 1, 1953 Herbert Cahoon
The Motion Picture Guide A–B page 195 (1985, Cinebooks) Jay Robert Nash and Stanley Ralph Ross
Nation page 434 November 21, 1953 Manny Farber
New York Times October 15, 1953 Bosley Crowther
Newsweek pages 90-91 November 2, 1953
Sight and Sound page 36 July-September 1954 Lindsay Anderson
Suicide Blonde pages 150-155 (1989,) Vincent Curcio
Thriller Movies page 146 (1974, Octopus) Lawrence Hammond
Time page 112 November 2, 1953

Gun Fury (1953)

The BFI Companion to the Western page 266 (1988, Da Capo) Edited by Edward Buscombe
Commonweal page 108 November 27, 1953 Philip T. Hartung
Hollywood Citizen-News October 29, 1953 Lowell E. Redelings
Hollywood Reporter October 23, 1953
Los Angeles Daily News October 29, 1953 Roy Ringer
Los Angeles Herald & Express October 29, 1953
Los Angeles Times October 29, 1953 G. K.
The Motion Picture Guide E–G page 1123 (1985, Cinebooks) Jay Robert Nash and Stanley Ralph Ross
Newsweek page 116 October 26, 1953
The Overlook Western Encyclopedia page 223 (1994, Overlook) Phil Hardy
Ten Against Caesar (1952, Houghton Mifflin) K.R.G. Granger novel upon which the screenplay is based
Time page 110 December 7, 1953
Variety October 23, 1953 Neal.

The Wild One (1954)

America page 407 January 16, 1954 Moira Walsh
Brando pages 337-348 (1994, Hyperion) Peter Manso
Brando pages 50-55 (1994, Studio Vista) Robert Tanitch
Brando: A Life in Our Times pages 81-86 (1991, Maxwell McMillan) Richard Schickel
Brando: Songs My Mother Taught Me pages 175-181 (1994, Random House) Marlon Brando with Robert Lindsey
Brando: The Unauthorized Biography pages 132-138 (1987, New American Library) Charles Higham

Catholic World page 304 January, 1954 Robert Kass
Chicago Reader Internet Archive Review (1997) Dave Kehr
Commonweal 59: page 449 February 5, 1954 Philip T. Hartung
The Films of the Fifties pages 86-87 (1976, Citadel) Douglas Brode
The 500 Best American Films to Buy, Rent or Videotape page 481 (1985, Pocket)
The Great Gangster Pictures page 418 (1976, Scarecrow) James Robert Parish and Michael R. Pitts
Guide for the Film Fanatic page 471 (1986, Fireside) Danny Peary
The I Was a Teenage Juvenile Delinquent Rock 'n' Roll Horror Beach Party Movie Book page 68 (1986, St. Martin's) Alan Betrock
Library Journal page 56 January 1, 1954 Gerald D. McDonald
Life pages 95-96 January 18, 1954
A Mad, Mad, Mad, Mad World pages 45-60 (1997, Harcourt Brace) Stanley Kramer with Thomas M. Coffey
The Motion Picture Guide W–Z pages 3858-3859 (1985, Cinebooks) Jay Robert Nash and Stanley Ralph Ross
New York Times December 31, 1953 Bosley Crowther
Newsweek page 88 December 14, 1953
Races, Chases & Crashes pages 135-136 (1994, Motorbooks International) Dave Mann and Ron Main
Retakes pages 372-373 (1989, Ballantine) John Eastman
Saturday Review page 58 January 2, 1954 Hollis Alpert
Sight and Sound Summer, 1955 pages 30-31 Gavin Lambert
Stanley Kramer: Film Maker pages 157-165 (1978, Samuel French) Donald Spoto
Time pages 100, 102 January 18, 1954
Wild and Young pages 46-47 (1983, Orbis) Edited by Ann Lloyd

Gorilla at Large (1954)

Hollywood Reporter April 30, 1954 M.L.
Hollywood Reporter May 13, 1982 Richard Hack
Hollywood Reporter July 5, 1983 Mamoru Ohba
Los Angeles Daily News May 27, 1954 Russ Burton
Los Angeles Times May 30, 1954
Los Angeles Times November 18, 1992
The Motion Picture Guide E–G page 1078 (1985, Cinebooks) Jay Robert Nash and Stanley Ralph Ross
New York Times June 12, 1954 Bosley Crowther
Time page 112 October 19, 1953

Variety April 30, 1954 Brog.
Variety June 9, 1982

The Caine Mutiny (1954)

America page 367 July 3, 1954 Moira Walsh
Bogart pages 478-485 (1997, William Morrow) A. M. Sperber and Eric Lax
Bogart: A Life in Hollywood pages 277-280, footnotes (1997, Houghton Mifflin) Jeffrey Meyers
Bogey pages 173-175 (1965, Citadel) Clifford McCarty
The Caine Mutiny (1951, Doubleday) Herman Wouk
Catholic World pages 221-222 June, 1954 Robert Kass
Commonweal pages 293-294 June 25, 1954 Philip T. Hartung
Guide for the Film Fanatic pages 79-80 (1986, Fireside) Danny Peary
Library Journal page 1304 July, 1954 Charlotte Bilkey Speicher
Life pages 67-70 May 3, 1954
Look pages 84-87 June 29, 1954
A Mad, Mad, Mad, Mad World pages 110-120 (1997, Harcourt Brace) Stanley Kramer with Thomas M. Coffey
The Motion Picture Guide C-D pages 329-330 (1985, Cinebooks) Jay Robert Nash and Stanley Ralph Ross
New York Times June 25, 1954 Bosley Crowther
New York Times July 4, 1954 Bosley Crowther
New York Times July 4, 1954 Howard H. Thompson
New Yorker pages 48-49 July 3, 1954 John McCarten
Newsweek page 72 June 28, 1954
Oscar A to Z pages 130-131 (1995, Doubleday) Charles Matthews
Reel Justice pages 63-68 (1996, Andrews and McMeel) Paul Bergman and Michael Asimow
Retakes pages 50-51 (1989, Ballantine) John Eastman
Saturday Review pages 28-30 June 26, 1954 Arthur Knight
Stanley Kramer: Film Maker pages 167-176 (1978, Samuel French) Donald Spoto
Time Cover, pages 66-72 June 7, 1954
Time page 90 June 28, 1954
War Movies pages 51-52 (1987, Facts On File) Brock Garland

The Raid (1954)

America page 601 September 8, 1954 Moira Walsh
The BFI Companion to the Western page 291 (1988, Da Capo) Edited by Edward Buscombe
The Blue & Gray on the Silver Screen pages 132-135 (1996, Birch Lane) Roy Kinnard
Commonweal pages 557-558 September 10, 1954 Philip T. Hartung
Confederate Battle Stories pages 149-161 (1992, August House) "Affair at St. Albans" Herbert R. Sass Original story upon which the screenplay is based
Historical Times Illustrated Encyclopedia of the Civil War page 651 (1991, Harper)
The Motion Picture Guide N-R pages 2527-2528 (1985, Cinebooks) Jay Robert Nash and Stanley Ralph Ross
New York Times August 21, 1955 Howard H. Thompson
Newsweek page 76 August 23, 1954
The Overlook Western Encyclopedia pages 233-234 (1994, Overlook) Phil Hardy

Bad Day at Black Rock (1955)

America pages 518-519 February 12, 1955 Moira Walsh
The BFI Companion to the Western page 248 (1988, Da Capo) Edited by Edward Buscombe
Catholic World pages 382-383 February, 1955 Robert Kass
Commonweal page 407 January 14, 1955 Philip T. Hartung
Film Culture page 26 May/June, 1955 G. N. Fenin
The Films of Spencer Tracy pages 221-223 (1968, Citadel) Donald Deschner
The Films of the Fifties pages 153-155 (1976, Citadel) Douglas Brode
The 500 Best American Films to Buy, Rent or Videotape page 33 (1985, Pocket)
The Great Western Pictures pages 14-16 (1976, Scarecrow) James Robert Parish and Michael R. Pitts
Kiss Kiss Bang Bang page 287 (1968, Bantam) Pauline Kael
The Motion Picture Guide A-B page 125 (1985, Cinebooks) Jay Robert Nash and Stanley Ralph Ross
Nation pages 165-166 February 19, 1955 Robert Hatch
Newsweek page 94 February 21, 1955
New Yorker pages 92-93 February 12, 1955 John McCarten
New York Times February 2, 1955 Bosley Crowther
New York Times February 6, 1955 Bosley Crowther
No, But I Saw the Movie pages 16-30 (1989, Penguin) "Bad Time At Honda" Howard Breslin Short Story upon which the screenplay is based
Oscar A to Z page 57 (1995, Doubleday) Charles Matthews

The Overlook Western Encyclopedia page 237 (1994, Overlook) Phil Hardy
Spencer Tracy: Tragic Idol pages 112-124 (1987, E. P. Dutton) Bill Davidson
Time page 74 January 17, 1955

Violent Saturday (1955)

America page 250 May 28, 1955 Moira Walsh
Catholic World page 221 June, 1955 Robert Kass
Film Comment pages 5-6+ May/June, 1985 Michael Sragow
The Films of the Fifties pages 156-157 (1976, Citadel) Douglas Brode
Great Gangster Pictures pages 407-408 (1976, Scarecrow) James Robert Parish and Michael R. Pitts
Library Journal pages 1105, 1157 May 1, 1955 Earle F. Walbridge
The Motion Picture Guide T-V page 3691 (1985, Cinebooks) Jay Robert Nash and Stanley Ralph Ross
New York Times May 12, 1955 Bosley Crowther
New Yorker page 130 May 21, 1955 John McCarten
Newsweek page 120 May 23, 1955
Saturday Review page 26 April 23, 1955 Lee Rogow
Time pages 106-110 May 16, 1955

Not as a Stranger (1955)

America page 399 July 16, 1955 Moira Walsh
Catholic World pages 221-222 June, 1955 Robert Kass
Commonweal page 371 July 15, 1955 Philip T. Hartung
Film Culture page 35 Winter, 1955 Martin Dworkin
The Films of Olivia de Havilland pages 227-228 (1983, Citadel) Tony Thomas
Library Journal page 1487 June 15, 1955 Gerald D. McDonald
Life pages 77-81 June 27, 1955
Look pages 87-88 May 31, 1955
A Mad, Mad, Mad, Mad World pages 121-133 (1997, Harcourt Brace) Stanley Kramer with Thomas M. Coffey
The Motion Picture Guide N-R page 2199 (1985, Cinebooks) Jay Robert Nash and Stanley Ralph Ross
Nation page 591 June 25, 1955 Robert Hatch
New Yorker pages 66-67 July 9, 1955 John McCarten
New York Times June 12, 1955 Oscar Godbout
New York Times June 29, 1955 Bosley Crowther
New York Times July 10, 1955 A. H. Weiler
Oscar A to Z pages 604-605 (1995, Doubleday) Charles Matthews

Robert Mitchum pages 181-182 (1984,) George Eells
Robert Mitchum on the Screen pages 138-139 (1978, A. S. Barnes) Alvin H. Marill
Saturday Review page 24 June 25, 1955 Arthur Knight
Stanley Kramer: Film Maker pages 177-185 (1978, Samuel French) Donald Spoto
Time pages 70-71 July 4, 1955

A Life in the Balance (1955)

Commonweal pages 503-504 February 11, 1955 Philip T. Hartung
Farm Journal page 89 April, 1955
The Motion Picture Guide L-M page 1669 (1985, Cinebooks) Jay Robert Nash and Stanley Ralph Ross
New York Times July 14, 1955 Howard H. Thompson

Pete Kelly's Blues (1955)

America page 575 September 10, 1955 Moira Walsh
Catholic World page 59 October, 1955 Robert Kass
Commonweal page 542 September 2, 1955 Philip T. Hartung
The Great Gangster Pictures page 309 (1976, Scarecrow) James Robert Parish and Michael R. Pitts
The Hollywood Musical page 346 (1981, Crown) Clive Hirschhorn
Life pages 109-110 August 29, 1955
The Motion Picture Guide N-R page 2379 (1985, Cinebooks) Jay Robert Nash and Stanley Ralph Ross
Newsweek pages 66-67 September 5, 1955
New Yorker pages 100-101 August 27, 1955 Philip Hamburger
New York Times August 19, 1955 Howard H. Thompson
Oscar A to Z pages 646-647 (1995, Doubleday) Charles Matthews
Saturday Review page 23 August 27, 1955 Lee Rogow
Time pages 114-116 September 12, 1955

I Died a Thousand Times (1955)

Commonweal page 228 December 2, 1955 Philip T. Hartung
Film Noir page 192 (1995, McFarland) Michael L. Stephens
The Great Gangster Pictures pages 201-203 (1976, Scarecrow) James Robert Parish and Michael R. Pitts

High Sierra (1979, University of Wisconsin) W. R. Burnett Screenplay upon which the screenplay is based
The Motion Picture Guide H–K page 1326 (1985, Cinebooks) Jay Robert Nash and Stanley Ralph Ross
Newsweek page 98 December 5, 1955
New York Times November 10, 1955 Bosley Crowther
Shelley II pages 118-122 (1989, Pocket) Shelley Winters
Time pages 102-104 November 28, 1955

Shack Out on 101 (1955)

Leonard Maltin's Movie and Video Guide 1995 (1994, Signet) Leonard Maltin
The Motion Picture Guide S page 2849 (1985, Cinebooks) Jay Robert Nash and Stanley Ralph Ross
Motion Picture Herald December 3, 1955 Samuel D. Berns
New York Times January 10, 1956 A. H. Weiler
Time page 92 February 13, 1956

Seven Men from Now (1956)

The BFI Companion to the Western page 297 (1988, Da Capo) Edited by Edward Buscombe
Guide for the Film Fanatic page 378 (1986, Fireside) Danny Peary
Los Angeles Times November 29, 1992 Michael Wilmington
The Motion Picture Guide S page 2838 (1985, Cinebooks) Jay Robert Nash and Stanley Ralph Ross
The Overlook Western Encyclopedia page 251 (1994, Overlook) Phil Hardy
Randolph Scott: A Film Biography page 149 (1994, Empire) Jefferson Brim Crow III

Pillars of the Sky (1956)

Frontier Fury (1953, Random House) Will Henry Novel, also known as *To Follow a Flag* and *Pillars of the Sky*, upon which the screenplay is based
The Motion Picture Guide N–R page 2399 (1985, Cinebooks) Jay Robert Nash and Stanley Ralph Ross
Motion Picture Herald 1956 Lawrence J. Quirk
New York Times October 13, 1956 Howard H. Thompson

The Rack (1956)

Catholic World pages 145-146 May, 1956 Robert Kass
Commonweal page 179 May 18, 1956 Philip T. Hartung
The Films of Paul Newman pages 48-52 (1971, Citadel) Lawrence J. Quirk
The Films of the Fifties pages 185-186 (1976, Citadel) Douglas Brode
Library Journal pages 2676-2677 November 15, 1956 Herbert Cahoon
The Motion Picture Guide N–R page 2521 (1985, Cinebooks) Jay Robert Nash and Stanley Ralph Ross
Nation page 467 November 24, 1956 Robert Hatch
New York Times November 6, 1956 Bosley Crowther
New Yorker page 102 November 17, 1956 John McCarten
Newsweek page 99 June 4, 1956
Paul Newman page 65 (1996, Taylor) Lawrence J. Quirk
Saturday Review page 47 May 19, 1956 Arthur Knight
Serling pages 108-109 (1992, E. P. Dutton) Gordon F. Sander
Variety Television Reviews 1954–1956 April 20, 1955 (1989, Garland) Hift.
War Movies page 165 (1987, Facts On File) Brock Garland

Attack (1956)

America page 632 September 29, 1956 Moira Walsh
Catholic World page 65 October, 1956 James Fenlon Finley, C.S.P.
Commonweal pages 16-17 October 5, 1956 Philip T. Hartung
The Films and Career of Robert Aldrich pages 60-75 (1986, University of Tennessee) Edwin T. Arnold and Eugene L. Miller, Jr.
The Great War Films pages 139-141 (1994, Citadel) Lawrence J. Quirk
Guide for the Film Fanatic page 34 (1986, Fireside) Danny Peary
Library Journal page 2315 October 15, 1956 Herbert Cahoon
The Lost Films of the Fifties pages 180-183 (1988, Citadel) Douglas Brode
The Motion Picture Guide A–B page 107 (1985, Cinebooks) Jay Robert Nash and Stanley Ralph Ross
Nation page 294 October 6, 1956 Robert Hatch
New York Times February 19, 1956 Oscar Godbout
New York Times September 20, 1956 Bosley Crowther
New Yorker page 88 September 29, 1956 John McCarten
Newsweek page 116 September 17, 1956
Saturday Review pages 25-26 September 1, 1956 Arthur Knight

The Star-Spangled Screen pages 252-253 (1985, University of Kentucky) Bernard F. Dick
Time page 116 September 10, 1956
War Movies pages 29-30 (1987, Facts on File) Brock Garland
What Ever Happened to Robert Aldrich? pages 119-124 (1995, Limelight) Alain Silver and James Ursini

Raintree County (1957)

America page 384 December 21, 1957 Moira Walsh
The Blue & Gray on the Silver Screen pages 164-167 (1996, Birch Lane) Roy Kinnard
Catholic World page 463 March, 1958 James Fenlon Finley, C.S.P.
Chicago Reader Internet Archive Review (1997) Jonathan Rosenbaum
Commonweal page 409 January 17, 1958 Philip T. Hartung
The Films of Montgomery Clift pages 157-165 (1979, Citadel) Judith M. Kass
Library Journal page 72 January 1, 1958 Gerald D. McDonald
Look pages 122-128 April 30, 1957
Montgomery Clift pages 291-312 (1978, Bantam) Patricia Bosworth
Monty pages 142-164 (1977, Avon) Robert LaGuardia
The Motion Picture Guide N-R page 2535 (1985, Cinebooks) Jay Robert Nash and Stanley Ralph Ross
New Republic page 22 November 11, 1957 Philip Roth
New York Times October 3, 1957 Bosley Crowther
New York Times December 21, 1957 Bosley Crowther
New Yorker page 102 January 11, 1958 John McCarten
Newsweek page 112 October 21, 1957
Oscar A to Z pages 696-697 (1995, Doubleday) Charles Matthews
Saturday Review page 23 November 2, 1957 Hollis Alpert
Time pages 76-77 January 6, 1958

The Missouri Traveler (1958)

Library Journal page 588 February 15, 1958 Charlotte Bilkey Speicher
The Missouri Traveler (1955, Vanguard) John Burress
The Motion Picture Guide L-M page 1977 (1985, Cinebooks) Jay Robert Nash and Stanley Ralph Ross
Newsweek page 116 May 21, 1956
Newsweek page 104 February 24, 1958

The Comancheros (1961)

America page 228 November 11, 1961 Moira Walsh
The BFI Companion to the Western page 256 (1988, Da Capo) Edited by Edward Buscombe
The Comancheros (1952, Doubleday) Paul I. Wellman
The Complete Films of John Wayne pages 233-236 (1983, Citadel) Mark Ricci, Boris Zmiejewski and Steve Zmiejewski
The Great Western Pictures pages 64-65 (1976, Scarecrow) James Robert Parish and Michael R. Pitts
John Wayne page 109 (1974, Pyramid) Alan G. Barbour
John Wayne and the Movies pages 180-182, 300 (1976, Grosset and Dunlap) Allen Eyles
The John Wayne Scrapbook pages 92-95 (1989, Citadel) Lee Pfeiffer
The Motion Picture Guide C-D page 459 (1985, Cinebooks) Jay Robert Nash and Stanley Ralph Ross
New York Times November 2, 1961 Bosley Crowther
Newsweek page 107 November 13, 1961
Time page 59 November 17, 1961

The Man Who Shot Liberty Valance (1962)

About John Ford pages 178-182 (1981, McGraw-Hill) Lindsay Anderson
America page 409 June 16, 1962 Moira Walsh
The BFI Companion to the Western pages 284-285 (1988, Da Capo) Edited by Edward Buscombe
Chicago Reader Internet Archive Review (1997) Dave Kehr
Cinema Journal pages 22-36 November 1, 1991 William Darby
Commonweal page 211 May 18, 1962 Philip T. Hartung
The Complete Films of John Wayne pages 236-238 (1983, Citadel) Mark Ricci, Boris Zmijewsky and Steve Zmijewsky
Esquire pages 126-127 July, 1962 Dwight McDonald
Film Comment pages 8-17 Fall, 1971 Robin Wood
Film Comment pages 18-20 Fall, 1971 David Bordwell
Film Culture 25 pages 13-15 Summer, 1962 Andrew Sarris
Film Quarterly pages 42-44 Winter, 1963/1964 Ernest Callenbach
The 500 Best American Films to Buy, Rent or Videotape page 239 (1985, Pocket)
Goal Dust pages 210-212 (1990, Madison) Woody Strode and Sam Young

Guide for the Film Fanatic pages 262-263 (1986, Fireside) Danny Peary
Gunfight! pages 38-51 (1996, University of Nebraska) "The Man Who Shot Liberty Valance" Dorothy Johnson
It's a Wonderful Life: The Films & Career of James Stewart pages 203-207 (1988, Citadel) Tony Thomas
James Stewart pages 412-414 (1996, Turner) Donald Dewey
James Stewart pages 153-155 (1984, Stein and Day) Allen Eyles
James Stewart pages 115-116 (1974, Pyramid) Howard Thompson
James Stewart: A Life in Film pages 150-152 (1992, St. Martin's) Roy Pickard
James Stewart: A Wonderful Life pages 166, 170 (1994, Little, Brown) Jonathan Coe
John Ford pages 175-189 (1974, Da Capo) Joseph McBride and Michael Wilmington
John Ford pages 194-198 (1979, Dial) Andrew Sinclair
John Ford: Hollywood's Old Master pages 307-311 (1995, University of Oklahoma) Ronald L. Davis
John Ford: The Man and His Films pages 384-413 (1986, University of California) Tag Gallagher
John Wayne pages 55-57 (1974, Pyramid) Alan G. Barbour
John Wayne and the Movies pages 182-186, 300-301 (1976, Grosset and Dunlap) Allen Eyles
The John Wayne Scrapbook pages 96-99 (1989, Citadel) Lee Pfeiffer
The Motion Picture Guide L–M pages 1857-1858 (1985, Cinebooks) Jay Robert Nash and Stanley Ralph Ross
New York Times May 24, 1962 A. H. Weiler
New York Times June 3, 1962 Bosley Crowther
Newsweek page 88 May 7, 1962
Oscar A to Z page 530 (1995, Doubleday) Charles Matthews
The Overlook Western Encyclopedia pages 281-282 (1994, Overlook) Phil Hardy
Retakes page 203 (1989, Ballantine) John Eastman
Screen World 1963 Annual page 27 (1964, Crown) John Willis
The Western Films of John Ford pages 214-227 (1974, Citadel) J. A. Place

Donovan's Reef (1963)

About John Ford pages 166, 167 (1981, McGraw-Hill) Lindsay Anderson
The Complete Films of John Wayne pages 246-247 (1983, Citadel) Mark Ricci, Boris Zmijewsky and Steve Zmijewsky
Film Comment pages 8-17 Fall, 1971 Robin Wood
Film Quarterly pages 42-44 Winter, 1963/1964 Ernest Callenbach

John Ford page 205 (1979, Dial) Andrew Sinclair
John Ford: Hollywood's Old Master pages 317-319 (1995, University of Oklahoma) Ronald L. Davis
John Ford: The Man and His Films pages 413-429 (1986, University of California) Tag Gallagher
John Wayne page 118 (1974, Pyramid) Alan G. Barbour
John Wayne and the Movies pages 193-194, 304 (1976, Grosset and Dunlap) Allen Eyles
The John Wayne Scrapbook pages 174-176 (1989, Citadel) Lee Pfeiffer
The Motion Picture Guide C–D page 690 (1985, Cinebooks) Jay Robert Nash and Stanley Ralph Ross
New York Times July 25, 1963 A. H. Weiler
New York Times July 28, 1963 A. H. Weiler
The Non-Western Films of John Ford pages 274-278 (1979, Citadel) J. A. Place

The Killers (1964)

The Films of Ronald Reagan pages 222-224 (1980, Citadel) Tony Thomas
The Great Gangster Pictures pages 223-225 (1976, Scarecrow) James Robert Parish and Michael R. Pitts
Guide for the Film Fanatic page 226 (1986, Fireside) Danny Peary
Hemingway's Short Stories pages 279-289 (1986, Scribners) "The Killers" Ernest Hemingway
The Motion Picture Guide H–K page 1526 (1985, Cinebooks) Jay Robert Nash and Stanley Ralph Ross
Newsweek page 72 August 3, 1964
New York Times July 18, 1964 Eugene Archer
Screen World 1965 Annual page 82 (1966, Crown) John Willis
Siegel Film, A pages 235-259 (1993, Faber and Faber) Don Siegel

Cat Ballou (1965)

Academy Awards: A Pictorial History page 309 (1978, Crown) Paul Michael
...And the Winner Is pages 173-175 (1991, Continuum) Emanuel Levy
The BFI Companion to the Western pages 253-254 (1988, Da Capo) Edited by Edward Buscombe
Chicago Reader Internet Archive Review (1997) Don Druker
Commonweal page 192 April 30, 1965 Philip T. Hartung
Esquire page 40 September, 1965 Dwight McDonald
Film Quarterly pages 54-55 Fall, 1965 Pauline Kael
The Great Western Pictures pages 49-51 (1976, Scarecrow) James Robert Parish and Michael R. Pitts

History of the Academy Award Winners—1974 Edition page 177 (1975, Ace) Nathalie Fredrik and Auriel Douglas
Horses in the Movies pages 67-68 (1979, A. S. Barnes) H. F. Hintz
Inside Oscar pages 381-382, 386-390 (1993, Ballantine) Mason Wiley and Damien Bona
Jane Fonda: All-American Anti-Heroine pages 57-60 (1980, Quick Fox) Gary Herman and David Downing
The Motion Picture Guide C-D page 378 (1985, Cinebooks) Jay Robert Nash and Stanley Ralph Ross
Nation page 68 August 2, 1965 Robert Hatch
New York Times June 25, 1965 Bosley Crowther
New York Times 1:8, 5:1 June 27, 1965 Bosley Crowther
Newsweek pages 118A, 120 May 10, 1965
Oscar A to Z pages 152-153 (1995, Doubleday) Charles Matthews
Oscar Stars from A to Z pages 230-231 (1996, Headline) Roy Pickard
The Overlook Western Encyclopedia pages 289-290 (1994, Overlook) Phil Hardy
The Private Eye, the Cowboy & the Very Naked Girl pages 123-126, 148-149 (1968, Holt, Rinehart and Winston) Judith Crist
Retakes page 55 (1989, Ballantine) John Eastman
Screen World 1966 Annual pages 56-57 (1967, Crown) John Willis
Time page 107 May 21, 1965
Tough Guys page 148 (1976, Arlington House) James Robert Parish
TV Guide page A-28 April 18, 1966 Academy Awards show listing
Unsold TV Pilots page 89 (1991, Citadel) Lee Goldberg

Ship of Fools (1965)

America page 170 August 14, 1965 Moira Walsh
Book of the Month Club News "Bookmark" Report by Clifton Fadiman
Chicago Reader Internet Archive Review (1997) Jonathan Rosenbaum
Christian Century page 1262 October 13, 1965 Malcolm Boyd
Commonweal pages 563-564 August 6, 1965 Philip T. Hartung
Film Quarterly pages 39-51 Fall, 1965 William Johnson
Kiss Kiss Bang Bang pages 249-263 (1968, Bantam) Pauline Kael
A Mad, Mad, Mad, Mad World pages 201-212 (1997, Harcourt Brace) Stanley Kramer with Thomas M. Coffey
The Motion Picture Guide S page 2988 (1985, Cinebooks) Jay Robert Nash and Stanley Ralph Ross
New York Times July 29, 1965 Bosley Crowther
New York Times August 1, 1965 Bosley Crowther
Oscar A to Z pages 768-769 (1995, Doubleday) Charles Matthews
The Private Eye, the Cowboy & the Very Naked Girl pages 135-138 (1968, Holt, Rinehart and Winston) Judith Crist
Retakes pages 310-311 (1989, Ballantine) John Eastman
Screen World 1966 Annual pages 82-83 (1967, Crown) John Willis
Ship of Fools (1945, Atlantic) Katherine Anne Porter
Stanley Kramer: Film Maker pages 265-271 (1978, Samuel French) Donald Spoto
Time page 85 August 6, 1965
Vivien pages 281-283 (1987, Grove) Alexander Walker
Vogue page 51 August 1, 1965 Elizabeth Hardwick

The Professionals (1966)

Against Type pages 243-245 (1995, Scribners) Gary Fishgall
The BFI Companion to the Western page 290 (1988, Da Capo) Edited by Edward Buscombe
Commonweal page 201 November 18, 1966 Philip T. Hartung
Film Quarterly page 62 Spring, 1967 Ernest Callenbach
The Films of the Sixties pages 173-174 (1980, Citadel) Douglas Brode
The 500 Best American Films to Buy, Rent Or Videotape page 337 (1985, Pocket)
Goal Dust pages 225-231 (1990, Madison) Woody Strode and Sam Young
The Great Western Pictures pages 275-277 (1976, Scarecrow) James Robert Parish and Michael R. Pitts
The Motion Picture Guide N-R page 2476 (1985, Cinebooks) Jay Robert Nash and Stanley Ralph Ross
A Mule for the Marquesa (1964, Pocket) Frank O'Rourke Novel upon which the screenplay is based
New Republic page 34 December 10, 1966 Pauline Kael
New York Times November 3, 1966 Bosley Crowther
New York Times November 13, 1966 Bosley Crowther
New Yorker page 199 November 5, 1966 Brendan Gill
Newsweek page 110 November 7, 1966 Joseph Morgenstern
Oscar A to Z pages 680-681 (1995, Doubleday) Charles Matthews

The Overlook Western Encyclopedia page 298 (1994, Overlook) Phil Hardy
The Private Eye, the Cowboy & the Very Naked Girl pages 200-203 (1968, Holt, Rinehart and Winston) Judith Crist
Retakes page 271 (1989, Ballantine) John Eastman
Saturday Review 49: page 74 December 3, 1966 Arthur Knight
Screen World 1967 Annual pages 104-105 (1968, Crown) John Willis

The Dirty Dozen (1967)

America pages 22-23 July 1, 1967 Moira Walsh
Chicago Reader Internet Archive Review (1997) Dave Kehr
The Dirty Dozen (1965, Random House) E. M. Nathanson
Film Quarterly page 58 Fall, 1967 Dennis Hunt
Film Quarterly pages 36-41 Winter, 1967 Stephen Farber
Film 67/68 pages 131-133 (1968, Simon & Schuster) Richard Schickel
Films and Career of Robert Aldrich pages 123-132 (1986, University of Tennessee) Edwin T. Arnold and Eugene L. Miller, Jr.
The Films of the Sixties pages 208-211 (1980, Citadel) Douglas Brode
Guide for the Film Fanatic page 124 (1986, Fireside) Danny Peary
The Motion Picture Guide C–D page 662 (1985, Cinebooks) Jay Robert Nash and Stanley Ralph Ross
The Movie List Book page 116 (1994, Better Way) Richard B. Armstrong and Mary Willems Armstrong
New York Times June 16, 1967 Bosley Crowther
New York Times July 9, 1967 Bosley Crowther
New York Times September 3, 1967 Robert Windeler
New Yorker pages 70, 73 July 22, 1967 Penelope Gilliatt
Newsweek page 78 July 3, 1967 Paul D. Zimmerman
Oscar A to Z page 227 (1995, Doubleday) Charles Matthews
Out of Bounds pages 212-216 (1989, Zebra) Jim Brown with Steve Delsohn
The Private Eye, the Cowboy & the Very Naked Girl pages 250-253 (1968, Holt, Rinehart and Winston) Judith Crist
Retakes pages 88-89 (1989, Ballantine) John Eastman
Saturday Review page 47 June 17, 1967 Arthur Knight
Screen World 1968 Annual pages 56-57 (1969, Crown) John Willis
Time page 70 June 30, 1967
War Movies pages 78-79 (1987, Facts On File) Brock Garland
What Ever Happened to Robert Aldrich? pages 26-27, 125-132 (1995, Limelight) Alain Silver and James Ursini
The World War II Combat Film pages 205-209 (1986, Columbia University) Jeanine Basinger

Point Blank (1967)

Chicago Reader Internet Archive Review (1997) Jonathan Rosenbaum
Chicago Tribune Friday Section page K February 7, 1997 Michael Wilmington
Commonweal page 24 October 6, 1967 Philip T. Hartung
Fatal Woman pages 95-107 (1996, Fairleigh Dickinson University) James F. Maxfield
Film Comment pages 13-17 July/Aug. 1981 David Thomson
Film Noir page 289 (1995, McFarland) Michael L. Stephens
Film Quarterly page 63 Winter, 1967/1968 Dan Bates
Film Quarterly pages 2-13 Summer, 1968 Stephen Farber
Film Quarterly pages 2-14 Winter, 1968/1969 Stephen Farber
The Great Gangster Pictures pages 314-315 (1976, Scarecrow) James Robert Parish and Michael R. Pitts
Guide for the Film Fanatic page 335 (1986, Fireside) Danny Peary
John Boorman pages 60-79 (1986) Michael Ciment
Los Angeles Times June 2, 1996 Steven Smith
The Motion Picture Guide N–R pages 2424-2425 (1985, Cinebooks) Jay Robert Nash and Stanley Ralph Ross
Newsweek page 107 September 25, 1967 Howard Junker
New Yorker pages 112, 114 September 30, 1967 Brendan Gill
Saturday Review page 36 September 30, 1967 Hollis Alpert
Screen World 1968 Annual page 76 (1969, Crown) John Willis
Second Sight pages 145-148 (1972, Simon and Schuster) Richard Schickel
Sight and Sound pages 14-17, Cover June, 1998 David Thomson
Stardom pages 345-346 (1970, Stein and Day) Alexander Walker

Sergeant Ryker (1968)
(Filmed in 1963)

Are You Anybody? pages 70-71 (1997, Fithian) Bradford Dillman
Harry & Wally's Favorite TV Shows page 106 (1989,

Prentice Hall) Harry Castleman and Walter J. Podrazik
The Motion Picture Guide S page 2826 (1985, Cinebooks) Jay Robert Nash and Stanley Ralph Ross
The Movie List Book page 102 (1994, Better Way) Richard B. Armstrong & Mary Willems Armstrong
New York Times March 21, 1968 Howard Thompson
Screen World 1969 Annual page 12 (1970, Crown) John Willis
Variety Television Reviews 1963-1965 October 16, 1963 (1989, Garland) Bill.
War Movies page 180 (1987, Facts on File) Brock Garland

Hell in the Pacific (1968)

America page 288 March 8, 1969 Vincent P. McCorry
Chicago Reader Internet Archive Review (1997) Jonathan Rosenbaum
Commonweal pages 707-708 March 7, 1969 Philip T. Hartung
Film Quarterly pages 52-56 Summer, 1969 Stephen Farber
John Boorman pages 80-93 (1986) Michel Ciment
The Motion Picture Guide H-K pages 1191-1192 (1985, Cinebooks) Jay Robert Nash and Stanley Ralph Ross
New York Times February 11, 1969 A. H. Weiler
New Yorker page 74 March 1, 1969 Pauline Kael
Newsweek page 98 February 25, 1969 Paul D. Zimmerman
Saturday Review page 48 December 14, 1968 Arthur Knight
Screen World 1969 Annual page 75 (1970, Crown) John Willis
Time page 87 February 21, 1969
War Movies pages 114-115 (1987, Facts on File) Brock Garland

Paint Your Wagon (1969)

America pages 474-475 November 15, 1969
Clint Eastwood pages 67-70 (1986, St. Martin's) Francois Guerif
Clint Eastwood pages 211-223 (1996, Knopf) Richard Schickel
Deeper Into Movies pages 33-39 (1973, Bantam) Pauline Kael
The Great Western Pictures pages 255-257 (1976, Scarecrow) James Robert Parish and Michael R. Pitts
The Hollywood Hall of Shame pages 154-160 (1984, Perigee) Harry and Michael Medved
The Hollywood Musical page 394 (1981, Crown) Clive Hirschhorn

The Motion Picture Guide N-R page 2323 (1985, Cinebooks) Jay Robert Nash and Stanley Ralph Ross
Movie Stars, Real People and Me pages 211-225 (1978, Delacorte) Joshua Logan
New York Times October 16, 1969 Vincent Canby
New York Times October 26, 1969 Vincent Canby
Newsweek pages 124-125 October 27, 1969 Joseph Morgenstern
Oscar A to Z pages 632-633 (1995, Doubleday) Charles Matthews
The Overlook Western Encyclopedia page 315 (1994, Overlook) Phil Hardy
Played Out: The Jean Seberg Story pages 175-193 (1981, Playboy) David Richards
Screen World 1970 Annual pages 78-79 (1971, Crown) John Willis
The Worst Movies of All Time pages 126-129 (1996, Citadel) Michael Sauter

Monte Walsh (1970)

The BFI Companion to the Western page 286 (1988, Da Capo) Edited by Edward Buscombe
Deeper Into Movies pages 204-205 (1973, Bantam) Pauline Kael
Guide for the Film Fanatic pages 279-280 (1986, Fireside) Danny Peary
Moreau pages 125-126 (1994, Donald I. Fine) Marianne Gray
The Motion Picture Guide L-M page 2017 (1985, Cinebooks) Jay Robert Nash and Stanley Ralph Ross
New York Times October 8, 1970 Vincent Canby
The Overlook Western Encyclopedia pages 326-327 (1994, Overlook) Phil Hardy
What Ever Happened to Robert Aldrich? page 336 (1995, Limelight) Alain Silver and James Ursini

Pocket Money (1972)

Film Facts pages 172-174
The Films of Paul Newman pages 197-200 (1971, Citadel) Lawrence J. Quirk
The Motion Picture Guide N-R page 2423 (1985, Cinebooks) Jay Robert Nash and Stanley Ralph Ross
New York Times April 20, 1972 Vincent Canby
The Overlook Western Encyclopedia page 340 (1994, Overlook) Phil Hardy
Paul and Joanne pages 171-172 (1988, Delacorte) Joe Morella and Edward Z. Epstein
Paul Newman pages 215-216 (1996, Taylor) Lawrence J. Quirk
Screen World 1973 Annual page 13 (1974, Crown) John Willis

Vogue pages 146-147, 196 April 1, 1971 Candice Bergen

Prime Cut (1972)
(aka *Kansas City Prime*)

Film Facts 15:13 pages 292-294
Gangster Movies page 17 (1974, Octopus) Harry Hossent
Gene Hackman pages 79-80 (1988, St. Martin's) Allan Hunter
Gene Hackman pages 55-57 (1997, Robert Hale) Michael Munn
The Great Gangster Pictures page 318 (1976, Scarecrow) James Robert Parish and Michael R. Pitts
Life page 16 June 23, 1972 Richard Schickel
Minneapolis Star page 14A June 30, 1972 Don Morrison
The Motion Picture Guide N–R page 2455 (1985, Cinebooks) Jay Robert Nash and Stanley Ralph Ross
New York Times June 29, 1972 Vincent Canby
New York Times July 9, 1972 Vincent Canby
Opening Shots pages 332-336 (1994, Workman) Damien Bona
Roger Ebert's Video Companion 1998 Edition pages 648-649 (1997, Andrews McMeel) Roger Ebert
Screen World 1973 Annual page 52 (1974, Crown) John Willis
Time page 41 July 31, 1972 J. C.

Emperor of the North (1973)
(aka *Emperor of the North Pole*)

Bloody Sam pages 222-223 (1991, Donald I. Fine) Marshall Fine
Chicago Reader Internet Archive Review (1997) Don Druker
The Films and Career of Robert Aldrich pages 174-180 (1986, University of Tennessee) Edwin T. Arnold and Eugene L. Miller
Guide for the Film Fanatic pages 138-139 (1986, Fireside) Danny Peary
The Motion Picture Guide E–G page 761 (1985, Cinebooks) Jay Robert Nash and Stanley Ralph Ross
New York Times May 25, 1973 Vincent Canby
New York Times June 3, 1973 Vincent Canby
Peckinpah pages 154-155 (1982, University of Texas) Garner Simmons
Screen World 1974 Annual page 31 (1975, Crown) John Willis
What Ever Happened to Robert Aldrich? pages 35-36, 101-105 (1995, Limelight) Alain Silver and James Ursini

The Iceman Cometh (1973)

Are You Anybody? page 194 (1997, Fithian) Bradford Dillman
John Frankenheimer: A Conversation pages 132-135 (1995, Riverwood) Charles Champlin
Los Angeles Times August 21, 1997 Susan King
The Motion Picture Guide H–K page 1352 (1985, Cinebooks) Jay Robert Nash and Stanley Ralph Ross
New York Times October 30, 1973 Nora Sayre
Reeling pages 270-277 (1977, Warner) Pauline Kael
Screen World 1974 Annual pages 76-77 (1975, Crown) Nash/Ross
Tough Guys page 583 (1976, Arlington House) James Robert Parish

The Spikes Gang (1974)

The Motion Picture Guide S page 3067 (1985, Cinebooks) Jay Robert Nash and Stanley Ralph Ross
New Statesman pages 811-812 June 7, 1974 John Coleman
New York Times May 2, 1974 Vincent Canby
The Overlook Western Encyclopedia page 346 (1994, Overlook) Phil Hardy
Screen World 1975 Annual page 106 (1976, Crown) John Willis

The Klansman (1974)
(aka *The Burning Cross and KKK*)

Ebony pages 148-150, 152, 154 December, 1974
The Motion Picture Guide H–K page 1554 (1985, Cinebooks) Jay Robert Nash and Stanley Ralph Ross
Movieline October, 1996 page 78 Edward Margulies
New York Times November 21, 1974 Vincent Canby
Screen World 1975 Annual page 79 (1976, Crown) John Willis

Shout at the Devil (1976)

The Motion Picture Guide S page 2902 (1985, Cinebooks) Jay Robert Nash and Stanley Ralph Ross
New Statesman page 517 April 16, 1976 John Coleman
New York Times November 25, 1976 Richard Eder
Screen World 1977 Annual page 197 (1978, Crown) John Willis
Shout at the Devil (1968, Dell) Wilbur Smith

The Great Scout and Cathouse Thursday (1976) (aka *Wildcat*)

The Motion Picture Guide E–G page 1103 (1985, Cinebooks) Jay Robert Nash and Stanley Ralph Ross
New York Times June 24, 1976 Richard Eder
The Overlook Western Encyclopedia page 349 (1994, Overlook) Phil Hardy
Screen World 1977 Annual page 139 (1978, Crown) John Willis

The Meanest Men in the West (1976)

No sources found

Avalanche Express (1979)

Avalanche Express (1977, Pan) Colin Forbes
Chicago Reader Internet Archive Review (1997) Jonathan Rosenbaum
The Motion Picture Guide A–B pages 110-111 (1985, Cinebooks) Jay Robert Nash and Stanley Ralph Ross
New York Times October 19, 1979 Vincent Canby
New York Times October 28, 1979 Vincent Canby
Screen World 1980 Annual page 79 (1981, Crown) John Willis

The Big Red One (1980)

American Film pages 20-24, 47, Cover June, 1979 Bruce Cook
Chicago Reader Internet Archive Review (1997) Jonathan Rosenbaum
Film Comment pages 25-31 January/February, 1977 Richard Thompson
The Films of the Eighties pages 44-46 (1990, Citadel) Douglas Brode
The Great War Films pages 229-230 (1994, Citadel) Lawrence J. Quirk
Guide for the Film Fanatic pages 52-53 (1986, Fireside) Danny Peary
The Motion Picture Guide A–B page 199 (1985, Cinebooks) Jay Robert Nash and Stanley Ralph Ross
New Statesman page 30 October 3, 1980 John Coleman
New York Times July 18, 1980 Vincent Canby
People pages 18-19 August 11, 1980
Roger Ebert's Video Companion 1998 Edition pages 64-65 (1997, Andrews McMeel) Roger Ebert

War Movies page 42 (1987, Facts on File) Brock Garland
The World War II Combat Film pages 216-219 (1986, Columbia University) Jeanine Basinger

Death Hunt (1981)

The Motion Picture Guide C–D page 602 (1985, Cinebooks) Jay Robert Nash and Stanley Ralph Ross
New York Times May 22, 1981 Vincent Canby
Overlook Western Encyclopedia page 361 (1994, Overlook) Phil Hardy
People page 25 June 22, 1981
Screen World 1982 Annual page 33 (1983, Crown) John Willis
What Ever Happened to Robert Aldrich? pages 45-46 (1995, Limelight) Alain Silver and James Ursini

Gorky Park (1983)

Chicago Reader Internet Archive Review (1997) Dave Kehr
Film Comment pages 29-32 January/February, 1984 Dan Yakir
Gorky Park (1981, Ballantine) Martin Cruz Smith
The Motion Picture Guide E–G pages 1078-1079 (1985, Cinebooks) Jay Robert Nash and Stanley Ralph Ross
New Statesman pages 26-27 January 6, 1984 John Coleman
New York Times December 16, 1983 Janet Maslin
People page 18 December 19, 1983
People pages 72-74 January 30, 1984 Fred Bernstein
Playboy August 1983 page 27 Bruce Williamson
Roger Ebert's Video Companion, 1998 Edition pages 323-324 (1997, Andrews McMeel) Roger Ebert
Screen World 1984 Annual page 90 (1985, Crown) John Willis
William Hurt pages 109-121 (1987, St. Martin's) Toby Goldstein

Dog Day (1984) (aka *Canicule*)

Internet Movie Database
The Motion Picture Guide W–Z 1984 Annual Section page 4032 (1985, Cinebooks) Jay Robert Nash and Stanley Ralph Ross

The Dirty Dozen: Next Mission (1985, TV Movie)

No sources found

The Delta Force (1986)

Chicago Tribune pages 2, 21 February 23, 1986 Kirk Honeycutt
The Motion Picture Guide 1987 Annual pages 67-68 (1988, Cinebooks) Jay Robert Nash and Stanley Ralph Ross
New York Times February 14, 1986 Vincent Canby
New York Times February 23, 1986 Vincent Canby
People page 13 March 17, 1986 David Hiltbrand
Roger Ebert's Video Companion, 1998 Edition page 211 (1997, Andrews McMeel) Roger Ebert
War Movies pages 74-75 (1987, Facts On File) Brock Garland

Documentaries, Short Films and Stage Plays

Internet Movie Database
Lee, a Romance (1998, Faber and Faber) Pamela Marvin
New York Times September 27, 1967 Bosley Crowther Review of *Tonite, Let's All Make Love in London*
People page 15 March 10, 1986 Jeff Jarvis Review of *The Spencer Tracy Legacy: A Tribute by Katharine Hepburn*
People pages 92-94, 97-98 March 17, 1986 Christopher P. Andersen Article on *The Spencer Tracy Legacy: A Tribute by Katharine Hepburn*

M Squad (1957-1960)

The Complete Directory to Prime Time Network and Cable TV Shows (1995, Ballantine) Tim Brooks and Earle Marsh
Harry and Wally's Favorite TV Shows page 305 (1989, Prentice Hall) Harry Castleman and Walter J. Podrazik
Total Television page 458 (1996, Penguin) Alex McNeil
TV Detectives pages 42-43 (1981, A. S. Barnes) Richard Meyers
TV Guide pages 17-19 February 7-13, 1959
TV Guide October 3-9, 1959

Lawbreaker (1963-1964)

The Complete Directory to Prime Time Network and Cable TV Shows (1995, Ballantine) Tim Brooks and Earle Marsh
Harry and Wally's Favorite TV Shows page 282 (1989, Prentice Hall) Harry Castleman and Walter J. Podrazik

Total Television (1996, Penguin) Alex McNeil
TV Guide page 20 September 14-20, 1963

Other Television Episodes

Bloody Sam pages 51-54, 77, 85 (1991, Donald I. Fine) Marshall Fine
The Complete Directory to Prime Time Network and Cable TV Shows (1995, Ballantine) Tim Brooks and Earle Marsh
Film Quarterly pages 3-9 Winter 1963/1964 Ernest Callenbach
Harry & Wally's Favorite TV Shows pages 106, 282, 305, 544-545 (1989, Prentice Hall) Harry Castleman and Walter J. Podrazik
Television Specials (1995, McFarland) Vincent Terrace
Total Television (1996, Penguin) Alex McNeil
TV Facts page 180 (1982, Vintage) Cobbett Steinberg
TV Guide
The Twilight Zone Companion pages 219, 220, 380-382 (1992, Silman-James) Marc Scott Zicree
Unsold TV Pilots page 131 (1991, Citadel) Lee Goldberg
Variety Presents: The Complete Book of Major U.S. Show Business Awards page 111 (1985, Garland)

Miscellaneous Marvin

All-Movie Guide (Internet)
The BFI Companion to the Western page 368 (1988, Da Capo) Edited by Edward Buscombe
Close-Ups pages 406-407 (1978, Workman) John Boorman
Current Biography 1966 Edition pages 265-267 (1967)
Esquire pages 148-149, 220 November, 1970 Roger Ebert
The Film Encyclopedia page 909 (1994, Harper Collins) Ephraim Katz
Gangster Movies page 65 (1974, Octopus) Harry Hossent
The Great Movie Stars: The International Years pages 355-358 (1995, Little, Brown) David Shipman
Hollywood's First Choices page 218 (1994, Crown) Jeff Burkhart and Bruce Stuart
The Illustrated Encyclopedia of the World's Great Movie Stars pages 201-202 (1979, Harmony) Ken Wlaschin
The International Directory of Films & Filmmakers (Actors & Actresses) pages 636-637 Joanne Abrams
Internet Movie Database
John Boorman page 233 (1986) Lee Marvin
John Frankenheimer: A Conversation page 23 (1995, Riverwood) Charles Champlin
Lee, a Romance (1998, Faber and Faber) Pamela Marvin

218 Bibliography

Leonard Maltin's Movie and Video Guide (1994, Signet) Leonard Maltin
Los Angeles Times February 21, 1995 Jim Washburn
Marvin (1980, St. Martin's) Donald Zec
Motor Boating and Sailing pages 72-75, 108, 110, 112 May, 1977 Roger Vaughan
Movie Stars pages 178-186 (1970) Roger Ebert
New York 13 pages 48, 50-52 Lewis Grossberger
New York Times May 23, 1965 Howard Thompson
New York Times September 24, 1967 Bosley Crowther
New York Times December 15, 1968 Roger Ebert
New York Times October 20, 1970 Reuters
Peckinpah pages 56-57, 84 (1982, University of Texas) Garner Simmons
People pages 65-66 October 13, 1980 Karen G. Jackovich
Playboy pages 59-60, 64, 66, 68, 70, 72, 74, 76, 78 January 1969 Richard Warren Lewis
The Private Eye, The Cowboy & the Very Naked Girl pages 145-147 (1968, Holt, Rinehart and Winston) Judith Crist
Projections pages 9-14 (1992, Faber and Faber) John Boorman
Projections 4 1/2 pages 23-27 (1995, Faber and Faber) John Boorman
Rating the Movie Stars pages 254-255 (1983, Beekman House) Joel Hirschhorn
Redbook pages 74-75, 125-126 November, 1967 Lee Marvin and Johnny Carson
Rolling Stone September 3, 1981 pages 29-32, 62 Robert Ward
Saturday Evening Post pages 76-79 August 14, 1965
Time page 58 June 4, 1965
Vogue pages 146-147+ October 1, 1971
What Ever Happened to Robert Aldrich? page 338 (1995, Limelight) Alain Silver and James Ursini
The World War II Combat Film page 343, note 18 (1986, Columbia University) Jeanine Basinger

The Palimony Case

Esquire pages 16, 18 May 9, 1978 Steven Brill
Ladies Home Journal pages 78-85 October, 1973 Ronnie Cowan
Macleans pages 25-26 April 30, 1979 William Lowther
New York pages 48, 50-52 August 25, 1980 Lewis Grossberger
New York pages 34-41 January 10, 1983 Patricia Morrisroe
New York Times July 26, 1973 AP
New York Times December 28, 1976 AP
New York Times February 12, 1977 Albin Krebs
New York Times January 9, 1979
New York Times January 13, 1979 UPI
New York Times January 31, 1979
New York Times February 21, 1979 AP
New York Times February 22, 1979 Sue Mittenthal
New York Times February 25, 1979
New York Times March 11, 1979
New York Times March 16, 1979 AP
New York Times April 1, 1979
New York Times April 19, 1979 Robert Lindsey
New York Times April 19, 1979
New York Times April 20, 1979 Lawrence Van Gelder
New York Times April 22, 1979 AP
New York Times July 20, 1979
New York Times August 6, 1980
New York Times August 13, 1981
New York Times August 15, 1981 Alvin Krebs and Robert McG. Thomas, Jr.
New York Times October 9, 1981 AP
Newsweek page 70 April 30, 1979 Jerrold K. Footlick with Martin Kasindorf
Newsweek pages 14, 19 October 8, 1979 Eileen Keerdoja with Jeff B. Copeland
People pages 85-88 May 7, 1979
Time page 24 March 5, 1979
Time page 25 April 30, 1979
Time page 57 May 7, 1979

Obituaries

New York Times August 30, 1987 Dennis Hevesi
Newsweek page 75 September 7, 1987
People page 42 September 14, 1987 Brad Darrach
Screen World 1988 Annual page 239 (1989, Crown) John Willis
Time page 64 September 7, 1987

Index

Entries in SMALL CAPS *are Lee Marvin films; numbers in* **bold** *represent photographs*

Abbott, Bud **197**
ABC television network 101, 122
Abrahams, Jim (director) 185
Acker, Sharon 116, **117**, 118
The Adventures of Robin Hood (1938) 86
An Affair to Remember (1957) 2, 113
Airport (1970) 178
Akins, Claude 45, 48, 95, 97
Albert, Eddie 4, 5, **70**, 71, 72, 74
Albert, Edward 195
Alcoa Premiere (television show) 70, 72, 73, 112, 115, 137, 139, 166, 198
Aldrich, Robert (director) 167
Alfie (1966) 108
Allen, Elizabeth 92, 94, 95
Allen, Fred 12
Allen, Mark 199
Alpert, Hollis (*Saturday Review* critic) 40
America magazine, review quotes 62
American International Pictures studios 131, 151, 154, 155
The Americans (television show) 196
America's Most Wanted (television show) 193
Anderson, James 14
Andes, Keith 75, 76
Andrews, Julie 1
Angeli, Pier 6, 7
Ankrum, Morris 185
Annual top ten box office stars list 1, 18, 110, 115
Ansara, Michael 11, 75, 76, 85
Apted, Michael (director) 169
Arctic Rampage (*Death Hunt*) 166
Arlington National Cemetery, Arlington, Virginia 179
Armstrong, Whitney 199
Arthur, Robert Alan (writer) 182
Ashley, Elizabeth 104, 105, 152, 153
ATTACK (1956) 69, **70**, 71, 72, **73**, 74
Attack, Department of Defense controversy 71, 72, 74
Audran, Stephanie 160
Austin, Charlotte 40
Avalanche Express (Colin Forbes novel) 159
AVALANCHE EXPRESS (1979) 156, 157, **158**, 159

The Bad and the Beautiful (1952) 36
Bad Company (1972) 145
BAD DAY AT BLACK ROCK (1955) 7, 48, **49**, 50, **51**, 52, 67, 181
Bad Day at Black Rock, Academy Award nominations 52
Baldwin, Janit 134
Balin, Ina 84
Balsam, Martin 178
Bancroft, Anne 40, 41, 47, 48, 58, 59
The Bank Robber (Giles Tippette novel) 143
Bannen, Ian **168**, 170
Barcroft, Roy 131
Barry, Donald 67, **68**
Basie, Count (composer/musician) 185
The Bastard Sons of Lee (organization) 2
Beckman, Henry 165
Bedoya, Alfonso 27
The Beetles 37, 39
Begley, Ed 5
Belford, Christine 133
Bellamy, Ralph 107
Ben Casey (television show) 199
Bennent, David 171
Berlin Film Festival Best Actor award (1965) 101
Best, James 22, 48
Bevans, Clem 17, 18
Bickford, Charles 56, 58
THE BIG HEAT (1953) 32, 33, **34**, **35**, 36, 67, 109
The Big Knife (1955) 72
THE BIG RED ONE (1980) 168
The Big Sleep (1946) 36
The Big Valley (television show) 182
Binder, Maurice (titles designer) 154
Binns, Edward 7
Biroc, Joseph (cinematographer) 139
Bishop, Joey 178
Bissell, Whit 65
Blow-Up (1966) 108
Blue, Monte 18
The Bob Hope Chrysler Theatre (television show) 202
Bochner, Lloyd 116, 118
Boetticher, Budd (director) 68, 69

219

Bogart, Humphrey 5, 42, 44, 45, 62, 64
Bombs Over China (Hong Kong) 8
Bonanza (television show) 182, 199
Bond, Ward 75, 76, 198
Bonnie and Clyde (1967) 114
Book of the Month Club 104
Booke, Sorrell 139
Boone, Richard 47, 48, 195, 196
Boorman, John (director) 97, 116, 118, 119, 122, 123, 124, 136, 181
Borgnine, Ernest 26, 27, 49, **51**, 52, 53, 111, 114, 137, 138, 172, 175
Bouchey, Willis 33, **34**, 75
Boxoffice magazine, review quotes 6, 142
Bracken, Eddie 12
Brando, Jocelyn 33
Brando, Marlon 37, **38**, 39, 40, 45, 78, 141
Brennan, Walter 49, 50, 52
Bridges, Jeff 139, 140
British Academy Award Best Actor award (1965) 101
Brode, Douglas (writer) 72
Broderick, Malcolm 195
Bronson, Charles 2, 4, 5, 11, 111, 113, 114, 149, **150**, 151, 165, 166, 185
Brooks, Hildy 140, **142**
Brooks, Norman (writer) 71
Brooks, Richard (writer/director) 108, 109, 110, 128
Brown, Jim 2, 111, 113
Bryan, William Jennings (politician) 153
Buchholz, Horst 159
Buchinski, Charles (aka Charles Bronson) 5, 11
Burnett, W.R. (writer) 64
Burr, Raymond 40, 41
Burress, John (writer) 82
Burton, Richard 101, 146, 148, 170
Burton, Robert 33, **34**
Bush, Billy Green 131
Butch Cassidy and the Sundance Kid (1969) 124

Caan, James 199
Cabot, Sebastian 198
Cabot, Susan 15
Cady, Frank 82
Caine, Michael 180
THE CAINE MUTINY (1954) 40, 42, 43, **44**, 45, 50, 56, 121, 165
The Caine Mutiny, Academy Award nominations 45; Pulitzer Prize for Fiction (1952) 42, 44
The Caine Mutiny Court Martial (1954 play) 45
Calhern, Louis 12
Callan, Michael 98, 100, **103**
Callenbach, Ernest (writer) 94
Camelot (1967) 127
Canby, Vincent (*N.Y. Times* critic) 131, 136, 159, 159
The Candidate (1972) 136
Canicule (*Dog Day*) 170, 172
Captain Blood (1935) 86

Cardinale, Claudia 107, 109
Carey, Phil 30, **31**, 32
Carlson, Richard 21, **22**, 23
Carmet, Jean 171
Carradine, John 88
Carradine, Keith 137, 138
Carradine, Robert 160, **161**, 163
Carter, Benny (composer/musician) 185
Casablanca (1943) 86
The Case Against Paul Ryker (television show) 119, 122
The Cassandra Crossing (1977) 157
Cassavetes, John 95, 97, 111, 112, 114, 115
Cassinelli, Claudio 159
Castle, Mary 20
CAT BALLOU (1965) 1, 13, 92, 98, **99**, 100, 101, **102**, **103**, 106, 107, 110, 143, 151, 156
Cat Ballou, Academy Award nominations 1, 98, 100, 101, 103, 106
Cat Ballou (television pilot) 101
Cathcart, Dick (musician) 61
Catholic World magazine, review quotes 20, 40
Catus, Gary 146
Center Stage (television show) 194
Champlin, Charles (*L.A. Times* critic) 143
Chandler, Jeff 74, **75**, 76, 84
Chaney, Lon, Jr. 62
Chang, Danny 8
Chaplin, Charlie 132
Chaplin, Sydney 76
The Charge at Feather River (1953) 26
Chayefsky, Paddy (writer) 52, 127, 182
Checkmate (television show) 198
Chicago Reader, review quotes 169
Christie, Julie 180
Christmas, Eric 130
Citizen Kane (1941) 92
Clark, Dane 195
Clark, Matt 130, 131
Clarke, Gary 149
Clift, Montgomery 80, **81**, 84
Climax (television show) 195, 196
Cobb, Lee J. 40, 41, 149, 199
Coburn, James 185
Cocks, Jay (*Time* critic) 136
Cole, Nat King 98, 100
Colleano, Bonar 19
Collier's magazine, review quotes 52
Collinge, Patrica 6
Collins, Ray 4, 5
Collins, Russell 52
Colon, Miriam 149
Colorado Territory (1949) 62
Columbia studios 45, 69, 102
THE COMANCHEROS (1961) 84, **85**, 86, **87**, 88
The Comancheros (Paul I. Wellman novel) 86
Combat (television show) 201
Combat Leadership: The Ultimate Challenge (1986) (U.S. Marine Corps film) 179

Commonweal magazine, review quotes 32, 48
Connery, Sean 1
Connors, Mike 157, **158**, 159
Conrad, Michael 149
Cool Hand Luke (1967) 114, 124
Cooper, Gary 3, 5, 76
Cooper, George 19
Corcoran, Donna 53
Corcoran, Kevin 53
Corcoran, Noreen 53
Corey, Wendell 77, 78, 79
Costner, Kevin 74
Counterpoint (television show) 194
Court Martial (television show) 122, 201
Craven award (for smokey in *Cat Ballou*) 101
Crawford, Broderick **57**, 58
Crist, Judith (critic) 100
Crosby, Bing 25
Crossfire (1947) 52
Crowther, Bosley (*N.Y. Times* critic) 6, 11, 39, 45, 55, 59, 87, 115
Cue magazine, review quotes 17, 129
Culp, Robert 152, 153
Curtiz, Michael (director) 86
The Cyclist's Raid (Frank Rooney short story) 36

Dahl, Roald (writer) 182
Dances with Wolves (1990) 74
Daniell, Henry 85
Dave Kehr (*Chicago Reader* critic) 169
Davis, Jim 130, 131
Dawson, Nancy Juno 140, **142**
Day, John 22
Dead Man (1997) 2
DEATH HUNT (1981) 148, 164, 165, **166**, 167
The Defenders (television show) 198
DeHaven, Gloria 25
de Havilland, Olivia 56, 58
Deliverance (1972) 116
THE DELTA FORCE (1986) 165, 175, 176, **177**, 178, 179
The Delta Force II (1990) 178
de Naut, Jud (musician) 61
Dennehy, Brian 168, 170
Denning, Richard 17
Denny, Reginald 98
De Palma, Brian (director) 118
Desilu Playhouse (television show) 196
The Devil's Brigade (1968) 110
Devine, Andy 88, 90
de Wilde, Brandon 82, **83**, 84
DiCicco, Bobby 160, **161**
Dick Powell Theatre (television show) 198, 201
Dickinson, Angie 96, 97, 116, 118, 165, 166
Dierkes, John 48
Dillman, Bradford **120**, 121, 122, 139, 142, 143, 201
DIPLOMATIC COURIER (1952) 9, **10**, 11
THE DIRTY DOZEN (1967) 1, 2, 74, 97, 107, 109, **110**, 111, **112**, 113, 114, **115**, 116, 119, 122, 172, 174, 175, 180
DIRTY DOZEN: THE NEXT MISSION (1985, TV Movie) 172, **173**, 174, 175
The Dirty Dozen (Academy Award nominations) 112, 115
The Dirty Dozen (comic book) **115**
The Dirty Dozen (*Eight Iron Men*) 21
The Dirty Dozen (Made for television sequels) 110, 172, 175
Dirty Harry (1971) 127
Divorce American Style (1967) 119
Dmytryk, Edward (director) 45
The Doctor (television show) 194
Dr. Kildare (television show) 199, 201
DOG DAY (1984) 170, 171, 172
Domergue, Faith 14, 16
DONOVAN'S REEF (1963) 86, 88, 92, **93**, 94, 95
Douglas, Kirk 98, 101
Douglas, Paul 12
DOWN AMONG THE SHELTERING PALMS (1953) 23, 24, 25
Dragnet (television show) 61, 182, 183, 185, 194
Dru, Joanne 196
Drury, James 149, 199
THE DUEL AT SILVER CREEK (1952) 14, **15**, 16
Dunn, Michael 104, 105, **106**
DuPont Show of the Month (television show) 199
Dykstra, John (models/special effects designer) 157

East of Eden (1955) 61
Eastwood, Clint 1, 2, 109, 125, 127, 128, 129, 171
Easy Chair Theatre (television show) 194
Easy Rider (1969) 40
Ebsen, Buddy 71, 72
Eder, Richard (*N.Y. Times* critic) 156
Edwards, Blake (writer/director) 182
Egan, Eddie 134
Egan Richard 53, 55
EIGHT IRON MEN (1952) 19, **20**, 21, 132
El Dorado (1967) 86
Elam, Jack 101
Ellison, Clint 134
Elphick, Michael 168, 170
EMPROR OF THE NORTH (1973) 136, 137, **138**, 139
Emperor of the North Pole (*Emperor of the North*) 138, 139
The End of the Trail (James Earle Fraser statue) 101
The Enemy (*Hell in the Pacific*) 122
Erdman, Richard 4
Ericson, John 6, 7, 50, 52
Evans, Evans 139
Evans, Linda 146, 157, **158**, 159

Fadiman, Clifton (writer) 104
Fairbanks, Douglas 132
Falana, Lola 146
Falk, Peter 198

Farnsworth, Richard 131
Fatool, Nick (musician) 61
Faylen, Frank 17, 18
Fell, Norman 95, 97, 120, 121, 122
Ferror, Jose 43, **44**, 104, 105
Film Quarterly magazine, review quotes 94
The Films of Ronald Reagan (Lawrence J. Quirk book) 8
Fireside Theater (television show) 195
First Artists production company 132, 134
First Infantry Division (*The Big Red One*) 160, 164
Fitzgerald, Ella 61
Fixed Bayonets (1951) 162
Flaming Feather (1952) 8
Fleet, Jo Van 61
Fleming, Rhonda 8
Flippen, Jay C. 38, 99
Fonda, Jane 98, 100, 102, **103**
Foote, Horton (writer) 182
Foran, Dick 94
Forbes, Colin (writer) 159
Forbidden Planet (1956) 64
Ford, Glenn 33, **34**, 35, 36
Ford, John (director) 68, 76, 88, 89, 92, 94, 95
Ford, Paul 82, 84
Forster, Robert 177
Fragile Fox (Norman Brooks play) 71, 72
Fraker, William A. (director) 130
Francis, Anne 50, 52, 77
Francis, Robert 42, 44
Frankenheimer, John (director) 139, 140, 141, 143, 195, 196
Franz, Arthur 20
Fraser, James Earle (artist) 101
Fregonese, Hugo (director) 48
From Here to Eternity (1953) 18, 32, 45, 50
Front Row Center (television show) 195
Frontier Fury (Will Henry novel) 76
Fuller, Samuel (director) 148, 160, 162, 163, 164, 180, 199

G.E. Theater (television show) 194, 195, 196, 198
Gabor, Zsa Zsa 12
Garfield, John 5
Garner, Peggy Ann 7
Gaynor, Mitzi 12, 25
Gehring, Ted 131
Gentleman Jim (1942) 31
Gilbert, Billy 25
Glen, John (editor/director) 154
THE GLORY BRIGADE (1953) 28, **29**, 30, 77
The Godfather (1972) 134, 135
Godzilla (1954) 41
Golden Globe Best Actor award (1965) 101
Goldstein, Leonard (producer) 58
Gomez, Maria 107
Gone with the Wind (1939) 79, 80, 81, 82
Gonzalez Gonzalez, Pedro 64

Goodwin, Jimmy 71
Gordon, Leo 30, 32
Gordon, Rita (singer) 127
GORILLA AT LARGE (1954) 40, **41**, 42, 65, 148
GORKY PARK (1983) 1, 159, 167, **168**, 169, 170, 172, 175
Grade, Sir Lew (producer) 159
The Graduate (1967) 114, 119
Grahame, Gloria 33, **35**, 36, 56, 58
Graves, Peter **46**, 48, 120, 121, 122, 201
Graziano, Rocky (boxer) 78
The Great Adventure (television show) 201
The Great Escape (1963) 113
THE GREAT SCOUT AND CATHOUSE THURSDAY (1976) 1, 151, **152**, 153, 154, 156
Green, Dorothy 33
Green, Martyn 140
Greer, Jane 4, 5, 25
Griffith, D.W. (director) 132
Griffith, James 20
Griffiths, Richard 170
Grimes, Gary **144**, 145
Gulager, Clu 95, 97
GUN FURY (1953) 26, 30, **31**, 32
Gunn, Moses 139
Gunsmoke (television show) 182

Hackman, Gene 134, 136, 141
Hagen, Jean 199
Hailey, Arthur (writer) 182
Hale, Barbara 21, 23
Hall, Conrad (cinematographer) 108, 110, 124
Hamburger, Philip (*New Yorker* critic) 61
Hamill, Mark 160, **161**, 163
Hamilton, Murray 121, 122
HANGMAN'S KNOT (1952) 16, 17, **18**, 19, 69
Hanks, Tom 2, 113
Hardy, Phil (writer) 109
Harper's magazine 36
Hartung, Phillip T. (*Commonweal* critic) 48
Hatari! (1962) 86, 94
Hathaway, Henry 5, 6, 11
Hawks, Howard (director) 94
Hayes, Alfred (writer) 7
Hayes, Ira (Iwo Jima soldier) 196
Hayes, Margaret 53
Haynes, Robert 30, **31**, 32
Hayworth, Rita 20
Heaton, Tom 130
Hecht, Harold (producer) 101
Heflin, Van **46**, 48
HELL IN THE PACIFIC (1968) 116, 119, 122, **123**, 124, 125, 132, 143, 181
Hemingway, Ernest (writer) 95, 97
Henry, Will (writer) 76
Hepburn, Katharine 178, 180, 181
Heston, Charlton 195
Hickey, Donna Lee (aka May Wynn) 44
Hickman, Dwayne 98, 100, **103**

High Noon (1952) 36
High Sierra (1941) 31, 62
Hill, George Roy (writer/director) 182
His Name Is ... Savage (comic book) 2
Hitchcock, Alfred (director) 118
Hoffman, Dustin 1, 132
Holliman, Earl 62, **63**, 64
Hollywood Citizen-News, review quotes 32
Hollywood Reporter, review quotes 6, 19, 32, 42
Holm, Ian 154, 156
Hondo (1953) 26
Hong Kong (1952) 8, 9
Hosford, Mary 82
Howard, Ron **144**, 145
Hudson, Rock 21, **22**, 23, 30, 32
Huggins, Roy (director) 17
Hughes, Kathleen **197**
Huie, William Bradford (writer) 146
Hunt, Peter (director) 154, 166
The Hunter (Richard Stark novel) 116
Hurt, William **168**, 169, 170
Huston, John (writer/director) 64

I Died a Thousand Times (1955) 62, **63**, 64, 67
The Iceman Cometh (1973) 114, 139, 140, 141, **142**, 143
The Iceman Cometh (Eugene O'Neill play) 140
Iglesias, Eugene 14, 16
In Cold Blood (1967) 114, 124
In Harm's Way (1965) 86
Invasion of the Body Snatchers (1956) 65
The Investigators (television show) 198

Jacks, Robert L. (producer) 42
Jaeckel, Richard 71, 72, 111, 113, 172, 174
Jagger, Dean **49**, 52
Jagger, Mick (singer/actor) 180
Jarman, Claude, Jr. 17, 18
Jarmusch, Jim (director) 2
Jeff's Collie (television show) 48
Jim Kane (*Pocket Money*) 132
Johnny North (*The Killers*) 95
Johnson, Dorothy M. (writer) 89
Johnson, Van 42, **44**
Jones, Shirley 196
Jory, Victor 199
Judge Advocate General's office (*Sergeant Ryker*) 122

Kael, Pauline (*New Republic/New Yorker* critic) 109, 127, 141, 142
Kahler, Wolf 172
Kane, Michael (writer) 174
Kansas City Prime (*Prime Cut*) 136
Kass, Robert (*Catholic World* critic) 20
Kaufman, Millard (writer) 52
Kaye, Stubby 98, 100
Kazan, Lainie 178

Keith, Brian 201
Keith, Robert 38
Kelley, DeForest 80
Kennedy, Arthur 198
Kennedy, Burt (writer/director) 68
Kennedy, George 114, 178
Kerwin, Lance 149
Kid Shelleen (prospective television show) 101
Kiley, Richard 19, 21, 195
The Killers (1946) 97
The Killers (1964) 2, 95, **96**, 97, 98, 118, 119, 167
Kjellin, Alf 104
The Klansman (1974) 1, 145, 146, **147**, 148, 171
The Klansman (William Bradford Hule novel) 146
Klemperer, Werner 104
Knight, Arthur (*Saturday Review* critic) 16, 45, 79
Knox, Alexander 170
Kohlmar, Fred (producer) 24
Kolldehoff, Rene 154
Korean War, collaborators during 78, 121
Korvin, Charles 105
Kovacs, Laszlo (cinematographer) 133
Kraft Suspense Theatre (television show) 119, 122, 201
Kraft Television Theatre (television show) 195
Kramer, Stanley (producer/director) 19, 21, 36, 37, 39, 44, 104, 105

Lamour, Dorothy 94
Lancaster, Burt 21, 97, **107**, 108, 109, 114
Lane, Sara 149
Lang, Fritz (director) 32, 34
Lannom, Les 134
Lanoux, Victor 171
Larch, John 67
Laughlin, Tom 185
Lauter, Ed 165
Lawbreaker (1963-1964) (television show) **193**, 194
Lee, Peggy 61
Lee Marvin: A Personal Portrait by John Boorman (1998) (Documentary) 181
Leigh, Janet 61
Leigh, Vivien 104, 105
Leith, Virginia 53, 55
Lembeck, Harvey 5
Lemmon, Jack 1
Lenz, Kay 152, 153
Lerner, Alan Jay (producer/lyricist) 125, 127, 128
A Letter to Three Wives (1949) 12
Lewis, Jerry 3
A Life in the Balance (1955) 58, **59**, 67
A Life in the Movies (Fred Zinnemann book) 7
Life magazine; review quotes 6, 13, 123, 136
Lindley, Audra 195

224   Index

Lockhart, Gene 25
Lockridge, Ross, Jr. (writer) 80
Loewe, Frederick (composer) 127
Logan, Joshua (director) 128
The Longest Day (1962) 164
Lopez, Perry 63
Lopez, Trini 111, 113
Los Angeles Daily News review quotes 11
Los Angeles Times 128; *Best of 1960s survey* 101; review quotes 16, 143
The Losers (prospective television show) 201
The Lost Films of the Fifties (Douglas Brode book) 72
Louise, Tina 171
Lovejoy, Frank 21, 65
Luna, Barbara 104, 106
Lundigan, William 24
Lupino, Ida (director) 201
Lyons, Cliff (director) 86

M Squad (1957–1960) (television series) 1, 81, 84, 98, 148, 182, 183, **184**, 185, 186, 187, 188, 189, 190, 191, 192, 193
M*A*S*H (1970) 74, 111
MacMurray, Fred 42, 44
Macready, George 26, 27
The Magnificent Seven (1960) 113
Maibaum, Richard (writer) 182
Mailer, Norman (writer) 72
Malden, Karl 9, 11
Malone, Dorothy 75, 76
Malouf, Jacqueline 94
Malpaso production company 129
Maltin, Leonard (writer) 8, 65
A Man for All Seasons (1966) 110
THE MAN WHO SHOT LIBERTY VALANCE (1962) 129
Mancini, Henry (composer) 97
Mann, Abby (writer) 104
Mann, Anthony (director) 68
Mantell, Joe 201
March, Fredric 44, 139, 141
The Mark (1961) 87
Marley, John 98, 100, **103**
Marshall, E.G. 11
Martin, Dean 3
Martin, Strother 88, 91, 132, 151
Marty (1955) 52
Marty (television show) 79
Marvin, Christopher (Lee's son) 179
Marvin, Claudia (Lee's daughter) 179
Marvin, Courtenay (Lee's daughter) 179
Marvin, Cynthia (Lee's daughter) 179
Marvin, Lee: Academy Award for *Cat Ballou* (1965) 1, 92, 98, 101, 103; career overview 1; death of 1, 179; death scenes 2, 48, 69, 81; Emmy nomination (1961) 198; gold record for "Wand'rin' Star" 127; palimony lawsuit 1, 106, 156, 157, 159, 178; portrait photographs **9**, **24**; screen persona 2, 32, 35, B96, 167; serviceman roles 3, 72; stage appearances 5, 181; television appearances 194, 195, 196, **197**, 198, 199, **200**, 201, 202; variety show/interview appearances 202; World War II service 5, 124
Marvin, Pamela (Lee's second wife) 156, 179, 181
Mason, James 170
Matheson, Richard (writer) 201
Matlock, Matty (musician) 61
A Matter of Life and Death (Georges Simenon story) 58
Mature, Victor 28, 29, 53, 55
Mauldin, Bill 7
Mazurki, Mike 185
MCA television (Universal) 182
McCarthy, Kevin 196
McClay, Howard (*L.A. Daily News* critic) 11
McClure, Doug 149
McCrea, Joel 62
McIntire, John 198
McLaglen, Andrew V. (director) 174
McLerie, Allyn Ann 130
McLintock! (1963) 86
McNally, Stephen 9, 11, 14, 16, 53
McNeil, Alex (writer) 194
McQueen, Steve 1, 2, 132
THE MEANEST MEN IN THE WEST (1976) 148, 149, **150**, 151, 199
Meddings, Derek (models/special effects designer) 154
The Medic (television show) 195
Meeker, Ralph 7, 114
Meril, Macha 199
Merrill, Gary 82, 84
Merrill's Marauders (1962) 162
MGM studios 79, 80, 116, 172
Mifune, Toshiro 122, **123**, 124
Miles, Sylvia 152
Miles, Vera 88, 90, 119, 121, 201
Miller, Eddie (musician) 61
Miller, Marvin 8
Millican, James 9, 62
Milner, Martin **60**, 199
Miou-Miou 171
THE MISSOURI TRAVELER (1958) 82, **83**, 84
Mister Roberts (1955) 3, 50
Mr. Smith Goes to Washington (1939) 90
Mitchell, Cameron 40, **41**, 146
Mitchell, Millard 4, 5
Mitchum, Robert 56, **57**
Mohr, Gerald 14, 16
Monroe, Marilyn 12
Montalban, Ricardo 58, 59, 201
MONTE WALSH (1970) 129, 130, **131**, 143
Moore, Roger 154, **155**, 156
Moore, Terry 65
Moore, Victor 11
Moreau, Jeanne 130, 131
Morey, William 134

Morganstern, Joseph (*Newsweek* critic) 109, 127
Morrison, Anne 53
Motion Picture Association of America 108, 114, 134
The Motion Picture Guide, review quotes 14
Motion Picture Herald, review quotes 65, 79
The Motorola TV Hour (television show) 194
Murder on the Orient Express (1974) 157
Murphy, Audie 14, 16, 76
Murphy, Mary 37
Murrow, Edward R. (television commentator) 193
Museum of Broadcast Communications, Chicago, IL 122

Naish, J. Carroll 53
The Naked and the Dead (Norman Mailer book) 72
The Naked City (television show) 182
The Naked Gun (1989) 185
Namath, Joe 157, 159
Nardini, Tom 98, 100, **103**
Nathanson, E.M. (writer) 110
National Board of Review Best Actor award (1965) 101
NBC television network 95, 119
Neal, Patricia 9, 11
Neff, Hildegard 9, 11
Nelson, Lori 62, 64
New Republic, review quotes 109
New York Times bestseller list 42
New York Times, review quotes 6, 8, 11, 13, 19, 32, 39, 45, 55, 59, 61, 65, 87, 122, 131, 136, 139, 142, 156, 159
New Yorker, review quotes 13, 61
Newborn, Ira (composer) 185
Newlan, Paul 183
Newman, Paul 77, 78, 79, 84, 121, 132, **133**
Newsweek, review quotes 82, 101, 109, 127
Nielson, Leslie 185
Nimoy, Leonard 185
Nolan, Jeanette 17, 18, 33, 88
Nolan, Lloyd 45, 120, 121, 122
Noonan, Tommy 53
Norris, Chuck 177
North, Alex (composer) 133
North to Alaska (1960) 86
NOT AS A STRANGER (1955) 55, 56, **57**, 58, 62

Objective Burma (1945) 31
O'Brian, Hugh 23, 23
O'Brien, Edmond 61, 77, 79, 88, 90
O'Connor, Carroll 116, 118
Octaman (1972) 7
O'Hara, John (*Colliers* critic) 52
O'Henry's Full House (1952) 12
Olivier, Laurence 101
On the Waterfront (1954) 45, 78
O'Neill, Eugene (writer) 139, 140, 141, 143
Oregon Pacific and Eastern Railroad (*Emperor of the North*) 139

Orion studios 169
Osceola (Seminole Indian leader) 23
Othello (1965) 101
Our Time in Hell (1966) (documentary) 180
Overlook Western Encyclopedia (Phil Hardy book) 109

Paar, Jack 25
Pacula, Joanna 168, 170
PAINT YOUR WAGON (1969) 2, 125, **126**, 127, **128**, 129, 137, 156
Paint Your Wagon (play) 126
Paint Your Wagon, production problems 127, 128
Palance, Jack 130, 131
Panaromic Productions company 42, 58
Panic in the Streets (1950) 7
Paramount studios 127, 129, 146
Parkins, Barbara 154, **155**, 156
The Pasadena Playhouse 5
Patrick, Nigel 80
Patterns (television show) 78, 79
Patton (1970) 165
The Pawnbroker (1965) 101, 114
Payne, John 195
Peck, Gregory 159
Peckinpah, Sam (director) 125, 137, 139, 201
Pedi, Tom 140
Pepsi Cola Playhouse (television show) 194
Perez, Jose 58, **59**
Perkins, Anthony 195
Perry Mason (television show) 182
Persoff, Nehemiah 85
Pete Kelly's Blues: Academy Award nominations 61; prospective television show 62
PETE KELLY'S BLUES (1955) **60**, 61, 62
Peter Gunn (television show) 182, 185
Phillips, Barney 19, **20**
Phone Call from a Stranger (1952) 12
Pickford, Mary 132
Pidgeon, Walter 77, 78, 79
PILLARS OF THE SKY (1956) 74, **75**, 76, 77, 165
Pink Floyd (band) 180
Platoon (1986) 74
Platt, Howard 134
Playboy magazine, review quotes 169
POCKET MONEY (1972) 132, **133**, 134
POINT BLANK (1967) 97, 110, 116, **117**, 118, 119, 122, 136, 167, 181
Poitier, Sidney 1, 132
Police Squad (television show) 185
Polonsky, Abraham (writer) 159
Porter, Katherine Anne (writer) 104
Porter, Robert 146
Potter, Dennis (writer) 169
Power, Tyrone 9, 11
Powers, Mala 198
Presnell, Harve 127, 128
Previn, Andre (composer) 127

Price, U.S. Representative Melvin (politician) 72
PRIME CUT (1972) 109, 134, **135**, 136
The Professionals, Academy Award nominations 110
THE PROFESSIONALS (1966) 1, 106, **107**, 108, **109**, 110, 114, 119, 124
Proft, Pat (writer) 185
Project 120 (television show) 95
Psycho (1960) 90

Qualen, John 88
Quinn, anthony 22, 23
Quirk, Lawrence J. (writer) 8, 79

THE RACK (1956) 28, 45, 77, **78**, 79, 121
THE RAID (1954) 2, 45, **46**, 47, 48, 165
RAINTREE COUNTY (1957) 79, 80, **81**
Raintree County, Academy Award nominations 81
Rawhide (television show) 127
Reagan, Ronald 8, 9, 84, 96, 97, 195
Rear Window (1954) 41
Rebecca (1940) 82
Rebound (television show) 194
Reed, Donna 17, **18**, 30, 32
Reed, Olvier 152, 153
Reed, Walter 67, **68**
Reservoir Dogs (1992) 2
Rettig, Tommy 47, 48
Reynolds, Burt 185
Rio Bravo (1959) 86
Ritchie, Michael (director) 136
RKO studios 73
The Roaring Twenties (1939) 31
Robards, Jason, Jr. 141, 142, 143
Robbins, Marty (singer) 139
Roberts, Pernell 199
Roberts, Stanley (writer) 45
Robson, Mark (director) 159
Rockwell, Norman (artist) 83
Rodgers and Hammerstein (composer/lyricist team) 24, 25
Rogers, Ginger 12
Rogers, Wayne 132
Rolfe, Sam (writer) 76
Rooney, Frank (writer) 36
Roope, Fay 22
Rose, Reginald (writer) 182
Ross, Ricco 175
Route 66 (television show) 198
Ruehmann, Heinz 104, 105
Russell, Gail 67, **68**
Ryan, Mitchell 130
Ryan, Robert **49**, 52, 107, 108, 111, 114, 139, 141

Saint, Eva Marie 80, 194
St. John, Howard 63
Samuel Fuller and The Big Red One (1979) (documentary) 180
Sande, Walter 52
Saturday Review, review quotes 16, 40, 45, 79
Savalas, Telly 111, 113, 114, 175
Saving Private Ryan (1998) 164
Sayre, Nora (*N.Y. Times* critic) 142
Schaefer, Jack (writer) 129
Schaffner, Franklin J. (director) 195
Schallert, William 48
Schell, Maximillian 157, 159
Scheuer, Philip K. (*L.A. Times* critic) 16
Schickel, Richard (*Time* critic) 136
Schlitz Playhouse of the Stars (television show) 196
Schmidtmer, Christine 104
Schneider, Moe (musician) 61
Schygulla, Hanna 177
Scott, Randolph 16, 17, **18**, 26, 27, 67, 68, 69
Scourby, Alexander 28, 33
The Sea Hawk (1941) 86
The Searchers (1956) 82, 90
Seberg, Jean 126, 127, 128
Segal, George 104, 105, **106**
SEMINOLE (1953) 21, **22**, 23
SERGEANT RYKER (1968) 28, 45, 77, 119, **120**, 121, 122, 149, 201
Serling, Rod (writer) 78, 182
SEVEN MEN FROM NOW (1956) 2, 66, 67, **68**, 69
SHACK OUT ON 101 (1955) 64, 65, **66**, 67
Shaft (1971) 146
Shane (1953) 48
Shane (Jack Schaefer book) 129
Shatner, William 196
Shaw, Irwin (writer) 72
Shaw, Robert 157, 159, 170
Sherman, Ray (musician) 61
SHIP OF FOOLS (1965) 101, 103, 104, 105, **106**, 107, 132
Ship of Fools, Academy Award nominations 104, 105
Ship of Fools (Katherine Anne Porter novel) 104, 105
SHOUT AT THE DEVIL (1976) 153, 154, **155**, 156
Sidney, Sylvia 53, **54**
Siegel, Don (director) 14, 15, 16, 97
Sierra, Gregory 132
Signoret, Simone 104, 105, 196
Sikking, James B. 116, 118
The Silver Chalice (1954) 78
Silverstein, Elliot (director) 101
Simenon, Georges (writer) 58, 59
Simpson, O.J. 146, 148
The Simpsons (television show) 2
Sinatra, Frank 56, **57**
Sleepless in Seattle (1993) 2, 113
Smith, Charles Martin **144**, 145
Smith, Martin Cruz (writer) 168
Smithers, William 71, 72, **73**
Smoky (*Cat Ballou* horse) 101, **102**
Somebody Up There Likes Me (1956) 78, 79

The Sons of Lee Marvin (organization) 2
A Sound of Hunting (Eight Iron Men) 19, 21
South Pacific (1958) 25
South Pacific (Rodgers and Hammerstein play) 24
Spacek, Sissy 134, 136
Spencer, Douglas 48
The Spencer Tracy Legacy: A Tribute by Katharine Hepburn (1987) (documentary) 178, 180
THE SPIKES GANG (1974) 143, **144**, 145
Spradlin, G.D. 131
The Spy Who Came In from the Cold 101
Stalag 17 (1953) 5
A Star Is Born (1937) 82
Star Wars (1977) 157, 163
Stark, Richard (writer) 116
The Steel Helmet (1951) 162
Steiger, Rod 7, 78, 101
Steptoe, Colonel Edward (army officer) 76
Stern, Stewart (writer) 7
Stevens, Andrew 165, 166
Stevens, Leith (composer) 39
Stewart, James 88, 90
The Story of G.I. Joe (1945) 73
THE STRANGER WORE A GUN (1953) 2, 25, **26**, 27, 30, 69
Strasberg, Susan 178
Strauss, Robert 71, 72
A Streetcar Named Desire (1951) 39
Streisand, Barbra 1, 132
Strode, Woody 88, 90, 107, 108, 114
Studio One (television show) 195
Sturges, John (director) 51, 52
Sunday Showcase (television show) 196
Superfly (1972) 146
Sutherland, Donald 113, 114
Swensen, Karl 195

Taft, William H. (politician/president) 153
Tales of Manhattan (1942) 12
Taylor, Elizabeth 80, 81, 148
Taylor, Rod 80
Teal, Ray 18
TERESA (1951) 6, **7**
Teresa, Academy Award nominations 7
The Terminator (1984) 119
They Died with Their Boots On (1941) 31
Thinnes, Roy 199
Thompson, Howard (*N.Y. Times* critic) 8, 59, 61, 122
Thompson, Marshall 78
Thompson, Morton (writer) 58
Thomson, David (writer) 118
3-D films 26, 27, 30, 31, 32, 40, 41, 42
3:10 to Yuma (1957) 48
Time, review quotes 13, 23, 32, 40, 52, 65, 101, 136, 141
Tippette, Giles (writer) 143
Title changes 6, 21
To Follow a Flag (Will Henry novel) 76

The Tomahawk and the Cross (Pillars of the Sky) 74
Tompkins, Angel 134
The Tonight Show (television show) 25
Tonite, Let's All Make Love in London (1967) (documentary) 180
Total Television (Alex McNeil book) 194
Touch of Evil (1958) 97
Tracy, Spencer 49, 52, 84, 178, 180, 181
Tremayne, Les 185
Trevor, Claire 26, 27
Triola, Michelle (sued Marvin for palimony) 106, 156
True Grit (1969) 86
Tucker, Forrest 101
Tully, Tom 42, 45
TV Guide magazine 183, 193
TV Movies and Video Guide (Leonard Maltin book) 9, 65
TV Reader's Digest (television show) 195
TV Soundstage (television show) 194
TWA Flight 847 hijacking 176
20th Century–Fox studios 11
The Twilight Zone (television show) 198, 201
Tyner, Charles 131

U.S. Marine Corps 179, 180, 181
U.S.S. Teakettle (You're in the Navy Now) 3
United Artists studios 132
United States Steel Hour (television show) 78, 196
Universal Studios 15, 95, 97, 119, 122, 151
Unsolved Mysteries (television show) 193
The Untouchables (television show) 192, 198, 199

Van Cleef, Lee 88, 91
Van Eps, George (musician) 61
Variety magazine, review quotes 6, 19, 32, 42, 141
Vaughn, Robert 178
Vernon, John 116, 118
Villa, Pancho (revolutionary) 107
VIOLENT SATURDAY (1955) 2, 52, 53, **54**, 55, 59
The Virginian (television show) 149, 150, 151, 199
Vogler, Karl Michael 154
Voskevoc, George 140

Wagon Train (television show) 196
Wahl, Ken 174
Walcott, Gregory 134, 136
Walker, Clint 113
Walsh, Moira (*America* critic) 62
Walsh, Raoul (director) 31
Walston, Ray 126, 127
Ward, Kelly 160, **161**
Warden, Jack 5, 92, 94
Warner Bros. studios 62, 97, 125
Wasserman, Dale (writer) 182
Wasserman, Lew (studio chief) 97
Watkin, Pierre 26
Wayne, David 12, 25

Wayne, John 3, 76, 84, 86, 87, 88, 90, 92, **93**, 94, 95, 148, 160, 164
Weathers, Carl 165, 166
Webb, Jack 4, 5, **60**, 61, 183, 185
Webber, Robert 114
Webster, Peggy 195
Weldon, Joan 26, 27
Wellman, Paul I. (writer) 86
Wendell, Howard 33
WE'RE NOT MARRIED (1952) 11, 12, **13**, 14, 28
Werner, Oskar 101, 104, 105
The Westerner (television show) 201
White Christmas (1954) 45
White Heat (1949) 31
Whitman, Stuart 84, 86, 87
Whitney, C.V. (producer) 82, 83, 84
Whitney, Peter 41
Who's Afraid of Virginia Woolf? (1966) 108, 114
Wilcox, Larry 174
The Wild Bunch (1969) 119, 125, 137
THE WILD ONE (1954) 36, **37**, **38**, 39, 40, 67, 109

Wildcat (*The Great Scout and Cathouse Thursday*) 151
Williams, Adam 33
Williams, John (composer) 97
Williamson, Bruce (*Playboy* critic) 169
Wilmer, Dr. Harry (psychotherapist) 198
Wilson, Rita 2, 113
Wilson, Stanley (composer/musician) 185
Winters, Shelley 62, **63**, 64, 178
Wouk, Herman (writer) 42, 43, **44**
The Wrong Man (1957) 90
Wynn, Keenan 39, 65, **66**, 116, 118, **200**
Wynn, May (aka Donna Lee Hickey) 44

Yankee Doodle Dandy (1942) 86
The Yearling (1946) 18
The Young Lions (Irwin Shaw book) 72
YOU'RE IN THE NAVY NOW (1951) 3, 4, 5, 6, 11, 21, 60, 61

Zinnemann, Fred (director) 6, 7
Zucker, David (director) 185
Zucker, Jerry (director) 185

www.ingramcontent.com/pod-product-compliance
Ingram Content Group UK Ltd.
Pitfield, Milton Keynes, MK11 3LW, UK
UKHW050531150426
5217IPUK00026B/1892